THE
WRITING PROCESS

THE WRITING PROCESS

A CONCISE RHETORIC

FOURTH EDITION

JOHN M. LANNON
University of Massachusetts—Dartmouth

HarperCollinsPublishers

Developmental Editor: Vicky Anderson Schiff
Project Coordinator: Donna Conte
Design Supervisor: Lucy Kirkorian
Text Design: North 7 Atelier, Ltd.
Cover Design and Illustration: Jan Kessner
Production Administrator: Linda Murray
Compositor: University Graphics
Printer and Binder: R.R. Donnelley & Sons Company
Cover Printer: Lehigh Press Lithographers

The Writing Process: A Concise Rhetoric, Fourth Edition

Library of Congress Cataloging-in-Publication Data

Lannon, John M.
    The writing process : a concise rhetoric / John M. Lannon. —4th
  ed.
      p.   cm.
    Includes index.
    ISBN 0-673-52133-8 (SE). —ISBN 0-673-52168-0 (IE)
    1. English language—Rhetoric.   I. Title.
PE1408.L3188   1992
808'.042—dc20   91-24907
                                                   CIP

    92 93 94 9 8 7 6 5 4 3 2

Brief Contents

v

Detailed Contents

Preface

This text fosters rhetorical awareness by treating the writing process as a set of deliberate and recursive decisions. It promotes rhetorical effectiveness by offering practice in the problem-solving skills essential to reader-centered discourse.

Organization

Section One, "The Process," covers planning, drafting, and revising. Students learn to invent, select, organize, and express their material recursively. They see how decisions about purpose and audience influence decisions about what will be said and how it will be said. They see that reading and writing are linked, and that writing is essentially a "thinking" process.

Section Two, "The Product," expands on composition and evaluation skills by focusing on content, organization, and style. Students learn to support their assertions; to organize for the reader; and to achieve prose maturity, precise diction, and appropriate tone.

Selection Three, "Essays for Various Goals," shows how the *strategies* (or modes) of discourse serve its particular *goals*, that is, how description, narration, exposition, and argument are variously employed for expressive, referential, or persuasive ends. Offering variations on the standard "formula-essay," a balance of student and professional selections touches on current and lasting issues. Beyond studying these samples as models, students are asked to respond to the issues presented, that is, to write in response to a specific rhetorical situation.

Section Four, "Research and Correspondence," expands rhetorical awareness beyond the traditional composition classroom. The chapter on library research covers the process, the resources, and the product (a fully annotated research report). A chapter on business letters and memoranda focuses on the audiences, the informational and persuasive considerations, and the composing decisions in writing in the work place.

Finally, for easy reference, the Appendix is a concise handbook, with exercises for the student.

The Foundations of *The Writing Process*

- Although it follows no single, predictable sequence, the writing process is not a collection of random activities; rather, it is a set of decisions in problem solving. Beyond studying model essays, students need to understand that effective writing can only come from effective thinking.

- Students initially are more comfortable with writer-centered discourse (description, narration) than with reader-centered discourse (exposition, argument), because they rarely write for any apparent audience other than teachers or for any apparent purpose other than to complete an assignment. To the extent that they view writing as an exercise in which writer and reader have no higher stake or interest, students cannot possibly understand that each writing situation poses its own unique rhetorical constraints. Outside the classroom, we write to create specific connections with specific audiences.

- Writers with no rhetorical awareness overlook the decisions that are crucial for effective writing. Only by sizing up their rhetorical problem and asking the important questions can writers discover the solution they need.

- Students at any level of ability can learn to incorporate within their writing the essential rhetorical features: worthwhile content, sensible organization, and readable style.

- Rather than reiterating information found in the course textbook, classroom workshops can apply textbook principles by focusing on the students' writing. The workshop then calls for a comprehensive, concise, and accessible text. (Suggestions for workshop design can be found in the *Instructor's Manual*.)

- Finally, most writing classes contain students who possess all types of strengths and weaknesses. Because books are ordered far in advance, instructors can only hope that their choices will match the general caliber of the classes they end up with. A textbook, then, should offer explanations that are thorough, examples and models that are broadly intelligible, and goals that are rigorous yet realistic. And the book should be flexible enough to allow for individualized assignments.

This book proceeds from writer-centered to reader-centered discourse. Beginning with personal topics and a basic essay structure, the focus shifts to increasingly complex rhetorical tasks, culminating in argument. Within this cumulative structure, however, each chapter is self-contained for flexible course planning. Exercises (or Applications) in each chapter offer various levels of challenge. All material has been class-tested.

New to This Edition

- A focus on writing as a means for authentic expression and exploration. Students learn that any effective writing "makes a difference," because it brings writer and reader closer together. (See Section One "Introduction.")

- Many more sample essays from students and professional writers, along with questions for analysis, discussion, and response. (See Chapters 11, 12, 13, 15, 18, and 19.)

- Greater emphasis throughout on the link between reading and writing, with provocative suggestions for "Responding to Your Reading." (See Applications 5-1, 10 3, 11-3, 12-2, 13-3, 15-3, 16-3, 17-4, 18-13, 19-1, and 19-2.)

- A wide range of challenging, class-tested ideas for essay topics. (See Applications 1-3, 3-6, 10-3, 11-3, 12-2, 13-3, 15-3, 18-13, 19-1, and 19-2.)

- Exercises in collaborative writing and revising. (See Applications 1-3, 2-12, 4-2, 6-5, 9-9, and 21-9.)

- A new section on the rhetorical implications of sexist language. (See Chapter 9, pages 212–214 and Applications 9-7, 9-8, and 9-9.)

- A fully revised Chapter 18, "Developing a Persuasive Argument," which emphasizes the rhetorical complexity of persuasive situations. New features include additional essays for analysis and response, sections on "Anticipating Audience Resistance" and "Supporting Your Claim," and class-tested suggestions for writing.

- A fully revised Chapter 19, "Composing Various Arguments," including new essays and ethical guidelines for argument.

- A fully revised Chapter 20, "Developing a Research Report," with an emphasis on critical thinking. Specific features include detailed treatment of the research report process ("Asking the Right Questions," "Focusing on Essential Viewpoints," and "Evaluating and Interpreting Findings"), more on using library resources and automated retrieval, new suggestions for research topics, and new applications for hands-on work with various print and electronic resources.

Much of the improvement in this edition was inspired by helpful reviews from Joe Boles, Northern Arizona University; Arnold Bradford, Northern Virginia Community College; Tim Dekin, Loyola University; Sarah Harrold, Southwest Oregon Community College; Garnett Kilberg, Columbia College; Robert McCoy, Kent State University; Luetta Milledge, Savannah State College; Marnie Prange, University of Montana; and Robert Schwegler, University of Rhode Island.

For examples, advice, and support, I thank colleagues and friends at University of Massachusetts—Dartmouth, especially Tish Dace, Barbara Jacobskind, Margaret Panos, Louise Habicht, and Richard Larschan. As always, Raymond Dumont helped in countless ways.

A special thanks to my students who allowed me to reproduce versions of their work: Chris Adey for selections on privacy in America, Mike Creeden for a paragraph on physical fitness, Kim Fonteneau for "Suffering Through Gym Class," Suzanne Gilbertson for selections on New Guinea, Shirley Haley for "Sailboats" and other excellent work, Jeff Leonard for "Walk but Don't Run," Liz Gonzales for her selection on rap music, and the many other writers whose selections and essays appear throughout.

I appreciate the gracious and expert help from my editors, Constance Rajala and Vicky Anderson Schiff. Donna Conte did a superb job of coordinating this project.

For Chega, Daniel, Sarah, and Patrick—without whom not.

John M. Lannon

THE
WRITING PROCESS

SECTION ONE

THE PROCESS— PLANNING, DRAFTING, REVISING

Introduction

Success comes from good decision making. People who succeed usually are those who make the right decisions—about a career, an investment, a relationship, or anything else. Instead of letting things happen, these decision makers take control of their situation—and they stay in control. In one respect, writing is no different from life in general: effective writers stay in control by making the right decisions.

How Writing Occurs

Like any decision making, good writing is hard work. If we had one recipe for all writing, one surefire way of doing it, our labors would be small. We could learn the recipe ("Do this; then do that"), and then apply it to every writing task—from love letters to lab reports. (With a cookbook approach of that kind, I might have spent only an hour or two writing this introduction, instead of almost a week!) But no two writing tasks are identical; we write about various subjects for various audiences for various purposes—at home, at school, on the job. For every task, writers have to make their own decisions.

Even though we have no one recipe for writing well, most writers in most situations face identical problems: they need to decide who their audience is and how to connect with it; they need to decide what goal they want their writing to achieve and how to make sure the writing achieves that goal; they need to decide what to say and how to say it. Each writer struggles alone, but there *are* decision-making strategies that work for most writing tasks. This book introduces strategies that help writers succeed.

Most writing is a conscious and deliberate process—not the result of divine intervention, magic, miracles, or last-minute inspiration. Nothing ever leaps from the mind to the page in one neat and painless motion—not even for creative geniuses. Instead, worthwhile writing progresses and improves in stages: we plan, draft, and revise—repeating this cycle of decisions until our thinking takes shape, until the writing does precisely what we want it to do. Sometimes we know exactly what we want to do and say as we begin to write, and sometimes we discover our purpose and meaning only as we write. But our finished product takes shape through the decisions we make at different stages in the writing process.

This book provides the ingredients for decision making, but you have to create your own recipes. So that you can make the right decisions, you will be shown how to plan, draft, and revise in a suggested sequence of activities. But just as no two people use an identical sequence of activities to drive, ski, or play tennis, no two people write in the same way. Good writing occurs in many ways, but *each* way requires careful decisions. How you decide to use this book's advice will depend on your writing task and on what works for you.

How Writing Looks

The neat and ordered writing samples throughout this book show the *products* of writing—not the process. Beneath every finished writing product (including this introduction) lie pages and pages of scribbling and things crossed out, lists, arrows, and fragments of ideas. Writing begins in disorder; decision making can be a messy business, as shown in Figure 1, a section from my first draft of this introduction. (Not until I'd written *four* equally messy drafts was it a finished product.) Messiness is a natural and often essential part of writing in its early stages.

Just as the writing process has no one recipe, the finished products have no one shape. In fact, very little writing published in books, magazines, and newspapers looks exactly like the basic college essay discussed in this book's early chapters (an introductory paragraph ending with a thesis statement; three or more support paragraphs, each beginning with a topic sentence; and a concluding paragraph). Published writing may have very short paragraphs, some no longer than one sentence, or even one word.

Despite the countless shapes among the *products* of writing, all

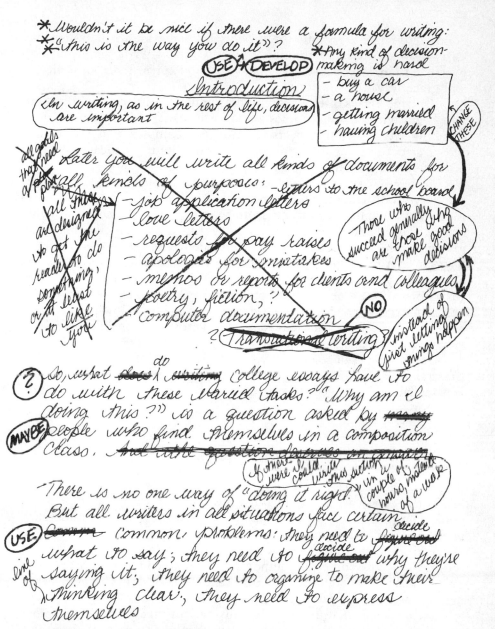

* Wouldn't it be nice if there were a formula for writing:
* "this is the way you do it"?

* Any kind of decision-making is hard

(USE) (DEVELOP)

Introduction

In writing, as in the rest of life, decisions are important

- buy a car
- a house
- getting married
- having children

CHANGE THESE

all goals that you need all purposes all letters are designed to get the reader to do something, or at least to like you

Later you will write all kinds of documents for all kinds of purposes: - letters to the school board
- job application letters
- love letters
- requests for pay raises
- apologies for mistakes
- memos or reports for clients and colleagues
- poetry, fiction,?
- computer documentation

? Transactional writing

NO

- Those who succeed generally are those who make good decisions

Instead of just letting things happen

(?) So, what do college essays have to do with these varied tasks? "Why am I doing this?" is a question asked by people who find themselves in a composition class.

MAYBE

If others were I could write this section in a couple of hours instead of a week

There is no one way of "doing it right." But all writers in all situations face certain common problems: they need to decide what to say; they need to decide why they're saying it; they need to organize to make their thinking clear; they need to express themselves

(USE)

Figure 1 Part of a Typical First Draft

effective writers carry out the *process* by using identical skills: they know how to discover something worthwhile to write about, how to organize their material sensibly, and how to express their ideas clearly and gracefully.

College essays offer a good model for developing these skills: first, you begin with personal topics and a basic structure for shaping your thinking; later, as your subjects become more complex, you develop different structures for different goals. Throughout, you learn to make order out of disorder.

College essays also provide you with an immediate, helpful audience—your instructor and classmates. Unlike many audiences who read only your final draft and from whom you could not reasonably expect helpful and sympathetic advice, your teacher and classmates can give you valuable feedback as you continue to shape and rework drafts of your writing. Like any audience, however, your classroom readers will expect you finally to give them something worthwhile—some useful information, a new insight on some topic, an unusual perspective or an entertaining story—in a form that is easy to follow and pleasing to read. Connect with these readers, and you should be able to connect with just about any reader.

In writing college essays, you practice ways of achieving control by attending to all the decisions in the writing process. Here you can learn what a writer needs to know before you set out to face other audiences on your own.

How Writing Makes a Difference

All through school, we write too often for *surface* reasons: to impress teachers, to show we can grind out a few hundred words on some topic, cook up a thesis, and organize paragraphs; to show we can punctuate, spell, and use grammar; to pass the course. Although essential for our survival in school, these surface reasons mask the *deeper* reasons we write: to explore something important to us, to connect with our readers, to be understood, to make a difference—as students, as employees, as citizens, or as friends.

What kind of difference can any writing make? It might move readers to act or reconsider their biases; it might increase their knowledge or win their support; it might broaden their understanding or their insight. Writing might do any of these things or other things. But whether you're giving instructions for running an electric toothbrush or pouring out your feelings to a friend, effective writing almost always brings writer and reader closer together.

Have you read anything lately that has made a difference to you?

Can you think of situations where your own writing could make a difference for others?

In reading the essays throughout this book, you will see how student and professional writers in all kinds of situations manage to make a difference with their readers. These models, along with the advice and assignments, should help your writing make a difference of its own.

1
Decisions in the Writing Process

How Writing Is Used • How Writing Is Shaped
• How an Essay Is Composed • Applications

How can writers bring readers closer? By anticipating their needs, by making the message matter, by making the right decisions.

How Writing Is Used

Readers will use your writing to learn something about you, to share your experience and insight, to see things as you do—and maybe even to judge you. Whether your writing succeeds will depend on *what* you decide to say and *how* you decide to say it. A Dear John or Jane letter, a job application, an essay exam, a letter to a newspaper, a note to a sick friend, your written testimony as a witness to a crime—these are just a sampling of the writing situations you might face.

In each of these situations, you write because you feel strongly enough to have a definite viewpoint, to take a definite position, to respond or speak out. Maybe you think X is good (or bad); or maybe you support (or oppose) X; or maybe you see something unique about X; or maybe you think something should be done about X. By asserting your viewpoint, you tell readers where you stand; you announce your position.

9

Here are just a few of the countless possible viewpoints any writer might assert:

College is not for everyone.

I deserve a raise.

Playing Monopoly makes me obsessed with winning.

My high school education was a waste of time.

I want my life to be better than that of my parents.

Later you will see how assertions like these serve as thesis statements for essays. But you can see here that the mere expression of a viewpoint is not in itself very useful to readers. To understand and appreciate any of these assertions, readers need an *explanation* of the writer's exact meaning. Whenever you express a viewpoint, you need to explain it. After telling your audience where you stand, show them why.

How Writing Is Shaped

No matter what the viewpoint and how detailed the explanation, writers have to shape their thinking so that readers can follow it. Any useful writing (whether in the form of a book, a chapter, a news article, a memo, a report, or an essay) most often reveals a sensible line of thinking by taking a shape like this:

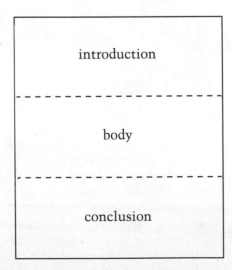

- The *introduction* attracts attention and makes readers take notice, announces the viewpoint, and previews what will follow. When readers know what to expect, they can more easily follow the message. Some introductions need to be long and involved; some, short and sweet. But all good introductions invite readers in.

- The *body* explains and supports the viewpoint. This section achieves unity by remaining focused on the viewpoint. And it achieves coherence by presenting a line of thinking carried from sentence to sentence in logical order. Body sections come in all different sizes, depending on how much readers need and expect.

- The *conclusion* sums up the meaning of the piece, or it points toward other meanings to be explored. If the issue is straightforward, the conclusion might be brief and definite. If the issue is complex or controversial, the conclusion might be lengthy and open-ended. But all good conclusions leave readers reflecting on what they have just read.

Just about any useful writing follows some version of this basic shape. The shape is most obvious in the form of the standard college essay—a piece of nonfiction writing whose writer develops and supports a viewpoint (expressed as a thesis) in one or more paragraphs. Practice in planning, drafting, and revising college essays will help you cope with many other kinds of writing during and after college.

How an Essay Is Composed

For naming the process that produces a useful essay, *composing* probably is a more accurate word than *writing*. Too many people think that *writing* involves little more than inscribing words on paper—as if some magical energy from the friction of pen on paper could create a finished essay. But getting the words down is only one small part of the writing process. Your real challenge lies with the other parts:

1. exploring for things you might want to say (in journals, lists of ideas, and so on) and then deciding what these things mean

2. deciding on your audience and how you expect them to use your message

3. deciding on a plan for helping the audience understand your meaning

4. discovering new meanings as you work and deciding on ways of revising your original plan and message to accommodate these new meanings

Writing is a process of transforming the material you discover—by inspiration, research, accident, trial and error, or whatever—into a message with a definite meaning. In short, *writing is a process of deliberate decisions.*

To see the difference between writing as a random act and writing as a deliberate process, let's follow one student writer through two approaches to the same writing situation: first, her quickest effort; then, her best effort. Shirley Haley has been assigned an essay on this topic: How do you want your life to be different from (or similar to) that of your parents? Haley's goal here is twofold: to explore her feelings about this topic and to share that exploration with us. Her first response is a random, off-the-top-of-the-head piece of freewriting that took her less than 30 minutes:

> When my mother was my age, life was simple. Women really didn't have to study in college. They came primarily to find a husband, and they majored in liberal arts or teaching. They knew they were going to be wives and mothers. My mother says she got an education so she would have "something to fall back on" in case something ever happened to my father—which was a good thing, I suppose. Maybe it was her attitude about "family first, me second" that made our home life so stable.
>
> I appreciate the fact that my parents have given me a stable home life, and I want parts of my life to turn out like theirs. But my parents are slaves to their house; they never go anywhere or do anything with their spare time. They just work on the house and yard. They never seem to do anything they want to do—only what other people expect of them.
>
> I wish my parents would allow themselves to enjoy life, have more adventure. They go to the same place every year for their vacation. They've never even seen a country outside the United States.
>
> I'll have a family some day, and I'll have responsibilities, but I never want to have a boring life. When I'm on my own, I want my life to soar. And even though I want to provide a stable home life for my children and husband some day, I hope I never forget my responsibility to myself as well.

Haley's draft has potential, but she hints at lots of things in general and points at nothing in particular. What exactly does she mean, and what is her purpose? Without a thesis to assert a controlling viewpoint, neither writer nor reader ever finds a point of reference, an orientation. We can't tell what this essay is *about*. We are confused.

At first, the essay seems to be about a change in women's roles, but none of Haley's generalizations (say, "Women . . . came . . . to find a husband") is supported by *evidence*. Then, the end of the first paragraph and the beginning of the second suggest that Haley's topic has shifted to ways in which she wants her life to resemble her parents'. But in the second, third, and fourth paragraphs, Haley goes on to discuss what she *dislikes* about her parents' lives. The final sentence adds to our confusion by looking back to one of the now-defunct topics in the first paragraph: stable family life. We have no idea where the emphasis belongs.

Not everything that comes to the writer's mind belongs in an essay, but Haley included everything, anyway. Without a definite purpose and thesis, she never could decide which material didn't belong, which was the most important, and which deserved careful development.

Besides its confusing array of material, the essay has problems in shape and style. We are frustrated by the lack of a definite introduction and conclusion. Without an introduction, we have trouble establishing a framework for reading, a way of narrowing the possible meanings we might take from the piece. Without a conclusion, we have trouble tying together what we have just read.

Also, the paragraphs either are poorly developed or fail to focus on one specific point. And some sentences (such as the last two in paragraph one) seem to have hardly any logical connection. In general, the sentences lack variety and make for dull reading.

Finally, Haley never seems to have decided on an appropriate tone. We get almost no sense of a real person speaking to real people, expressing a definite attitude toward her subject. Instead of writing for an audience, Haley has written only for herself—as if writing a journal or diary. Although Haley's quickest effort seems to be a promising beginning, her writing needs much more work before it can connect with readers.

A quick effort (as in a journal or diary) can be a good way of getting started, a good source of material for an essay. But rarely will a quick effort alone be adequate. When writers do nothing more than *draft* whatever comes to mind (as Haley does on page 12), they bypass the most essential stages in the writing process, *planning* and *revising*.

In fact, planning and revising should take much longer than drafting. Getting some material down on the page is easy. Getting the piece to work, to make a difference to readers—this is where the toughest decisions are made. Indeed, I'm struggling right now to say things that will make a difference to my readers. And if Haley hopes to make contact, she, too, will have to struggle with decisions such as these:

- *Planning decisions*: about *exactly* what she wants her topic to be and what she wants her essay to accomplish; about what her position is and how she will support that viewpoint; about which material, organization, and tone will work best for her specified audience.

- *Drafting decisions*: about how to write an introduction that opens doors to her world, her way of seeing; about how to develop the middle so that it shows a real mind at work and in control; about how to conclude memorably, with emphasis and insight and imagination.

- *Revising decisions*: about whether her material is worth reading; her organization sensible; her style readable; her grammar, spelling, and punctuation correct—rethinking and polishing until the essay represents her best effort, until it conveys the exact point or feeling she wanted to get across.

Figure 1.1 shows how we might diagram the kinds of decisions Haley has to make during the writing process. Of course none of these decisions necessarily occurs in the neat sequence shown here. Writing can hardly ever be reduced to a "by-the-numbers" activity. But at some point before turning in a final draft, Haley—or any writer—will need to answer all these questions.

For a clear sense of a writer's decision making, let's follow Haley's thinking as she struggles through her planning decisions:

> **What exactly is my topic, and why am I writing about it?** My intended topic was "How I Want My Life to Be Different from That of My Parents," but somehow my first draft got off the track. I need to focus on the specific differences!
>
> I'm writing this essay to discover my own feelings and to help readers understand these feelings by showing them specific parts of my parents' life-style that I hope will be different for me.
>
> **What is my thesis?** After countless tries, I think I've finally settled on my thesis: "As I look at my parents' life, I hope my own will be less ordinary, less duty-bound, and less predictable."
>
> **Who is my audience, and what do they need to know?** My audience consists of my teacher and classmates (this essay will be discussed in class). Each reader already is familiar with this topic in her or his

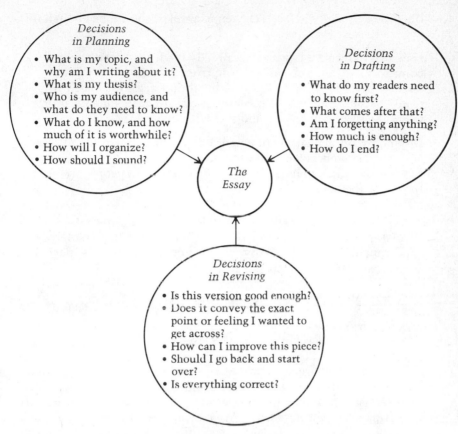

Figure 1.1   Typical Decisions During the Writing Process

own way. Everyone, after all, is someone's son or daughter! But I want my audience to understand specifically the differences *I* envision.

What do I know about this topic? A better question might be, "What *don't* I know?" I've spent my life with this topic, and so I certainly don't have to do any research.

Of all the material I've been able to discover on this topic, how much of it is worthwhile (considering my purpose and audience)? Because I could write volumes here, I'll have to resist getting carried away. My readers don't want a life story. They can tolerate only a few paragraphs. I certainly don't want to bury readers under mountains of needless detail. I've already decided to focus on the feeling that my parents' lives are too ordinary, duty-bound, and predictable. One paragraph explaining each of these supporting points (and illustrating them with well-chosen examples) should be enough for my readers.

How will I organize? I guess I've already made this decision by coming up with my thesis: moving from "ordinary" to "duty-bound" to "predictable." The predictability belongs at the end, I think, because this is the characteristic that bothers me most. It's what I want to emphasize, and so I will save it for last.

How do I want my writing to sound? I'm sharing something intimate with my classmates here, and so I want to sound like one of them. My tone should be relaxed and personal, as when people are talking to people they trust.

In completing her essay, Haley went on to make the same kind of deliberate decisions for drafting and revising. And among her many decisions and revisions, Haley discovered in her original draft (page 12) a path worth following. Here is her final draft:

Life in Full Color

I'm probably the only person I know who still has the same two parents she was born with. We have a traditional American family: we go to church and football games; we watch the Olympics on television and argue about politics; and we have Thanksgiving dinner at my grandmother Clancy's and Christmas dinner with my father's sister Jess, who used to let us kids put pitted olives on our fingertips when we were little. Most of my friends are struggling with the problems of broken homes; I'll always be grateful to my parents for giving me a loving and stable background. But sometimes I look at my parents' life and hope my life will be less ordinary, less duty-bound, and less predictable.

I want my life to be imaginative, not ordinary. Instead of honeymooning at Niagara Falls, I want to go to Paris. In my parents' neighborhood, all the houses were built alike about twenty years ago. Different owners have added on or shingled or painted, but the houses basically all look the same. The first thing we did when we moved into our house was plant trees; everyone did. Now the neighborhood is full of family homes on tree-lined streets, which is nice; but I'd prefer a condo in a renovated brick building in Boston. I'd have dozens of plants, and I'd buy great furniture one piece at a time at auctions and dusty shops and not by the roomful from the local furniture store. Instead of spending my time trying to be similar to everyone else, I'd like to explore ways of being different.

My parents have so many obligations, they barely have time for themselves; I don't want to live like that. I'm never quite sure whether they own the house or the house owns them. They worry constantly about taxes, or the old furnace, or the new deck, or mowing the lawn, or weeding the garden. After spending every weekend slaving over their beautiful yard, they have no time left to enjoy it. And when they're not buried in household chores, other people are making endless demands on their time. My mother will stay up past midnight because she promised some telephone voice 3 cakes for the church bazaar, or 5 dozen cookies for the Girl Scout meeting, or 76 little sandwiches for the women's club Christmas party. My father coaches Little League, wears a clown suit for the Lions' flea markets, and both he and my mother are volunteer firefighters. In fact, both my parents get talked into volunteering for everything. I hate to sound selfish, but my first duty is to myself. I'd rather live in a tent than be owned by my house. And I don't want my life to end up being measured out in endless chores.

Although it's nice to be able to take things such as regular meals and paychecks for granted, many other events in my parents' life are too predictable for me. Every Sunday at two o'clock we dine on overdone roast beef, mashed potatoes and gravy, a faded green vegetable, and sometimes that mushy orange squash that comes frozen in bricks. It's not that either of my parents is a bad cook, but Sunday dinner isn't *food* any more; it's a habit. Mom and Dad have become so predictable that they can order each other's food in restaurants. Just once I'd like to see them pack up and go away for a weekend, without telling anybody; they couldn't do it. They can't even go crazy and try a new place for their summer vacation. They've been spending the first two weeks in August on Cape Cod since I was 2 years old. I want variety in my life. I want to travel, see this country and see Europe, do things spontaneously. No one will ever be able to predict my order in a restaurant.

Before long, Christmas will be here, and we'll be going to Aunt Jess's. Mom will bake a walnut pie, and Grandpa Frank will say, "Michelle, you sure know how to spoil an old man." It's nice to know that some things never change. In fact, some of the ordinary, obligatory, predictable things in life are the most comfortable. But too much of any routine can make life seem dull and gray. I hope my choices lead to a life in full color.

Haley's deliberate decisions about planning, drafting, and revising have produced a far better essay than her first, random version on page 12. Notice the clear and distinctive shape of this essay:

Introductory
paragraph (leads into
the thesis)

Thesis statement
_____ But sometimes I look at my parents' life and hope my life will be less ordinary, less duty-bound, and less predictable.

Topic statement and first support paragraph
I want my life to be imaginative, not ordinary. _____
_____
_____
_____

Topic statement and second support paragraph
My parents have so many obligations, they barely have time for themselves; I don't want to live like that. _____
_____
_____
_____

Topic statement and third support paragraph
Although it's nice to be able to take things such as regular meals and paychecks for granted, many other things in my parents' life are too predictable for me. _____
_____
_____
_____

Concluding paragraph
_____
_____
_____
_____

Essays can vary from this shape in countless ways, but a good first step for gaining control is to master the standard shape.

Besides seeing how the design of Haley's whole essay has evolved, we recognize other improvements. Above all, we're no longer confused. Somewhere between her first draft and this last one, Haley discovered her exact meaning and found a way of making it clear to us as well. We know *where* she stands because she tells us, with a definite thesis; and we know *why* because she shows us, with plenty of examples. But even though we get real substance here, nothing is wasted; everything seems to belong, and everything sticks together.

Within the larger design of Haley's whole essay, each paragraph offers a smaller design, a place for things that belong together. The introduction reveals the writer's way of seeing; each middle paragraph brings us close enough to see and touch things; and the conclusion lets us look back on everything, lets us finish. Each paragraph does its job, enriching the whole.

The style, too, is improved. We now see real variety in the ways in which sentences begin and words are put together. We now hear a genuine voice. Haley's tone helps create contact.

Because she knew how to go about making the right decisions, Haley produced a final draft that has the qualities typical of any good writing: *content* that makes it worth reading; *organization* that reveals the line of thinking and emphasizes what is most important; and *style* that is economical and convincingly human.

Every writer struggles with the same decisions about planning, drafting, and revising, but rarely in a predictable sequence. Instead, each writer chooses a sequence that works best for *that* person. And no single stage of decisions is complete until *all three* stages are complete. Figure 1.2 shows how we might diagram this looping structure of the writing process.

You might write a draft before or after you have a clear plan, but if the draft has no real potential, you will have to loop back and draft again or even return to your planning stage. Once you do have a usable draft, you revise; but if the revision still fails to convey your exact point or feeling, you may have to return to the planning or drafting stage. This looping continues until you achieve an essay that does exactly what you want it to do.

Although decisions about planning, drafting, and revising are treated separately and sequentially in the next three chapters, during the actual writing these decisions often are indistinguishable parts of a writer's thinking.

Application 1–1

The essay that follows (a third draft) was written in response to this assignment:

> Identify a personal trait that is so strong you cannot control it (a quick temper, the need for acceptance, a fear of failure, shyness, a bad habit, a phobia, an obsession, or the like). In a serious or humorous essay, show how this trait affects your behavior. Provide enough details for readers to understand clearly this part of your personality.

Our writer, Thom Harrigan, decided to show a humorous side of his personality: his obsession with winning at Monopoly.

Read the essay once or twice. Then read it again, trying to identify specific ways the writer connects with his audience. Use the questions that follow the essay as a guide for your analysis.

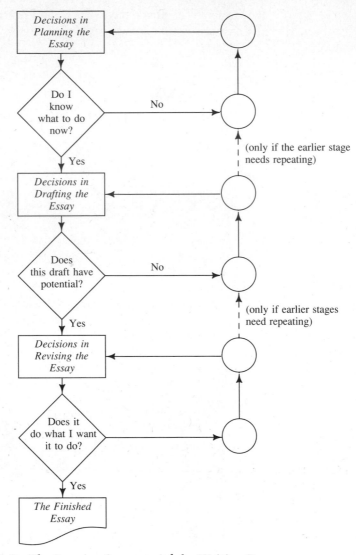

Figure 1.2   The Looping Structure of the Writing Process

Tycoon for a Day

Money really doesn't interest me. I don't dream about it at night. Never have I had the goal of being a corporate czar or owning a controlling interest in the Chase Manhattan Bank. I never would knowingly hurt anyone—much less try to destroy them financially and then seize their remaining pitiful assets. But somehow, when I play Parker Brothers' legendary game, Monopoly, I become obsessed with winning, a person to be feared.

Monopoly brings out the raging tycoon that lies buried somewhere deep inside me. When I play, I truly enjoy wiping out the opposition. Sworn enemies, casual acquaintances, relatives, or close friends—it makes no difference; everyone must lose to me. I can remember being ruthless as early as my first game back in 1982, but my blind drive to win reached its height five years ago, when my mother played me for her first and only time. I gave her deliberately bad advice, deceived her with smooth, underhanded rhetoric, and then mercilessly broke her, using her measly property to increase my fortune—my own mother.

Playing Monopoly gives me security because, unlike real life, it offers clear rules. Here, my actions have a consistent purpose, and I control my own destiny. My particular purpose is to win; my destiny is to control everyone else's destiny. In the rules of Monopoly's universe, only one person can be the victor. And if I win, I can pat myself on my play-money wallet and say, "I am now lord of all I survey"—simple and absolute. Lesser gods have no place in Monopoly; you either win or lose. And I'll do anything to be a winner for a few minutes. After all, I'm just a guy named Thom all the rest of the time.

As heartless as the game can be, Monopoly portrays the ultimate world of equal opportunity. Assuming all the players understand the rules, everyone stands the same chance of winning. Two dice are the only random discriminators. But winning is not simply a matter of luck. If Johnny has been foolish enough to mortgage his four railroads to finance a hotel on Illinois Avenue and then lands on my Boardwalk property—too bad, Johnny. The rent is two grand. Suddenly, demolition occurs on Illinois Avenue. Only my crafty financial decisions and a little timely help from the dice have secured my victory— another Bigtime success story.

I can't help myself. I love to win, and now I know a little more about why. It all sounds childish, I know, but . . . maybe I'm on to something here. Monopoly has been a bestseller every year since it was first marketed in 1934. The impulse toward victory and power seems to be alive and well in the game-playing public. The next time you play Monopoly, take a close look at your behavior. You might be surprised at what you see.

QUESTIONS

Does the Content of the Essay Make It Worth Reading?

- Can you find a definite thesis that announces the writer's viewpoint?

- Are you given enough information to understand the viewpoint?
- Do you learn something new and useful?
- Does everything belong, or should any material be cut?

Does the Organization Reveal the Writer's Line of Thinking?

- Is there an introduction that sets the scene, a middle that walks us through, and a conclusion that sums up the meaning?
- Does each support paragraph begin with a topic statement?
- Does each paragraph stick to the point and stick together?

Is the Style Economical and Convincing?

- Can you understand each sentence the first time you read it?
- Should any words be cut?
- Do sentences have variety in the way they're put together?
- Is the writer's meaning always clear?
- Can you hear a real person speaking?
- Do you like the person you hear?

In one or two paragraphs, suggest *as specifically as you can* how Thom Harrigan might improve his essay. Be prepared to discuss your suggestions in class.

Application 1–2

Compare Shirley Haley's first draft (page 12) with her final draft (page 16). Discuss the specific improvements, and give examples. Use the questions from Application 1–1 as a guide for your discussion.

Application 1–3

ESSAY PRACTICE

In class, write your "quickest effort" essay about a personal trait, or about this subject: "Important Differences or Similarities Between My Life and That of My Parents." Exchange papers with another student, and evaluate your classmate's paper, using the questions from

Application 1–1. In one or two paragraphs, give your classmate advice for improving the essay. Don't be afraid to mark up (with your own questions, comments, and suggestions) the paper you're evaluating. Discuss with your classmate your evaluation of his/her paper.

At home, read the evaluation of your paper carefully, and write your "best" version of your original essay. List the improvements you made in moving from your quickest effort to your best effort. Be prepared to discuss your improvements in class.

Also, in two or three paragraphs, trace your own writing process for this essay by describing the decisions you made. Be prepared to discuss your decisions in class.

Note: Don't expect miracles at this stage. You're bound to feel some degree of frustration and confusion. If you find even your best effort disappointing, don't be surprised. Things will improve quickly.

OPTIONS FOR ESSAY WRITING

The following topics offer some ideas for essays that will get you started. People write best about things they know best, and so we begin with personal forms of writing. These topics ask you to explore your feelings, opinions, attitudes, and experience—to discover your insights and viewpoints and to share your thinking with readers. You might want to return to this long list for topic ideas when essays are assigned throughout the early chapters of this book.

Whichever topic(s) you choose, be sure the best version of your essay has a clear thesis supported by a discussion readers will find worthwhile, easy to follow, and understandable. (Save all your writing for revision work in later chapters.)

1. What major effects has television had on your life (your ambitions, hopes, fears, values, consumer habits, awareness of the world, beliefs, outlook, faith in people, and so on)? Overall, has television been a positive or negative influence? Have you learned anything from TV that you couldn't have learned elsewhere? Be sure to support your thesis with specific details.

2. Are today's children growing up too fast by learning so early about sex, violence, drugs, alcohol, money, divorce, suffering, injustice, and death? Or do they need such knowledge in order to cope with an increasingly complex and dangerous world? Discuss this issue in an essay that offers detailed support for your viewpoint. (You might use yourself or a younger sibling as an example here.)

3. How do advertising and commercials shape or mold our values (notions about looking young, being athletic, being thin, smoking, beer drinking, the brands of shoes we wear, and so on)? Does advertising present an unrealistic view of life? In what ways? What kinds of human weaknesses and aspirations do commercials exploit? Support your viewpoint with examples your readers will recognize. (You might focus on how you or someone you know has been victimized by the hype.)

4. How do your notions of "feminine" and "masculine" differ from those of your parents' generation? What do you suppose these changing notions mean for future generations? Support your thesis with specific details.

5. If you had the chance to repeat your high school years, what three or four things would you do differently? Write for a younger brother or sister who is entering high school, and provide enough detail to get your viewpoint across.

6. Has peer pressure had mostly a positive or a negative influence on you? Explain why and how, and give specific examples. Be sure your essay supports a definite viewpoint.

7. Do some music videos communicate distorted and dangerous messages? Discuss specific examples and their effect on viewers. What should be done? Support your viewpoint in a detailed essay.

8. Think about your favorite sport or activity. Identify at least three special features of that activity that contribute to your enjoyment. Describe these features in enough detail to make your classmates share your enjoyment.

9. Americans often are criticized for their emphasis on *competing* and *succeeding* (academically, financially, physically, socially, and so on). Is this criticism valid? Discuss the specific pressures you have experienced. Has emphasis on competition and success been mostly helpful or harmful for you? Why? Support your viewpoint with specific details.

10. Perhaps you belong to a club, sorority, fraternity, environmental or political group, or the like. Encourage your classmates to consider joining the group by writing an essay that describes the organization in terms of its history, goals, philosophy, achievements, activities, or benefits that will have meaning for your readers.

11. Our public schools have been accused of failing to educate America's students. Does your high school typify the so-called failure of American education? Why, or why not? How well did your school prepare you for college—and for life? Give clear and convincing examples to support your thesis.

12. Identify three things that make you angry. Why? Provide enough detail for readers to understand your feelings.

13. Assume that your classmates are about to buy some fairly expensive or specialized item such as ski boots, a stereo, running shoes, a trail bike, roller blades, or the like. Help them make the best choice by giving them clear and useful advice about what qualities and features to look for and what deficiencies to avoid.

14. If a genie could grant you three wishes, what would they be? Describe exactly what you would want, and explain why. Be sure to leave no room for your wishes to be *misinterpreted*.

2
Planning the Essay

Deciding on Your Topic • Deciding on Your Purpose
• Deciding on Your Thesis • Deciding on Your Audience
• Discovering Useful Material • Selecting Your Best Material
• Organizing for Readers • Deciding on Your Tone
• The Writer's Planning Guide • Applications

Writing is a battle with impatience, a fight against the natural urge to "be done with it." Effective writers know how to win this battle; they spend plenty of time working out a plan for their writing. Of course, "planning" continues throughout the writing process; as your thinking changes, as you explore and discover new meanings and new expressions, your plan might change many times. But an initial plan gives you something to aim for, a place to start, and something to hold onto as you make your way through the process.

Writers plan their essays by deciding on answers to all these questions:

What, exactly, is my topic?

Why do I want to write about it?

What is my viewpoint (expressed as a thesis)?

Who is my audience, and how much information do they need?

What do I know about this topic?

26

Of all the material I've discovered, how much is worthwhile—considering my purpose and audience?

How will I organize this material?

How do I want my writing to sound?

Although these decisions (about topic, purpose, thesis, audience, material, organization, and tone) are covered here in order, rarely will you make them in the same order for planning your own writing. In Chapter 1, Shirley Haley comes up with her thesis *before* brainstorming for material. Other writers begin with an outline. The key is to *make all the decisions*—in whichever order works best for your writing task.

As with any stage in the writing process, you might have to return again and again to your plan while you work toward the finished essay.

Deciding on Your Topic

If the topic is dictated by your situation, you have no problem; this decision is already made in most out-of-school writing ("Why I deserve a promotion"; "Why you should marry me"; "How we repaired your computer"). In school, you might be assigned a topic or asked to choose your own. When the topic decision *is* left to you, remember this one word: *focus.*

Never tackle too broad a topic. Instead of describing your social life last summer or telling how to play tennis, tell us about last night's blind date or how to serve a tennis ball. Begin with a *focused* topic, something you know and can really talk about, something that has real meaning for *you.*

One big fear among inexperienced writers is of having too little to say, and so they mistakenly choose the broadest possible topic. But in reality, a limited topic provides *more* to write about by allowing for the nitty-gritty details that help readers see what you mean.

Our world is full of subjects: love, work, sex, drugs, money, lifestyles, or whatever. But none of these huge subjects can be covered in a brief essay. Without a specific angle we end up looking at everything in general and at nothing in particular. Suppose, for instance, you really wanted to know the "personality" of a particular town; walking around and talking with the people would tell you a lot more than if you flew over the place at 10,000 feet.

If you try to write about why love is important, we won't get to read about anything we haven't heard or seen or read many times before; if, instead, you share with us your experience in learning to cope with the death of a loved one, we will get to know something about you, about pain, and maybe about courage as well. Reading is hard work; try to reward your readers for their labors. Don't waste their time and yours with a topic you know is too broad.

Within any subject, you need to discover a *topic*, your own angle of vision, a viewpoint. First, make the subject narrow:

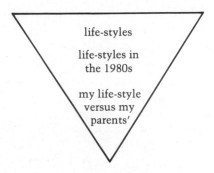

Even the limited subject "my life-style versus my parents' " could be narrowed again—say, to one specific difference (in respective attitudes about money or work or education or the like).

Narrow your subject until you get to where you can take a definite position; then make it a topic by inserting your viewpoint.

Subject	My life-style versus my parents'
	↓
Topic	How I want my life to differ from that of my parents

Suppose your instructor asks for an essay about a vivid memory. This time, part of your focusing job already is done (memory → a vivid memory). But you need even more focus:

A vivid memory
↓
A memory from high school
↓
High school gym class
↓
Unpleasant memories of my gym class

The last subject seems focused enough for a short essay. But what in this subject do you wish to explore? What do you want readers to know and understand? Make the subject a topic by inserting a viewpoint:

Why I hated high school gym class

Once you have a topic you can live with, you're on your way. You might get stuck later and have to throw the whole thing out, but for now you have something to work from.

Deciding on Your Purpose

During all stages in the writing process, you will be making decisions about priorities: What's most important? What can I leave out? What should I say first? How much is enough? And so on. How you answer those questions will depend on how you answer this one: *Why am I writing this piece?* Once you decide on your exact *purpose*, all your other decisions become much easier.

Each writing situation has a specific goal. Perhaps you want your audience to see what you saw, to feel what you felt, or to otherwise understand or accept your viewpoint—your own way of seeing. For your writing to achieve the goal, you need to make the right decisions. But to make these decisions you need more than just a goal for guidance; you need some kind of plan.

A *purpose* is any goal that can be reached through a specific plan. To define your purpose, then, you need a definite view of your goal and a clear sense of how to reach it. Consider these answers one writer gave to the familiar question, "Why am I writing this paper?"

I'm writing this to pass the course.

My goal is to write an essay about yoga.

My goal is to write an essay to persuade my classmates to try yoga.

The first response tells nothing about the writer's specific goal, and the second isn't much better; don't expect to get the job done if you don't take time initially to figure out first what the job *is*. The third statement defines the goal all right, but it suggests no plan for tackling it. Here, finally, is our writer's statement of purpose (goal plus plan):

My purpose is to write an essay persuading my classmates to try yoga by showing them how it relaxes the body, clears the mind, and stimulates the imagination.*

With a place to begin at and a path to follow, you beat the problem of trying to make something from nothing—a problem all writers face

---

*The purpose statement, of course, is not included in the essay; it merely gives the writer a definite orientation.

always. Trying to write anything definite *before* you spell out your purpose is like trying to cross a wilderness without map and compass. Knowing neither your destination nor your route, you're bound to get lost.

Sometimes you won't be able to figure out your purpose right away. You might need to jot down as many purposes as possible until one pops up. Or you might need to write a rough draft first or make some type of outline. Assume that you're writing the essay "Why I Hated High School Gym Class." To share with your classmates that painful memory, you will need a plan. Because the essay examines "Why," you organize a rough outline to follow the sequence of causes and effects in your unpleasant experience:

> What the class was like
>
> How I performed
>
> How my peers and teachers reacted to my performance
>
> How I ended up feeling

Now you can compose your statement of purpose:

> My purpose is to explain to my classmates why I have such a painful memory of high school gym class. I'll have to show what the class was like, how I performed, how everyone reacted, and how I ended up feeling.

Besides having a clear direction, you now have a rough map for reaching your goal.

Deciding on Your Thesis

In your purpose statement, you identify exactly what you want to *do*. In your thesis, you announce what you want to *say* to your readers. Your thesis statement makes a definite commitment. Think of the thesis as the one sentence you would keep if you could keep only one. A clear thesis is the Great Connector between your exact meaning and the reader's exact understanding; a foggy thesis leaves everyone confused. Tell readers what to expect by making your viewpoint absolutely clear. The viewpoint itself can be expressed in any of several forms:

As an opinion	College is not for everyone.
As an observation	My high school education was a waste of time.

As a suggestion	Computer literacy should be a requirement for all undergraduates.
As an attitude	I want my life to be better than that of my parents.
As a question	What is friendship?

Any of these thesis statements creates clear expectations. Readers don't like to be kept guessing. Make your point, and make it early.

THE THESIS AS FRAMEWORK

Consciously or unconsciously, readers look for a thesis,* and they look for it in the first or second paragraph in your essay. When they don't know what the essay is about, readers struggle to grasp your meaning. Even one paragraph is hard to understand if the main point is missing. Read this paragraph once, only—and then try answering the questions that follow.

> His [or her] job is not to punish, but to heal. Most students are bad writers, but the more serious the injuries, the more confusing the symptoms, the greater the need for effective diagnostic work. When an accident victim is carried into the hospital emergency ward, the doctor does not start treating the patient at the top and slowly work down without a sense of priority, spending a great deal of time on the black eye before [getting] to the punctured lung. Yet that is exactly what the English teacher too often does. The doctor looks for the most vital problem; he [or she] wants to keep the patient alive, and . . . goes to work on the critical injury.
>
> —Donald Murray

What is the main point in this paragraph? Can you tell after one reading? Could you restate the message in your own words? Probably not—even after a second reading. Without a main point, you have no framework for understanding this information in its larger meaning. And because you can't tell what to look for, you have no way of sorting out the more important details from the less important. Should you place the emphasis on doctors and hospitals, on students, or on English teachers? Without the organizing thread provided by a topic statement, you can't tell.

---

*Although readers may not *consciously* ask, "Where is the thesis?" they do expect some clear signal to help them approach the whole message and to help them narrow the range of meanings they can create from the essay.

Now, after inserting the following topic statement at the beginning, reread the paragraph.

The writing teacher must be not a judge, but a physician.

With this organizing point, the exact meaning of the message becomes obvious.

In the framework for the *basic* essay, each paragraph in the body of the essay is controlled by its own topic statement, which focuses on one aspect of the thesis. In other words, the thesis is the *big idea.* And each topic statement treats one part of the big idea, as diagramed here:

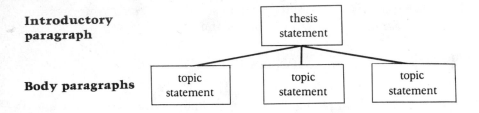

The thesis statement announces the most important point—the writer's reason for writing. It is a commitment that everything to follow will support that point.

Some writers include in the thesis a *preview* of the main supporting points; some don't. An essay titled "Beef Cost and the Cattle Rancher" might have this thesis statement:

Because of rising costs, unpredictable weather, and long hours, many cattle ranchers have trouble staying in business.

An alternative is to omit such a preview:

Cattle ranchers' biggest challenge is survival for their business.

Inexperienced writers often find that including a preview in their thesis helps them stay on track as they develop each support paragraph. Use whichever version works best for you—as long as your thesis announces exactly where you stand. And with or without the preview, be sure to express the supporting points as topic statements in subsequent paragraphs.

FROM PURPOSE STATEMENT TO THESIS

You can make your meaning clear to readers only if you've already made it clear to yourself. Your thesis statement, therefore, often grows out of your statement of purpose. Here again is the purpose statement for your gym class essay:

> My purpose is to explain to my classmates why I have such a painful memory of high school gym class. I'll have to show what the class was like, how I performed, how everyone reacted, and how I ended up feeling.

Keep in mind that the purpose statement is part of the discovery process, but the thesis is part of the finished essay. Here is the thesis you've derived from your purpose statement:

Introductory paragraph	_____ _____ _____
Thesis statement	_____ For three long years, gym class was my weekly exercise in failure.

Although you decided not to preview the main supporting points, you do announce each in the topic statements:

First supporting paragraph	Although I respected my gym teacher's focus on excellence, the standards in this class were beyond my ability. [topic statement] _____ _____ _____
Second supporting paragraph	Whatever sport we played, I could count on being the loser, even when my team won. [topic statement] _____ _____ _____
Third supporting paragraph	I was continually reminded of my failures. [topic statement] _____ _____ _____
Concluding paragraph	The whole experience left me feeling defeated. [topic statement] _____ _____ _____

EVALUATING YOUR THESIS

Always check to see that your thesis has a sharp focus and a definite and significant viewpoint.

Is the Topic Sharply and Appropriately Focused?   Have you focused on a topic limited enough to cover in a short essay? Avoid broad topics such as this one:

Too broad   Some experiences can be unforgettable.

The topic (unforgettable experiences) would require volumes!

Also, keep your focus appropriate to your purpose. Instead of cataloging your disasters in gym class, you might want to focus on the caste system that grew among the students. You might come up with this thesis:

> Because of the fierce competition in my gym class, each student quickly and indelibly earned the label of "achiever" or of "reject."

Depending on your purpose, you can adjust your thesis to focus on smaller and smaller parts of a topic.

Is a Definite and Informative Viewpoint Expressed?   Let readers know immediately where you stand. Preview your exact meaning. These thesis statements are inadequate, because they offer no such preview:

No clear viewpoint   I will discuss a memory of high school gym class.
expressed
                            In high school, I had a weekly gym class.

                            High school experiences can be complex.

The first sentence identifies a limited subject but says nothing about the writer's viewpoint. The second is a mere statement of fact. The third signals no exact meaning, thereby arousing no definite expectations in the reader. Always give readers a clear sense of what to look for.

Is the Viewpoint Significant?   Whether your thesis is expressed as an opinion, attitude, observation, suggestion, or question, it should trigger some fresh insight or have some kind of value or importance for your readers. A thesis that holds no surprise is worthless:

Insignificant   The high school years can be traumatic. [*Everyone*
viewpoints   *would agree, and so why discuss it?*]

> Everyone has some vivid memories of high
> school. [*No big surprise here!*]

Worthless thesis statements usually are a prelude to worthless essays. A worthwhile thesis is the spark that ignites the fuel. Without a strong spark, the engine never will turn over, no matter how much cranking you do.

To measure the value of your thesis, ask yourself this question: Is my thesis saying something my audience will want to read about?

VARIATIONS IN THE THESIS STATEMENT

The standard thesis statement can have several variations; we've seen that writers do not always preview the main supporting points, as in the gym class thesis.

Also, remember that you are not automatically restricted to a thesis that calls for only *three* supporting points. Three is a good minimum, but only if the topic really has only three main supporting points for consideration. In later essays, some topics call for more, some for less.

The thesis is most often the last sentence in the introduction. In this position it serves as a bridge between the introduction and the body. But for some purposes it can be placed elsewhere in the introduction (as shown on page 64). Finally, the thesis need not always be expressed in *one* sentence only (as shown in the paragraph on abortion on page 69).

How you phrase your thesis and where you place it depends on your situation, purpose, and audience.

WHEN TO COMPOSE YOUR THESIS

You might spell out your thesis before or after listing ideas or outlining or writing a first draft. Use whichever order works best. Usually you identify a focused topic as a first step. Then, ideally, you compose your statement of purpose and your thesis. But writers rarely follow these steps in neat order. *If you have trouble coming up with a thesis right away, don't worry.* Simply go on to some other activity; list some ideas, or work on an outline. Writing, after all, is *discovering* what you want to say—or, writing expert Peter Elbow says, "a way to end up thinking something you couldn't have started out thinking."* If you can begin with a definite goal, sooner or later you will discover a purpose and a

---

*Writing Without Teachers (New York: Oxford University Press, 1973), p. 15.

thesis. Then your later drafts can follow a definite plan. The order of steps is not important—as long as you complete them all.

Even if you begin with a workable thesis, it might not be the one you end up with. As you discover new meanings while you work, you might need to revise your thesis—or even discard it and start over. Remember that *nothing in the writing process is finished until everything is finished.*

Deciding on Your Audience

Except for a diary or a journal, everything you write is for readers who will *use* your information, who will react to what you have written. You might write to a prospective employer who wants to know why you quit a recent job; or to a committee who wants to know why you deserve a scholarship; or to a classmate who wants to know you better; or to a professor who wants to know whether you understand the material. For any audience, your task is to deliver a useful message, one that makes a difference with readers, that enables them to see things your way. You need to make readers appreciate the worth of what you have to say.

Out of school, of course, you will write for real-world audiences (customers, employers, politicians, and so on). But in school, you can envision a definite audience besides your instructor: your classmates. Like any audience, they will expect your writing to be clear, informative, and persuasive. If you can learn to write for a college audience, you will be reasonably well prepared for the real-world audiences you will face later (see Chapter 21).

Whether your audience is the company president or the person sitting next to you in your English class, people will read your writing because they expect a worthwhile message. They might need it to solve a problem, make a decision, evaluate your performance, or just entertain themselves. Whatever their motives, readers need enough material to understand your position and to react appropriately. Readers *don't* need repetition of material they already know. Instead of telling readers everything you know about the topic, tell them only what they need to know. A message that is useless to your readers is useless, period.

According to what they need to know, readers approach any piece of writing with questions:

What is it?

What does it look like?

What are its parts?

What happened?

How does it make you feel?

Who was involved?

When, where, and why did it happen?

How do I do it?

How did you do it?

What are its effects?

Is X better than Y?

How are they similar or different?

Can you give examples?

What does it mean?

Can you prove it?

Says who?

Why should I?

Who cares?

How am I supposed to react?

To put readers in *your* place, first put yourself in *theirs.* Anticipate their most probable questions.

As author of the gym class essay, you face your own special task: to make an experience that meant a lot to *you* mean just as much to your *audience.* Specifically, you need to answer at least these reader questions:

What was it?

What happened?

When, where, and why did it happen?

How did it make you feel?

Who was involved?

Who cares?

If you can anticipate with any accuracy your readers' questions, you stand a much better chance of discovering and selecting material that really will make a difference—that will give readers what they need and expect.

Discovering Useful Material

Discovering useful material is called *invention*. Your decisions about purpose, thesis, and audience are all part of invention. These decisions direct your search for content and help you select what to include and what to leave out. In turn, the material you discover may cause you to revise your original purpose and thesis.

When you begin working with an idea or exploring a topic, you search for useful material, for content: insights, facts, statistics, opinions, examples, images. In short, you search for anything that might advance your meaning, that might help you answer this question: How can I find something worthwhile to say—something that will convey my exact meaning?

The strategies for invention covered in this section are all based on one principle: *No writer can make something from nothing.* Even professional writers have to dredge from memory and imagination things that might otherwise have gone unrecognized. The goal of invention is to get as much material as possible down on paper. Here are some ways of doing it.

KEEPING A JOURNAL

A journal is an excellent way to build an inventory of ideas and topics that mean a great deal to you. Here you can write purely *for yourself.*

To start, buy a hardcover notebook with a sewn binding (so that whatever you write becomes a permanent part of your journal). From here on, the journal entries are up to you. Record your reactions to something you've read or seen; ask questions or describe people, places, things, feelings; explore fantasies, daydreams, nightmares, fears, hopes; write conversations or letters that never will be heard or read; examine the things you hate or love. Write several times a day or once a week or whenever you get the urge—or put aside some regular time to write. Every so often, go back and look over your entries—you might be surprised by the things you find.

FREEWRITING

Freewriting is a version of the "quickest-effort" approach discussed in Chapter 1. Shirley Haley's first attempt (page 12) is the product of freewriting. As the term suggests, when freewriting you just write whatever comes to mind, hoping that the very act of putting words on paper will help you come up with useful content.

Try freewriting by exploring what makes you angry or happy or frightened or worried. Write about what surprises you or what you think is unfair or what you would like to see happen. Don't stop writing until you've filled one or two pages, and don't worry about organization, grammar, spelling, and the like—just get it down. Although your product will be nowhere near a finished essay, freewriting can give you a good start by uncovering all kinds of buried ideas. It can be especially useful if you're suffering from "writer's block."

USING JOURNALISTS' QUESTIONS

To probe the many angles of a topic, journalists are taught to ask these questions.

> Who was involved?
>
> What happened?
>
> When did it happen?
>
> Where did it happen?
>
> How did it happen?
>
> Why did it happen?

Answering these questions for your gym class essay will enable you to share your experience of the people and events. Unlike freewriting, the journalists' questions offer a built in organizing strategy—a series of six "perspectives" for looking at something from different angles.

ASKING YOURSELF QUESTIONS

If you can't seem to settle on a definite viewpoint, try answering any of these questions that apply to your topic.

> **What is my opinion of X?**
>
> Is it good or bad?
>
> Is it beneficial or harmful?
>
> Is it valuable or worthless?
>
> Will it work or fail?
>
> Does it make sense?

What is my attitude toward *X*?

Am I for it or against it?

Do I like it or dislike it?

Do I accept it or reject it?

Does it make me happy or sad?

Do I approve or disapprove?

What have I observed about *X*?

What have I seen happen?

What is special or unique about it?

What strikes me about it?

What can I suggest about *X*?

What would I like to see happen?

What should be done?

What should not be done?

From your answers, you can zero in on the viewpoint that will provide the organizing insight for your essay.

BRAINSTORMING

If you're uncomfortable with freewriting and prefer not to answer a list of questions, try brainstorming—a sure bet for coming up with useful material. Here are the steps:

1. Find a quiet spot, and bring an alarm clock, a pencil, and plenty of paper.

2. Set the alarm to ring in 30 minutes.

3. Try to protect yourself from any interruptions—from anxieties, sleepiness, ringing phones, music. Sit with your eyes closed for two minutes, thinking about *absolutely nothing*.

4. Now, concentrate on your writing situation. If you've already spelled out your purpose and your audience's questions, focus on these. Otherwise, repeat this question: *What can I say about my topic, at all?*

5. As fragments of ideas begin to flow, write *every* one down. Don't stop to judge relevance or worth, and don't worry about complete sentences (or even correct spelling). Simply get everything on paper. The more ideas, the better your chance of finding a winner. Trust your imagination. Even the wildest idea might lead to some valuable insight.

6. Keep pushing and sweating until the alarm rings.

7. If the ideas are still flowing, reset the alarm and go on.

8. At the end of this session, you should have a chaotic mixture of nonsense, irrelevancies, and useful material.

9. Take a break.

10. Now confront your list. Strike out the useless material, and sort what's left into categories. If other ideas crop up, include them as well. Your finished list should provide an ample supply of raw material.

For your gym class essay, assume you've developed the brainstorming list that follows.

1. gym teacher expected too much

2. terror every Monday morning

3. like a walk to the guillotine

4. teachers should learn to control their biases

5. they should take courses in dealing with students of all abilities

6. winning was everything

7. drums beating

8. losing teams punished

9. teachers teach *students*, not phys. ed. or other subjects

10. always one of the last players picked

11. always the loser

12. trying hard only made me feel incompetent

13. teacher liked only the athletes

14. fun—instead of victory—should be the goal in athletics

15.   teammates groaned at my efforts

16.   my gift grade was a C minus

17.   I felt blacklisted

18.   effort versus performance

19.   nicknamed "the athlete"

20.   I laughed, but it wasn't funny

21.   missed the backboard

22.   I had no talent

23.   sure to fail

With your raw material collected, you can now move into the selection phase—leaving open the possibility that new material may surface.

Some people use invention as a very early step in writing, just as a way of getting started. Others save the invention stage until they've made other decisions. But regardless of the sequence, all writers use invention throughout the writing process; they do so to ensure that they will discover *all* the possible material they might want to include in their final draft.

Selecting Your Best Material

From the broad inventory of facts and ideas you've assembled, you will want to select *only* your best material. Invention invariably produces more material than a writer needs. Never expect to use *everything*.

As you review your brainstorming list (page 41) for the gym class essay, let's say you decide to cut items 4, 5, 9, and 14.

- Item 4 sounds too much like a sermon and doesn't relate to the purpose (to describe a memory—not to argue for changes in teaching approaches).

- Item 5, again, is not directly related to experiences in the gym. Also, the notion of such "courses" is too abstract to have real meaning in this context.

- Item 9 is a cliché, which again is too abstract to have real meaning—much less any relevance — to this essay.

- Item 14 is overstated. Athletics could have value other than fun (exercise, relaxation, team spirit, and so on).

Selection is a vital step. Without it, your writing is merely an emptying of your head onto paper. If you do find yourself trying to include *all* the material you've discovered, you probably need to refocus on your purpose and audience.*

Organizing for Readers

After selecting material that readers will find worthwhile, you need to organize it so they can follow your thinking. With an outline, you move from a random listing of items as they occurred to you to a deliberate map of information that will guide your readers from point to point. Readers more easily understand and remember material that has been organized in a sequence they find logical.

But *how* should you organize to make your writing logical—from your audience's point of view? What do all readers expect in a logically organized piece of writing? They expect a clear beginning, middle, and ending:

- a beginning (or introduction) that provides orientation by telling readers what they need to know first,

- a middle section (or body) that reveals the writer's exact meaning, with one item naturally following another,

- an ending (or conclusion) that emphasizes what is most important and leaves readers reflecting on the material they have just read.

When material is left in its original, unstructured form, readers waste a great deal of time trying to understand your meaning.

Readers generally expect writing to be organized into orientation, discussion, and review sections, such as those listed above. But your specific readers will want these sections tailored to their expectations. You can identify readers' expectations by (1) anticipating questions readers are likely to have about your thesis, and (2) visualizing the sequence in which readers would want these questions answered.

Let's try to anticipate readers' questions (and their sequence) about the gym-class thesis. Here again is the thesis: *For three long*

---

*In Chapter 6 you'll find detailed advice about selecting material that will be fresh and worthwhile for your readers.

years, high school gym class was my weekly exercise in failure. And here are the readers' questions, in the sequence we might anticipate:

Can you set the scene for us, and re-create your feelings or mood?

What were the teacher and the class like?

What did you do that was so bad?

How did everyone react to what you did?

How did you react?

You might think of slightly different questions. But we can assume that most readers would have questions much like these and would want them answered in a similar sequence.

What you have just learned about your readers' expectations gives you a basis for organizing your brainstorming material into definite categories:

   I. How I Dreaded Monday Morning Gym Class
  II. How Our Teacher's Standards Were Too High
 III. How I Failed to Meet These Standards
 IV. How I Was Continually Reminded of My Failures
  V. How the Experience Left Me Feeling Defeated

Within each category, you arrange your brainstorming items, along with any other worthwhile material you've since discovered. Your final outline might resemble this one:

   I. I dreaded Monday morning gym class.
     A. I knew what was waiting for me.
     B. I could sense the dampness and the stale smell.
     C. My hands would tremble, and I would sweat.
     D. Monday was physical education day.
     E. I had no athletic talent, and so was terrified.
     F. It felt like a walk to the guillotine, with drums in the background.
     G. *Thesis:* For three long years, my high school gym class was my weekly exercise in failure.

  II. Our teacher's standards were too high.
     A. She was not unkind, but not realistic, either.
     B. Athletic prowess was expected of each student.
     C. Only the athletes were liked.

      D.   Winning meant everything.
      E.   All fun disappeared.

III.   I never could measure up to the high standards.
      A.   I always lost—even when my team won.
      B.   I couldn't hit the backboard.
      C.   I tripped over my own feet.
      D.   Any sport meant failure.
      E.   The more I tried, the more I felt inferior.

IV.   I was continually reminded of my failures.
      A.   My classmates grew to expect the worst from me.
      B.   I was always one of the last picked for teams.
      C.   People groaned when I came up to bat.
      D.   My friends nicknamed me "the athlete."
      E.   I laughed on the outside, but not inside.
      F.   My C— "gift grade" killed my otherwise high average.

 V.   The whole experience left me feeling defeated.
      A.   I should have been able to learn something about self-confidence.
      B.   But I only felt "blacklisted."
      C.   Intimidated, I developed a kind of mental paralysis.
      D.   I accepted the certainty of failure.
      E.   Never have my personal shortcomings received such public display.

Notice that this outline is in the form of short, kernel sentences that include key ideas for later expansion in the essay. Some writers instead might have used a less formal outline—simply a rough list of phrases without numerals or letters. Use the form that works best for you.

At any stage in the writing process, writers can discover new and worthwhile material. Here are some thoughts that might have occurred as you outlined:

My stomach tightened as I walked through the school door. (belongs in IA)

Many classmates seemed to reflect the teacher's attitude. (belongs in IIC)

In baseball, I was the sure strikeout, the right fielder who dropped every fly ball. (belongs in IIIC)

Later, during various drafts, you will discover even more material, and you will probably delete some of your original material as well (as shown in the final draft on pages 71–73).

Once you have an outline you can live with, check it for *unity* and *coherence*. An outline has unity when everything directly supports the thesis. Items 4, 5, 9, and 14 were deleted from the earlier brainstorming list (page 41) because none of that material related directly to the thesis. An outline has coherence when the thesis and all supporting material form one connected line of thought, like links in a chain. Coherence would suffer in the gym class essay if, say, description of the teacher's standards *followed* description of the writer's failures. Readers need to know about the standards in order to appreciate the writer's sense of failure.

Finally, check your outline for emphasis. An outline has good emphasis when the important things stand out. Last things are best remembered; then, first; middles are too easily forgotten. Our gym class outline is organized to emphasize first the writer's fear and last her sense of paralysis. The middle explains the cause of these feelings, but readers will identify most vividly with the feelings themselves.*

Some writers can organize merely by working from a good thesis statement. Other writers prefer to begin with some sort of outline. And some write a draft and then outline to be sure the line of thinking will make sense to readers. For your own writing, you might outline early or later. But before submitting a final draft, you will need to move from a random collection of ideas to some kind of organized list that makes sense to your readers. Organize in the way that will be best for readers to approach your material.

Deciding on Your Tone

With most of your planning decisions made, your inventory is nearly complete: you have a topic and a thesis, a clear sense of your purpose and audience, a stock of material, and some kind of outline. In fact, if your reason for writing were merely *to get your message across*, you could begin drafting the essay right now. But you write not only to transmit information; you also write to connect with readers.

Unlike computers, writers can't be programmed to complete their profoundly human task. Except for diaries or some technical reports,

---

*Because unity, coherence, and emphasis are best illustrated at the paragraph level, they are covered in detail in Chapter 7.

all writers have to decide how they want their writing to sound—the attitude they want to convey about their reader and their topic. The way your writing sounds will depend on your *tone*, your personal mark—the voice readers hear between the lines. If readers respect and like the tone, they like the writer; they sense a sincere person talking; they allow contact. Always labor to get your message across, but never be afraid to give it real feeling.

All readers, consciously or unconsciously, ask themselves three big questions about the writer:

1. *Who is this person* (somebody businesslike, serious, silly, sincere, phony, boring, bored, intense, stuck-up, meek, confident, friendly, hostile, or what)?

2. *How is this person treating me* (as a friend, acquaintance, stranger, enemy, nobody, superior, subordinate, bozo, somebody with a brain and feelings, or what)?

3. *What does this person really think about the topic* (does the writer genuinely care, or is the writer simply "going through the motions")?

The readers' answers will depend on your tone. Readers expect you to be attentive to them as well as to what you're doing. Think hard about your words and the meanings they suggest.

Some inexperienced writers mistakenly think that fancy words are better than simple words for sounding more intelligent and important. And sometimes, of course, only the fancy word will convey your exact meaning. Instead of saying "Sexist language *contributes to the ongoing existence of* stereotypes," you could say more accurately and concisely, "Sexist language *perpetuates* stereotypes." One "fancy" word effectively replaces six "simpler" words. But when you use fancy words needlessly, and only to impress, your writing sounds stuffy and pretentious.

Readers expect to hear a real person behind the lines, just as you do when reading this book or almost anything else. And so when you write, "For three long years, gym class was my weekly exercise in failure," you invite us into your experience, make us want to read on; but not when you write, "During the seemingly interminable course of three years, my physical education curriculum served as an effrontery to my self-esteem." This second version probably means more or less the same as the first, but nothing here is inviting.

For most personal essays you would want to use a *conversational* tone, that is, to write to your audience as if you were speaking to them.

For instance, here again are the opening lines from Shirley Haley's final draft on page 16:

> I'm probably the only person I know who still has the same two parents she was born with. We have a traditional American family: we go to church and football games; we watch the Olympics on television and argue about politics; and we have Thanksgiving dinner at my grandmother Clancy's and Christmas dinner with my father's sister Jess, who used to let us kids put pitted olives on our fingertips when we were little.

Haley's tone is friendly and relaxed—the voice of a writer who seems at home with herself, her subject, and her readers. We are treated to comfortable images of family things. But we sense something else here, too: the long list of "traditional" family activities hints at the writer's restlessness, lets us share her mixed feelings of attraction and repulsion.

Imagine, instead, that Haley had decided to sound "academic" throughout her essay:

> Among my friends and acquaintances, I am apparently the only individual with the good fortune to have parents who remain married. Our family activities are grounded in American tradition: we attend church services and football games; we watch televised sporting events and engage in political debates; at Thanksgiving, we dine at Grandmother's, and at Christmas, with an aunt who has always been quite tolerant of children's behavior.

We can agree, I think, that the voice in this second version is much less likeable and inviting than the voice in the original. Here, the writer has disappeared, and so apparently has her awareness of her audience. To see for yourself, test each version against readers' three big questions on page 47. This second version has words that seemingly were written by no one in particular, about nothing special, for no one who matters—words that deny contact. Let your readers hear your voice.*

The Writer's Planning Guide

Decisions and strategies covered in this chapter apply to almost any writing situation. You can make sure your own planning decisions are complete by following the Planning Guide whenever you write. Items in the Planning Guide are reminders of things to be done.

---

*For specific ways of adjusting the tone of your writing, see Chapter 9.

PLANNING GUIDE

Broad subject:

Limited topic:

Purpose statement:

Thesis statement:

Audience:

Probable audience questions:

Brainstorming list (with irrelevant items deleted):

Outline:

Appropriate tone for audience and purpose:

This next Planning Guide has been completed to show a typical set of decisions for the gym class essay.

PLANNING GUIDE

Broad subject: A vivid memory

Limited topic: Why I hated high school gym class

Purpose statement (what you want to do): My purpose is to explain to my classmates why I have such a painful memory of high school gym class. I'll have to show what the class was like, how I performed, how everyone reacted, and how I ended up feeling.

Thesis statement (what you want to say): For three long years, gym class was my weekly exercise in failure.

Audience: Classmates

Probable audience questions:
  Can you set the scene for us, and re-create your feelings or mood?
  What were the teacher and the class like?
  What did you do that was so bad?
  How did everyone react to what you did?

How did you react?
Who cares?

Brainstorming list:
1. gym teacher expected too much
2. terror every Monday morning
3. like a walk to the guillotine
   . . . and so on

Outline:
I. I dreaded Monday morning gym class.
    A. I knew what was waiting for me.
    B. I could sense the dampness and the stale smell.
    C. My hands would tremble, and I would sweat.
    D. Monday was physical education day
        . . . and so on.

Appropriate tone for audience and purpose: personal and serious

Remember that your decisions for completing the Planning Guide need not follow the strict order of the items listed—so long as you make all the necessary decisions.

Your instructor might ask you to use the Planning Guide for early assignments and to submit your responses along with your essay.

Application 2–1

Narrow two or three of the subjects in this list to a topic suitable for a short essay. (Review pages 27–29.)

Example

movies
↓
how movies influence viewers
↓
how some movies depict sex
↓
how some movies shown on prime-time television encourage sexual permissiveness

SUBJECTS TO BE NARROWED

television	money	careers	sailing
war	family life	sports	crime
energy	sex	science fiction	automobiles
fashion	forests	animals	music
marriage	jobs	weather	alcohol
camping	studying	junk food	drugs

NOTE: The Options for Essay Writing on pages 23–25 contain certain topics that have been narrowed from some of the subjects listed above (say, "television" or "music"). You might review those topics to get some ideas for this application.

Application 2–2

Compose statements of purpose for essays on three or more of the topics in Application 2–1. (Review pages 29–30.)

Example

Topic

Prime-time television movies that encourage sexual permissiveness

Statement of purpose

My purpose is to show a general reading audience how some movies shown on prime-time television encourage sexual permissiveness among immature viewers. I will discuss four misleading ways in which such movies often depict sex: as a ritual of introduction, an educational experience, a device for achieving personal gain, and a form of recreation.

Application 2–3

Convert your statements of purpose from Application 2–2 into thesis statements. (Review pages 31–35.)

Example

Statement of purpose	My purpose is to show a general reading audience how some movies shown on prime-time television encourage sexual permissiveness among immature viewers. I will discuss four misleading ways in which such movies often depict sex: as a ritual of introduction, an educational experience, a device for achieving personal gain, and a form of recreation.
Thesis statement	Too many movies shown on prime-time television encourage sexual permissiveness by depicting sex without love in a variety of superficial encounters.

Application 2–4

For each thesis statement in Application 2–3, brainstorm and write three or four topic statements for individual supporting paragraphs. Arrange your topic statements in logical order. (Review pages 31–33.)

Example

Thesis statement	Too many movies shown on prime-time television encourage sexual permissiveness by depicting sex without love in a variety of superficial encounters.
First topic statement	One of the most common forms of sexual encounter I've seen on television is the "first-date" syndrome, where sex becomes part of the ritual of introduction.
Second topic statement	Other movies recently shown on television depict sex as an educational experience.
Third topic statement	Some films degrade the act of love by showing characters who use sex as a device for obtaining something.
Fourth topic statement	The most demeaning portrayal, however, occurs when sex is treated as casual recreation.

Application 2–5

From Application 2–4, select the most promising set of materials, and write your best essay. Use selected items from your brainstorming list to develop each support paragraph. Outline as necessary. Provide an engaging introduction and a definite conclusion. Use the questions on pages 21–22 as guidelines for revising your essay.

Application 2–6

From this list of broad subjects, select *four* about which you would have something worthwhile to say to your classmates. (Review pages 27–29.)

animals	drinking	life-styles	old age
cars	drugs	love	television
college	ecology	marriage	travel
dating	families	money	sex
death	jobs	nuclear power	war

After limiting these four subjects, make up *one* thesis statement for each. (You may wish to freewrite or to compose a statement of purpose beforehand.) Your thesis can be expressed as an opinion, an attitude, an observation, or a suggestion. (Use the questions on pages 39–40 to get started.) Revise each statement until it meets the standards on pages 34–35.

Examples

Broad subject	television
Limited subject	certain effects of television commercials
Thesis statement	Television commercials prey on the insecurities of consumers. [*gives an informed opinion*]
Broad subject	marriage
Limited subject	fear of parenthood
Thesis statement	The prospect of becoming a parent in the 1990s frightens me. [*expresses an attitude*]
Broad subject	life-styles
Limited subject	the pace of American life
Thesis statement	Americans everywhere are obsessed with speed. [*shares an observation*]
Broad subject	money

Limited subject	one way to save money
Thesis statement	Becoming a vegetarian is a great way to save money. [*makes a suggestion*]

Application 2–7

From the thesis statements you composed in Application 2–6, select one that seems the best candidate for an essay. List the questions you could expect readers to have about this thesis statement. (Review pages 36–37.)

Example

Thesis statement	Americans everywhere are obsessed with speed.
Readers' questions	Can you show me how?
	Can you give me some examples?
	Says who?

Now, brainstorm for answers to readers' questions. Be sure to delete the items that do not relate directly to your purpose.

Example

Brainstorming list	
	1. big engines in cars
	2. ten-minute oil changes offered by service stations
	3. shoes repaired "while you wait"
	4. fast-food restaurants are booming
	5. jets that can cross the Atlantic in two hours
	6. life in the fast lane
	7. drive-in church services
	8. people gobbling their hamburgers
	9. spitting out your prayer and hitting the road

Using your selected brainstorming materials, compose an essay that explains the viewpoint in your thesis statement. Revise until the essay represents your best effort. Use the questions on pages 21–22 as revision guidelines.

Application 2–8

List the questions you or any reader probably would have about each viewpoint expressed here. If the thesis is a contract with the reader, what must the writer provide to fulfill that contract? (Review pages 36–37.)

Example

Viewpoint	America's income tax structure exploits the middle-class citizen.
Questions	Why do you think so?
	In what specific ways?
	What do you mean by "middle-class citizen"?
	Can you give examples?
	(List any additional questions you or any reader would have.)

1. There is no such thing as a "winnable" nuclear war.
2. "Growing up" means learning to compromise and conform.
3. Today's younger generation is rightly called the "me" generation.
4. Downhill skiing is more dangerous than cross-country skiing
5. Some students have good reason for finding their freshman year boring.

Application 2–9

Revise any four of these assertions that do not already meet the following standards. (Review pages 34–35.)

- focus on a limited topic
- establish a definite viewpoint
- express a significant viewpoint
- preview, in order, the supporting ideas*

---

*For practice, this exercise specifies that each thesis statement include a preview. Remember that some of your own thesis statements will not require a preview.

Mark an X next to those that are adequate.

Example

Faulty thesis   Grades are a way of life in college. [*expresses no definite or significant viewpoint and fails to preview the main supporting points*]

Revised thesis   Grades are an aid to education because they motivate students, provide an objective measure of performance, and prepare people to compete successfully in their careers.

1. My academic adviser is a new professor.
2. Less than one semester in college has changed my outlook.
3. My last blind date was childish, repulsive, and boring.
4. I would love to spend a year in (name a country).
5. Nuclear power is a controversial issue.
6. I have three great fears.
7. In this essay, I will discuss my attitude toward abortion.
8. Elvis Presley had an amazing career.
9. The Batmobile is a good car because it's inexpensive, fuel efficient, and dependable.
10. I (look forward to, dread) marriage.
11. Education enriches our world.

Application 2–10

Write thesis statements for *five* of these subjects. Include a preview of main supporting points in each, if your instructor so requests. (Review pages 30–35.)

your opinion of college life

your opinion of today's teenagers

why you like or dislike pets

someone you love

what you would like your life to be like in ten years

what worries you most about the future

why animals should or should not be allowed on campus

why your hometown is a good or bad place to live

what makes a good teacher

why you came to college

an improvement your college needs

why you enjoy a specified activity

your biggest complaint

anything else you can think of

Application 2-11

Assume you are preparing the body of a paper titled "The Negative Effects of Strip Mining on the Cumberland Plateau Region of Kentucky." This is your thesis (review pages 43–46):

> Decades of strip mining on the Cumberland Plateau have devastated this region's environment, economy, and social structure.

After brainstorming, you settle on these four categories for subtopics:

> social and economic effects of strip mining
>
> description of the strip-mining process
>
> environmental effects of strip mining
>
> description of the Cumberland Plateau

Arrange these categories in the most effective sequence.
Now that your categories are arranged, assume that you have written out (as full sentences) these items from your brainstorming list:

> Contour mining consists of shaving down all ground cover to expose the coal deposits.
>
> Silt dams, designed to trap sediment in ponds rather than downstream, quickly fill and break, causing extensive flood damage and loss of life.

A recent census showed that 19 to 25 percent of the adult population of this region could neither read nor write.

Strip mining is ruining many other areas besides Kentucky.

The Cumberland Plateau was formed approximately 200 million years ago from a plain that had risen from a dried-up inland sea.

One danger of coal as a fuel source is the sulfur dioxide it produces.

This poverty-level existence leaves many families always hungry.

Auger mining employs huge drills that bore through the earth into the coal seam to draw out the coal.

Strip mining scars and pollutes hundreds of acres each week.

Strip-mining processes vary according to the type of terrain.

Using coal for fuel is one way of ending our dependence on imported oil.

Strip mining in the Cumberland Plateau continues to have far-reaching and irreversible effects on the environment.

Strip-mining technology has rendered the skills of farmers and conventional coal miners obsolete, and it has laid waste to a good deal of America's tillable land.

Open-pit mining consists of excavating a terraced, inverted cone into the earth from 100 to 3,000 feet deep; or, this method may employ a series of parallel trenches.

The Cumberland Plateau is a land of jagged hills and narrow, winding valleys covering 10,000 square miles and located 300 miles west of Washington, D.C.

In the Cumberland region of Kentucky and elsewhere in the Appalachians, more than 1 million Americans live in squalor, ignorance, and demoralization.

Soil erosion from strip-mined surfaces occurs at a rate one thousand times greater than that of undisturbed adjacent land.

Air pollution is the terrible price we have to pay for burning coal.

Most of the region's counties show a vast population decrease over the last decade.

Before exploitation, the original plateau held the richest forest on the planet, along with extensive deposits of oil, gas, and coal.

Streams, rivers, and watersheds are polluted by acids and other chemicals, and some become swamps because of mud slides.

Chronic illnesses often result from inadequate diets.

After deleting irrelevant items, arrange the remaining items in order under the appropriate categories. Concentrate on unity, coherence, and emphasis. To increase your control, use this system of notation:

I.   (for a major category)

    A.   (for a topic in that category)
       1.   (for any subtopics)
    B.   2.

II.
    A.   . . . and so on.

Application 2–12

In class: Organize into small groups. Choose a subject from this list. Then decide on a thesis statement and (*not* necessarily in this order) brainstorm. Identify a specific audience. Group similar items under the same major categories, and develop an outline. When each group completes this procedure, one representative can write the outline on the board for class suggestions about revision. (Review pages 38–46.)

    a description of the ideal classroom

    instructions for surviving the first semester of college

    instructions for surviving a blind date

    suggestions for improving one's college experience

    causes of teenage suicide

    arguments for or against a formal grading system

    an argument for an improvement you think this college needs most

    the qualities of a good parent

    what you expect the world to be like in ten years

    young people's needs that parents often ignore

Application 2–13

Using the Planning Guide on pages 49–50 as a model, do all the planning for an essay on one of these two topics:

> Look back on a painful or frightening memory from your childhood or high school years—some event or experience that left you with a feeling of failure, guilt, anger, rejection, embarrassment, or inadequacy. Maybe you remember making a serious mistake or having incredibly bad luck or trying to make a good impression. Describe for classmates how you tried but failed, how you reacted, and what you learned. Whether you write from a serious or humorous perspective, readers will need enough details to visualize what happened and to identify with your feelings about the event or experience.

> As an alternative topic, look back on a pleasant memory, on some event or experience in which you tried and succeeded and which left you with a feeling of triumph or confidence or achievement or satisfaction. Maybe you faced a seemingly impossible challenge or did something courageous. Share this experience with your readers, and tell them what you learned from it.

As your instructor requests, you might move beyond the planning stage and compose your best draft of the essay. Or you might read Chapter 3 before you submit your best draft. Either way, don't be afraid to write one or more *rough* drafts (such as Haley's freewriting on page 12) as part of your planning.

3
Drafting the Essay

Drafting the Title and Introduction • Drafting the Body Section • Drafting the Conclusion • Applications

Once you have a definite plan, you are ready to draft your essay. Here is where you decide on answers to some tough questions:

How do I begin the essay?

What does my reader need to know first?

What comes after that?

How much is enough?

Am I forgetting anything?

How do I end the essay?

Write at least two drafts, revising until the essay represents your best work. Keep in mind that Shirley Haley drafted and revised four times to reach her best version (pages 16–17). And each writing sample in this book is the product of multiple drafts and revisions. None of these writers expected to get it right the first time—neither should you.

Drafting the Title and Introduction

A title should forecast an essay's subject and approach. Shirley Haley's title, "Life in Full Color" (pages 16–17), leads us to expect a vivid discussion about something that makes life interesting. Clear titles, such

61

as "A Terrifying Experience," "Let's Shorten the Baseball Season," or "Instead of Running, Try Walking," help readers plan how to interpret the essay. Phrase your title in a way that attracts attention but doesn't sound like a commercial or a sideshow gimmick. A "catchy" title can be a real attention grabber, but it also can make a serious essay seem trivial. To be sure you give an accurate forecast, write your title's final version *after* completing the essay.

THE INTRODUCTORY PARAGRAPH

Your introduction tells readers what they need to know first. An introductory paragraph opens an essay in three ways: it leads into the thesis and main discussion; it arouses readers' interest; and it creates a setting and a tone for the whole essay. Above all, your introduction must be *clear* and *vivid* enough to invite readers in. If you lose readers here, chances are you've lost them for good.

Introductory paragraphs differ in shape and size; however, many basic introductory paragraphs seem to have a funnel shape:

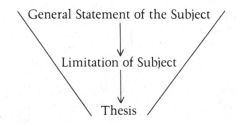

Assume you are continuing your work from Chapter 2 on "Suffering Through Gym Class." To introduce the final draft of your essay, you use a funnel pattern:

Suffering Through Gym Class

General statement (1)
Limitation of subject (2–4)

[1]In high school my Monday mornings were awful. [2]Even before the school's front door had slammed behind me, I could sense a nauseating dampness rising up from the locker room, a mist of stale sweat. [3]Monday for me was physical education day. [4]And because I was no athlete, each of my 8:00 a.m. trips downstairs to the gym seemed like a clammy and quivering walk to the guillotine, my heartbeat like a drumbeat, my ego

Thesis (5)   about to suffer its ritual of public execution. [5]For three long years, gym class was my weekly exercise in failure.

This account of a painful experience is written for classmates. And so its tone is personal and urgent, created by the first-person *I* and *my*, *our*, and by images such as "a clammy and quivering walk to the guillotine."

If your only aim were to lead into the main discussion, you might have given this introduction instead:

I always did poorly in high school gym class.

But this version contains none of the vivid images ("nauseating dampness," "a mist of stale sweat") that make the original engage our attention, make us want to read on. And this version is toneless. What kind of attitude is expressed here? We can't possibly tell. Because the writer seems not to care much about the topic or the audience, we don't care, either.

Worse than a lifeless opening is one that exaggerates to attract attention:

In high school gym class, I had the most incredible experiences of my life, experiences that burned deeply into my soul. Never will I forget those humiliating moments spent trying to be an athlete.

Any introduction you write for your first draft probably will be only a *tentative* one. You almost always need to revise it in your final draft.

PLACING THE THESIS

Where you place your thesis depends on the way in which you want readers to perceive and react to your introduction. Ordinarily, readers expect some kind of background that sets the scene for your thesis, but sometimes they want to know where you stand right away.

The thesis in a standard essay usually comes at the end of the introductory paragraph, as a connector to the discussion. Also, with the thesis statement at the end, the earlier sentences draw readers into the writer's world. If it had begun flatly with the thesis, the introduction to "Suffering Through Gym Class" would be much less inviting. Without background, we are less prepared to understand the message, and less interested.

Some introductions, however, do call for a thesis statement that leads off the paragraph. For a controversial topic especially, the writer's position might be expressed immediately:

> *Corporal punishment does not belong in our public schools, because it creates a regimented atmosphere that stifles the desire to learn, generates hostility toward the teacher, and causes antisocial behavior.* A school, after all, is not a prison. And among the varied learning experiences it should provide its students is the opportunity to learn through mistakes.

To evoke an immediate reader response, this writer decided to open with a direct statement of his position. The paragraph then expands the thesis.

Sometimes, even a highly personal piece can open directly with the thesis, especially when the writer is expressing a surprising or controversial viewpoint:

> *I hate summer beaches.* Ocean swimming is impossible; upon conquering a wave, I simply lose to the next, getting pushed back onto the hard-packed, abrasive sand. Booby-traps of bottles, soda cans, toys, and rocks make walking hazardous. Heavy with the stench of suntan lotion, greasy French fries, dead fish, and sweat, the thick, searing air hangs motionless about the scorching sand. Blasting radios and growling hot rods cut the slap-swoosh of the green-gray surf to a weak hiss. People devour a summer beach, gouging the sand with umbrella spikes and gripping it with oiled limbs, leaving only trampled debris at summer's end.

By opening directly with your thesis, you alert readers immediately to where you stand.

THE MULTIPLE-PARAGRAPH INTRODUCTION

Although single paragraphs can serve for most introductions, you might use two or more paragraphs, especially in developing some kind of comparison. In the next introduction the first paragraph offers a view of "primitive" New Guinea, in contrast to the second paragraph's focus on the "modern" aspect of this island nation.

> Poised like an ungainly bird over the north coast of Australia, the island of New Guinea is one of the few remaining "final frontiers" on earth. Hundreds of stone-age tribes survive in the highlands, isolated from each other by massive mountain ranges. Here, in valleys and rain forests still fresh and undiscovered by

modern science, live people intimate with the supernatural, skilled in potent sorcery. They are garden people, communing with the land and bound by a complex web of interlocking kinships.

But while the twentieth century is slowly finding its way into these primeval highland villages, it has hurled itself full force on the coastlands. *Port Moresby, New Guinea's capital city, is a symbol of a nation in transition, where the old and the new exist side by side, sometimes in conflict, often in harmony.*

SELECTING AN OPENING STRATEGY

The specific shape and content of your introduction are determined by what you know about your readers and your purpose.

How interested in this topic are my readers likely to be?

How can I make them want to read on?

Are they likely to react defensively?

Is my purpose to describe something, to tell a story, to explain something, to entertain, to change somebody's mind, or something else?

The opening strategies here are designed to serve varied purposes. Whichever approach you choose, make it *inviting.*

Open with an Anecdote   A brief, personal story that makes a point (leads to the thesis*) is a good way to invite readers in.

Last weekend, I gave a friend's younger brother a ride from the mall. As we drove, I asked him the same old questions about high school, grades, football, and girlfriends. He answered me in one-word sentences and then pulled out a cassette tape. "Wanna hear somethin' cool?" I shrugged and popped it into the tape player. What came pouring through my car speakers made me run a stop sign. The "rap" song spelled out, in elaborate detail, 101 ways to violate a woman's body. Needless to say, it was a long ride across town.

I borrowed the tape and listened to every song, horrified by their recurrent theme of sexual violence and domination. But most horrifying is that a 15-year-old kid actually considers this music "cool."

---

*Many narratives will have no explicit thesis.

In this brief but forceful anecdote, the writer's straightforward approach to a vital contemporary issue is sure to make readers take notice.

Open with a Background Story   In an essay that challenges or argues against a popular attitude, telling how and why that attitude became prevalent sometimes helps.

> In 1945, an unearthly blast shook the New Mexico desert. Shortly afterward, the new, awesome force was used, at the cost of hundreds of thousands of lives, to end World War II. Thus began the atomic era, and because of its horrid beginning, it has met with increasing criticism. Now in the 90s the nuclear breeder reactor is our most promising energy alternative, but atomic energy critics have drastically reduced its development and production. *We need the breeder reactor, because it is presently our best long-range source of energy.*

The vivid images here attract our attention. This kind of opening is especially effective in persuasive writing, because it anticipates opposing views and, by acknowledging them, creates a tone of empathy (identification with the reader's attitude).

Open with a Question   A question or series of questions can get readers thinking, especially when you are writing instructions, giving advice, or persuading someone to act.

> What do you do when you find yourself in the produce room cooler with your manager and he nonchalantly wraps his arm around your waist? Or how about when the guys you work with come out with a distasteful remark that makes you seem like a piece of meat? These are just a couple of problems you might face as the only female in a department. *There are, however, ways of dealing with this kind of harassment.*

Any reader who needs this advice would be likely to take it seriously, for the writer clearly has identified with her audience.

Open with a Quotation   Use a quotation summarizing the point you are making or disputing. Always use a *short* quotation, and discuss its significance immediately afterward; don't leave to readers the task of making the connection.

> "The XL Roadster—anything else is just a car," *unless the XL happens to be mine. In that case, it's just a piece of junk.*

Notice how this writer uses the words of the ad ironically to make her point. The abrupt opening reflects her anger and creates a forceful tone.

Open with a Direct Address   Readers generally pay more attention when addressed directly. Using the second-person *you* can be a good way to involve the reader—especially when giving instructions or advice or when writing persuasively.

> Does the thought of artificially preserved, chemically treated food make you lose your appetite? Do limp, tasteless, frozen vegetables leave you cold? *Then you should try your hand at organic gardening.*

This opening combines direct address with questions. The enthusiastic tone is reinforced by concrete images. *Caution:* Use *you* only when writing *directly* to the audience—only when the subject is something *about* your audience. Avoid using second person with a subject that calls for third-person point of view. Otherwise, you could make this kind of error:

Incorrect use of *you*   When you are a freshman in college, you soon discover that increased freedom also means increased responsibility for you.

Revised   College freshmen soon discover that increased freedom also means increased responsibility.

Direct address usually works well in ads, popular articles, and brochures—but not in academic reports or most business and technical documents.

Open with a Description   The saying "One picture is worth more than ten thousand words" certainly holds true in writing. A brief, vivid picture is an excellent way to set the scene or create a mood. Instead of including a standard thesis statement in the introduction, some descriptive essays simply have an *orienting sentence* to place readers at the center of things. This introduction ends with an orienting sentence that leads into the essay:

> The raft bobs gently on the ocean as the four divers help each other with scuba gear. We joke and laugh casually as we struggle in the cramped space; but a restlessness is in the air because we want to be on our way. Finally, everyone is ready, and we split into pairs. I steal a last glance over the blue ocean. I hear the waves slap gently against the boat, the mournful cry of a seagull, and a steady murmur

from the crowded beach a mile away. With three splashes my friends jump in. I follow. There is a splash and then silence. The water presses in on me, and all I can hear is the sound of my regulator as I take my first breath. All I see is blue water, yellow light, and endless space. It feels as if we are suspended in time while the world rushes on. *Then my buddy taps me on the shoulder, and we begin a tour of a hidden world.*

Notice how the sharp images draw us into the scene and how choice of words ("restlessness," "steal a last glance," "finally") contributes to a suspenseful tone.

Although commonly used in narrative and descriptive essays, descriptive openings can also serve in explanatory essays, as with this opening:

They appear each workday morning from 7:00 to 9:00, role models for millions of career-minded women. Their crisp, clear diction and articulate reporting are second only to their appearance. Slender and lovely, the female co-hosts of "Today" and other morning news shows radiate that businesslike "chic" that networks consider essential in their newswomen. Such perfection is precisely why the networks hire these women as anchors. *Network television rarely tolerates women commentators who are other than young, slim, and attractive.*

Notice the businesslike tone that parallels the topic itself.

Open with Examples   Examples can immediately engage and alert your readers to an issue or problem by enabling them to *visualize* the topic.

Privacy in America seems to be disappearing. New technologies enable users to unearth the health, credit, and legal records of almost anyone at the punch of a computer key. Beyond these computerized records, our telephones, television sets, and even our trash can be monitored by government agencies, banks, businesses, political groups—or just plain nosy people. *Current United States law does disturbingly little to protect our right to privacy.*

Notice how the list of brief but vivid examples causes us to pay close attention to the thesis.

Open with a Definition   An essay on an abstract subject such as *patriotism* or *courage* almost inevitably requires an opening that defines the abstract term for both writer and reader. This writer begins an essay on abortion by defining the key issue: life.

> What is "life"? A tree is alive, a dog is alive, a fish is alive; yet we willfully eliminate these life forms in favor of building a house, controlling the stray dog population, or catching a fish for dinner. Some of the reasoning behind this form of murder is that these beings lack sophisticated thought processes. They do not question why they are alive; they merely exist. Psychologists claim that without consistent symbols to apply to meanings, there can be no evaluative thoughts on life. In other words, a dog cannot think in an abstract way about why he is a dog or about how being a dog differs from being a cat. He "thinks" in the symbols he knows—hunger, food, pain, or chasing rabbits. But he cannot analyze how he could improve his rabbit chase next time; no symbols are there for him to apply to a time sequence. A human embryo also has no symbols to apply to its growing life form (given the supposition that a developing brain can partially function). Nothing is there to distinguish "I" from "them" or "life" from "death." The embryo is growing into a complete life form but does not yet have the awareness of a functioning human being. *Is it possible, then, for an embryo to recognize its own existence? And is that embryonic existence more important than the life of a stray dog, if its future will consist of being unwanted in an already overcrowded world?*

These openings have things in common. Each has some description, several carry a brief background story. Even so, your own introduction might resemble none of these. So much the better—as long as it makes us keep reading.

Some Final Hints

- Many writers consider the introduction the hardest part of an essay; therefore they often write the final version of their introduction *last*. If you do write your introduction first, be sure to go back and revise it afterward.

- In most college writing, you will want to avoid introducing your discussion with personal qualifiers such as "it is my opinion that," "I believe that," "I will now discuss," and "in this paper I will."

- Try to let your introduction create some kind of suspense that is resolved by your thesis statement, usually at the end of the paragraph(s).

- Think about the chemistry you want with your reader. If the opening is boring, coy, vague, or long-winded, your audience may not read on. Give your opening the voice of a real human being. Don't waste readers' time with needless background.

- Keep the tone in your introduction consistent with the tone in your essay. For instance, don't use a humorous opening for a serious piece, or vice versa.

Drafting the Body Section

The body of the essay reveals the substance and shape of your thinking. Here you deliver on the commitment made in your thesis. Readers always expect a clear line of thought and enough details to understand your exact meaning. Readers never expect details that just get in the way, or a jigsaw puzzle they will have to unscramble for themselves. Developing the body, therefore, requires decisive answers to these questions:

How much is enough?

How much information or detail should I provide?

How can I keep myself and my readers from getting off the track?

What shape will reveal my line of thought?

You need enough of the right material to make your point, and you need to organize that material so readers can follow it.

Decide about the essay's substance (or content). Focus on ways of rethinking your draft. How much is enough? Here is where you throw out some material you thought you'd keep, and maybe come up with additional material. Take a hard look at everything you've discovered during your freewriting, brainstorming, or questioning. Think about your purpose. Stand in the reader's place. Think about unity. Keep what belongs, and discard what doesn't. Maybe you need to sweat again, until you find what you need.

Decide about the essay's shape. How many support paragraphs will you need? From page 32, we recall that each support paragraph has its own *topic statement*, focusing on one aspect of the thesis. A support paragraph, in fact, is usually a mini-essay, with its own introduction, body, and conclusion (or transition to the next paragraph). The body of a college essay typically has three or more support paragraphs. But three is by no means a magic number. Use as few or as many paragraphs as it takes to get the message across.

Besides determining the *number* of support paragraphs, you have other shaping decisions as well. How should you develop each support paragraph? What order should you follow to make the most sense, to give the best emphasis? Before discussing these decisions, let's look at the final draft of the body for "Suffering Through Gym Class." Assume you've revised twice, to improve content and organization as well as style. (In Chapter 4 we will look at the steps in revision that created this finished version.) For ease of reading, the introductory paragraph from page 62 is included here.

Suffering Through Gym Class

Introductory paragraph

    In high school my Monday mornings were awful. Even before the school's front door had slammed behind me, I could sense a nauseating dampness rising up from the locker room, a mist of stale sweat. Monday for me was physical education day. And because I was no athlete, each of my 8:00 a.m. trips downstairs to the gym seemed like a clammy and quivering walk to the guillotine, my heartbeat like a drumbeat, my ego about to suffer its ritual of public execution. *For*

Thesis

three long years, gym class was my weekly exercise in failure.

Topic statement

    Although I respected my gym teacher's focus on excellence, *the standards in this class were beyond my ability.* Everybody was expected to be an athlete—and nothing less would do. Effort was

First body paragraph

ignored in favor of performance. Winning became all-important, and losing teams were punished with extra laps. The fun in any game quickly disappeared. To make matters worse, some gung-ho classmates seemed to mirror our teacher's attitude; in a few short weeks, a kind of caste system had developed: jocks on top, the marginally acceptable in the middle, and klutzes like me—the untouchables—at the very bottom.

Topic statement

    Whatever sport we played, I could count on being the loser, even when my team won. In

Second body paragraph

baseball, I was the sure strikeout, the right fielder whose glove had a hole in it. In basketball, I had a hard time hitting the backboard, much less scoring a basket. In soccer, I tripped over my own feet. No less disastrous than team sports were

those emphasizing individual performance.
Parallel bars, hurdles, broad jumps, or high
jumps—all were occasions for my world-class
embarrassment. The more pathetic attempts I
made, the more I came to feel incompetent and
inferior.

Topic statement

Third body paragraph

I was continually reminded of my failures.
Whenever players were picked for teams, I was
sure to be last—huddled among the few
remaining rejects trying to look nonchalant.
Bracing myself at home plate for the inevitable
swing-and-miss, I could count on hearing a few
hisses and groans from teammates, and at least
one reassuring "easy out!" from opponents. Even
my friends affectionately nicknamed me "the
athlete." More charitable than my peers, our
teacher simply ignored, for the most part, those of
us who qualified as wimps. And, as if to certify
my incompetence, my C-minus grade (a gift, I
guess, for passing "showers") would destroy an
otherwise impressive grade average. At all these
indignities I laughed on the outside, but not on
the inside.*

This piece works because it is the product of careful decisions
about content. The essay's body gives a sharply focused picture,
enabling readers to feel what the writer felt. And the picture is unified:
nothing gets in the way; everything belongs.

But content alone cannot ensure contact. Things need shaping as
well. Only the orderly development of your thoughts can allow us into
the reality you remember, help us grasp your experience and appreciate
its importance. Each paragraph, richly supported by details, leads us
through your weekly sequence of anxiety, alienation, inadequacy, and
then humiliation. Throughout, the shape reveals and reinforces your
meaning.

We've covered here only briefly matters affecting the shape of
your writing: unity, coherence, emphasis, and transition; all are discussed fully in Chapter 7, "Shaping the Paragraphs." Principles of the
individual paragraph are principles as well of the whole essay—or of
writing at any length.

---

*The concluding paragraph is on page 73.

Drafting the Conclusion

A good conclusion *closes* an essay. It refocuses on the thesis and leaves a final—and lasting—impression on the readers. Your conclusion might evaluate the meaning or significance of the material in the body, restate your position, predict an outcome, offer a solution, request an action, make a recommendation, or pave the way for further exploration. Never just stop, having run out of things to say.

Create a sense of completeness by summing up, interpreting, evaluating, driving home the point you want to impress on your readers. Tell us what to make of the words we've just read. What should we be thinking or feeling or doing? Should we be angry or curious or supportive, or what? Keep your conclusion brief, but always help us finish.

Provide emphasis without repeating, apologizing, or belaboring the obvious. Avoid conclusions like these:

> I have just discussed my reasons for disliking gym class. I never did well at any sport I played. [*repeats*]

> Although some readers might be bored reading about my experiences in gym class, they mean a lot to me. [*apologizes*]

> Now that you've read my essay, you should have a clear picture of what my gym class was like. [*belabors the obvious*]

Flat, toneless endings such as these drain the life from any writing. Their biggest flaw is lack of concreteness: nothing about them sticks in the memory. Here, in contrast, is a forceful conclusion to the final draft of "Suffering Through Gym Class":

> The whole experience left me feeling defeated. Instead of having fun and gaining self-confidence, I felt blacklisted. Intimidated by a standard of performance impossible for me to achieve, I never gave myself the chance to discover my personal best. Taking fewer and fewer risks, I grew to accept the certainty of failure in sports. Those painful years are now behind me, but I still have trouble playing even a sport as casual as volleyball without feeling self-conscious. Looking back, I can appreciate the value of challenge in any class, but I can't help resenting a system that so relentlessly forces personal shortcomings into public display.

This conclusion explores the significance of what happened to you in gym class. The first four sentences tell us how repeated failures affected your sense of self-worth. The fifth sentence tells us about the lasting effects of such an experience. The final sentence brings everything together by reemphasizing your way of seeing: ambivalence and resentment toward an experience that challenges all students but humiliates some.

Readers remember last things best, and this conclusion leaves us with something worth remembering.

SELECTING A CLOSING STRATEGY

This list of strategies is by no means exhaustive, but it samples common ways of signaling that a discussion has ended.

Close with an Insightful Look Backward   You might want to pull things together with a concluding insight about your main point, as in the gym class essay above.

Close with a Question   Forcing readers to confront a closing question can be a good way to nail down an argument:

> Overall, the advantages of the breeder reactor strike me as immeasurable. Because it can produce more fuel than it uses, it will theoretically be an infinite source of energy. And efficient use of the fuel it does burn makes it highly desirable in this energy-tight era. What other source promises so much for our long-range energy future?

This closing also summarizes the major points in the body. Summaries are especially effective in argumentative essays.

Close with a Call to Action   Make a specific suggestion for action:

> Just imagine yourself eating a salad of crisp green lettuce, juicy red tomato chunks, firm white slices of cucumber, and crunchy strips of green pepper—all picked fresh from your own garden. If this picture appeals to you, begin planning your summer garden now, and by July the picture of you eating that salad will become a reality. *Bon appétit!*

Direct address, of course, will cause readers to pay more attention to your advice.

Close with a Quotation   If you are writing in response to something you've read, you might close with a relevant quote from the author. This writer quotes from journalist Ellen Goodman's essay, "Blame the Victim."

I agree with Ellen Goodman's assertion that there is "something malignant about some of the extremists who make a public virtue of their health." The cancer is in the superior attitudes of the "health elite"—an attitude that actually discourages exercise and healthy habits by making average people feel too intimidated and inferior even to begin a fitness program.

Close with an Interpretation or Evaluation   Save readers work by interpreting facts and evaluating evidence.

A growing array of so-called private information about American citizens is collected daily. And few laws protect one's right to be left alone. In the interest of pursuing criminals, government too often sacrifices the privacy of innocent people, and new technology is making old laws obsolete. Huge collections of data are becoming available to your insurance company, to prospective employers, to companies doing mass mailings, and even to your neighbor. The invasion continues, and no one seems to know how to stop our world from fulfilling the prophecy in George Orwell's *1984*.

Close by Creating a Mood   If you have just narrated an event or described a place, you may want to leave readers with a final impression about what being there was like. This writer closes her description of New Guinea by sharing with us a tropical sunset.

Tonight as the sun slips into the Coral Sea, the tropical sky shimmers with pastel shades then fades to the soft light of the southern constellations. Standing in the twilight on Gabutu Point, you can hear the gecko lizards squabbling in the grass, and farther off, the tide steadily rising against the cliffs, and perhaps farther still, rhythmic drums and voices raised in a tribal song of celebration for a South Pacific night.

These strategies all rely on rich, vivid description for concreteness. Whichever strategy or combination of strategies you select, be sure that your conclusion is in some way memorable and that it refocuses on your main point without repeating it.

Application 3–1

Plan and draft an essay about something *special* to you; it might be a place, a person, an experience, an activity, or anything else—but it has to be something you're sure is worth writing about. Decide on an audience: your classmates, a friend, readers of the campus paper, or someone close to you. Your purpose here is to *share* your way of seeing, and so be sure your audience comes to understand *why* the thing is special. Let them see it and let them feel your responses to it. Be vivid but not melodramatic. Have a thesis, and deliver on it.

Think about a voice that will appeal to your readers. Think about unity so that your writing sticks to the point, and about order and transition so that it sticks together. Have a beginning, a middle, and an ending.

(Use the questions on pages 21–22 for guidance in improving your essay.)

Application 3–2

Now you know more about how to begin, how to develop and shape the middle, and how to finish. Return to an essay you wrote earlier (maybe your first, or one your instructor recommends), and write a better draft. List the improvements you make, and be prepared to discuss them.

Application 3–3

Locate a good introduction to a short article in a popular magazine such as *Time, Newsweek,* or *Reader's Digest.* In one paragraph discuss the strategies that make the introduction effective. Bring a copy of the article to class. (Review pages 61–70.)

Application 3–4

Locate a good conclusion to a short article in a popular magazine. In one paragraph discuss the strategies that make the conclusion effective. Bring a copy of the article to class. (Review pages 73–75.)

Application 3–5

Complete the essay you began in Application 2–13.

Application 3–6

Write an essay to next year's incoming freshmen, explaining how to survive the early weeks of college. You might focus on what seems to go wrong, how to avoid some common mistakes, and what freshmen can look forward to—once life settles down to something normal. Be sure your essay supports a clear viewpoint. (Your tone here will be important; you don't want this to sound like a sermon. Give it some personality!)

4

Revising
the Essay

The Meaning of Revision • Revision Checklist
• Using the Checklist • Applications

Besides being a battle with impatience, writing is a battle with inertia: once we've rested after writing a draft, we usually want to *continue* resting, too easily satisfied with what we've written. Good writers win the battle by revising as often as needed to make real contact.

For the sake of clarity, earlier chapters have presented a single sequence of steps for composing an essay. To review:

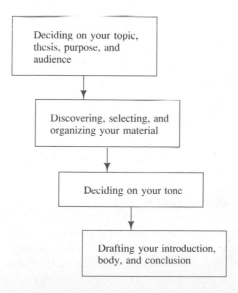

Figure 4.1

But writers rarely follow this exact sequence. Finished essays are reached in more ways than one. Some writers begin by brainstorming or freewriting. Some come up with a solid thesis immediately, without having to struggle over their purpose. Some make an outline and then write a thesis. Others use no outline at all; instead they write and rewrite, using scissors and tape to organize their material. Some even write a whole draft of an essay before coming up with their thesis. Often the best introductions and titles are written last. And so on. In short, it would be nonsense to suggest that the writing process follows one lockstep approach: first do this; then do that. The "process" is a lot more mysterious and unpredictable than that.

No matter what the sequence, a fact of life for any effective writer is *revision*—the one constant in the writing process. When you have finished a first draft, you have really only begun; don't give in to inertia. Take the time to make a poor essay adequate, or an adequate essay excellent. We might say there are no good writers—only good rewriters.

The Meaning of Revision

Revision involves more than proofreading to fix spelling or to insert a comma or to attend to other mechanical details (all covered in the Appendix). Although mechanical correctness is essential, you need to attend, as well, to your essay's *rhetorical* features: worthwhile content, sensible organization, and readable style. Specifically, you might need to cut needless details or add needed ones; to find the exact word or improve coherence; to sharpen the focus, alter the tone, or eliminate wordiness; to improve the organization or eliminate trite expressions. Your instructor might write suggestions on your first draft or might ask you to revise on your own. In any case, revision never means merely *recopying*; it always means *rethinking.*

Before you can improve your draft, you have to decide what in the draft is effective and what is not so effective. Useful revision happens only when you can evaluate accurately what you have already written:

How does this draft measure up?

Does it achieve what I want it to achieve?

Is it the best I can do?

How can I improve it?

These general questions suggest many more specific questions for evaluating an essay. Nobody can solve problems they cannot identify. You can pretty much pinpoint the problems in any writing by evaluating it for three essential features: content that makes the piece worthwhile; organization that makes it easy to follow; and style that makes it read-

Revision Checklist

WORTHWHILE CONTENT
1. *The essay's main point is clear and sharply focused.*
    a. Does the title attract attention and give a forecast? (61)
    b. Is the topic limited enough? (27)
    c. Do you get to your main point quickly? (62)
    d. Is the thesis definite, informative, and easy to find? (30)

2. *The discussion delivers on the promise of your thesis.*
    a. Will readers learn something new and useful? (36)
    b. Do you support every assertion with enough details? (105)
    c   Does everything belong, or can anything be cut? (42)
    d. Have you used only your *best* material? (108)

SENSIBLE ORGANIZATION
3. *The essay has a definite introduction, body, and conclusion.*
    a. Will your introduction make readers want to read on? (69)
    b. Does each body paragraph develop *one* supporting point? (70)
    c. Does the order of body paragraphs reveal a clear line of thought
        and emphasize what is most important? (72)
    d. Does the conclusion give a real sense of an ending? (73)
    e. Is everything connected? (132)
    f. If you varied this organization, was it for good reason? (224)

4. *Except for paragraphs of transition or special emphasis, each
    body (or support) paragraph usually is a mini-essay.*
    a. Does the paragraph have a topic (or orienting) statement? (126)
    b. Does the topic statement come at the beginning or end,
        depending on your emphasis? (135)
    c. Does everything stick to the point (unity), and stick together
        (coherence)? (130)
    d. Is the paragraph developed enough to support the point? (113)

READABLE STYLE
5. *Sentences are clear, concise, and fluent.*
    a. Can each sentence be understood the first time it is read? (158)
    b. Is the information expressed in the fewest words? (174)
    c. Are sentences put together with enough variety? (184)

6. *Each word does its job.*
    a. Is a real person speaking, and is the voice likable? (46)
    b. Is everything in plain English? (206)
    c. Is your meaning precise, concrete, and specific? (197)
    d. Is your tone appropriate for this situation and audience? (204)

able, clear, and engaging. These features are detailed in the Revision Checklist. (Numbers refer to the first page of discussion.)

Using the Checklist

Unless you are writing an in-class essay, your instructor may ask you to revise your first draft before handing in the essay. You can use the Revision Checklist as a guide for rethinking your essay by asking yourself questions such as these:

- Have I conveyed the exact point or feeling I wanted to get across?

- Do vivid details from the event come to mind now that I've finished writing?

- What facts or figures or ideas do I now remember as I read what I've written?

- Can I reorganize anything for greater emphasis or clarity?

- Can I find a better way of saying what I want to?

- Does this draft sound as I wanted it to sound, or is it too corny or detached or arrogant or humble or what?

Eventually you should find that you can revise almost automatically, without following the checklist item by item.

Assume you've written this early draft of "Suffering Through Gym Class":

> Like any other student, I feel that many of my high school experiences were memorable. Few of them, however, were as memorable as my gym class. Every Monday morning, I would feel my anxiety rising as I thought about facing the most hateful part of my week.
>
> In all fairness, I'm sure my gym teacher was kind. But athletic prowess was expected of every student, and nothing less would do. The fun in any game quickly disappeared. The students' effort was ignored in favor of performance. The students seemed to take on the same attitude as the teacher; students with athletic skill were seen as superior to those who lacked athletic skill. The whole thing made me sick. Physical education teachers should learn to control their biases and accept students who lack athletic abilities. The whole system otherwise ends up doing more harm than good.

Whatever sport we played, I could count on being the loser, even when my team won. In both team sports and individual sports, all I seemed to be able to do in each gym class was to make some kind of pathetic attempt. Some people simply have little or no athletic ability, and I'm one of them. It seemed as if every effort I made resulted in embarrassment. All I could do on these occasions was feel incompetent.

I was always one of the last players picked for teams. As I waited at home plate to swing and miss, I could already hear the hisses and groans from other players on my team, and the "easy-out" chant from members of the opposing team. Even people who were my friends nicknamed me "the athlete." Although these friends were only joking, they nevertheless caused me to suffer emotionally. My teacher seemed to ignore all those students who failed to excel in the achievement of athletic goals. At semester's end, I always received a C-minus grade.

What really are the underlying elements of sports? I would say that the elements are these: rules, teamwork, and tolerance. Combining all these concepts into a grade makes more sense than counting the number of home runs in a semester. Faculty, students, and administrators should work together to improve the system.

We can see that this draft needs a good deal of revision. First, the content leaves lots of reader questions unanswered:

- What, exactly, was the class like?

- What, exactly, did you do that was so bad?

- What was the meaning of this whole experience for you?

And although the organization of this draft hints at an introduction, body, and conclusion, some paragraphs lack topic sentences and clear connections between ideas. Finally, the style has problems: sentences that are too similar in the way they're put together, causing a monotonous tone; other sentences that sound stuffy or too much like a sermon instead of like a person speaking.

On the following pages you will see how the checklist can help you revise to achieve the finished essay shown on pages 71–73. (Notice that this revision treats only the *rhetorical* features: content, organization, and style. A checklist for correcting grammar, punctuation, and mechanics appears on page 529.)

For reference, the paragraphs from the essay are labeled A through E. Specific needed improvements are explained on the facing page. References (such as "3-a") on the facing pages lead you to items in the checklist.

Suffering through Gym Class

(circled margin note: Rewrite introduction to invite readers in)

~~Like every student, I feel that many of my high~~ ~~school experiences were memorable.~~ ~~Few of them,~~ ~~however, were as memorable as my gym class.~~ Every

[A]

(circled margin note: Give more of a forecast in the thesis)

Tuesday morning, I would feel my anxiety rising as

I thought about facing the most hateful part of my

week. *Although I respected my gym teacher's commitment to excellence,*
the standards in this class simply were impossible for me to reach.
~~In all fairness, I'm sure my gym teacher was kind.~~
Everybody was expected to be an athlete
~~But athletic prowess was expected of every student~~, and

(circled margin note: Sentence variety)

nothing less would do. (The) fun in any game quickly
                                                    E
disappeared. ~~(The) students¹~~ éffort was ignored in favor

of performance. (The) students seemed to take on the

[B]

same attitude as the teacher; students with athletic

(circled margin note: More description here)

skill were seen as superior to those who lacked athletic

skill. (The) whole thing made me sick. ~~Physical educa-~~

~~tion teachers should learn to control their biases~~ and

~~accept students who lack athletic abilities.~~ (The) ~~whole~~

~~system otherwise ends up doing more harm than good.~~

Whatever sport we played, I could count on being

(circled margin note: give examples)

the loser, even when my team won. ⟨ In both team sports
            (parallel bars, hurdles, etc.)
and individual sports ∧ all I seemed to be able to do ~~in~~

[C]

~~each gym class~~ was to make some kind of pathetic attempt.
In baseball, I was the sure strike-out, the right-fielder whose
glove had a hole in it. In basketball, I had a hard time hitting the
backboard, much less scoring a basket. In soccer, I tripped over my
own feet.

Figure 4.2

Paragraph A: The essay lacks a title (1-a), and the introduction needs more development (3-a) to give readers an orientation, a clear sense of what they can expect. The opening sentence is so general and obvious as to be meaningless (2-a). The second sentence seems to beat around the bush, doing little to advance meaning (1-c). Presumably the thesis, the final sentence suggests an attitude, but readers are not sure why gym class was such a hateful experience (because it was boring, too hard, too easy, or what?). The thesis needs to be more definite and informative (1-d).

Paragraph B: This first support paragraph needs a topic statement (4-a) that forecasts the content of the paragraph. Sentences throughout need greater variety (5-c), especially to cut down on the many "the" sentence openers that create a monotonous tone. The final two sentences don't really belong (2-c); they sound too much like a sermon (6-d). And readers need some kind of transition (3-e) to the paragraph that follows.

Paragraph C: This paragraph contains too many needless words (5-b) and too few details (2-b). Because it merely repeats earlier material, the third sentence can be cut (2-c). Concrete and specific details are needed throughout to make meaning clear (4-d and 6-c). What were some of the "pathetic attempts"? To share the writer's embarrassment, readers need to *visualize* what happened.

~~Some people simply have little or no athletic ability,~~

~~and I'm one of them.~~   ~~It seemed as if~~ every effort I
seemed to

made~~resulted~~ in embarrassment. All I could do ~~on~~
and inferior

~~these occasions~~ was ~~to~~ feel incompetent.
I was continually reminded of my failures.

I was always one of the last players picked for
along with the other rejects

teams. As I waited at home plate to swing and miss, I

could already hear the hisses and groans from other

players on my team, and the "easy-out" chant from ~~mem~~
opponents.

~~bers of the opposing team.~~ Even ~~people who were~~ my
affectionately

friends nicknamed me "the athlete." Although ~~these~~
hurt

~~friends were~~ only joking, they nevertheless ~~caused~~
my feelings

~~me to suffer emotionally.~~ My teacher seemed to ignore
qualified as wimps

all those students who ~~failed to excel in the achieve-~~

~~ment of athletic goals.~~ At semester's end, I always

recieved a C~~-~~minus grade. *(a gift for passing "showers" I guess)*
At all these indignities I laughed on the outside, but not on the inside.

~~What really are the underlying elements of sports?~~

~~I would say that the elements are these: rules, team-~~

~~work, and tolerance. Combining all these concepts into~~

~~a grade makes more sense than counting the number of~~

~~home runs in a semester. Faculty, students, and admin-~~

~~istrators should work together to improve the system.~~
The whole experience left me feeling defeated.

(margin notes)
Loosen the tone

D

E

Relate the ending directly to the painful memory.

show the overall meaning of the experience

Talk about this detail

Paragraph D: Although this paragraph seems adequately developed with informative details, it lacks a topic sentence (4-a) that would give readers a framework for understanding these details. The tone (6-d) often seems stuffy: "caused me to suffer emotionally" instead of "hurt my feelings." For this kind of personal topic and audience especially, the tone should be more like that of a person speaking. Lightening the tone also would help eliminate many needlessly big or just plain needless words (5-b). And some sort of transition (3-e) to the concluding paragraph is needed.

Paragraph E: This conclusion strays from your essay's purpose: to share with us your painful memory. Instead of giving a real sense of an ending (3-d), the paragraph seems more like part of some other essay about how gym classes should be run and evaluated. A good conclusion here would sum up the *meaning* of your experience. Also, the tone seems much too *preachy* (6-d), inconsistent with your earlier reminiscence.

To give yourself scribbling room as you revise your own work, write longhand drafts on every other line (or, if you type your drafts, use triple spacing).

Although the final version of "Suffering Through Gym Class" (pages 71–73) isn't "perfect," it is still a respectable piece of writing—by anyone's standards. By using the checklist, you have revised to create an essay that makes contact through worthwhile content, sensible organization, and readable style. (For detailed advice on achieving these qualities in any final draft, see Chapters 6–9.)

Application 4–1

Now you know more about what to look for when evaluating an essay—and you have more to think about as well! Using the page 81 Revision Checklist as a guide, return to an essay you have written earlier, and do your best job of revising it.

At this early stage, you are bound to feel a little confused about the finer points of content, organization, and style. But try not to worry; just do your best. Later chapters will help improve your skill for diagnosing problems and prescribing cures.

Along with your revised essay, submit an explanation of the improvements you've made, together with the original essay.

Application 4–2

Take an essay you have written earlier, and exchange it for a classmate's. Write a detailed evaluation of your classmate's essay, making specific suggestions for revision. Use the page 81 checklist as your guide. Be sure to look at all three rhetorical features: content, organization, and style. Use the Appendix to recommend any improvements in grammar, punctuation, and mechanics. Do plenty of scribbling on the essay, and sign your evaluation.

Hint: Assume your classmate's essay has been written specifically for *you* as the audience. Do you find it worth reading and easy to follow? Can you understand it easily? Do you like the voice you hear? Does the essay do what it is supposed to do? Why, or why not? The Revision Checklist should help you produce an effective evaluation.

5
Writing About Reading

Different Levels of Reading
- **Different Readers, Different Meanings**
- **Responding to Reading** • **Suggestions for Reading and Writing**
- **Application**

Throughout college you are asked to write about things you've read. In a psychology assignment you may be asked to summarize a textbook definition of *paranoid schizophrenia* or *superego*. For this type of writing, you read to retrieve and understand the facts. Then you write to demonstrate your knowledge or understanding. To summarize your reading, you write to answer this question:

- What are the main ideas?

Some other assignments require that you go beyond merely retrieving information. You might be asked to read several chapters and articles and to write on this topic: "Explain the role of the id, ego, and superego in human behavior." Here you would write to analyze your reading by answering these questions:

- What are the basic principles?

- What are the parts?

- How do the parts relate?

In this chapter we focus on yet another type of writing about reading—writing to answer questions that are more personal:

- What particular meaning does this reading have for me?

- How do I want to reply?

In this third type of writing, you are more like an active participant in a conversation: reacting to something that was said, you respond with something of your own.

Different Levels of Reading

These different types of writing call for different levels of reading or interacting with the text. To *summarize*, you read to record information. To *analyze*, you read to examine the information. But to *respond*, you read to discover and explore how your own thinking can take shape, or to make up your mind about something, or to get in touch with buried feelings or ideas. As a responding reader, you discover something that makes a difference to you personally, and you *reinvent* it so as to make a difference to readers of your own.

Writing in response to reading, then, can add another way of seeing, another way of expanding and enriching the possibilities for real connection. By helping you discover and explore the things you may want to say, reading can enrich the decisions you make throughout the writing process.

Different Readers, Different Meanings

The connection that writing creates is both public and private. On the one hand, a piece of writing makes a public connection with *all* its readers; on the other hand, the writing makes a private connection with *each* of its readers. Recall, for a moment, "Suffering Through Gym Class" (pages 71–73): Many of us who read this essay can feel the writer's anxiety and alienation and sense of failure. Beyond our common reaction, however, *each* of us has a unique and personal reaction as well—special things that we ended up feeling or remembering or thinking about.

If your whole class were to describe their individual reactions to the gym class essay ("What it means to me"), no two responses would be much alike. The essay might cause one reader to remember how competition in high school helped her develop self-confidence; some other reader might remember with regret how he made fun of someone less able. And so on.

You as reader interpret and complete the "private" meaning of the text you read. And, like you, all other readers come away from the same text with a personal meaning of their own. It is this personal meaning that can serve as inspiration for your own writing.

Responding to Reading

This essay by Judy Syfers was published in the very first issue of *Ms.* magazine, in Spring 1972. Even though Syfers seems to write for married readers in particular, in her essay she speaks to anyone who is at all familiar with married people in general. Please read the essay carefully.

I Want a Wife

I belong to that classification of people known as wives. I am A Wife. And, not altogether incidentally, I am a mother.

Not too long ago a male friend of mine appeared on the scene fresh from a recent divorce. He had one child, who is, of course, with his ex-wife. He is looking for another wife. As I thought about him while I was ironing one evening, it suddenly occurred to me that I, too, would like to have a wife. Why do I want a wife?

I would like to go back to school so that I can become economically independent, support myself, and, if need be, support those dependent upon me. I want a wife who will work and send me to school. And while I am going to school I want a wife to take care of my children. I want a wife to keep track of the children's doctor and dentist appointments. And to keep track of mine, too. I want a wife to make sure my children eat properly and are kept clean. I want a wife who will wash the children's clothes and keep them mended. I want a wife who is a good nurturant attendant to my children, who arranges for their schooling, makes sure that they have an adequate social life with their peers, takes them to the park, the zoo, etc. I want a wife who takes care of the children when they are sick, a wife who arranges to be around when the children need special care, because, of course, I cannot miss classes at school. My wife must arrange to lose time at work and not lose the job. It may mean a small cut in my wife's income from time to time, but I guess I can tolerate that. Needless to say, my wife will arrange and pay for the care of the children while my wife is working.

I want a wife who will take care of *my* physical needs. I want a wife who will keep my house clean. A wife who will pick up after my children, a wife who will pick up after me. I want a wife who will keep my clothes clean, ironed, mended, replaced when need be, and who will see to it that my personal things are kept in their proper place so that I can find what I need the minute I need it. I want a wife who cooks the meals, a wife who is a *good* cook. I want a wife who will plan the menus, do the necessary grocery shopping, prepare the meals, serve them pleasantly, and then do the cleaning up while I do my studying. I want a wife who will care for me when I am sick and sympathize with my pain and loss of time from school. I want a wife to go along when our family takes a vacation so that someone can continue to care for me and my children when I need a rest and change of scene.

I want a wife who will not bother me with rambling complaints about a wife's duties. But I want a wife who will listen to me when I feel the need to explain a rather difficult point I have come across in my course of studies. And I want a wife who will type my papers for me when I have written them.

I want a wife who will take care of the details of my social life. When my wife and I are invited out by my friends, I want a wife who will take care of the babysitting arrangements. When I meet people at school that I like and want to entertain, I want a wife who will have the house clean, will prepare a special meal, serve it to me and my friends, and not interrupt when I talk about things that interest me and my friends. I want a wife who will have arranged that the children are fed and ready for bed before my guests arrive so that the children do not bother us. I want a wife who takes care of the needs of my guests so that they feel comfortable, who makes sure that they have an ashtray, that they are passed the hors d'oeuvres, that they are offered a second helping of the food, that their wine glasses are replenished when necessary, that their coffee is served to them as they like it. And I want a wife who knows that sometimes I need a night out by myself.

I want a wife who is sensitive to my sexual needs, a wife who makes love passionately and eagerly when I feel like it, a wife who makes sure that I am satisfied. And, of course, I want a wife who will not demand sexual attention when I am not in the mood for it. I want a wife who assumes the complete responsibility for birth control, because I do not want more children. I want a wife who will remain sexually faithful to me so that I do not have to clutter up my intellectual life with jealousies. And I want a wife who understands that *my* sexual needs may entail more than strict adherence to monogamy. I must, after all, be able to relate to people as fully as possible.

If, by chance, I find another person more suitable as a wife than the wife I already have, I want the liberty to replace my present wife with another one. Naturally, I will expect a fresh, new life; my wife will take the children and be solely responsible for them so that I am left free.

When I am through with school and have a job, I want my wife to quit working and remain at home so that my wife can more fully and completely take care of a wife's duties.

My God, who *wouldn't* want a wife?

Now let's examine our reactions to "I Want A Wife." We can all presumably extract a common meaning from this piece: namely the viewpoint that women in the traditional "wifely" role are overworked and underappreciated. But, beyond its bleak portrait of the "housewife's" destiny, what particular meaning does this essay have for you?

Maybe Syfers's essay makes you feel angry with (1) men, (2) the writer, (3) yourself, or (4) someone else. Or maybe you feel threatened or offended. Or maybe you feel amused or confused about your own attitudes toward gender roles. Or maybe you feel all these things at once—or maybe none. Here are some questions that may help you explore your reactions to the reading:

1 • How do I feel about this reading? Angry, defensive, supportive, or what?

2 • Why do I feel this way?

3 • Does the piece present an accurate picture?

4 • With what statements do I agree or disagree?

5 • What is the most striking part of this essay?

6 • Do I like the way the writing sounds (the tone)?

7 • Has it reminded me of something, made me aware of something new, or changed my mind about anything?

8 • What does this essay make me want to think and talk about?

In your answers to these questions, you should be able to discover what you are thinking or feeling or remembering. A good way to explore your reactions and collect your thoughts is by keeping a reading journal in which you record your impressions.

Once you have discovered the particular meaning Syfers's essay has for you, how will you respond? Among all the things you could say, which will be your exact reply? Before you decide, read how two other writers responded.

Here are some of the notes that Jacqueline LeBlanc wrote in her journal after first reading Syfers's essay:

This essay makes me angry because it reminds me too much of some women in my own generation who seem to want nothing more than a wifely role for themselves. For all we hear about "equal rights," women still feel the pressure to conform to old-fashioned notions. I can really take this essay personally.

After rereading the essay and reviewing her journal entries, Jackie decided to write from the viewpoint that the stereotypical role condemned by Syfers two decades ago continues to be disturbingly evident. Jackie expresses her viewpoint in this thesis statement:

Although today's "equality-minded" generation presumably sees marriage as more than just an occupation, the wifely stereotype persists.

Here, after several revisions, is the essay that explains Jackie's viewpoint:

A Long Way to Go

Judy Syfers's portrait of a servile wife might appear somewhat dated—until we examine some of today's views about marriage. Syfers defines a wife by the work she does for her husband: she is a secretary, housemaid, babysitter, and sex object. She is, in a word, her husband's employee. Although today's "equality-minded" generation presumably sees marriage as more than an occupation, the wifely stereotype persists.

Among my women friends, I continue to encounter surprisingly traditional attitudes. Last week, for instance, I was discussing my career possibilities with my roommate, who added to the list of my choices by saying, "You can always get married." In her view, becoming a wife seems no different from becoming a teacher or journalist. She implied that marriage is merely another way of making a living. But where do I apply for the position of wife? The notion struck me as absurd. I thought to myself, "Surely, this person is an isolated case. We are, after all, in the nineties. Women no longer get married as a substitute for a job—do they?"

Of course many women do have both job and marriage, but as I look closely at others' attitudes, I find that my roommate's view is not so rare. Before the recent wedding of a female friend, my conversations with the future bride revolved around her meal plans and laundry schedule. To her vows "to love, honor, and cherish" she could have added, "to cook, serve, and clean up." She had been anticipating the first meal she would prepare for her husband. Granted, nothing is wrong with wanting to serve and provide for the one you love—but she spoke of this meal as if it were a pass-or-fail exam given by her employer on her first day on the job. Following the big day of judgment, she was elated to have passed with flying colors.

I couldn't help wondering what would have happened if her meal had been a flop. Would she have lost her marriage as an employee loses a job? As long as my friend retains such a narrow and materialistic view of wifely duties, her marriage is not likely to be anything more than a job.

Not all my friends are obsessed with wifely duties, but some do have a definite sense of husbandly duties. A potential husband must measure up to the qualifications of the position, foremost of which is wealth. One of the first questions about any male is "What does he do?" Engineering majors or premed students usually get highest ranking, and humanities or music majors end up at the bottom. College women are by no means opposed to marriage based on true love, but, as we grow older, the fantasy of a Prince Charming gives way to the reality of an affluent provider. Some women look for high-paying marriages just as they look for high-paying jobs.

Some of my peers may see marriage as one of many career choices, but my parents see it as the *only* choice. To my parents, my not finding a husband is a much more terrifying fate than my not finding a job. In their view, being a wife is no mere occupation, but a natural vocation for all women. But not just any man will do as a husband. My parents have a built-in screening procedure for each man I date. Appearance, money, and general background are the highest qualifications. They ignore domestic traits because they assume that his parents will be screening me for such qualifications.

I have always tried to avoid considering male friends simply as prospective husbands; likewise, I never think of myself as filling the stereotypical position of wife. But sometimes I fall into my parents' way of thinking. When I invite a friend to dinner at my house, I suddenly find myself fretting about his hair, his religion, or his job. Will he pass the screening test? Is he the right man for the role of husband? In some ways my attitudes seem no more liberated than those of my peers or parents.

Today's women have made a good deal of progress, but apparently not enough. Allowing the practical implications of marriage to overshadow its emotional implications, a surprising number of us seem to feel that we still have to fit the stereotype that Syfers condemns.

As an active reader, Jackie discovered in Syfers's essay something that made a difference. As the writer, in turn, she responded so as to make a difference to readers of her own.

Our second writer, David Galuski, discovered in the Syfers essay the possibility for humor, summed up in this thesis:

Instead of a wife, I need an assistant.

He uses his response to poke fun at his own inability for coping with an impossibly busy schedule and to discover that (like all of us, at times) he is just looking for a little sympathy.

I Need an Assistant

I am much too busy. Being eighteen takes a lot out of a person—especially anyone who attends college full time, works two part-time jobs, plays sports, and tries to have a social life. I need someone to help me get through the day. Instead of a wife, I need an assistant.

For one thing, my assistant would help with school chores. Although I usually find time to do my homework, it is never without a good deal of pain. My assistant could ease the pain by doing some of my reading, which he could then summarize and explain to me. Maybe he could do some of my research and type the papers I write, as well. Fluent in all subjects, my assistant would be able to transfer his knowledge to me.

Studying is easy—when I have enough time. But keeping up grades while holding down two part-time jobs is another story. I spend twenty hours a week at Max's, a gourmet restaurant, where I am expected to continuously cater to my customers. But when I'm exhausted from studying, I'm likely to be forgetful and irritable. I want an assistant who will stand by me at all times at work. He could help with the work and also cover for any lapses in my patience or attention.

My work as timekeeper for hockey games at the skating rink consumes five hours weekly out of my busy schedule. I need an assistant to cover the games I cannot time because of homework or conflicting hours at the restaurant. My assistant also would stand by my side and take over when I fall asleep because of the late hours at which the games are scheduled. Although I must work at these jobs to pay college expenses, my life isn't all work and studying.

Sports are a big part of my life. I set aside at least one hour every day to run, cycle, or swim. No matter what my other commitments are, without daily exercise I feel I've accomplished nothing. I need an assistant to encourage me to run that extra step or to swim one more pool length. He would push me out the door to exercise in the cold and in the rain. My assistant would compete alongside me in the six triathlons I do each year. He would also be a good hockey player, who would attend practice sessions in my place, leaving the team happy and giving me time to finish homework or earn money.

Besides school, work, and sports, I have other commitments to consider. I try—without much success—to maintain an active social life. I need an assistant to keep me up to date on my friends and girlfriend. I never have time to call them. When I do manage to see them, it is briefly. Even though they understand my obligations, they can't help being annoyed occasionally. My assistant would make my phone calls and arrange dates for me at times when I can squeeze them in.

Dates are something I really can't make with my family. But I see my parents as much as possible. I try to help out at home, but that would be a job for my assistant. He would do my household chores, wash the cars, and mow the lawn. My assistant would make my bed and wash my clothes while I hurry off to some pressing engagement.

Finally, I need an assistant who will give me emotional support. I want an assistant to whisper in my ear, telling me that everything will turn out all right—one who will sing me to sleep and hold me when I cry. Maybe all I'm looking for after all is a little pity.

Beyond the two samples shown here, the range of possible responses to Syfers's essay is almost infinite. Can you think of other possibilities for your own response?

Suggestions for Reading and Writing

In many later chapters you will be invited to write in response to this or that reading. Some of the readings are professionally written; others are student written. All these readings are selected as enjoyable ways of showing how other writers can connect with you. Besides triggering ideas for your own writing, each reading provides a model of worthwhile content, sensible organization, and readable style.

Here are a few suggestions for reading to respond to the selections assigned throughout the semester:

1. Read the essay at least three times: first, to get a sense of the geography; next, to explore your reactions; finally, to see what you find most striking or important or outrageous.

2. List (or underline) the statements that strike you or set you off.

3. Answer any questions on page 93 that are relevant here.

4. Once you've identified your reaction, think of all the things you would like to say in reply.

5. Settle on the main thing you want to say—your viewpoint.

6. Write out your viewpoint in a thesis statement.

Keep in mind that these are *only* suggestions—not commandments.

Like everything else in the writing process, reading to write calls for an intimate involvement that follows no simple formula. You might read something and want to begin writing immediately, without lists or other helps. Sometimes you won't even have a thesis as you begin, but you will want to write anyway, maybe to tell a story or to describe something personal.

In writing about reading, each of us reinvents a special way of seeing. Maybe, like Jackie LeBlanc, you will respond in a way that sticks closely to what you've read. Or maybe, like David Galuski, you will want to have fun and try something different. Or maybe you will decide to use the reading as a launching toward *new* exploration, as Shirley Haley did after reading this selection from Annie Dillard's prizewinning book, *Pilgrim at Tinker Creek*. (Haley's essay appears on pages 100–101.)

Seeing

It is still the first week in January, and I've got great plans. I've been thinking about seeing. There are lots of things to see, unwrapped gifts and free surprises. The world is fairly studded and strewn with pennies cast broadside from a generous hand. But—and this is the point—who gets excited by a mere penny? If you follow one arrow, if you crouch motionless on a bank to watch a tremulous ripple thrill on the water and are rewarded by the sight of a muskrat kit paddling from its den, will you count that sight a chip of copper only, and go your rueful way? It is dire poverty indeed when a man is so malnourished and fatigued that he won't stoop to pick up a penny. But if you cultivate a healthy poverty and simplicity, so that finding a penny will literally make your day, then, since the world is in fact planted in pennies, you have with your poverty bought a lifetime of days. It is that simple. What you see is what you get.

I used to be able to see flying insects in the air. I'd look ahead and see, not the row of hemlocks across the road, but the air in front of it. My eyes would focus along that column of air, picking out flying insects. But I lost interest, I guess, for I dropped the habit.

Now I can see birds. Probably some people can look at the grass at their feet and discover all the crawling creatures. I would like to know grasses and sedges—and care. Then my least journey into the world would be a field trip, a series of happy recognitions. Thoreau, in an expansive mood, exulted, "What a rich book might be made about buds, including, perhaps, sprouts!" It would be nice to think so. I cherish mental images I have of three perfectly happy people. One collects stones. Another—an Englishman, say—watches clouds. The third lives on a coast and collects drops of seawater which he examines microscopically and mounts. But I don't see what the specialist sees, and so I cut myself off, not only from the total picture, but from the various forms of happiness.

Unfortunately, nature is very much a now-you-see-it, now-you-don't affair: A fish flashes, then dissolves in the water before my eyes like so much salt. Deer apparently ascend bodily into heaven; the brightest oriole fades into leaves. These disappearances stun me into stillness and concentration; they say of nature that it conceals with a grand nonchalance, and they say of vision that it is a deliberate gift, the revelation of a dancer who for my eyes only flings away her seven veils. For nature does reveal as well as conceal: now-you-don't-see-it, now-you-do. For a week last September migrating red-winged blackbirds were feeding heavily down by the creek at the back of the house. One day I went out to investigate the racket; I walked up to a tree, an Osage orange, and a hundred birds flew away. They simply materialized out of the tree. I saw a tree, then a whisk of color, then a tree again. I walked closer and another hundred blackbirds took flight. Not a branch, not a twig budged: the birds were apparently weightless as well as invisible. Or, it was as if the leaves of the Osage orange had been freed from a spell in the form of red-winged blackbirds; they flew from the tree, caught my eye in the sky, and vanished. When I looked again at the tree the leaves had reassembled as if nothing had happened. Finally I walked directly to the trunk of the tree and a final hundred, the real diehards, appeared, spread, and vanished. How could so many hide in the tree without my seeing them? The Osage orange, unruffled, looked just as it had looked from the house, when three hundred red-winged blackbirds cried from its crown. I looked downstream where they flew, and they were gone. Searching, I couldn't spot one. I wandered downstream to force them to play their hand, but they'd crossed the creek and scattered. One show to a customer. These appearances catch at my throat; they are the free gifts, the bright coppers at the roots of the trees.

In her response to Annie Dillard, Haley sets out to reinvent the meaning of "Seeing," for herself and her readers. Even though Haley gives us no explicit thesis, her writing clearly enough implies one: Things we truly see outside ourselves can sometimes help ease the pain we feel inside.

Sailboats

On an afternoon in late June I stomped out of the house to walk off the frustration of an argument. White fists jammed into my pockets, I rehearsed what I should have said as I tromped fiercely away from the people, the village, the wharf, and the lifeguarded beaches toward the path. A fringe benefit of putting in town sewage four or five years ago, the path begins with the gravel road to the pumping station and moves on around the deepest curve of the harbor, tracing the old railroad bed. It is by no means private there, but by mutual understanding, speaking is optional, nodding preferable; the illusion of privacy is preserved. It's where I walk when I walk and fancy I'll run when I take up running, and today it was where I was stomping.

Like a child more determined to stay angry the harder you coax and tickle, I was determined to stay hurt. The walk would do no good beyond creating space between me and the house. *Pilgrim at Tinker Creek* lay on the table by my bed, and I was angry at Annie Dillard, too. She makes such work of simply being here: marveling at caterpillar foreheads and all the time refocusing to "see." When I refocus, I see places that need cleaning; better to glance and be happy in my ignorance. I cannot see the universe in a drop of water. Hers is not a gift for seeing; it's a gift for applying imagination. I walked the path that day wanting not to think, or feel or see, wishing to be transformed, melted away like the Little Mermaid into the foam at the tip of a wave.

Not far along the way, the raised bed falls away to bracken water (neither salt nor fresh); on either side, the eel pond. It's only a baby pond on the left connected to the expanse of water on the right by a culvert, a giant corrugated tunnel for boys to hoot into and make echos. The bright sky paled against the vivid blue of the pond. The warming air had freed the scent of beach rose and marsh grass. And across the pond, across the buckskin marsh not yet turned jewel green, was the swans' nest. The swans were there like plastic swans on a wedding cake, one on the giant nest, one swimming near with wings slightly raised in a gesture of vigilance.

The growth of land separating pond and marsh from harbor and beach is called Goodspeed Island. It's not really an island, of course, but it's a good place to pretend and to camp out if you're careful about poison ivy. As the path curves from behind it, dissolving from packed dirt to sand, the harbor opens up on the left. A sandy isthmus between pond and ocean, the path continues; I digressed to my destination. The beach is cluttered with beachy clutter: seaweed, shells, waterlogged wood, and plastic rings from six-packs. Aged quarry stones strewn in odd arrangement make ideal seats for the contemplation of universes, if you're so inclined—or of hurts.

The view is of sailboats, mostly moored; the curve of the shore with houses, shops, wharves, and beaches; and, at the farthest point on the far side, the lighthouse, white. Above, the trees, which from here are a solid green rolling back from the harbor, hiding the village, reach the tips of the steeples, a Congregational Church, white, Center School, yellow, marking the block where I live.

I wonder about the boats sometimes; they never seem to go out. Dangling there at their moorings all summer, they float like vanes into the wind. And when weather comes, and it blows, one always slips its mooring and runs with the storm across the harbor to the rocks. I remember clearly going out like ghouls once in the rain to see such a one, its side torn open, and a lady in a yellow slicker picking up silverware in the dark in the surf.

I stayed a while, nursing my hurts and contemplating boats. Dog walkers passed behind me. A resolute lady strode briskly by in warm-up suit zipped to the chin, and the tide began to change. I headed home by the populated route. Still hurt but no longer angry, I walked quietly, carrying beach roses for the dining-room table. At the wharf a 40-foot wooden sailboat, a mahogany beauty, slid into the water and then motored to the dock to have her mast and rigging fitted. At home I took care in arranging my flowers and felt better.

We have seen how three student writers reached deep into their reading and into themselves to make something happen, to discover a real connection. Their writing, in turn, makes us part of that connection.

Application 5–1

Respond to any of the essays in this chapter with an essay of your own. Share with us a new way of seeing.

In planning your response, imagine that you are conversing with the writer: How would you reply if someone had just spoken what you have read? In responding to Judy Syfers's essay (pages 91–93), you might ask yourself questions such as:

- Has anything changed since this essay was written (1972)?

- Is this what my mother is like?

- What do I want for myself in a marriage?
- How do I see my role as a wife or husband?
- What are my expectations?

Ask these questions, those on page 93, and any others that will help you reach deep into your reading experience.

As you read, record your impressions in a reading journal. In reviewing these journal entries, you should be able to discover the seeds that can grow into a truly worthwhile essay.

SECTION TWO

THE PRODUCT— SUBSTANCE, SHAPE, STYLE

6

Achieving
Worthwhile
Content

Credibility • Informative Value • Completeness • Applications

Readers hate to waste time. They want writing that is worth the effort. They expect an insightful thesis backed by solid support. To make contact, writing has to say something worthwhile. If the content is worthless, nothing else matters.

From all the material you develop during planning and drafting, you want to select only what is worthwhile. The first requirement of worthwhile content is *unity*: every word, every detail advances the writer's exact meaning. In addition to unity, three other qualities are essential to worthwhile content: *credibility, informative value,* and *completeness.**

Credibility

How believable and convincing is your draft? Anybody can make assertions; *supporting* your assertions is the real challenge. When you assert an opinion, readers expect it to be *informed*. We all have opinions about political candidates, cars, controversial subjects such as abortion

---

*Adapted from James L. Kinneavy's assertion that discourse should be factual, unpredictable, and comprehensive. See James L. Kinneavy, *A Theory of Discourse* (Englewood Cliffs, N.J.: Prentice Hall, 1971).

or nuclear energy, and anything else that touches our lives. But sometimes we forget that many of our opinions are *uninformed*; instead of resting on *facts*, they lean mostly on a chaotic collection of beliefs repeated around us, notions we've inherited from advertising, things we've read but never checked, and so on.

Uninformed opinions   Ronald Reagan was a reckless president.

Ronald Reagan was a courageous president.

Grindo toothpaste is best for making teeth whiter.

In a democracy, religion deserves a voice in government.

Uninformed opinion is merely a belief that hasn't been verified (shown to be valid).

Informed opinion, in contrast, rests on fact or good sense. Any fact *(my hair is brown; Professor Glum fails more than 50 percent of his freshmen; Americans have more televisions than bathtubs)* can be verified by anyone. A fact might be verified by observation *(I saw Felix murder his wife)*; by research *(wood smoke contains the deadly chemical dioxin)*; by experience *(I was mugged this morning)*; or by measurement *(fewer than 60 percent of our freshmen eventually earn a degree)*. Opinions based on these facts would be informed opinions.

Informed opinions   Felix is guilty of murder.

Homes with woodstoves need good ventilation.

This has been a bad day for me.

College clearly is not for everyone.

To support your opinions, you often must consider a variety of facts. You might be able to support with facts the claim that Grindo toothpaste makes teeth whiter; but a related fact may be that Grindo contains tiny silicone particles—an abrasive that "whitens" by scraping enamel from teeth. The second fact could change your opinion about Grindo.

As we see from the Grindo example, no two facts about *anything* are likely to have the same value. Assume you've asserted this opinion:

The Diablo Canyon nuclear plant is dangerous.

In deciding how to support this opinion, you compare the relative value of each of these facts:

1.   The road system is inadequate for rapid evacuation of local residents.

2.   Nuclear plants have found no suitable way to dispose of radioactive wastes.

3.   The plant is little more than 100 miles from sizable population centers.

4.   The plant is built near a major earthquake fault.

Although all these facts support the label *dangerous,* the first three can apply to almost any nuclear plant. Only the fourth addresses the danger specific to the Diablo Canyon plant—and therefore has most value here. When your space *and* your reader's tolerance are limited—and they usually are—you need to decide which of your collected facts best support your assertion, thus offering greatest unity.

Besides unifying your facts, you need to present them in an order that reflects the most vivid and appropriate emphasis. Consider this opening passage from an essay on pages 404–405.

Passage A

Opening opinion

Supporting facts

> *Child abuse has become our national disgrace.* In the past decade, its incidence has increased by an average 20 percent yearly. This year alone, more than 500,000 children (fewer than 20 percent of cases) will be the *reported* victims of physical, sexual, or emotional violence by one or both parents. And among the reported offenders, only 3 *percent* are ever convicted. Even more tragic, the pattern of violence is cyclical, with many abused children later becoming abusive parents themselves.

Notice how the facts are ordered: from the increase in the past decade to the cases this year to the conviction rate to the cyclical pattern; we move from the disquieting numbers to the tragically cyclical process.

Not all opinions, however, can be supported by facts. Take moral or emotional issues (prayer in public schools, the existence of God, the distribution of wealth). Opinions on issues such as these rest mainly on good sense and on solid insights. Here is a passage supporting the opinion that Americans should do more to help the world's hungry.

Passage B

   If we as a nation allow people to starve while we could, through some sacrifice, make more food available to them, what hope can any person have for the future of international relations? If we cannot agree on this most basic of values—feed the hungry— what hopes for the future can we entertain? Technology is imitable and nuclear weaponry certain to proliferate. What appeals to trust and respect can be made if the most rudimentary of moral impulses—feed the hungry—is not strenuously incorporated into national policy?

—James R. Kelly

   Although the passage offers no statistics, research data, or observable facts (except for technology being imitable), the support is credible because of its basis in sensible reasons. Granted, we cannot *prove* the writer's opinion valid by measurement or research, but we can find support for it in our own feelings about our shared humanity.

Informative Value

Relevant facts and sensible insights make your writing convincing, but readers don't need every item you can think of. Maybe you're one of those writers who enter college as experts in the art of "stuffing." The stuffing expert knows how to fill pages quickly by cramming into the essay every thought that will pile up 500 words (or any required total) with minimal pain. Early drafts almost always need radical surgery to trim away the stuff that serves no purpose.

   Readers always expect to learn something *new and useful* from your writing; they never want filler that wastes their time. If your reader already knows or finds obvious everything you've written, then your message is worthless. To have informative value, your writing needs to make some kind of difference by

- sharing something new and significant with an audience, or

- reminding the audience about something they know but ignore, or

- offering fresh insight about something the audience already knows, thus helping readers see things in a new way.

In short, informative writing gives readers exactly what they need.

   In any writing situation, you can safely make some assumptions about your readers. You know that readers approach your topic with some prior knowledge or old information. These readers don't need a rehash of old information; they can "fill in the blanks" for themselves. But readers may need reminding about something they've ignored or forgotten. On the other hand, readers don't need every bit of *new* information you can think of, either.

How, then, do you zero in on readers' exact needs for information in your writing situation? By anticipating their questions. Imagine this situation: You have no formal computer background (only general knowledge); you are trying to decide whether to take an introductory computer course, and I want to offer some information that might help. In this situation, which of these bits of information would you find useful?

a. Interest in computers has grown immensely in the past decade.

b. By 1995, over 75 percent of businesses will depend on computers.

c. The first digital computer was built by Howard Aiken.

d. Information can be transmitted rapidly by computer.

I can make a pretty good guess about how useful each item is by anticipating the questions you need answered: "What are the benefits?" and "Why should I?" I would guess that fact **b** would be new to many freshmen, and this fact seems relevant to your needs and my purpose. Fact **a**, in contrast, has no informative value here, because it is self-evident to anyone exposed to our media culture. Although **c** is news to anyone with no computer background, the information is not immediately relevant to this situation. (It could be, say, if you already were taking a computer course.) And **d** is a statement everyone would find obvious. Mere facts, then, are not enough; they have to be facts readers can use.

Sometimes a message can have informative value if it reminds us about something familiar or gives us fresh insight into a familiar subject. As a reader of this book, you expect to learn something worthwhile about writing, and my purpose is to help you do that. In this situation, which of these bits of information would you find useful?

a. Writing is hard and frustrating work.

b. Writing is a process of deliberate decisions.

Statement **a** offers no news to anyone who's ever picked up a pencil. But **b** offers a *new way* of seeing something familiar. It reminds you that producing good writing can be a lot more painful than we would like. No matter how much you have struggled over decisions about punctuation or spelling or grammar, chances are you haven't viewed writing as entailing the many kinds of deliberate decisions treated in this book. Because **b** offers new insight into a familiar process, then, we can say it has informative value.

Rereading Passages A and B (pages 107, 108), we see that each satisfies our criteria for informative value. Passage A offers surprising but convincing evidence about child abuse; Passage B gives fresh insight into the crucial but familiar issue of international relations.

So far in this section, we've looked at writing situations in which the audience's needs were relatively easy to identify. But sometimes we have to write for an audience whose members have varied needs. How, then, do we serve the needs of a mixed audience so that our writing has informative value for each reader?

Imagine you are an ex-jogger and a convert to walking for aerobic exercise. You decide to write an essay explaining to your classmates the advantages of walking over running. You can assume a few classmates are runners; others swim, cycle, lift weights, or do some type of exercise; some don't do much, but are thinking of starting; and the rest have little interest in any kind of exercise.

Your problem is to address all these readers (the informed or more interested, and the uninformed or less interested) in one essay that *each* reader will find worthwhile in some way. Specifically, you hope your essay will

- persuade runners and other exercisers to consider walking as an alternative,
- encourage the interested nonexercisers to try walking, and
- create at least a spark of interest among the diehard nonexercisers—and maybe even inspire them to rise up out of their easy chairs and hit the bricks.

To achieve your ambitious purpose, in this essay you will need to answer questions shared by all readers:

Why is walking better than running?

How are they similar or different?

What are the benefits in walking?

Can you give examples?

Why should I?

But some readers will have special questions of their own. Nonexercisers might ask, "What exactly is aerobic exercise, anyway?" And the true couch potatoes might ask, "Who cares?" For your essay to work, it will have to answer all these questions.

Assume that many hours of planning, drafting, and revising have enabled you to produce this final draft:

Walk but Don't Run

Our bodies gain aerobic benefits when we exercise at a fast enough pace for muscles to demand oxygen-rich blood from the heart and lungs. During effective aerobic exercise, the heart rate increases roughly 80 percent above normal. Besides strengthening muscle groups—especially the heart—aerobic exercise makes blood vessels stronger and larger.

Running, or jogging, has become a most popular form of aerobic exercise. But millions of Americans who began running to get in shape are now limping to their doctors for treatment of running injuries. To keep yourself in one piece as you keep yourself in shape, try walking instead of running.

All the aerobic benefits of running can be yours if you merely take brisk walks. Consider this comparison. For enough aerobic training to increase cardiovascular (heart, lungs, and blood vessels) efficiency, you need to run three times weekly for roughly thirty minutes. (Like any efficient system, an efficient cardiovascular system produces maximum work with minimum effort.) You can gain cardiovascular benefits equivalent to running, however, by taking a brisk walk three times weekly for roughly sixty minutes. Granted, walking takes up more time than running, but it carries fewer risks.

Because of its more controlled and deliberate pace, walking is safer than running. A walker stands far less chance of tripping, stepping in potholes, or slipping and falling. And the slower pace causes less physical trauma. Anyone who has ever run at all knows that a runner's foot strikes the ground with sizable impact. But the shock of this impact travels beyond the foot—to the shins, knees, hips, internal organs, and spine. Walking, of course, creates an impact of its own, but the walker's foot strikes the ground with only half as much force as the runner's foot.

Beyond its apparent physical dangers, running can provoke subtle stress for the devoted exerciser. Because running is generally seen as more competitive than just walking, we too easily can be tempted to push our bodies too far, too fast. Even though we might not compete in races or marathons, we often tend to compete against ourselves—maybe just to keep up with a jock neighbor or to

As a guide to developing complete and unified support, anticipate readers' questions about your thesis. Assume that a friend now living in another state is thinking of taking a job similar to one you held last summer. Your friend has written to ask how you liked the job and will base his or her decision on your information. Here is a passage from the first draft of your response:

> My job last summer as a flagger for a road construction company was boring, tiresome, dirty, and painful. All I did was stand in the road and flag cars. Every day I stood there for hours, getting sore feet. I was always covered with dirt and breathing it in. To make matters worse, the sun, wind, and insects ruined my skin. By the end of summer, I vowed never to do this kind of work again.

This passage *tells* but doesn't *show*. It has only limited informative value because it fails to get readers *into* the experience, to make them feel a part of it all. Granted, the opening sentence expresses the main point, and the remaining sentences provide a glimpse of the writer's ordeal; but a glimpse is all we get. Because its details are too sketchy, the passage fails to answer the obvious questions:

Can you show me what the job was like?

What, exactly, made it boring, tiresome, dirty, and painful?

This revised version (a one-paragraph essay) includes graphic details that *show*, that make readers feel as if they were there:

> My job last summer as a flagger for a road construction company was boring, tiresome, dirty, and painful. With nothing to do but wave a red flag at oncoming traffic, I stood like a robot, the deafening roar of road machinery at my back, each day dragging by more slowly than the last. My feet would swell, and my legs would ache from standing on the hard-packed earth for as long as fifteen hours a day. And the filth was overwhelming. The fumes, oil, and grime from the heavy machines and the exhaust from passing cars became my second skin. Each breath was filled with dust, clogging my sinuses, irritating my eyes. But the worst part of all was my poor body's exposure to the ravages of the weather. If I was not blistering all over from severe sunburn, or being pounded by hail, my skin was being sandblasted and rubbed raw by windstorms or chewed and bitten by mosquitoes and horseflies. By the end of the summer, I was a mess: swollen feet and ankles, the skin of a leper, and a chronic case of sinusitis. I vowed to starve before taking that kind of job again.

This version is complete; it delivers on the writer's opening promise. Compare these columns to see how the writer made the message more detailed.

First draft	Revision
I stood there for hours.	I stood like a robot, the deafening roar of road machinery at my back, each day dragging by more slowly than the last.
getting sore feet	My feet would swell, and my legs would ache from standing on the hard-packed earth for as long as fifteen hours a day.
I was always covered with road dirt and breathing it in.	The fumes, oil, and grime from the heavy machines and the exhaust from passing cars became my second skin. Each breath was filled with dust, clogging my sinuses, irritating my eyes.
The sun, wind, and insects ruined my skin.	If I was not blistered all over from a severe sunburn, or being pounded by hail, my skin was being sandblasted and rubbed raw by windstorms or chewed and bitten by mosquitoes and horseflies.
By the end of summer, I vowed never to do this kind of work again.	By the end of summer, I was a mess: swollen feet and ankles, the skin of a leper, and a chronic case of sinusitis. I vowed to starve before taking that kind of job again.

The support here can be considered complete and appropriate for this situation. More specific treatment (say, a day-by-day description of every event) would only clutter the message. The reader here needed and *wanted* just enough information to make an informed decision, not a diary of someone's summer on the road. Readers are busy and impatient people; think hard how much your reader can tolerate. Don't confuse needless details with legitimate support.

Every item of legitimate support advances the writer's exact meaning. But developing support does not mean simply adding words. Whatever does nothing but fill the page is puffery, as in this example:

> My job last summer as a flagger for a road construction company was boring, tiresome, dirty, and painful. Day in and day out, I stood ~~on that road~~ for endless hours getting ~~a severe case of~~ sore feet. My face and body were ~~always completely~~ covered with ~~the~~ dust blown up from the ~~passing cars and various other~~ vehicles, and I was forced to breathe in all ~~of~~ this ~~horrible~~ junk ~~day after day~~. ~~To add to the problems of boredom, fatigue, and dirt,~~ the weather did ~~the most~~ horrible things to my skin. ~~Let me tell you that~~ by the time the summer ended, I ~~had~~ made ~~myself~~ a solemn promise never to ~~victimize myself by~~ taking this kind of awful job again.

Although this version is almost twice as long as the original, it adds nothing to the writer's meaning; we are given many needless words (shown crossed out) but not much real information. Make every word, phrase, and sentence carry its weight. Replace all puffed-up expressions with sharp details.

Details are the lifeblood of good writing. Details are the facts, ideas, examples, numbers, names, events, dates, or reasons that do the *showing*. They advance the writer's exact meaning. They make a piece of writing complete by answering questions such as these:

Who, what, when, where, and why?

What did you see, feel, hear, taste, smell?

What would a camera record?

What are the dates, numbers, percentages?

Can you compare it to something more familiar?

In the next passage, a noted American writer describes with brutal clarity how a professional boxer was beaten to death during a prizefight. See for yourself how the details here make contact.

The Death of Benny Paret

> Paret was a Cuban, a proud club fighter who had become welterweight champion because of his unusual ability to take a punch. His style of fighting was to take three punches to the head in order to give back two. At the end of ten rounds, he would still be bouncing; his opponent would have a headache. But in the last two

years, over the fifteen-round fights, he had started to take some bad maulings.

This fight had its turns. Griffith won most of the early rounds, but Paret knocked Griffith down in the sixth. Griffith had trouble getting up, but made it, came alive and was dominating Paret again before the round was over. Then Paret began to wilt. In the middle of the eighth round, after a clubbing punch had turned his back to Griffith, Paret walked three disgusted steps away, showing his hindquarters. For a champion, he took much too long to turn back around. It was the first hint of weakness Paret had ever shown, and it must have inspired a particular shame, because he fought the rest of the fight as if he were seeking to demonstrate that he could take more punishment than any man alive. In the twelfth, Griffith caught him. Paret got trapped in a corner. Trying to duck away, his left arm and his head became tangled on the wrong side of the top rope. Griffith was in like a cat ready to rip the life out of a huge boxed rat. He hit him eighteen right hands in a row, an act which took perhaps three or four seconds, Griffith making a pent-up whimpering sound all the while he attacked, the right hand whipping like a piston rod which has broken through the crankcase, or like a baseball bat demolishing a pumpkin.

I was sitting in the second row of that corner. They were not ten feet away from me, and like everybody else, I was hypnotized. I had never seen one man hit another so hard and so many times. Over the referee's face came a look of woe as if some spasm had passed its way through him, and then he leaped on Griffith to pull him away. It was the act of a brave man. Griffith was uncontrollable. His trainer leaped into the ring, his manager, his cut man. There were four people holding Griffith, but he was off on an orgy; he had left the garden; he was back on a hoodlum's street. If he had been able to break loose from his handlers and the referee, he would have jumped Paret to the floor and whaled on him there.

And Paret? Paret died on his feet. As he took those eighteen punches, something happened to everyone who was in psychic range of the event. Some part of his death reached out to us. One felt it hover in the air. He was still standing in the ropes, trapped as he had been before. He gave some little half-smile of regret, as if he were saying, "I didn't know I was going to die just yet," and then, his head leaning back but still erect, his death came to breathe about him. He began to pass away. As he passed, so his limbs descended beneath him, and he sank slowly to the floor. He went down more slowly than any fighter had ever gone down; he went down like a large ship which turns on end and slides second by second into its grave. As he went down, the sound of Griffith's punches echoed in the mind like a heavy axe in the distance chopping into a wet log.

—Norman Mailer

As illustration of how vivid details advance a writer's meaning, consider this version of Mailer's final paragraph—this one without detailed support:

> Paret died on his feet and all the spectators were affected. Standing trapped in the ropes, he almost seemed to smile regretfully, and then sank very slowly to the floor. As he went down, we all remembered the sound of Griffith's punches.

To measure the completeness of your own writing, use these guidelines:

1. The often-stipulated 500 to 1000 words is a realistic length for giving a well-focused topic respectable treatment. Quality, however, is far more important than quantity. Once you have begun the writing process (searching for details, rephrasing in your own words, making connections), you probably will find it harder to *stay within* the limit than to reach it.

2. Your major purpose is to make your point—not to show how smart you are. Don't feel married to every word, fact, and idea that crosses your mind. Instead of writing *everything* you know, learn to cut.

3. Don't write something unless your reader needs to know it. If you've written just to get *something* down on the page, most of it probably doesn't belong.

4. Sometimes one detail is enough to support and clarify a point. To make the point about a "boring" job, the passage on page 114 describes the writer standing like a robot, waving a red flag. Some points, however, call for many details. When Norman Mailer shows how "Paret began to wilt," he lays out a gruesome catalog of the events, blow by blow—but nothing is wasted.

"Completeness" doesn't mean using every detail you can think of. Use only those that advance your meaning.

Application 6–1

Each sentence below states either a fact or an opinion. Rewrite all statements of opinion as statements of fact. Remember that a fact can be verified. (Review pages 105–108.)

Example

Opinion	My roommate isn't taking college work seriously.
Fact	My roommate never studies, sleeps through most classes, and has missed every exam.

1. Professor X grades unfairly.

2. My vacation was too short.

3. The salary for this position is $15,000 yearly.

4. This bicycle is reasonably priced.

5. We walked 5 miles last Saturday.

6. He drives recklessly.

7. My motorcycle gets great gas mileage.

8. This course has been very helpful.

9. German shepherds eat more than cocker spaniels do.

10. This apartment is much too small for our family.

Application 6–2

Return to Shirley Haley's essay on pages 16–17. Underline all statements of fact, and circle all statements of opinion. Are all the opinions supported by facts or by good sense? Now, perform the same evaluation on an essay you have written. (Review pages 105–108.)

Application 6–3

Assume you live in the Northeast, and citizens in your state are voting on a solar energy referendum that would channel millions of tax dollars toward solar technology. These two paragraphs are designed to help you, as a voter, make an educated decision. Do both these versions of the same message have informative value? Explain. (Review pages 108–113.)

Solar power offers a realistic solution to the Northeast's energy problems. In recent years the cost of fossil fuels (oil, coal, and natural gas) has risen rapidly while the supply has continued to decline. High prices and short supply will continue to cause a worsening energy crisis. Because solar energy comes directly from the sun, it is an inexhaustible resource. By using this energy to heat and air-condition our buildings, as well as to provide electricity, we could decrease substantially our consumption of fossil fuels. In turn, we would be less dependent on the unstable Middle East for our oil supplies. Clearly, solar power is a good alternative to conventional energy sources.

Solar power offers a realistic solution to the Northeast's energy problems. To begin with, solar power is efficient. Solar collectors installed on fewer than 30 percent of roofs in the Northeast would provide more than 70 percent of the area's heating and air-conditioning needs. Moreover, solar heat collectors are economical, operating for up to twenty years with little or no maintenance. These savings recoup the initial cost of installment within only ten years. Most important, solar power is safe. It can be transformed into electricity through photovoltaic cells (a type of storage battery) noiselessly and with no air pollution—unlike coal, oil, and wood combustion. In sharp contrast to its nuclear counterpart, solar power produces no toxic wastes and poses no catastrophic danger of meltdown. Thus, massive conversion to solar power would ensure abundant energy and a safe, clean environment for future generations.

Application 6–4

We've all had our own experiences—for better or worse—in a competitive society and are thus familiar with the subject of *competition.* The authors of this paragraph explain how the American character is rooted in competition. Are you familiar with experiences like those described here? Does the paragraph have informative value for you? Explain. (Review pages 108–113.)

The drive to compete and to be a "winner" has always been part of the American psyche. Our early ancestors were aggressive and competitive to begin with. They knew they were pitted against amazing odds, but they also felt they were a select and chosen group. They defied their mother country and were successful. Later came the "frontier spirit," the belief in survival of the fittest, and the growing American fetish for figures, statistics, records, and winners. Over forty years ago, John R. Tunis wrote, in *The American Way in Sport:* "We worship the victors. But why? The Dutch don't especially, nor the Swedes, neither do the Danes, the Swiss, or the English, and they all seem fairly civilized people." We devised an international "scoreboard" to chart our successes in the Olympics as well as in our wars, an obsession that was tragically reflected in our approach to Vietnam, where both President Johnson and President Nixon vowed that they were not going down in history as "the first American President who lost a war."

—Thomas Tutko and William Bruns

Application 6–5

Review one of your earlier essays (or a classmate's essay), and eliminate all statements that have no informative value (those that offer commonly known, irrelevant, or insignificant material). Be careful *not* to cut material the audience needs to understand the essay. (Review pages 108–113.)

Application 6–6

Reread Norman Mailer's essay (pages 116–117), and list the details that do these kinds of *showing:*

1. Details that help us see. *Example:* Paret began to wilt.

2. Details that help us feel. *Example:* a clubbing punch.

3. Numerical details. *Example:* He hit him eighteen right hands in a row.

4. Vivid comparisons. *Example:* the right hand whipping like a piston rod which has broken through the crankcase.

5. Details that a camera would record.

6. A detail that helps us hear.

Application 6–7

Return to one of your earlier essays. Study it carefully, then brainstorm again to sharpen your details. Now write a revised version. (Review pages 40–42.)

Application 6–8

Assume that your English teacher has just won $15 million in the state lottery. As a final grand gesture before retiring to a life of sailing, fine wines, and other expensive hobbies, your soon-to-be ex-teacher makes this announcement to the class:

> After years of agonizing over ways to motivate my writing students, I've discovered what could be the ultimate solution. I'm going to hold a contest offering one million dollars to the student who can write the best essay on this topic: How I Would Spend One Million Dollars. Essays will be evaluated on the basis of originality, richness of detail, and quality of explanation. The whole class will pick the winner from among the five finalists I select.

Write your essay, revising as often as needed to make it a winner.

Application 6–9

Assume a point of view similar to Norman Mailer's (pages 116–117), and describe something you witnessed and will never forget. Write for your classmates.

Application 6–10

Choose one of the essay options from pages 23–25.

7

Shaping
the Paragraphs

Support Paragraphs as Mini-Essays • Paragraph Function
• Paragraph Length • The Topic Statement
• Structural Variations in Support Paragraphs
• When to Compose Your Topic Statement • Paragraph Unity
• Paragraph Coherence • Applications

Beyond saying something worthwhile, writers must decide how to shape their thinking, to make it *accessible* for readers. For its larger design (introduction, body, conclusion), the essay depends on the smaller design of each paragraph. A paragraph is a place for things that belong together.

Support Paragraphs as Mini-Essays

We've seen how paragraphs in any essay differ in shape and purpose. Introductory paragraphs draw us into the writer's reality; concluding paragraphs ease us out; transitional paragraphs help hold things together. But here the subject is *support paragraphs*—those middle blocks of thought, each often a mini-shape of the whole essay. Just as the thesis is sustained by its supporting points, each major supporting point is sustained by its paragraph.

Although the support paragraphs in an essay are most often part of a larger design, each usually can stand alone in meaning and emphasis. Consider this paragraph by a well-known psychiatrist:

123

Introduction (topic statement, 1)

Body (2–9)

Conclusion (10–12)

¹Crime is everybody's temptation. ²It is easy to look with proud disdain upon "those people" who get caught—the stupid ones, the unlucky ones, the blatant ones. ³But who does not get nervous when a police car follows closely? ⁴We squirm over our income-tax statements and make some "adjustments." ⁵We tell the customs official that we have nothing to declare—well, practically nothing. ⁶Some of us who have never been convicted of any crime picked up over two billion dollars' worth of merchandise last year from the stores we patronize. ⁷Over a billion dollars was embezzled by employees last year. ⁸One hotel in New York lost over seventy-five thousand finger bowls, demitasse spoons, and other objects in its first ten months of operation. ⁹The Claims Bureau of the American Insurance Association estimates that 75 percent of all claims are dishonest in some respect and the amount of overpayment more than $350,000,000 a year. ¹⁰These facts disturb us or should. ¹¹They give us an uneasy feeling that we are all indicted. ¹²"Let him who is without sin cast the first stone."

—Karl Menninger

Menninger's paragraph is part of a much larger design: a chapter in his book *The Crime of Punishment*. But the paragraph's shape is familiar enough: the introduction asserts a definite viewpoint; the body walks us through the writer's reasoning; the conclusion helps us interpret and evaluate what we've read. As a unit of meaning, Menninger's paragraph is complete.

Paragraph Function

Writers need definite paragraph divisions for *control*; readers need them for *access*.

Paragraphs increase your writing control. Each support paragraph is an idea unit, one distinct space for developing one supporting point. If Menninger begins his paragraph with the point that crime tempts everyone, he can stay on track. He can tailor everything in the paragraph to help readers understand his point. And if he ends up talking, say, about neurotic anxiety by the third or fourth sentence, he will know he has strayed from the point. No matter how long your message, you can stay in control by shaping your brainstorming materials into one paragraph at a time. To organize, you look for things that belong together—you think in terms of paragraphs.

Beyond giving you a shape for your thinking, paragraphs give readers access. Readers look for orientation, for a shape they can recognize; they need to know where they are and where they're going. Paragraphs keep them on the path. By dividing a long piece of writing, paragraphs allow readers to focus on each point. The indention (five spaces) gives a breathing space, a signal that the geography is changing and that it's time to look ahead.

Paragraph Length

How long you make any paragraph depends on your purpose and your reader's needs. In writing that carries highly technical information or complex instructions, short paragraphs (perhaps in a list) give readers plenty of breathing space. In a newspaper article, paragraphs of only one or two sentences keep the reader's attention. In writing that explains concepts, attitudes, or viewpoints (as in college essays), support paragraphs generally run from 100 to 300 words.

But word count really means nothing. What matters is how *thoroughly* the paragraph makes your point. A flabby paragraph buries readers in needless words and details, but just skin-and-bones leaves readers looking for the meat. Each paragraph requires new decisions.

Try to avoid too much of anything. A clump of short paragraphs can make some writing seem choppy and poorly organized, but a stretch of long ones is tiring. Attract attention with a well-placed short paragraph, sometimes—for special emphasis—just one sentence:

More than 30 percent of our state's groundwater contains toxic wastes.

Or even just one word:

Exactly.

Decide on a shape and length for every paragraph; don't just let things happen. Make the paragraph just long enough to deliver on the promise expressed by your topic statement.

The Topic Statement

A college essay almost always needs a thesis that asserts the main point; and each support paragraph usually needs a topic statement that asserts a supporting point. Sometimes the topic statement comes at the end of the paragraph; sometimes in the middle; but usually it comes first. A paragraph's first sentence should orient readers, tell them what to expect. Without some sort of orientation, readers have no clue.

TOPIC STATEMENT AS READERS' FRAMEWORK

Most paragraphs in college writing begin by telling readers what to look for. Don't write *Some jobs are less stressful than others* when you mean *Mortuary management is an ideal major for anyone craving a stress-free job.* The first topic statement doesn't give a very clear forecast; the second helps us focus, tells us what to expect. Don't write *Summers in Goonville are awful* when you mean *I hate Goonville summers because of the chiggers, ticks, scorpions, and rattlesnakes.* Try not to keep readers guessing.

Avoid creating topic statements that are boring or vague or that lead nowhere. Don't write *In this paragraph, I will discuss whale intelligence.* Announcements like that invite boredom. Don't write *Whales are interesting animals,* thereby sticking readers with the job of figuring out your meaning for *interesting.* And don't close the door before you've opened it by making dead-end statements such as these: *Whales live only in salt water* or *Whales are a species of mammal.* Without a viewpoint, these simple expressions of fact lead nowhere, leave nothing to be explained. Lead your readers in; give them a definite signal about what to expect.

Let your purpose and audience's needs guide your adjustment of focus. Say you're writing an essay about whales for readers you'd like to recruit for the Save-the-Whales movement. First, you need to decide on the exact point about whales that you want to make in this paragraph. Suppose you decide to talk about whale intelligence. What is your *exact* viewpoint?

Whales seem to exhibit real intelligence.

Whales are measurably intelligent.

Whales are highly intelligent.

You decide that the final version is closest to what you mean. Now you think about ways of making the assertion more informative. Your readers will be asking: "Highly intelligent, relative to what?" Your answer:

Whales are among the most intelligent of the mammals.

Now you have a clear direction for developing your support. The finished paragraph might look like this:

> *Whales are among the most intelligent of the mammals.*
> Scientists rank whale intelligence with that of higher primates
> because of whales' sophisticated group behavior. These impressive
> mammals have been seen teaching and disciplining their young,
> helping their wounded comrades, engaging in elaborate courtship
> rituals, and playing in definite gamelike patterns. They are able to
> coordinate such complex activities through their highly effective
> communication system of sonar clicks and pings. This remarkable
> social organization apparently grows out of the almost human
> devotion that whales seem to have toward one another.

With the framework provided by your topic statement, we can under-stand your message easily.

Let's imagine other directions your topic statement on whale intelligence might have taken. If your purpose were even *more* specific, you might have come up with this topic statement:

> A good indication of whales' intelligence is the way they play
> in gamelike patterns.

Or, for a different purpose, you might narrow your focus to *one* game:

> Like children, a group of whales can spend hours playing tag.

Depending on your purpose and your readers' needs, you can make any topic statement more and more specific by focusing on smaller and smaller parts of it.

TOPIC STATEMENT AS WRITER'S FRAMEWORK

Without a topic statement, readers usually struggle to understand a paragraph, and the writer struggles to shape it—to make it more than a collection of *stuff*. Always take a definite stand; assert something significant.

Imagine that you are a member of Congress, about to vote on abortion legislation. One of your constituents has responded to your request for citizens' viewpoints with a letter that begins like this:

> *Abortion is a very complex issue.* There is a sharp division
> between those who are for it and those who are against it. Very few

people take a neutral stand on this issue. The battle between
supporters and opponents has raged for years. This is only one of the
serious problems in our society. Every day, things seem to get worse.

Because this writer never identified his purpose, never discovered his
own exact meaning, this paragraph merely parrots a number of unre-
lated thoughts that are all common knowledge. Without a definite
topic, the writer had no framework, no place to go. Having ignored
some essential early decisions, he was forced to borrow partial meanings from here and there.

If, instead, our writer had refined his meaning by asserting a definite viewpoint, he might have written a worthwhile paragraph.
Depending on his purpose, he might have begun with, say:

Abortion laws in our state discriminate against the poor.

or

Abortion is wrong because of the irresponsibility it allows.

Before you can explain yourself, you have to figure out exactly what it
is that you mean.

Structural Variations in Support Paragraphs

So far we've seen a standard structure for support paragraphs: topic
statement → support → conclusion or transition. First, master this
structure, but remember that all kinds of variations are possible. Some
topic statements require more than one sentence. Or your point might
have several distinct parts, which would result in an excessively long
paragraph. You might then break up the paragraph, letting your topic
statement stand as a brief introductory paragraph that serves the various subparts, which are set off as independent paragraphs for the reader's convenience.

*Common types of strip-mining procedures include open-pit
mining, contour mining, and auger mining. The specific type
employed will depend on the type of terrain covering the coal.*

Open-pit mining is employed in the relatively flat lands in
western Kentucky, Oklahoma, and Kansas. Here, draglines and
scoops operate directly on the coal seams. This process produces
long parallel rows of packed spoil banks, 10 to 30 feet high, with
steep slopes. Between the spoil banks are large pits that soon fill
with water to produce pollution and flood hazards.

Contour mining is most widely practiced in the mountainous terrain of the Cumberland Plateau and eastern Kentucky. Here, bulldozers and explosives cut and blast the earth and rock covering a coal seam. Wide bands are removed from the mountain's circumference to reach the embedded coal beneath. The cutting and blasting result in a shelf along with a man-made cliff some 60 feet high at a right angle to the shelf. The blasted and churned earth is pushed over the shelf to form a massive and unstable spoil bank that creates a danger of mud slides.

Auger mining is employed when the mountain has been cut so thin that it no longer can be stripped. It is also used in other difficult-access terrain. Here, large augers bore parallel rows of holes into the hidden coal seams to extract the embedded coal. Among the three strip-mining processes, auger mining causes least damage to the surrounding landscape.

As you can see, each paragraph begins with a clear statement of the sub-topic discussed in it.

Countless other variations are possible. Topic statements aren't always the first sentences. And some paragraphs have no explicit conclusion. Any such variations, however, should be based on good reason.

When to Compose Your Topic Statement

No writer's thinking ever is neat. You won't always be able to think *first* of the right topic statement, and *then* of your support. Your actual framework might not appear until you've done some freewriting or brainstorming. Say you're writing about the dangers of acid rain in your state. To help make one supporting point, you've isolated and arranged from your brainstorming materials these details:

1. Acid rain carries toxic metals.

2. It also leaches other materials from the soil.

3. Mercury and other toxins invade surface water and build up in fish tissues.

4. People or animals who drink the water or eat the fish risk heavy-metal poisoning.

5. Acidified water releases lead, copper, and other toxins from metal plumbing, thus making even tap water hazardous.

Let's say that in another paragraph you've discussed how acid rain is killing lakes and forests and damaging buildings, statues, and almost anything else it falls on. But your list of details suggests its own larger meaning: namely, that *acid rain threatens human health*. Now you can sharpen your meaning: acid rain doesn't directly harm the people it falls on (at least as far as we know), but its threat to humans is *indirect*. Now you've discovered your exact meaning. With the organizing viewpoint provided by the topic statement, you can write a sensible paragraph.

> *Acid rain indirectly threatens human health.* Besides bearing several toxic metals, it percolates through the soil, leaching out naturally present metals. Pollutants such as mercury invade surface water, accumulating in fish tissues. Any organism eating the fish— or drinking the water—in turn faces the risk of heavy-metal poisoning. Moreover, acidified water can release heavy concentrations of lead, copper, and aluminum from metal plumbing, making ordinary tap water hazardous.

You might come up with a topic statement, then your support, or vice versa. The sequence is unimportant—as long as the finished paragraph offers a definite framework and solid support.

Paragraph Unity

Each paragraph in an essay requires *external unity* and *internal unity*. A paragraph has external unity when (as on pages 71–72) it belongs with all the other paragraphs in an essay. But each paragraph requires internal unity as well: everything in the paragraph should belong there.

Internal unity occurs when all the material in a paragraph directly supports the topic statement. Imagine that you're composing a paragraph beginning with this topic statement:

> Chemical pesticides and herbicides are both ineffective and hazardous.

The words that signal the meaning here are *ineffective* and *hazardous*; everything in the paragraph should directly advance that meaning. Here is the unified paragraph:

A unified paragraph

> *Chemical pesticides and herbicides are both ineffective and hazardous.* Because none of these chemicals has permanent effects, pest populations invariably recover and need to be resprayed. Repeated applications cause pests to develop immunity to the chemicals. Furthermore, most pesticides and herbicides attack

species other than the intended pest, killing off its natural predators, thus actually increasing the pest population. Above all, chemical residues survive in the environment (and in living tissue) for years and are often carried hundreds of miles by wind and water. This toxic legacy includes such biological effects as birth deformities, reproductive failures, brain damage, and cancer. Although intended to control pest populations, these chemicals ironically threaten to make the human population their ultimate victims.

One way to destroy unity in this paragraph would be to discuss the cost of the chemicals or their unpleasant odor or the number of people who oppose their use. Although those matters do broadly relate to the pesticide and herbicide issue, none directly advances the meaning of *ineffective* and *hazardous*.

Every topic statement has a signal term, a key word or phrase that announces the writer's viewpoint. In the whale paragraph (page 127), the signal term is *intelligent*, causing readers to expect material about whale intelligence. Anything that fails to advance the meaning of *intelligence* throws the paragraph—and the reader—off track:

A disunified paragraph

Whales are among the most intelligent of all mammals. Scientists rank whale intelligence with that of higher primates because of whales' sophisticated group behavior. These impressive mammals have been seen teaching and disciplining their young, helping their wounded comrades, engaging in elaborate courtship rituals, and playing in definite gamelike patterns. *Whales continually need to search for food in order to survive. Their search for krill and other sea organisms can cause them to migrate thousands of miles yearly.*

The shift from intelligence to food problems frustrates the reader's expectations.

Disunity is commonly the product of a writer who neglects to brainstorm or who settles for a foggy topic statement. Lacking either enough material or a definite purpose, writers are tempted to throw in anything that comes to mind, whether or not the material really belongs. Here's what can happen when the topic statement lacks a definite signal of the writer's viewpoint:

A disunified paragraph

Divorce rates have been climbing for the last decade. People are deciding they want individual freedom after they are married. In the United States, divorces are easy to obtain, and not only young couples are getting divorced. There are many middle-aged people who find themselves unhappy in their situations and who change them. Statistics show that divorce rates are higher for couples who marry young. The breakup of a marriage will always affect children. But children themselves now are growing up with the same view of marriage that their parents have: if it doesn't work, get a divorce.

Without an exact viewpoint to work from, the writer skipped from one half-formed idea to another. Only when you're sure of what you want to say can you decide whether something really belongs.

Paragraph Coherence

In a unified paragraph, everything belongs. In a coherent paragraph, everything sticks together: topic statement and support form a connected line of thought, like links in a chain. To convey exact meaning, a paragraph must be unified. To be readable, a paragraph must be coherent, as well.

This paragraph (written by a track team veteran addressing new runners) is both unified and coherent: everything relates to the topic in a continuous line of thinking.

[1]To be among the first out of the starting blocks in any race, follow these instructions. [2]First, when the starter says "Into your blocks," make sure you are the last runner down. [3]Take your sweet time; make all the others wait for you. [4]You take your time for three good reasons: one, you get a little more stretching than your competitors do; two, they are down in the blocks getting cold and nervous while you're still warm and relaxed from stretching; and three, your deliberate manner tends to weaken other runners' confidence. [5]The second step is to lean forward over your shoulders, in the "set" position. [6]This way, you will come out of the blocks forward and low, meeting less wind resistance. [7]The third and final step is to pump your arms as fast as you can when you come off the blocks. [8]The faster your arms pump, the faster your legs will move. [9]By concentrating on each of these steps, you can expect your quickest possible start.

The material in this paragraph seems easy enough to follow. Here's how the thinking goes:

1.   The topic statement sets a clear direction.

2.   The first step is introduced.

3–4. The importance of "taking your time" is emphasized and explained.

5–6. The second step is introduced and its importance explained.

7–8. The third step is introduced and its importance explained.

9.   The conclusion sums up.

Within this line of thinking, each sentence follows logically from the one before it. Because the material follows a logical order (in this case, chronological), readers know exactly where they are at any place in the paragraph. And because everything is connected (by parallelism, repetition of key words, pronouns, and transitions), the whole paragraph sticks together. Let's now examine specific ways of achieving coherence.

ORDERING IDEAS FOR COHERENCE

The mind works in structured ways to sort out, arrange, and make sense of its many perceptions. If you decide you like a class (a general observation), you then identify your particular reasons (friendly atmosphere, interesting subject, dynamic teacher, and so on); your thinking has followed a *general-to-specific order*. Or, if you tell a friend about your terrific weekend, you follow the order of events, how things happened over the weekend; your thinking has followed a *chronological order*. These are just two of several ordering patterns the mind uses to filter out that which is not immediately important and to create a sensible sequence of information. Here are the most common ordering patterns that help us think and write clearly.

- general-to-specific order
- specific-to-general order
- emphatic order
- spatial order
- chronological order

Of course, thinking and writing do not always fall neatly into one of these categories. On the whole, though, these ordering patterns can help you sort out your ideas and answer these questions:

What comes first?

What comes next?

Does the subject have any features that suggest an order?

Answers will be based on your subject and purpose. In a letter describing your new car (subject) to a friend, you might decide to move from outside to inside in a spatial order, as one would first see the car. A description that skipped around (say, from hubcaps to seats to tires to carpeting) would be confusing. Or, if you decided to concentrate on the car's computerized dashboard (subject), you might move from left to right (as one would see it from the driver's seat). If, instead, you were trying to persuade someone to stay in school or to quit smoking, you probably would present your reasons in an emphatic order, from least to most important or vice versa. Choosing the appropriate order makes your message easy to follow.

As we will see, some kinds of order call for your topic statement to come last instead of first. Even then, your opening sentence should tell readers what to expect. Before considering those variations, however, let's begin with the standard ordering pattern: general to specific.

General-to-Specific Order   The commonest way of arranging a paragraph is general to specific: a general topic statement supported by specific details. Most sample paragraphs we've seen so far follow a general-to-specific order, as this one does:

General assertion (topic statement, 1)	[1]Americans everywhere are obsessed with speed. [2]The airlines think it's so important that they've developed jets that can cross the ocean in a few hours. [3]Despite energy shortages, Detroit often makes the speed of a car and the power of its engine a focal point of its advertising campaign. [4]Ads for oil companies boast of ten-minute oil changes at their gas stations. [5]Even pedestrians aren't spared: some shoemakers will put soles and heels on shoes "while you wait." [6]Fast-food restaurants prosper as increasing millions gobble increasing billions of "all-beef" hamburgers and guzzle their Cokes in seconds flat. [7]And the Day of Rest, too, has given way to the stopwatch as more and more churches offer brief evening services or customize their offerings to suit "people on the go." [8]Some churches even offer drive-in ceremonies—pay your money, spit out your prayer, and hit the road, streaking toward salvation with Ronald McDonald. [9]These days, even the road to eternity has a fast lane.
Specific support (2-8)	
Conclusion (9)	

Paragraphs of general-to-specific order are the workhorses of virtually all nonfiction writing: first, the big picture; then, the close-ups—everything sticking together.

Specific-to-General Order For some purposes, instead of narrowing and restricting your meaning, you will generalize and extend it. Thus, your support will come first, and your topic statement last. A specific-to-general order is especially useful for showing how pieces of evidence add up to a convincing conclusion, as in this paragraph.

Orienting statements
(1-2)

Specific details (3-4)

General conclusion
(topic statement, 5)

[1]For thousands of years, the single species *Homo sapiens*, to which you and I have the dubious honor of belonging, has been increasing in numbers. [2]In the past couple of centuries, the rate of increase has itself increased explosively. [3]At the time of Julius Caesar, when Earth's human population is estimated to have been 150 million, that population was increasing at a rate such that it would double in 1,000 years if that rate remained steady. [4]Today, with Earth's population estimated at about 4,000 million (26 times what it was in Caesar's time), it is increasing at a rate which, if steady, will cause it to double in 35 years. [5]The present rate of increase of Earth's swarming human population qualifies *Homo sapiens* as an ecological cancer, which will destroy the ecology just as sure as any ordinary cancer would destroy an organism.

—Isaac Asimov

Even though the topic statement is saved for last, the opening statements give readers a forecast of the paragraph. Whenever you decide to delay your topic sentence, be sure the paragraph's opening sentence gives readers enough orientation for them to know what's going on.

A specific-to-general order works well for supporting a position that some readers might disagree with, as in this example.

Specific observation in
orienting statement
(1)

Specific arguments
(2-7)

[1]Strange that so few ever come to the woods to see how the pine lives and grows and spires, lifting its evergreen arms to the light—to see its perfect success; but most are content to behold it in the shape of many broad boards brought to market, and deem *that* its true success! [2]But the pine is no more lumber than man is, and to be made into boards and houses is no more its true and highest use than the truest use of a man is to be cut down and made into manure. [3]There is a higher law affecting our relations to pine as well as to men. [4]A pine cut down, a dead pine, is no

more a pine than a dead human carcass is a man. [5]Can he who has discovered only some of the values of whalebone and whale oil be said to have discovered the true use of the whale? [6]Can he who slays the elephant for his ivory be said to have "seen the elephant"?[7] These are petty and accidental uses; just as if a stronger race were to kill us in order to make buttons and flutes of our bones; for everything may serve a lower as well as

General conclusion (topic statement, 8)

a higher use. [8]Every creature is better alive than dead, men and moose and pine trees, and he who understands it correctly will rather preserve its life than destroy it.

—Henry David Thoreau

Some readers (especially those in the paper and lumber industry, as well as hunters) would find Thoreau's main point harder to accept if it were placed at the beginning, without the full paragraph lead-in. By moving from the specific to the general, Thoreau presents his evidence before drawing his conclusion. Also, things that come last (last word in a sentence, last sentence in a paragraph, last paragraph in an essay) are the things readers remember best. The order of Thoreau's material increases its persuasiveness.

Emphatic Order   In earlier chapters, we've seen how emphasis can make important things stand out, become easier to remember. Writers achieve emphasis within paragraphs by positioning material in two common ways: (1) from least to most important or serious or dramatic, and (2) vice versa. The next paragraph is from an essay analyzing television advertisements for toys of violence. Joe Bolton offers dramatic support for his opening assertion by saving his strongest example for last.

Topic statement (1-2)

[1]Too many toys advertised during television programs for children are of what I call the "death and destruction" variety: toys that simulate the killing of humans by humans. [2]Such toys make children's "war games" seem far too real. [3]During the pre-Christmas season, children are bombarded

Examples in increasing order of importance (3-5)

with ads promoting all the new weapons: guns, tanks, boats, subs, jets, helicopters, lasers, and more. [4]One new warplane is described as "the wickedest weapon yet," and a new satellite resembles an old "Nike" missile and is designed to be moved around on railroad tracks to avoid an enemy strike. [5]One of the enemy dolls is even dubbed a "paranoid schizophrenic killer" and advertised as such on the side of the box.

Because last things are best remembered, the end position of Bolton's most dramatic example fixes it in the reader's mind.

In another paragraph from the same essay, Bolton reverses the emphasis: he begins with his most serious material (a statement of the problem) and then proposes a solution that becomes increasingly farfetched.

Topic statement (1)	[1]Today, as always, children learn about killing before they understand the concept of death. [2]Seeing we still are a violent, warlike species, maybe we should try a new approach. [3]Children might be less likely to enjoy playing "war" if they could first be shown how guns blow holes in their targets; then they could be made to understand that, when the targets are *people*, those bloody holes cause pain and death. [4]If toy manufacturers introduced a "sounds and smells of death" accessory for their toys of violence, for instance, more parents and children might object to the nature of the "game" these toys simulate.
Support in decreasing order of seriousness (2-4)	

The increasingly grotesque solution is meant not to be taken seriously, but only to focus attention on the problem asserted in the topic statement.

Spatial Order Sometimes, instead of explaining something, you will want to describe it with a word picture. You treat the parts of your subject in the same order that readers would follow if they actually were looking at it. In this paragraph, the writer describes a missing friend to the police.

Topic statement	My missing friend should be easy to recognize. When I last saw Roger, he was wearing dark blue jeans, a pair of dark brown hunting boots with red laces, and a light blue cableknit sweater with a turtleneck; he was carrying a red daypack with black trim filled with books. He stands about 6 feet 4 inches, has broad, slouching shoulders, and carries roughly 190 pounds on a medium frame. He walks in excessively long strides, like a cowboy. His hair is sunstreaked,
A gradually narrowing focus	

sandy blond, cut just below his ears and feathered back on the sides. He has deep purple eyes framed by dark brown eyelashes and brows set into a clear, tanned complexion. The bridge of his nose carries a half-inch scar in the shape of an inverted crescent. His right front tooth has a small chip in the left corner.

Notice the writer's decisions in organizing this piece, based on her knowledge of the readers' needs: she begins with Roger's clothing and accessories and moves to his height, posture, weight, body build, stride, and finally his facial features, from hair down to mouth. This sequence is particularly effective because it follows the order of features that readers would recognize as they approached Roger: first, from a distance, by his clothing, size, posture, and stride; next, from a closer view—the hair, eye color, and so on; and, finally, from right up close—the scar on his nose and the chip on his tooth. The earlier details, visible from a distance, would alert readers, and the later ones would confirm their early impression as they moved up close. The details here were selected to answer these reader questions:

What does he look like?

How could we recognize him?

Whenever we describe something, we have to make these kinds of decisions about content and organization, about the kinds and sequence of details that will be clearest. The writer above decided to take the angle of a movie camera gradually closing in.

Many descriptive paragraphs begin with no topic statement at all. Instead, the opening sentence puts us immediately in the writer's place, as in this sample:

The tarpaulin is down, and a midafternoon rain is falling steadily. Play has been halted. The lights are on, and the wet, pale-green tarp throws off wiggly, reptilian gleams. The players are back in their locker rooms, and both dugouts are empty. A few fans have stayed in their seats, huddling under big, brightly colored golf umbrellas, but almost everybody else has moved back under the shelter of the upper decks, standing there quietly, watching the rain. The huge park, the countless rows of shiny-blue wet seats, the long emerald outfield—all stand silent and waiting. By the look of it, this shower may hold things up for a good half-hour or more. Time for a few baseball stories.

—Roger Angell

This paragraph places us in a setting, *showing* the scene as the writer saw and felt it. Because the paragraph is designed to create a dominant impression of the whole ballpark in the rain, the details are presented from an elevated angle of vision—like that of a television camera scanning the park from up in the press box.

Chronological Order   Another common order in a paragraph follows time. A chronological paragraph follows the natural order in which something happens. Writers use chronological order to give instructions (how to be first out of the starting blocks), to explain how something works (how the heart pumps blood), or to show how something happened. This paragraph from George Orwell's "Shooting an Elephant" shows how something brutal happened. As with many paragraphs that tell a story, this one has no topic statement. Instead, the opening sentence places us in the middle of the action.

Orienting statement
(1-2)

[1]When I pulled the trigger I did not hear the bang or feel the kick—one never does when a shot goes home—but I heard the devilish roar of glee that went up from the crowd. [2]In that instant, in too short a time, one would have thought, even for the bullet to get there, a mysterious, terrible change had come over the elephant. [3]He neither stirred nor fell, but every line on his body had altered. [4]He looked suddenly stricken, shrunken, immensely old, as though the frightful impact of the bullet had paralyzed him without knocking him down. [5]At last, after what seemed like a long time—it might have been five seconds, I dare say—he sagged flabbily to his knees. [6]His mouth slobbered. [7]An enormous senility seemed to have settled upon him. [8]One could have imagined him thousands of years old. [9]I fired again into the same spot. [10]At the second shot he did not collapse but climbed with desperate slowness to his feet and stood weakly upright, with legs sagging and head drooping. [11]I fired a third time. [12]That was the shot that did it for him. [13]You could see the agony of it jolt his whole body and knock the last remnant of strength from his legs. [14]But in falling he seemed for a moment to rise, for as his hind legs collapsed beneath him he seemed to tower upwards like a huge rock toppling, his trunk reaching skywards like a tree. [15]He trumpeted, for the first and only

> time. [16]And then down he came, his belly towards me, with a crash that seemed to shake the ground even where I lay.

Besides a series of events ordered in time, Orwell's paragraph contains the writer's *impressions* of what happened at various moments. The actual chronology is simple enough:

1. With the first shot, the elephant falls to its knees.

2. With the second shot, instead of collapsing, the elephant drags itself up.

3. With the third shot, the elephant falls, rises, and then falls for good.

If narrating these events in order were the writer's only purpose, the paragraph might look like this:

> When I pulled the trigger, a change came over the elephant. He neither stirred nor fell, but every line on his body had altered as if the impact of the bullet had paralyzed him without knocking him down. At last, he sagged to his knees. His mouth slobbered. I fired again into the same spot. At the second shot, he did not collapse but climbed slowly to his feet and stood with legs sagging and head drooping. I fired a third time. That was the shot that did it for him. But in falling he seemed for a moment to rise. And then, down he came, with his belly towards me, with a crash that shook the ground.

This paragraph lists the details a camera would record. It lacks the strength of the original, where personal comments create a vivid angle of vision. The author's purpose is not simply to narrate the shooting of an elephant; it is to express horror over his actions, to record the animal's dignity in dying, to make us confront the senseless brutality of this kind of slaughter. Yet despite these digressions in the original version, we are able to follow the events because they are narrated in chronological order. And despite the absence of a topic statement, the author's attitude toward his actions is clearly implied.

Keep in mind that paragraph order is just another device to help writer and reader stay on track. Any specific order or combination of orders will depend on your subject and purpose. Writers don't begin by saying, "I've decided to write a spatial paragraph, and so now I need to find a subject that will fit that order." Instead, they say, "I want to discuss *X*; therefore, I need to select the most logical order to make my message sensible." Granted, in the exercises here you are asked to follow this or that specific order in writing a paragraph, but only to give you practice in improving coherence. In all later writing, you will make such decisions for yourself.

COMBINED TYPES OF ORDER

Often your subject and purpose will call for combining types of order. This paragraph combines general-to-specific and chronological order.

> [1]Television is the most effective brainwashing medium ever invented by man. [2]Advertisers know this to be true. [3]Children are affected by television in ways we scarcely understand. [4]In the fall of 1973 I was assigned a story involving a young white woman living on the fringe of Boston's black ghetto. [5]Her car had run out of gas. [6]She had gone to a filling station with a can and was returning to her car when she was trapped in an alley by a gang of black youths. [7]The gang poured gasoline over her and set fire to her. [8]She died of her burns. [9]It was later established that some of the youths involved had, on the night before the killing, watched on television a rerun of an old movie in which a drifter is set on fire by an adolescent gang. [10]There is some kind of strange reductive process at work here. [11]To see something on television robs it of its reality, and then when the same thing is acted out, it is like the reenactment of something unreal. [12]In other words, when the gang set fire to the girl, they were imitating what they had seen on a screen, as if they themselves were on a screen, and in a story. [13]I don't think we have even begun to realize how powerful a medium television is.
>
> —Ted Morgan

The overall order of this paragraph is general to specific. In the topic statement the author expresses a general viewpoint about television. The remaining sentences provide supporting points and a detailed example. But the example itself (sentences 4 to 9) follows chronological order.

PARALLELISM

Along with paragraph order, several other devices are useful for increasing coherence. The first is parallelism—similar grammatical structures and word order for similar items, or for items of equal importance. Note how parallelism is employed in this paragraph:

> [1]What is the *shape* of my life? [2]The *shape* of my life today starts with a family. [3]I *have* a husband, five children, and a home

just beyond the suburbs of New York. [4]I *have* also a craft, writing, and therefore work I want to pursue. [5]The *shape* of my life is, of course, determined by many other things: my *background and childhood*, *my mind and* its education, *my conscience and* its pressures, *my heart and* its desires. [6]I want *to give and take* from my children and husband, *to share* with friends and community, *to carry out* my obligations *to man* and *to the world*, *as a woman*, *as an artist*, *as a citizen*. [emphasis added]

—Anne Morrow Lindbergh

This writer uses parallelism *between* as well as *within* sentences. Sentences 2 and 5 open with identical structures ("The shape of my life . . . ") to show that in both sentences she will treat the same subject. Sentences 3 and 4, too, have parallel openings ("I have a husband . . . I have also a craft . . . ") to reflect their close relationship. Sentence 5 has four parallel phrases ("my background and . . . my mind and . . . , my conscience and . . . , my heart and . . . "). Sentence 6 has three sets of parallel phrases: (1) "to give and take . . . to share . . . to carry out . . . ," (2) "to man . . . to the world . . . ," and (3) "as a woman, as an artist, as a citizen." These similar structures emphasize similarity between ideas, thereby tying the paragraph together. See pages 163–165 for further discussion of parallelism.

REPETITION, RESTATEMENT, AND VARIATION

Repeating key words or phrases or rephrasing them in different ways helps link ideas, as in this paragraph (emphasis added):

[1]The ultimate threat posed by nuclear *weapons* is not only *death* but *meaninglessness:* an unknown *death* by an unimaginable weapon. [2]War with such *weapons* is no longer heroic; *death* from such *weapons* is without valor. [3]*Meaninglessness* has become almost a stereotyped characterization of twentieth-century *life*, a central theme in modern art, theater, and politics. [4]The roots of this *meaninglessness* are many. [5]But crucial, we believe, is the anxiety deriving from the sense that all forms of human associations are perhaps *pointless* because subject to sudden *irrational* ends. [6]Cultural *life* thus becomes still more *formless*. [7]No one form, no single *meaning* or style, appears to have any ultimate claim. [8]The psychological implications of this *formlessness* are not fully clear; while there seem to be more *life* choices available, fewer are inwardly compelling.

—Robert J. Lifton and Eric Olson

The signal word *meaninglessness* in the topic statement is repeated in sentences 3, 4, and 7 (its variant: *meaning*). *Formless* (or its variants), here treated as a symptom of meaninglessness, is used in 5, 6, 7, and 8. Repetition of these two key words helps tie the paragraph together. In 5, *pointless* and *irrational* serve as synonyms (different words with similar meaning) for the idea of meaninglessness that dominates the paragraph. And, throughout, the antonyms (words with opposite senses) *life* and *death* seem to clash, each uncertain of ultimate victory. Both clauses in 2 have parallel structure ("War with such weapons is . . . ; death from such weapons is . . . "). The similar structure reflects the similarity of ideas, linking them neatly. And, of course, the repetition of *weapon* from 1 further clarifies the connection. Such repetition and restatement help keep our attention where it belongs: on the writer's view of a world threatened with annihilation.

Needless repetition, of course, makes writing seem tedious, juvenile, and annoying to read. For a clear distinction between effective and ineffective repetition, see page 176.

PRONOUNS FOR COHERENCE

Instead of repeating certain nouns, it is sometimes more natural to use pronouns that refer to an earlier key noun. Pronouns improve coherence by relating sentences, clauses, and phrases to one another. This paragraph uses pronouns to avoid repeating *the bull fighters*.

> The bull fighters march in across the sand to the president's box. *They* march with easy professional stride, swinging along, not in the least theatrical except for *their* clothes. *They* all have the easy grace and slight slouch of the professional athlete. From *their* faces *they* might be major league ball players. *They* salute the president's box then spread out along the barrera, exchanging *their* heavy brocaded capes for the fighting capes that have been laid along the red fence by the attendants. [emphasis added]
>
> —Ernest Hemingway

Without the pronouns *they* and *their*, the writer would have to repeat *the bull fighters* as many as seven times. Such repetition in this short paragraph would be awkward and excessive. The pronouns in this paragraph clearly refer to *the bull fighters*. When you do use pronouns, be sure they refer clearly to the appropriate nouns. See page 161 for a full discussion of pronoun-antecedent agreement.

CONSISTENCY FOR COHERENCE

Underlying all these strategies for coherence is the need for consistent tense, point of view, and number. Do not shift from past to present tense, from third- to first-person point of view, or from singular to plural nouns or pronouns—unless your meaning requires you to do so. See the Appendix for a discussion of shifts that destroy coherence.

TRANSITIONS

The devices we have studied for achieving coherence (order, parallelism, repetition and restatement, pronouns) *suggest* specific relations between ideas. Transitional expressions, on the other hand, *state* those relations. These are words and phrases that work like bridges between thoughts. Here are a few transitional phrases that give readers definite signals: *for example, meanwhile, however, moreover, thus.* Each transition indicates a definite relation between ideas. Each has a definite meaning—even without a specific context—as shown below.

Transition	Relation
X; meanwhile, Y	X and Y are occurring at the same time.
X; however, Y	Y is in contrast or exception to X.
X; moreover, Y	Y is in addition to X.
X; thus, Y	Y is a result of X.

Here is a paragraph in which these transitions are used to clarify the writer's line of thinking:

> Psychological and social problems of aging too often are aggravated by the final humiliation: poverty. One of every three older Americans lives near or below the poverty level. *Meanwhile,* only one of every nine younger people lives in poverty. The American public assumes that Social Security and Medicare provide adequate support for the aged. These benefits alone, *however,* rarely are enough to raise an older person's living standards above the poverty level. *Moreover,* older people are the only group living in poverty whose population recently has increased rather than decreased. More and more of our aging citizens *thus* confront the horror of poverty.

Transitions help make your meaning clear. They announce that you are in a specific time or place, or that you are giving an example, showing a contrast, concluding your discussion, or shifting gears. Here are some common transitions and the relations they indicate.

An addition: *moreover, in addition, and, also*

I am majoring in naval architecture; *furthermore,* I spent three years crewing on a racing yawl.

Results: *thus, hence, therefore, accordingly, thereupon, as a result, and so, as a consequence*

Mary enjoyed all her courses; *therefore,* she worked especially hard last semester.

An example or illustration: *for instance, to illustrate, namely, specifically*

Competition for part-time jobs is fierce; *for example,* 80 students applied for the clerk's job at Sears.

An explanation: *in other words, simply stated, in fact*

She had a terrible semester; *in fact,* she flunked four courses.

A summary or conclusion: *in closing, to conclude, to summarize, in brief, in summary, to sum up, all in all, on the whole, in retrospect, in conclusion*

Our credit is destroyed, our bank account is overdrawn, and our debts are piling up; *in short,* we are bankrupt.

Time: *first, next, second, then, meanwhile, at length, later, now, the next day, in the meantime, in turn, subsequently*

Mow the ball field this morning; *then* clean the dugouts.

A comparison: *likewise, in the same way, in comparison*

Our reservoir is drying up because of the drought; *similarly,* water supplies in neighboring towns are dangerously low.

A contrast or alternative: *however, nevertheless, yet, still, in contrast, otherwise, but, on the other hand, to the contrary, notwithstanding, conversely*

Felix worked hard *yet* received poor grades.

Note: Transitional expressions should be a limited option for improving coherence. Use them sparingly, and only when a relationship is not already made clear by the devices discussed earlier.

Besides the transitional expressions that increase coherence *within* a paragraph, whole sentences serve as transitions *between* paragraphs. Here is a transitional sentence that could end one paragraph, begin another, or stand alone for emphasis as a single-sentence paragraph:

> Because the AKS cartridge increases album life by 15 percent, our company should install it as a standard item in all our turntables.

This kind of transitional sentence both looks back and looks ahead, providing a clear direction for following the discussion.

Sometimes a whole paragraph can serve as a transition between sections of your writing. Assume that you have a summer job as a marketing intern for a manufacturer of stereo components. You have just completed a section of a memo on the advantages of the new AKS cartridge and are now moving to a section on selling the idea to consumers. Here is a paragraph that might link the two sections:

> Because the AKS cartridge increases album life by 15 percent, it should be installed as a standard item in all our turntables. Tooling and installation adjustments, however, will add roughly $50 to the list price of each model. We must, therefore, explain the cartridge's long-range advantages to consumers. Let's look at ways of explaining these advantages.

Notice that this paragraph has transitional expressions *within* it as well.

ALL DEVICES FOR ACHIEVING COHERENCE COMBINED

Devices for achieving coherence include logical order, parallelism, repetition and restatement, pronouns, and transitional expressions. Although most paragraphs employ some combination of these devices, not every paragraph employs all of them. Because the next paragraph has a variety of transitional devices, it is a good model for summarizing our discussion about coherence. How many specific devices can you identify?

> [1]*In a society based on self-reliance and free will, the institutionalization of life scares me.* [2]Today, America has government-funded programs to treat all society's ills. [3]We have day-care centers for the young, nursing homes for the old, psychologists in schools who use mental health as an instrument of discipline, and mental hospitals for those whose behavior does not conform to the norm. [4]We have drug-abuse programs, methadone-maintenance

programs, alcohol programs, vocational programs, rehabilitation programs, learning-how-to-cope-with-death-for-the-terminally-ill programs, make-friends-with-your-neighborhood-policeman programs, helping-emotionally-disturbed-children programs, and how-to-accept-divorce programs. [5]Unemployment benefits and welfare are programs designed to institutionalize a growing body of citizens whose purpose in life is the avoidance of work. [6]They are dependent on the state for their livelihood. [7]We can't even let people die in peace. [8]We put them in hospitals for the dying, so that they can be programmed into dying correctly. [9]They don't need to be hospitalized; they would be better off with their families, dying with dignity instead of in these macabre halfway houses. [10]All this is a displacement of confidence from the individual to the program. [11]We can't rely on people to take care of themselves anymore so we have to funnel them into programs. [12]This is a self-perpetuating thing, for the more programs we make available, the more people will become accustomed to seeking help from the government. [emphasis added]

—Ted Morgan

Application 7–1

This essay is shown without proper paragraph divisions. Mark the spot where each new paragraph should begin. *Hint:* Here is a rough (six-paragraph) outline: (1) introduction, (2) description of the plant, (3) a typical night shift, (4) the writer's specific job, (5) overview, (6) concluding story. Remember that things that belong together—not length—should dictate specific paragraph divisions. (Review pages 124–125.)

Swing Shift

Have you ever worked in a factory? Have you ever worked swing shift? Can you stand to function like a machine in 95-degree heat or more? Let alone stand it—can you work in it for eight hours of endless repetition and mindless labor? I did, for more than eight years. The Acme Tire and Rubber Company, about 5 miles east of our campus, resembles a prison. (Look for a massive and forbidding three-story building occupying two city blocks on Orchard Street.) The plant was built 50 years ago, and its windows, coated by the soot and grit of a half-century, admit no light, no hope of seeing in or out. Add to this dismal picture the drab red bricks and the stench of burned rubber. This is what I faced five nights a week at 10:00 P.M. when I reported for work. A worker's life inside the plant is arranged so as not to tax the mind. At exactly 10:00 P.M. a loud bell rings. Get to work. The bell has to be loud in order to be heard over the roar of machinery and hissing steam escaping from the high-pressure lines. In time you don't even notice the noise. It took me about two weeks. At midnight the bell rings again: a ten-minute break. At 2:00 A.M. it rings again: lunch, 20 minutes. Two hours later, it rings for the last break of the night. At 6:00 A.M. the final bell announces that the long night is over; it's time to go home. My dreary job was stocking tires. (I say "was" because I quit the job last year.) I had to load push trucks, the kind you see in railroad depots. I picked the tires up from the curing presses. A curing press is an 8-foot-high by 6-foot-wide by 6-foot-deep pressure cooker. There are 18 curing presses all in a row, and the temperature around them is over 100 degrees. Clouds of steam hang just below the 20-foot ceiling. By the time I had worked for ten minutes, my clothes were drenched with sweat and reeked with the acrid stench of steamed rubber. Once the truck was full, I'd push it to the shipping department on the other side of the plant. It's quiet there; they ship only during the day. And it's much cooler. I'd feel chilled even though the temperature was around 75 degrees. Here I would leave the full truck, look for an empty one, push it back, and start again. It was the same routine every night: endless truckloads of tires, five nights a week—every week. Nothing ever changed except the workers; they got older and worn out. I wasn't surprised to hear that a worker had hanged himself there a few weeks ago. He was a friend of mine. Another friend told me that the work went on anyway. The police said to leave the body hanging until the medical examiner could clear it—like so much meat hanging on a hook. Someone put a blanket around the hanging body. They had to move around it. The work went on.

—Glenn Silverberg

Application 7–2

The following topic statements are inadequate in some way. Some fail to focus on a limited subject; others express no definite viewpoint; others fail to say anything significant. Identify the deficiencies, and revise the statements to sharpen their meaning. (Review pages 126–128.)

Examples

Inadequate   My town has a population of 10,000. [*no viewpoint*]

Revised	Growing up in a small town has given me a sense of "belonging."
Inadequate	Boa constrictors are fascinating pets. [*subject not sufficiently limited*]
Revised	My boa Tyrone is a friend, a protector, and a companion.
Inadequate	Grades are a controversial subject. [*obvious, therefore not significant*]
Revised	Grades encourage excellence.

1. Women have changed radically over the years.

2. My best friend's name is Sally.

3. A part-time job really cuts down on a student's study time.

4. My college enrolls more men than women.

5. Cross-country skiing is a popular sport.

6. I have strong feelings about television.

7. College is a complex experience.

8. Some college requirements are silly.

Application 7–3

Your assignment is to assume a situation in which you would write a paragraph about some limited aspect of college life for a specific audience who will use your information for a definite purpose. Here are some possible situations.

1. The Student Senate has published a request in the school newspaper for nominations for the Teacher of the Year award. This request stipulates that all nominations be accompanied by a paragraph of 200 words or fewer, showing why that teacher should be nominated. After several weeks of delightful and informative classes with Professor X, you decide to nominate him or her. Write the paragraph.

2. You've decided to apply for a scholarship offered by your college. Among other application materials requested by the Scholarship Committee is a paragraph explaining your reasons for attending this college. Write the paragraph.

Before composing your paragraph, read the material below carefully. The topic statements (in italics) limit the subject *college life* so that the writer's viewpoint can be supported in one paragraph. The first paragraph is written to a friend who cares especially about his identity, and thus about attending a college that will appreciate him as an individual.

Because you're a person who hates the idea of being lost in the crowd, I know you would like Grunter College. In a school such as this one, with limited enrollment and small classes, it's easy to make friends and to get to know your professors well. In no time you will find that all the faces look familiar and that everyone is on a first-name basis. Also, there will be lots of people asking you to join various organizations and activities. You can count on being welcomed here, on having a real sense of belonging, on making a difference. So why not give it a try? You won't be sorry.

The writer of the next paragraph had a different purpose. Helping to write a college brochure, she wanted to emphasize the varied activities and organizations at Grunter College. Because the focus of her topic statement is narrower than in the first paragraph, the details themselves are more specific.

Whether your interests are social, political, artistic, or athletic, you'll find many ways to keep busy at Grunter College. In addition to our eight sororities and seven fraternities, we have a social club that sponsors dances, parties, concerts, and whatever else might be needed to liven up even the dreariest weekend. If you like politics, run for the Student Senate or join the Visitors' Council, which brings social and political celebrities to campus. If you're musically inclined, join the marching band, chamber orchestra, or rock group. Also, the various clubs for painters, writers, and dancers are always looking for new talent. To stay in shape, try out for varsity baseball, soccer, or track (all have both men's and women's teams), or join an intramural team. In short, if you seek involvement and challenge, Grunter College is for you.

Depending on the writer's purpose and the audience's needs, a topic statement about college life might be narrowed even further—say, for a paragraph describing a sorority or fraternity or the activities of the Visitors' Council.

Application 7–4

Identify the subject and the signal term in each of these sentences. (Review pages 130–131.)

Example

The pressures of the sexual revolution are everywhere.

—Joyce Maynard

Subject	pressures of the sexual revolution
Signal term	everywhere

1. High voltage from utility transmission lines can cause bizarre human and animal behavior.

2. Nuclear power plants need stricter supervision.

3. Producers of television commercials have created a loathsome gallery of men and women patterned, presumably, on Mr. and Mrs. America.

    —Marya Mannes

4. From the very beginning of school, we make books and reading a constant source of possible failure and possible humiliation.

    —John Holt

5. High interest rates cripple the auto and housing industries.

6. America's population centers are inevitably shifting to the Sunbelt states.

Application 7–5

This paragraph is an early draft of part of an open letter to the governor published in a college newspaper. Read it carefully, and answer the questions that follow.

[1]Conditions in the state mental hospital are shameful. [2]The big brick building is two miles from the main highway, and many people do not even know that there is such a place. [3]It is surrounded by spacious grounds. [4]Hundreds of patients are left in filthy conditions, never receiving the care they desperately need. [5]When my sociology class toured the hospital, we spent the entire morning

walking through the wards and talking to the attendants. [6]Because the windows are kept tightly closed, the air is damp and musty. [7]Geraniums and African violets in small flowerpots are growing on the windowsills. [8]Patients lie for long hours staring vacantly at the dirty ceiling. [9]Some of them listen to the radio or watch television hour after hour. [10]The food is too cold and is always unappetizing. [11]Some people are ashamed when a relative must go to the hospital, but mental illness is no disgrace. [12]The hospital has only four physicians for more than 500 patients. [13]A doctor in a mental institution should be a trained psychiatrist. [14]Straitjackets, ropes, and leather straps are used to tie down violent patients. [15]Sedatives, soothing baths, occupational therapy, and individual counseling are rarely used, because the hospital cannot afford them. [16]Patients who are recovering are allowed to work outdoors, and most of them seem to enjoy gardening. [17]But, on the whole, anyone who tours the mental hospital feels ashamed of this state.

1. What is the subject of the paragraph?

2. What is the signal term?

3. Which sentences do not relate to the main idea? (List the numbers.)

Application 7–6

Think about a place in your town or on campus that needs improvement. Describe the problem in one paragraph to a specified audience who will use your information as a basis for action.

Application 7–7

The paragraph below is unified but not coherent, because the sentences are not in logical order. Rearrange the sentences so that the line of thinking is clear. Be prepared to discuss reasons for your order.

[1]The Supreme Court's ruling against sex discrimination has touched all parts of American life—even the doll industry. [2]For example, Mattel, a large manufacturer of dolls, decided to change its ways—and make a little profit as well. [3]Now, little girl mommies might not have realized the significance of this arrival had it not been for the television announcement that "No family is complete without a tender Baby Brother." [4]Where would they find that little boy before Christmas? [5]In short, the doll was one small step for

Mattel, but one giant leap for man. [6]Thus sexism died, and a new doll was born: Mattel's Baby Brother Tender Love, a soft, lovable doll complete with boy parts. [7]Not only did it give children a dose of sex education, but it also made men grin with satisfaction upon having invaded the doll industry. [8]As a consequence, parents quivered with anxiety that they would be unable to meet the demands of little mothers. [9]Yes, Baby Brother Tender Love was Mattel's gift to society that year.

Application 7–8

Select one of these assignments, and write a paragraph organized from the general to the specific.

1. Study the paragraph about America's obsession with speed, on page 134. Then compose your own paragraph about some other obsession you have witnessed among friends, students, coworkers, family, or others. Give plenty of examples.

2. Select a writing situation from this list, or make up one of your own.

   - Picture the ideal summer job. Explain to an employer why you would like the job.

   - Assume that it's time for end-of-semester student evaluations of courses. Write a one paragraph evaluation of your favorite course to be read by the professor's department chairperson.

   - Explain your views on video games. Write for your classmates.

   - Describe the job outlook in your chosen field. Write for a high school senior interested in your major.

Application 7–9

Identify someone who you think undervalues something, as in these possibilities:

- a brother who fails to appreciate your parents' sacrifices
- a neighbor who is cutting down his trees for firewood

- a roommate who doesn't appreciate the social or educational opportunities offered by your college

- a friend who dislikes another friend

- a friend who wants to drop out of school

- someone close who needs more exercise

- any other situation

Using Thoreau's paragraph (page 135) as a model, write a paragraph alerting your reader to the importance of X. Save your main point for last, with your support leading up to it. Be sure your opening sentence provides an orientation.

Application 7–10

Identify a problem in a group to which you belong (such as family, club, sorority). Or select a topic from the list, or make up one of your own. With the paragraphs on pages 136–137 as models, write your own emphatic paragraph.

- advice to an entering freshman about surviving in college

- your life goal, to your academic adviser, who is recommending you for a scholarship

- your reasons for wanting to live off campus, to the dean of students

Application 7–11

Using Angell's paragraph (page 138) as a model, describe to your classmates a memorable scene. Include details about *who, what, when, where,* and *why,* as well as any details that will help readers *see, feel, hear, taste,* or *smell.* Decide on the best angle of vision (such as outside to inside, near to far, right to left) to provide the clearest possible picture.

As an alternate assignment, choose a situation from this list, or make up one of your own.

- Show your classmates that a room in which you spend much of your time is pleasant or depressing.

- Show the local animal officer how to recognize your lost pet.

- Show a friend that the view from a favorite spot is worth the trip.

Your paragraph may or may not have a topic statement. But be sure your opening sentence (or sentences) provides a clear orientation.

Application 7–12

Using Orwell's paragraph (page 139) as a model, tell your classmates of a striking event in which you were involved. Use sharp details to make the scene vivid. Including your *impressions* will create a definite angle of vision. Instead of beginning with a topic statement, you might begin with an orienting statement that places readers immediately in the action. You might conclude with a topic statement or let the details of your story imply your main point. Be sure, though, that your story conveys a definite point.

As an alternate assignment, select a situation from this list, or make up one of your own. Write for your classmates.

1. Tell about the worst (or best) hour of your life.

2. Tell about how you said good-bye to someone close to you.

3. Tell about something frightening that happened in your childhood.

Application 7–13

In a logically ordered paragraph addressed to someone whose child watches television constantly, discuss one major effect television has had on you or someone you know. Use Morgan's paragraph (page 141) as a model.

Application 7–14

Supply the transitional expression that best connects each pair of sentences or clauses. (Review pages 144–146.)

An addition

1. Most elderly people wish to preserve their skills and possessions; _____, they wish to maintain their sense of freedom and prestige in the family, group, and community.

Time

2. Between ages 60 and 70, one feels the physical effects of aging;
_____, retirement causes changes in an older person's social
status, income, and self-concept.

A comparison

3. Minorities in America often are treated as people who must be
tolerated but who ought to stay out of the way. The elderly,
_____, often suffer discrimination and stereotyping and are
thought to have little social worth.

A contrast or alternative

4. Old age should be a time of comfort and leisure for those who
are still healthy; _____, society's indifference toward the
elderly often breeds depression and dependency.

A result

5. Our society values what is young and beautiful but discards what
is old and unattractive. It is, _____, no surprise that we find
ways to ignore the fact that people age and die.

An example

6. Active community support can make a great difference in the
quality of life for the elderly; _____, clubs, community centers,
public housing, and other services can help ease the burden of
aging.

An explanation

7. By segregating the aged through neglect, society itself suffers
great losses; _____, the loss of purchasing power, taxes, and
talent can often outweigh the cost of providing services to the
aged.

Application 7–15

Reread Morgan's paragraph (page 141), and identify the features that
help make it coherent.

1. Identify the topic statement.

2. What is the ordering pattern?

3. Identify all examples of parallel structure.

4. Identify the key words that are repeated, and explain how this repetition helps clarify the author's meaning.

5. Identify the synonyms in the paragraph.

6. Do the pronouns all refer to the same noun?

7. Identify any transitional expressions, and briefly explain the relationship signaled by each. Should there be any transitions in this paragraph?

Application 7–16

Select the best paragraph or essay you have written thus far (or one that your instructor suggests). Using the strategies in this chapter, revise the paragraph or essay for improved coherence. After revising, list the specific strategies you've used (logical order, parallelism, repetition of key terms, restatement, pronouns, transitions).

8

Writing
Effective Sentences

Making Sentences Clear • Making Sentences Concise
• Making Sentences Fluent • Applications

Every bit as important as *what* you have to say is *how* you say it. No matter how vital your content and how sensible your organization, your message will mean little unless it is easy to understand—in a word, *readable.* Any paragraph can be only as readable as the sentences that form it. And a readable sentence is one that can be understood in a *single* reading.

One requirement for readable sentences, of course, is that they have correct grammar, punctuation, and mechanics. Basic errors, such as fragments and comma splices (all covered in the Appendix), distract readers. But "correctness" alone is no guarantee that a sentence will be readable. Readers also can be distracted by sentences that are hard to interpret, that take too long to make the point, or that seem choppy. Besides being grammatical, effective sentences emphasize relationships, waste no words, and make for smooth reading. In short, effective sentences are *clear, concise,* and *fluent.*

Before working with this section, you may wish to review some basic grammatical terms (clauses, phrases, and the like) in the Appendix.

Making Sentences Clear

A clear sentence conveys the writer's meaning on the first reading. It signals relationships among its parts, and it emphasizes the main idea. These guidelines will help you write clear sentences.

158

AVOID FAULTY MODIFIERS

Modifiers explain, define, or add detail to other words or ideas. Prepositional phrases usually define or limit adjacent words:

the foundation **with the cracked wall**

the repair job **on the old Ford**

the journey **to the moon**

the party **for our manager**

Phrases with "-ing" verb forms limit:

the student **painting the portrait**

Opening the door, we entered quietly.

Phrases with "to + verb" form limit:

To succeed, one must work hard.

Some clauses limit:

the man **who came to dinner**

the job **that I recently accepted**

If a modifier is too far from the words it modifies, the message can be ambiguous.

Misplaced modifier   At our campsite, **devouring the bacon,** I saw a huge bear.

Was it I who was devouring the bacon? Of course not. But placing the modifier *devouring the bacon* next to *I* conveys that message. Moving the modifier next to *bear* clarifies the sentence:

Revised   At our campsite, I saw a huge bear **devouring the bacon.**

The order of adjectives and adverbs in a sentence is as important as the order of modifying phrases and clauses. Notice how changing word order affects the meaning of these sentences:

I **often** remind myself of the need to balance my checkbook.

I remind myself of the need to balance my checkbook **often.**

Be sure that modifiers and the words they modify follow an order that reflects your meaning.

Misplaced modifier	Harry typed another memo on our new electric typewriter **that was useless.** [*Was the typewriter or the memo useless?*]
Revised	Harry typed another useless memo on our new electric typewriter. or Harry typed another memo on our new, useless electric typewriter.
Misplaced modifier	She read a report on using nonchemical pesticides **in our conference room.** [*Are the pesticides to be used in the conference room?*]
Revised	In our conference room, she read a report on using nonchemical pesticides.
Misplaced modifier	*Only* press the red button in an emergency. (Does **only** modify **press** or **emergency?**)
Revised	Press **only** the red button in an emergency. or Press the red button in an emergency **only**.
Misplaced modifier	Nonsmokers are harmed by tobacco smoke **as well as smokers.** [*Do smokers harm nonsmokers?*]
Revised	Nonsmokers **as well as smokers** are harmed by tobacco smoke.

Another problem with word order occurs when the modifier has no word to modify. This problem can occur when a sentence begins with a modifying phrase:

Dangling modifier	**Answering the telephone,** the cat ran out the door.

The cat obviously did not answer the telephone. But because the modifier **Answering the telephone** has no word to modify, the word order suggests that the noun beginning the main clause (**cat**) names the one who answered the phone. Without any word to join itself to, the modifier *dangles*. By inserting a subject, we can repair this absurd message:

Revised	**As Mary answered the telephone,** the cat ran out the door.

A dangling modifier also can obscure the meaning in your message.

Dangling modifier	**After completing the student financial aid application form,** the Financial Aid Office will forward it to the appropriate state agency.

Who completes the form—the student or the financial aid office?
    Here are some other dangling modifiers that make the message confusing, inaccurate, or downright absurd:

Dangling modifier	**While walking,** a cold chill ran through my body.
Revised	While I walked, a cold chill ran through my body.
Dangling modifier	**After a night of worry,** the lights came on.
Revised	**After we had worried all night,** the lights came on.
Dangling modifier	Impurities have entered our bodies **by eating chemically processed foods**.
Revised	Impurities have entered our bodies by **our** eating chemically processed foods.
Dangling modifier	**By planting different varieties of crops,** the pests were unable to adapt.
Revised	By planting different varieties of crops, **farmers** prevented the pests from adapting.
Dangling modifier	An an **expert in this field,** I'm sure your advice will help.
Revised	**Because you are an expert in this field,** I'm sure your advice will help.

KEEP YOUR PRONOUN REFERENCES CLEAR

A pronoun takes the place of a noun. Whenever you use a pronoun (**she, it, his, their,** and so on), that pronoun must refer to one clearly identified noun. If the pronoun's referent (or antecedent) is vague, readers will find your sentence confusing.

Vague referent	Our patients are enjoying the warm days while **they** last. [*Are the patients or the warm days on the way out?*]

Depending on whether the referent for **they** is **days** or **patients,** the sentence can be clarified:

Clear referent	While these warm days last, our patients are enjoying them.
	or
	Our terminal patients are enjoying the warm days.

Be sure readers can identify the noun your pronoun replaces.

Ambiguous	**Sally** told **Sarah** that **she was obsessed** with her job.

Does **she** refer to **Sally** or **Sarah?** Many interpretations are possible:

1. Sally is obsessed with her own job.

2. Sally thinks that Sarah is obsessed with her (Sally's) job. (Sarah is envious.)

3. Sally thinks that Sarah is obsessed with her own (Sarah's) job.

4. Sally is obsessed with Sarah's job.

5. Sally thinks that someone else is obsessed with her (Sally's) job.

6. Sally thinks that someone else is obsessed with Sarah's job.

7. Sally thinks that someone else is obsessed with some other person's job.

8. Sally thinks that someone else is obsessed with her own job.

Revised	Sally told Sarah, "I'm obsessed with my job."
	Sally told Sarah, "I'm obsessed with your job."
	Sally told Sarah, "You're obsessed with [your, my] job."
	Sally told Sarah, "She's obsessed with [her, my, your] job."

Avoid using **this, that,** or **it**—especially to begin a sentence—unless the pronoun refers to a specific antecedent (referent).

Vague	As he drove away from his menial **job,** boring **lifestyle,** and damp **apartment,** he was happy to be leaving it behind.

Revised	As he drove away, he was happy to be leaving his menial job, boring life-style, and damp apartment behind.
Vague	The problem with our **defective machinery** is only compounded by the new **operator's incompetence.** This annoys me!
Revised	I am annoyed by the problem with our defective machinery as well as by the new operator's incompetence.
Inaccurate	Increased blood pressure is caused by narrowing of the blood vessels, making the pressure higher as **it** flows through the blood vessels.

Here, **it** seems to refer to **pressure,** which is absurd.

Revised	Increased blood pressure is caused by narrowing of the blood vessels, which makes the pressure higher as the blood flows through the vessels.

AVOID OVERSTUFFING

A sentence that crams in too many ideas forces the reader to struggle over its meaning.

Overstuffed	A smoke-filled room causes not only teary eyes and runny noses but also can alter people's hearing and vision, as well as creating dangerous levels of carbon monoxide, especially for people with heart and lung ailments, whose health is particularly threatened by "second-hand" smoke.

Clear things up by sorting out the relationships:

Revised	Besides causing teary eyes and runny noses, a smoke-filled room can alter people's hearing and vision. One of "second-hand" smoke's biggest dangers, however, is high levels of carbon monoxide, a particular health threat for people with heart and lung ailments.

KEEP EQUAL ITEMS PARALLEL

To reflect relationships among items of equal importance, express them in parallel grammatical form (see also page 141).

Correct   We here highly resolve . . . that government **of the people, by the people, for the people** shall not perish from the earth.

This statement describes the government with three modifiers equal in importance. Because the first modifier is a prepositional phrase, the others must be also. Otherwise, the message would be garbled, like this:

Faulty   We here highly resolve . . . that government **of the people, which the people created and maintain, serving the people** shall not perish from the earth.

If you begin the series with a noun, use nouns throughout the series; likewise for adjectives, adverbs, and specific types of clauses and phrases.

Faulty   The new tutor is **enthusiastic, skilled,** and **you can depend on her.**

Revised   The new tutor is **enthusiastic, skilled,** and **dependable.** [*all subjective complements*]

Faulty   In his new job he felt **lonely** and **without a friend.**

Revised   In his new job he felt **lonely** and **friendless.** [*both adjectives*]

Faulty   She plans **to study** all this month and **on scoring well** in her licensing examination.

Revised   She plans **to study** all this month and **to score** well in her licensing examination. [*both infinitive phrases*]

Faulty   She **sleeps well** and jogs daily, **as well as eating** high-protein foods.

Revised   She **sleeps** well, **jogs** daily, and **eats** high-protein foods. [*all verbs*]

To improve coherence in long sentences, repeat words that introduce parallel expressions:

Faulty   Before buying this property, you should decide whether you plan to settle down and raise a family, travel for a few years, or pursue a graduate degree.

Revised	Before buying this property, you should decide whether you plan **to settle** down and raise a family, **to travel** for a few years, or **to pursue** a graduate degree.

ARRANGE WORDS FOR COHERENCE AND EMPHASIS

In coherent writing, everything sticks together; each sentence builds on the preceding sentence and looks ahead to the following sentence. Many sentences work best when the beginning looks back at familiar information and the end provides the new information. Here is how sentences progress from familiar to unfamiliar:

Familiar		Unfamiliar
My dog	has	fleas.
Our boss	just won	the lottery.
This company	is planning	a merger.

Besides helping a message stick together, the familiar-to-unfamiliar structure emphasizes the new information. Just as every paragraph has a key sentence, every sentence has a key word or phrase that sums up the new information. That key word or phrase is best emphasized at the end of the sentence.

Faulty emphasis	We expect a **refund** because of your error in our shipment.
Correct	Because of your error in our shipment, we expect a **refund.**
Faulty emphasis	After your awful behavior, an **apology** is something I expect. But I'll probably get an excuse.
Correct	After your awful behavior, I expect an **apology.** But I'll probably get an excuse.

One exception to placing key words last occurs with *instructions.* Each step in a list of instructions ordinarily begins with an action verb (**insert, open, close, turn, remove, press**). To provide readers with a forecast, place the verb in that instruction at the beginning.

Correct	**Insert** the diskette before activating the system.
	Remove the protective seal.

With the key word at the beginning of the instruction, readers know immediately the action they need to take.

USE PROPER COORDINATION

Give equal emphasis to ideas of equal importance by joining them, within simple or compound sentences, with coordinating conjunctions: **and, but, or, nor, for, so,** and **yet.**

Correct	This course is difficult, **but** it is worthwhile. My horse is old **and** gray. We must decide to support **or** reject the dean's plan.

Do not, however, confound your meaning by coordinating excessively.

Excessive coordination	The climax in jogging comes after a few miles **and** I can no longer feel stride after stride **and** it seems as if I am floating **and** jogging becomes almost a reflex **and** my arms **and** legs continue to move **and** my mind no longer has to control their actions.
Revised	The climax in jogging comes after a few miles, when I can no longer feel stride after stride. By then I am jogging almost by reflex, nearly floating, my arms and legs still moving, my mind no longer having to control their actions.

Notice how the meaning becomes clear when the less important ideas (**nearly floating, arms and legs still moving, my mind no longer having**) are shown as dependent on, rather than equal to, the most important idea (**jogging almost by reflex**)—the idea that contains the lesser ones.

Avoid coordinating ideas that cannot be sensibly connected:

Faulty	John had a weight problem and dropped out of school.
Revised	John's weight problem made him so depressed that he couldn't study, and so he dropped out of school.
Faulty	I was late for work and wrecked my car.
Revised	Late for work, I backed out of the driveway too quickly, hit a truck, and wrecked my car.

In the faulty sentences above, the **and** is made to do too much work.

Do not use **try and.** Use **try to** instead.

Faulty   I will try and help you.

Revised   I will try to help you.

USE PROPER SUBORDINATION

Proper subordination shows that a less important idea is dependent on a more important idea. By using subordination, you can combine related simple sentences into complex sentences and also emphasize the most important idea. Consider these complete thoughts:

Joe studies diligently. He has a learning disability.

Because these ideas are expressed as simple sentences, they appear to be coordinate (equal in importance). But if you wanted to express your opinion of Joe's chances of succeeding, you would need a third sentence: **His handicap probably will prevent him from succeeding** or **His willpower will help him succeed** or some such. An easier and more concise way to communicate the intended meaning is by combining the two original thoughts and subordinating the one that deserves less emphasis:

Despite his learning disability [*subordinate thought*], Joe studies diligently [*independent thought*].

This first version suggests that Joe will succeed. Below, subordination is used to suggest the opposite meaning:

Despite his diligent study [*subordinate thought*], Joe is unlikely to overcome his learning disability.

A dependent (or subordinate) clause in a sentence is signaled by a subordinating conjunction: **because, so that, if, unless, after, until, since, while, as,** and **although.** Be sure to place the idea you want emphasized in the independent (main) clause; do not write

Although Alfred is receiving excellent medical treatment, he is seriously ill.

if you mean to suggest that Alfred has a good chance of recovering.
Do not coordinate when you should subordinate:

Faulty   Television viewers can relate to a person they idolize, and they feel obliged to buy the product endorsed by their hero.

Of the two ideas in this sentence, one is the cause, the other the effect. Emphasize this relationship through subordination:

Revised	Because television viewers can relate to a person they idolize, they feel obliged to buy the product endorsed by their hero.

When combining several ideas within a sentence, decide which is the most important, and make the other ideas subordinate to it.

Faulty	This employee is often late for work, and he writes illogical reports, and he is a poor manager, and he should be fired.
Revised	Because this employee is often late for work, writes illogical reports, and is a poor manager, **he should be fired.** [*The last clause is independent.*]

Do not overstuff sentences by subordinating excessively:

Faulty	This job, which I took when I graduated from college, while I waited for a better one to come along, which is boring, where I've gained no useful experience, makes me eager to quit.
Revised	Upon college graduation, I took this job while waiting for a better one to come along. Because I find it boring and have gained no useful experience, I am eager to quit.

USE ACTIVE VOICE OFTEN, PASSIVE VOICE SELECTIVELY

The active voice (**I did it**) is more direct, concise, and forceful than the passive voice (**It was done by me**). In the active voice, the agent performing the action serves as subject:

	Agent	Action	Recipient
Active	Joe	lost	your report.
	Subject	Verb	Object

The passive voice reverses the pattern, making the recipient of an action serve as subject:

	Recipient	Action	Agent
Passive	Your report	was lost	by Joe.
	Subject	Verb	Prepositional phrase

Sometimes the passive eliminates the agent altogether:

Passive   Your report was lost. [*Who lost it?*]

Some writers mistakenly rely on the passive voice because they think it sounds more objective and important. But the passive voice often makes writing seem merely wordy or evasive. Consider the effect when an active statement is recast in the passive voice:

Concise and direct   I underestimated expenses for this semester. [7
(active)   *words*]

Wordy and indirect   Expenses for this semester were underestimated
(passive)   by me. [9 *words*]

Evasive (passive)   Expenses for this semester were underestimated.

For economy, directness, and clarity, use the active voice in most of your writing.

Do not evade responsibility by hiding behind the passive voice:

Passive   **A mistake was made** in your shipment. [*By
"irresponsibles"   whom?*]

                            It was decided not to hire you. [*Who decided?*]

                            A layoff is recommended. [*By whom?*]

Acknowledge responsibility for your actions:

Active   **I made** a mistake in your shipment.

                            I decided not to hire you.

                            Our committee recommends a layoff.

In reporting errors or bad news, use the active voice. Readers appreciate clarity and sincerity.

But do use the passive voice if the person behind the action has reason for being protected:

Correct passive   The criminal was identified.

                           The embezzlement scheme was exposed.

Here, the passive protects the innocent person who identified the criminal or who exposed the scheme.

Use the passive only when your audience does not need to know the agent:

| Correct passive | Mr. Jones was brought to the emergency room. |
| | The bank failure was publicized statewide. |

Readers do not need to know *who* brought Mr. Jones or *who* publicized the bank failure. Notice again how the passive voice focuses on the *recipient* rather than the *agent.*

Use the passive voice to focus on events or results when the agent is unknown, unapparent, or unimportant:

| Correct passive | The victim was asked to testify. |
| | Mary's article was published last week. |

The information that will interest readers here is *that* the victim was asked to testify or *that* Fred's article was published.

Prefer the passive when you deliberately wish to be indirect or inoffensive (as in requesting the customer's payment or the employee's cooperation):

Active but offensive	**You** have not paid your bill.
	You need to overhaul our filing system.
Inoffensive passive	**This bill** has not been paid.
	Our filing system needs overhauling.

By focusing on the recipient rather than the agent, these passive versions help retain the audience's goodwill.

The passive voice is weaker than the active voice and creates an impersonal tone:

| **Weak and impersonal** | An invitation will be sent next week. |
| **Strong and personal** | We will send you an invitation next week. |

Use the active voice when you want action. Otherwise, your statement will have no power:

| **Weak passive** | If my claim is not settled by May 15, the Better Business Bureau will be contacted, and their advice on legal action will be taken. |

This passive and tentative statement is unlikely to move readers to action: *Who* is making the claim? *Who* should settle the claim? *Who* will contact the Bureau? *Who* will take action? Nobody is here! Here is a more direct, concise, and forceful version, in the active voice:

Strong active	If you do not settle my claim by May 15, I will contact the Better Business Bureau for advice on legal action.

Notice how this active version emphasizes the new and significant information by placing it at the end.

Ordinarily, use the active voice for giving instructions.

Faulty passive	The door to the cobra's cage should be closed.
	Care should be taken with the dynamite.
Correct active	**Close** the door to the cobra's cage.
	Be careful with the dynamite.

Avoid shifts from active to passive voice in the same sentence:

Faulty shift	During the meeting, project members spoke and presentations were given.
Correct	During the meeting, project members spoke and gave presentations.

By using the active voice, you direct the reader's attention to the subject of your sentence. Unless you have a deliberate reason for choosing the passive voice, prefer the *active* voice in most of your writing.

Application 8–1

These sentences are unclear because of faulty modification, unclear pronoun reference, or overstuffing. Revise them so that their meaning is clear. For sentences suggesting two meanings, write separate versions—one for each meaning intended. (Review pages 159–163.)

1.   Bill told Fred that he was wrong.
2.   I bought a house from a real estate agent full of termites.
3.   Only use this phone in a red alert.

4. Making the shelves look neater was another of my tasks at X-Mart that is very important to a store's business because if the merchandise is not always neatly arranged, customers will not have a good impression, whereas if it is neat they will probably return.

5. Wearing high boots, the snake could not hurt me.

6. Having more than an hour left to travel, the weather kept getting worse.

7. When my ninth-grade teacher caught daydreamers, she would jab them in the shoulder with gritted teeth and a fierce eye.

8. While they eat dead fish, our students enjoy watching the alligators.

9. After being late for work twice in one week, my boss is annoyed with me.

Application 8–2

These sentences are unclear because of faulty parallelism or key words buried in midsentence. Revise them so that their meaning is clear. (Review pages 163–166.)

1. Education enables us to recognize excellence and to achieve it.

2. Student nurses are required to identify diseases and how to treat them.

3. My car needs an oil change, a grease job, and the carburetor should be adjusted.

4. In a business relationship, trust makes it work.

5. I have a critical need for financial aid.

6. In all writing, revision is required.

Application 8–3

Use coordination or subordination as appropriate to clarify relationships in these sentences. (Review pages 166–168.)

1. Martha loves John. She also loves Bruno.

2. You will succeed. Work hard.

3. I worked hard in calculus and flunked the course.

4. Now I have no privacy. My cousin moved into my room.

5. I will try and get a refund on my defective watch.

6. The instructor entered the classroom. Some students were asleep.

Application 8–4

These sentences are wordy, weak, or evasive because of passive voice. Revise each sentence as a concise, forceful, and direct expression in the active voice, in order to identify the person or agent performing the action. (Review pages 168–171.)

1. The evaluation was performed by us.

2. The essay was written by me.

3. Unless you pay me within three days, my lawyer will be contacted.

4. Hard hats should be worn at all times.

5. It was decided to decline your invitation.

6. Gasoline was spilled on your Ferrari's leather seats.

7. The manager was kissed.

Application 8–5

These sentences lack proper emphasis because of active voice. Revise each ineffective active as an appropriate passive, emphasizing the recipient rather than the agent. (Review pages 168–171.)

1. Joe's company fired him.

2. A rockslide buried the mine entrance.

3. Someone on the maintenance crew has just discovered a crack in the nuclear-core containment unit.

4. A power surge destroyed more than 2000 lines of our new computer program.

5. Your essay confused me.

6. You are paying inadequate attention to students' safety.

7. You are checking temperatures too infrequently.

Making Sentences Concise

Writing can suffer from two kinds of wordiness: one kind occurs when readers are given information they don't need. (See Chapter 6, or watch a typical weather report on local television news.) The other kind of wordiness occurs when too many words are used to convey the information readers *do* need (as in saying **a great deal of potential for the future** instead of **great potential**). A concise sentence conveys most information in fewest words. It gets right to the point without clutter; however, conciseness does not mean omitting specific details necessary for clarity. A brief but vague message is useless.

Brief but vague	Clarence's grades for last semester were poor.
Brief but informative	Last semester Clarence received one **C**, two **D's**, and two **F's**.

Be sure your information is adequate, but use fewer words whenever fewer will do.

Cluttered	At this point in time I must say that I need a vacation.
Concise	I need a vacation **now**.

First drafts rarely are concise. Always revise parts that are wordy, repetitious, or vague. Trim the fat by getting rid of anything that adds no meaning.

AVOID NEEDLESS PHRASES

Don't use a whole phrase when one word will do. Instead of **in this day and age**, write **today**. Each needless phrase here can be reduced to one word—without any loss in meaning.

at this point in time	= now
has the ability to	= can
aware of the fact that	= know

due to the fact that	= because
on a personal basis	= personally
dislike very much	= hate
athletic person	= athlete
the majority of	= most
take the place of	= substitute
being in good health	= healthy
on a daily basis	= daily
each and every one	= all
in close proximity to	= near

ELIMINATE REDUNDANCY

A redundant expression says the same thing twice, in different words, as in **fellow classmates**. Each bracketed word or phrase below merely adds clutter, because its meaning is included in the other word.

a [dead] corpse	enter [into]
the reason [why]	[totally] monopolize
the [final] conclusion	[totally] oblivious
[utmost] perfection	[very] vital
[mental] awareness	[past] experience
[the month of] August	correct [amount of] change
[the color] green	stands out [the most]
[basic] essentials	[future] prospects
[mutual] cooperation	[valuable] asset
mix [together]	[close] scrutiny
[viable] alternative	[free] gift

AVOID NEEDLESS REPETITION

Unnecessary repetition of words or phrases can clutter your writing and dilute your meaning.

| Repetitious | In trauma victims, breathing is restored by **artificial respiration**. Techniques of **artificial respiration** include mouth-to-mouth **respiration** and mouth-to-nose **respiration**. |

Repetition in that passage can be eliminated when sentences are combined.

| Concise | In trauma victims, breathing is restored by artificial respiration, either mouth-to-mouth or mouth-to-nose. |

Keep in mind, however, that repetition can be useful. Don't hesitate to repeat, or at least rephrase, material (even whole paragraphs in a longer piece) if you feel that readers need reminders.

AVOID *THERE* SENTENCE OPENERS

Save words, add force, and improve your emphasis by not using **there is** and **there are** to begin sentences—whenever your intended meaning allows.

Faulty	There are several good reasons why Boris dropped out of school.*
Concise	Boris dropped out of school for several good reasons.
Faulty	There is a serious fire danger created by your smoking in bed.
Concise	Your smoking in bed creates danger of fire.

Dropping these openers places the key words at the end of the sentence, where they are best emphasized.

AVOID SOME *IT* SENTENCE OPENERS

Try not to begin a sentence with It—unless the It clearly refers to something specific in the preceding sentence.

---

*Of course, in some contexts, proper emphasis would call for a **There** opener.

Correct People often have wondered about the rationale behind Boris's sudden decision. Actually, there are several good reasons for his dropping out of school.

Most often, however, **There** openers are best dropped.

Wordy	[It was] his negative attitude [that] caused him to fail.
Wordy	It gives me great pleasure to introduce our speaker.
Concise	I am pleased to introduce our speaker.

AVOID WEAK VERBS

Try to choose verbs that express a definite action: **open, close, move, continue, begin.** These strong verbs advance your meaning. Avoid verbs that express no specific action: **is, was, are, has, give, make, come, take.** These weak verbs add words without advancing your meaning. All forms of the verb **to be** are weak. This sentence achieves conciseness because of the strong verb **consider:**

Concise	Please **consider** my application.

Here is what happens with a weak verb in the same sentence:

Weak and wordy	Please **take into consideration** my application.

Don't let yourself disappear behind weak verbs—along with their baggage of needless nouns and prepositions.

Weak	My recommendation **is** for a larger budget.
Strong	I **recommend** a larger budget.

Strong verbs, or action verbs, suggest an assertive, positive, and confident writer. Here are some weak verbs converted to strong:

is in conflict with	= conflicts
give a summary of	= summarize
make an assumption	= assume
come to the conclusion	= conclude
take action	= act
make a decision	= decide
come to the realization	= realize

DELETE NEEDLESS *TO BE* CONSTRUCTIONS

In the preceding section we saw that all forms of the verb **to be** (is, was, are, and so on) are weak. Sometimes the **to be** form itself mistakenly appears behind such verbs as **appears**, **seems**, and **find**.

Wordy	She seems [to be] upset.
Wordy	I find some of my classmates [to be] brilliant.

By eliminating **to be** in these examples, we save words without loss in meaning.

AVOID EXCESSIVE PREPOSITIONS

Needless prepositions (especially **of**) interfere with a writer's meaning.

Wordy	A dog by the name of Fido is missing.
Concise	A dog named Fido is missing.
Wordy	Some of the members of the committee made these recommendations.
Concise	Some committee members made these recommendations.
Wordy	I gave the money to Sarah.
Concise	I gave Sarah the money.

USE *THAT* AND *WHICH* SPARINGLY

Excessive use of **is** often drags along a needless **that** or **which**.

Wordy	The Batmobile is a car [that is] worth buying.
Wordy	This [is a] math problem [that] is impossible to solve.
Wordy	The book[, which is] about Hemingway[,] is fascinating.

FIGHT NOUN ADDICTION

Nouns manufactured from verbs (nominalizations) make your sentences weak and wordy. Nominalizations often accompany weak verbs and needless propositions.

Weak and wordy	We ask for the **cooperation** of all students.
Strong and concise	We ask that all students **cooperate**.
Weak and wordy	Give **consideration** to the possibility of a career change.
Strong and concise	**Consider** a career change.

Besides causing wordiness, nominalizations can be vague—by hiding the agent of an action.

| Wordy and vague | A **need for immediate action exists**. [*Who should take the action? We can't tell.*] |
| Precise | **We must act** immediately. |

Here are nominalizations restored to their verb forms:

conduct an investigation of	= investigate
provide a description of	= describe
conduct a test of	= test
engage in the preparation of	= prepare
make a discovery of	= discover

Along with weak verbs and needless prepositions, nominalizations take the life out of your style. In cheering for your favorite team, you wouldn't say

Blocking of that kick is a necessity!
instead of
Block that kick!

Write as you would speak.

MAKE NEGATIVES POSITIVE

A positive expression is more easily understood than a negative one. As writing expert Joseph Williams points out, "To understand the negative, we have to translate it into an affirmative, because the negative only implies what we should do by telling us what we shouldn't do. The affirmative states it directly."

| Indirect and wordy | I did not gain anything from this course. |

Direct and concise   I gained nothing from this course.

Readers have to work even harder to translate sentences with two or more negative expressions:

Confusing and wordy   Do **not** distribute this memo to employees who
have **not** received security clearance.

Clear and concise   Distribute this memo only to employees who
have received security clearance.

Besides the directly negative words (**no, not, never**), some words are indirectly negative (**except, forget, mistake, lose, uncooperative**). When these indirectly negative words combine with directly negative words, readers are forced to translate.

Confusing and wordy   **Do not neglect** to activate the alarm system.

My conclusion was **not inaccurate.**

The second example above shows how multiple negatives can make the writer seem evasive.

Clear and concise   **Be sure** to activate the alarm system.

My conclusion was **accurate.**

Some negative expressions, of course, are perfectly correct, as in expressing disagreement.

Correct negatives   This is **not** the best plan.

Your offer is **unacceptable.**

This project **never** will succeed.

Prefer positives to negatives, however, whenever your meaning allows.
Here are some negative expressions translated into their positive versions:

did not succeed   = failed

does not have   = lacks

did not prevent   = allowed

not unless   = only if

not until   = only when

not absent   = present

CLEAR OUT THE CLUTTER WORDS

Clutter words stretch a message without adding meaning. Here are some of the commonest: **very, definitely, quite, extremely, rather, some-what, really, actually, situation, aspect, factor.** Use such words only when they **actually** advance your meaning.

Cluttered	**Actually,** one **aspect** of a marriage **situation** that could **definitely** make me **very** happy would be to have a **somewhat** adventurous partner who **really** shared my **extreme** love of traveling.
Concise	I'd like to marry an adventurous person who loves traveling.

Again, if you must use one of these words, be sure it advances your meaning.

DELETE NEEDLESS PREFACES

Instead of keeping readers waiting for the new information in your sentence, get right to the point. Deliver the pitch without a long windup.

Wordy	[I am writing this letter because] I wish to apply for the position of dorm counselor.
Wordy	[The conclusion we can draw is that] writing is hard work.

DELETE NEEDLESS QUALIFIERS

Qualifiers are expressions such as **I feel, it would seem, I believe, in my opinion,** and **I think.** Use them only to emphasize that your assertion is one of uninformed opinion, without factual support—an opinion subject to change.

Appropriate qualifiers	Despite Frank's poor academic performance last semester, he will, **I think,** do well in college.
	Your product **seems to be** what I need.

If you are certain of your assertion, however, eliminate the qualifier. It waters down your meaning.

Needless qualifiers   [It seems that] I've wrecked the family car.

[It would appear that] I've lost your credit card.

[In my opinion,] you've done a good job.

Application 8–6

Make these sentences more concise by eliminating redundancies and needless repetition. (Review pages 174–176.)

1. She is a woman who works hard.
2. This book is the best book I've read in months.
3. I am aware of the fact that Sam is a trustworthy person.
4. The college is imposing a curfew due to the fact that several students have been mugged.
5. On previous occasions we have worked together.
6. Albert's outlook on life is optimistic.
7. Clarence completed his assignment in a short period of time.
8. Bruno has a stocky build.
9. Sally is a close friend of mine.
10. I've been able to rely on my parents in the past.

Application 8–7

Make these sentences more concise by eliminating **There is** and **There are** sentence openers, and the needless use of **it, to be, is, of, that,** and **which.** (Review pages 176–178.)

1. I consider Martha to be a good friend.
2. Our summer house, which is located on Cape Cod, is for sale.
3. The static electricity that is generated by the human body is measurable.
4. Writing must be practiced in order for it to become effective.

5. Another reason the job is attractive is because the salary is excellent.

6. There are many activities and sports that I enjoy very much, but the one that stands out in my mind is the sport of jogging.

7. Friendship is something that people should be honest about.

8. Smoking of cigarettes is considered by many people to be the worst habit of all habits of human beings.

9. There are many students who are immature.

10. It is necessary for me to leave immediately.

Application 8–8

Revise each wordy and vague sentence to eliminate weak verbs. (Review pages 177–178.)

1. I have a preference for Ferraris.

2. Please make a decision today.

3. We need to have a discussion about the problem.

4. I have just come to the realization that I was mistaken.

5. We certainly can make use of this information.

6. Your conclusion is in agreement with mine.

Application 8–9

Make these sentences more concise by replacing nouns with verbs, by changing negatives to positives, and by clearing out clutter words, needless prefatory expressions, and needless qualifiers. (Review pages 179–182.)

1. We request the formation of a committee of students for the review of grading discrepancies.

2. I am not unappreciative of your help.

3. Actually, I am very definitely in love with you.

4. I find Susan to be an industrious and competent employee.

5. Bill made the suggestion that we get an additional roommate.

6. It seems that I've made a mistake in your order.

7. My mother's quick wit is an extremely impressive aspect of her personality.

8. Igor does not have any friends at this schoool.

9. In my opinion, winter is an awful season.

10. As this academic year comes upon us, I realize that I will have trouble commuting to school this semester.

11. There is an undergraduate student attrition causes study needed at our school.

12. A need for your caution exists.

13. Never fail to attend classes.

14. Our acceptance of the offer is a necessity.

Making Sentences Fluent

Fluent sentences are easy to read because of clear connections, variety, and emphasis. Their varied length and word order eliminate choppiness and monotony. Fluent sentences enhance *clarity*, allowing readers to see ideas that are most important, with no struggle to sort out relationships. Fluent sentences enhance *conciseness*, often replacing several short, repetitious sentences with one longer, more economical sentence. The strategies discussed here will help you write fluent sentences.

COMBINE RELATED IDEAS

A series of short, disconnected sentences is not only choppy and wordy, but it is unclear as well.

Disconnected	Jogging can be healthful. You have to have the right equipment. Most necessary are well-fitting shoes. Without this equipment you take the chance of injuring your legs. Your knees are especially prone to injury. [5 *sentences*]
Clear, concise, and fluent	Jogging can be healthful if you have the right equipment. Shoes that fit well are most necessary

> because they prevent injury to your legs,
> especially your knees. [2 *sentences*]

Never force readers to figure out connections for themselves.

Most sets of information can be combined in different patterns, depending on what you want to emphasize. Imagine that this group of facts is about an applicant for a ski instructor's position:

- Roy James has been skiing since age 3.

- He has no experience teaching skiing.

- He has won several slalom competitions.

Assume that you are Snow Mountain Ski Area's head instructor writing to the manager to convey your impression of this candidate. To give your reader a negative impression, you might combine the facts in this way:

Strongly negative emphasis   Although Roy James has been skiing since age 3 and has won several slalom competitions, **he has no experience teaching skiing.**

The *independent* idea (in boldface) receives the emphasis. Earlier ideas are made dependent on (or subordinate to) the independent idea by the subordinating word **although**. When a sentence has two or more ideas of unequal importance, the less important idea is signaled by a subordinating word such as **often, as, because, if, unless, until,** or **while**.

Let's continue with our Roy James example. If you are undecided but leaning in a negative direction, you might combine the information in this way:

Slightly negative emphasis   Roy James has been skiing since age 3 and has won several slalom competitions, **but** he has no experience teaching skiing.

In the sentence above, both the ideas before and after **but** are independent. These independent ideas are joined by the coordinating word **but**, which suggests that both sides of the issue are equally important (or "coordinate"). Placing the negative idea last, however, gives it a slight emphasis. When a sentence has two or more ideas equal in importance, their equality is signaled by coordinating words such as **and, but, for, nor, or, so,** or **yet**.

Consider once again our Roy James example. To emphasize strong support for the candidate, you could use this combination:

Positive emphasis	Although Roy James has no experience teaching skiing, **he has been skiing since age 3 and has won several slalom competitions.**

In the version above, the earlier idea is subordinated by **although,** leaving the two final ideas independent.

Readers interpret our meaning not only by what we say, but by how we put our sentences together. The following sentences, excerpted from a student pilot's description of "Taking Off," further illustrate that fluent sentences are both more readable and meaningful.

First draft	My mind's eye is locked on the runway's center line. My eyes flash from the windshield to the instruments. They read and calculate, and they miss nothing.

Because these actions took place at the same time, the writer decided to emphasize that relationship by combining her information in one sentence:

More fluent	My mind's eye is locked on the runway's center line, while my eyes flash from the windshield to instruments, reading, calculating, missing nothing.

The revised version captures the mood that the writer set out to convey: one of immediacy, of excitement, of all things happening at once.

Here, from the same writer, is another illustration of how sentence structure can be revised to emphasize a particular meaning.

First draft	Gravity pulls at us. It insists that we are bound to the earth. It makes us slaves of its laws. This vibrating second seems like an eternity.

Because the idea of pulling deserves most emphasis here, the writer combines her information to reflect that sense:

More fluent	Gravity pulls at us, insisting that we are bound to the earth, slaves of its laws, this vibrating second like an eternity.

The lead verb, **pulls,** is placed in an independent clause, and the three subsequent ideas are subordinated—pulled along by the first clause.

Caution: Combine sentences only to advance your meaning, to ease the reader's task. A sentence with too much information and too many connections can be impossible for readers to sort out.

| Overstuffed | The night supervisor's orders from upper management to repair the overheated circuit were misunderstood by Harvey Kidd, who gave the wrong instructions to the emergency crew, thereby causing the fire. |

Notice how many times you have to read the following overstuffed instruction in order to understand what to do.

| Overstuffed | In developing less than a tankful of film, be sure to put in enough empty reels to fill all the space in the tank so that the film-loaded reels won't slide around when the tank is agitated. |

Readability is affected less by the number of words in a sentence than by the amount of information. Even relatively short sentences can be unreadable if they carry too many details:

| Overstuffed | Send three copies of Form 17-e to all six departments, unless Departments A or B or both request Form 16-w. |

Although effective combining *enhances* and *streamlines* your meaning, overcombining makes your meaning impenetrable.

VARY SENTENCE CONSTRUCTION AND LENGTH

Long and short sentences each have their purpose: to express ideas logically or forcefully.* We have just seen how related ideas often need to be linked in one sentence so that readers can grasp the connections:

| Disconnected | The nuclear core reached critical temperature. The loss-of-coolant alarm was triggered. The operator shut down the reactor. |

---

*My thanks to Professor Edith K. Weinstein, University of Akron, for suggesting this distinction.

Connected   As the nuclear core reached critical temperature, triggering the loss-of-coolant alarm, the operator shut down the reactor.

The ideas above have been combined to show that one action resulted from another. But an idea that should stand alone for emphasis needs a whole sentence of its own:

Correct   Core meltdown seemed inevitable.

Too much of anything loses effect. An unbroken string of long or short sentences can bore and confuse readers; so too can a series with identical openings:

Dreary   There are some drawbacks about diesel engines. They are difficult to start in cold weather. They cause vibration. They also give off an unpleasant odor. They cause sulfur dioxide pollution.

Varied   Diesel engines have some drawbacks. Most obvious are their noisiness, cold-weather starting difficulties, vibration, odor, and sulfur dioxide emission.

Opening sentences repeatedly with **The, This, He, She,** or **I** creates monotony. When you write in the first person, overusing **I** makes you seem self-centered.

  Do not, however, avoid personal pronouns if they make the writing more readable (say, by eliminating passive constructions). Instead, to avoid repetitious openings, combine ideas and shift word order.

USE SHORT SENTENCES FOR SPECIAL EMPHASIS

With all this talk about combining ideas, one might conclude that short sentences have no place in good writing. Wrong. Short sentences (even one-word sentences) provide vivid emphasis. Consider another part of the student pilot's description of taking off:

Our airspeed increases. The plane vibrates. We reach the point where the battle begins.

Instead, the student might have written: **As our airspeed increases, the plane vibrates, and we reach the point where the battle begins.** However, she wanted to emphasize three discrete instances here: (1) the acceleration, (2) the vibration, and (3) the critical point of lifting off the ground.

Whereas long sentences combine ideas to clarify relationships, short sentences isolate a thought for special focus. They drive home a crucial point. They stick in a reader's mind.

Application 8–10

Combine each set of sentences into one fluent sentence.

1. John was in love.
   He was in love with Martha.
   He walked with her through the night.
   He was holding Martha's hand.

2. The Red Sox are an exciting team.
   The Red Sox are supported by loyal fans.
   The Red Sox sometimes win the pennant.
   The Red Sox have not won the World Series in decades.

3. On summer nights the breeze from the lake cools the bedroom of our cabin.
   It helps us forget the sweltering nights in the city.
   It makes us curl up under warm blankets.
   It lulls us to sleep.

4. Boats with excessive horsepower should be banned from our lakes and ponds.
   This would be one way to decrease noise and water pollution.
   It could also save precious fuel.

5. I was employed by the Food Mart supermarket.
   I held the position of service clerk.
   It was my job to operate a cash register.
   I priced items and stocked shelves.

Application 8–11

Improve the fluency in the next paragraph by combining related ideas; by varying sentence structure, openings, and length; and by using short sentences for special emphasis. (*Note:* When rephrasing to achieve conciseness, be sure to preserve the meaning of the original.)

Each summer, semitropical fish appear in New England salt ponds. They are carried northward by the Gulf Stream. The Gulf Stream is a warm ocean current. It flows like a river through the cold Atlantic. It originates in the Caribbean. It winds through the Florida straits. It meanders northward along the eastern coast of the United States. Off the shore of Cape Hatteras, North Carolina, the Gulf Stream's northerly course veers. It veers slightly eastward. This veering moves the stream and its warming influence farther from the coast. Semitropical fish are swept into the Gulf Stream from their breeding ground. The breeding ground is south of Cape Hatteras. The fish are carried northward. The strong current carries them. The current is often 20 degrees warmer than adjacent waters. Some of these fish are trapped in eddies. Eddies are pools of warm water that split from the Gulf Stream. These pools drift shoreward. By midsummer the ocean water off the New England coast is warm. It is warm enough to attract some fish out of the eddies and nearer to shore. In turn, even warmer water flows from the salt ponds. It flows to the ocean. It attracts these warm-water fish. They are attracted into the ponds. Here they spend the rest of the summer. They die off in the fall. The ponds cool in the fall.

Application 8-12

The sentence sets below lack fluency because they are disconnected, have no variety, or have no emphasis. Combine each set into one or two fluent sentences.

Choppy	The world's forests are now disappearing. The rate of disappearance is 18 to 20 million hectares a year (an area half the size of California). Most of this loss occurs in humid tropical forests. These forests are in Asia, Africa, and South America.
Revised	The world's forests are now disappearing at the rate of 18 to 20 million hectares a year (an area half the size of California). Most of this loss is occurring in the humid tropical forests of Africa, Asia, and South America.*

1. The world's population will grow.
   It will grow from 4 billion in 1975.

*Sample sentences are adapted from *Global Year 2000 Report to the President: Entering the 21st Century* (Washington: GPO, 1980).

It will reach 6.5 billion in 2000.
This will be an increase of more than 50 percent.

2. In sheer numbers, population will be growing.
    It will be growing faster in 2000 than it is today.
    It will add 100 million people each year.
    This figure compares with 75 million in 1975.

3. Energy prices are expected to increase.
    Many less-developed countries will have increasing difficulty.
    Their difficulty will be in meeting energy needs.

4. One-quarter of humanity depends primarily on wood.
    They depend on wood for fuel.
    For them, the outlook is bleak.

5. The world has finite fuel resources.
    These include coal, oil, gas, oil shale, and uranium.
    These resources, theoretically, are sufficient for centuries.
    These resources are not evenly distributed.

6. Already the populations in parts of Africa and Asia have
    exceeded the carrying capacity of the immediate area.
    This overpopulation has triggered erosion.
    This erosion has reduced the land's capacity to support life.

Application 8–13

Combine each set of sentences below into one or two fluent sentences
that provide the requested emphasis.

Sentence set	John is a loyal employee. John is a motivated employee. John is short-tempered with his colleagues.
Combined for positive emphasis	Even though John is short-tempered with his colleagues, he is a loyal and motivated employee.
Sentence set	This word processor has many excellent features. It includes a spelling checker. It includes a thesaurus. It includes a grammar checker.
Combined to emphasize the thesaurus	Among its many excellent features, such as spelling and grammar checkers, this word processor includes a thesaurus.

1. The job offers an attractive salary.
   It demands long work hours.
   Promotions are rapid.
   (Combine for negative emphasis.)

2. The job offers an attractive salary.
   It demands long work hours.
   Promotions are rapid.
   (Combine for positive emphasis.)

3. Company X gave us the lowest bid.
   Company Y has an excellent reputation.
   (Combine to emphasize Company Y.)

4. Superinsulated homes are energy efficient.
   Superinsulated homes create a danger of indoor air pollution.
   The toxic substances include radon gas and urea formaldehyde.
   (Combine for negative emphasis.)

5. Computers cannot *think* for the writer.
   Computers eliminate many mechanical writing tasks.
   They speed the flow of information.
   (Combine to emphasize the first assertion.)

9

Choosing
the Right Words

Word choice ultimately determines the quality of your writing. After all, any sentence is only as effective as the words it contains. The range of what we see, think, and feel is infinite, and finding words to label these experiences is not easy. The following suggestions will, however, help you choose words that are convincing, precise, informative, and engaging.

Making Your Message Convincing

Our underlying purpose in all writing is to convince readers that a message is original, sensible, and sincere. Readers will consider worthless any message that is trite, slang-ridden, overstated, or devious. Observe the suggestions here to make your writing more convincing.

AVOID TRITENESS

Writers who rely on tired old phrases (clichés) come across as too lazy or too careless to find convincing or exact ways to say what they mean. Here are just a few of the countless expressions worn out by overuse.

193

first and foremost	tough as nails
in the final analysis	holding the bag
it is interesting to note	getting the shaft
needless to say	water over the dam
work like a dog	up the creek
last but not least	over the hill
hard as a rock	bite the bullet
dry as a bone	fly off the handle
victim of circumstance	get on the stick

If it sounds like a "catchy phrase" you've heard before, don't write it.

AVOID OVERSTATEMENT

Writers lose credibility when they exaggerate to make a point. Be cautious when using words such as **best, biggest, brightest, most,** and **worst.**

Overstated	If you try skiing, you will find it to be one of the most memorable experiences of your life.
Revised	If you try skiing, you will enjoy it.
Overstated	If you hire me, I will be the best worker you have ever had.
Revised	If you hire me, I will do a good job.

AVOID UNSUPPORTABLE GENERALIZATIONS

Unsupported or sweeping generalizations (see also page 364) harm your credibility because they have no way of being proved.

Sweeping	Television is rotting everyone's brain.
Revised	Many authorities argue that television is one cause of declining literacy.
Sweeping	Democracy in America is collapsing.
Revised	American democracy is threatened by fanatical groups—both from the left and from the right.

Be sure your conclusions are based on adequate evidence.

| Unsupported generalization | In 1983, 21 murderers were executed, and the murder rate dropped 8.1 percent for that year. These figures prove that the death penalty should be reinstated. |

This isolated piece of evidence does not justify such a sweeping generalization.

| Reasonable generalization | In 1983, 21 murderers were executed, and the murder rate dropped 8.1 percent for that year. These figures suggest that the death penalty may deter violent crimes. |

Be aware of the vast differences in meaning among these words:

few	never
some	rarely
many	sometimes
most	often
all	always

Unless you specify **few, some, many,** or **most,** readers can interpret your statement as meaning **all.**

| Misleading | Classmates are doing shabby work. |

Unless you mean **all** classmates, be sure to qualify your generalization with **some, most,** or another limiting word.

AVOID MISLEADING EUPHEMISMS

Euphemisms are expressions that are aimed at politeness or at making unpleasant subjects seem less offensive. Thus, we **powder our nose** or **use the boys' room** instead of **using the toilet;** we **pass away** or **meet our Maker** instead of **dying.**

When euphemisms avoid offending or embarrassing our audience, they are perfectly legitimate. Instead of telling a job applicant that he or she is **unqualified,** we might say, **Your background doesn't meet our needs.**

One danger with euphemisms, however, is that they can understate the truth when only the truth will serve. In the sugar-coated world of misleading euphemisms, bad news disappears:

- Instead of being **laid off** or **fired,** workers are **surplused** or **deselected,** or the company is **downsized.**

- Instead of **lying** to the public, the government **engages in a policy of disinformation.**

- Instead of **wars** and **civilian casualties,** we have **conflicts** and **collateral damage.**

Even the prospect of a nuclear holocaust becomes more digestible when one U.S. senator calls it a **nuclear exchange.**

But benign as **conflicts** and **nuclear exchange** may sound, they kill people just as effectively as do **wars** and a **nuclear holocaust.** Plain talk is always better than deception. If someone offers you a job **with limited opportunity for promotion,** you will have a **dead-end job.**

Application 9–1

Revise these sentences to eliminate triteness, overstatements, sweeping generalizations, and euphemisms.

1. This course gives me a pain in the neck.

2. We'll have to swallow our pride and admit our mistake.

3. There is never a dull moment in my dorm.

4. Last night's party was out of sight.

5. When it comes to neatness, my roommate is a hopeless case.

6. I was less than candid.

7. This student is poorly motivated.

8. You are the world's most beautiful woman.

9. Marriage in America is a dying institution.

10. She expropriated company funds.

11. When the grenade exploded, his arm was traumatically amputated.

12. I love you more than life itself.

13. We have decided to terminate your employment.

14. People of our generation are all selfish.

I SMOKE A lot OF DOPE

Making Your Language Precise

Be sure that what you say is what you mean. A word used carelessly can offend readers. Even words listed as synonyms have different shades of meaning. Do you mean to say "I'm slender; you're slim; he's lean; and she's scrawny"? The wrong choice could be disastrous. Did you **walk, stroll, shuffle,** or **amble** into the party? No two words mean exactly the same thing; don't use one word when you mean another. Don't write to apply for college admission with a statement like this:

> Another attractive feature of the college is its **adequate** track program.

The writer later explained his choice of **adequate:** the program, he said, wasn't highly ranked, and so he tried to choose a word that would be sincere. But his choice has two liabilities:

1. **Adequate** is insulting in this context. After all, who likes to be called adequate?

2. The word suggests that the writer has placed himself in an elevated position of judgment, overstepping his bounds as an applicant.

Any of several alternatives (**solid, respectable, growing**) sounds sincere without offending anyone or overstating the point.

Be especially aware of similar words with dissimilar meanings, as in these examples:

affect/effect	farther/further
all ready/already	fewer/less
almost dead/dying	healthy/healthful
among/between	imply/infer
continual/continuous	invariably/inevitably
eager/anxious	uninterested/disinterested
fearful/fearsome	worse/worst

Do not write **Skiing is healthy** when you mean that skiing is good for your health (healthful). **Healthy** means to be in a state of health. **Healthful** things help keep you healthy.

Be on the lookout for imprecise (and therefore illogical) comparisons:

Faulty	Your rate of interest is higher than the First National Bank. [*Can an interest rate be higher than a bank?*]
Revised	Your rate of interest is higher than that of the First National Bank.
Faulty	This bonus arrangement is unlike most waiters who are paid by the hour. [*Can a bonus arrangement be like a waiter?*]
Revised	This bonus arrangement is unlike that with most waiters, who are paid by the hour.

Finally, be sure your phrasing is not ambiguous. A statement suggesting more than one meaning will confuse readers. For instance, is **send us more personal information** a request for more information that is personal or for information that is more personal?

Ambiguous	I cannot recommend Professor Harvey too highly. [*Is the writer recommending or not?*]
Revised	Professor Harvey has my highest recommendation. **or** I cannot highly recommend Professor Harvey.
Ambiguous	Visiting relatives can be fun. [*Who's visiting whom?*]
Revised	It can be fun to visit relatives. **or** Visits from relatives can be fun.

Precision is essential above all to the informative value of your writing. Imprecise language can be misleading. Consider how meanings differ in these sentences:

Differing meanings	Include **less** technical detail in your essay. Include **fewer** technical details in your essay.

Precision ultimately enhances conciseness, when one *exact* word replaces multiple inexact words.

Wordy and less exact	I have **put together** all the financial information.
	Keep doing this exercise for ten seconds.
	It occurred to me that I had had the same problem earlier.
Concise and more exact	I have **assembled** all the financial information.
	Continue this exercise for ten seconds.
	I **remembered** having the same problem earlier.

Application 9–2

Revise these sentences to make them precise.

1. Our outlet does more business than San Francisco.

2. Low-fat foods are healthy.

3. Fred quickly got used to college life.

4. Anaerobic fermentation is used in this report.

5. Her license is for driving an automatic car only.

6. My mind became alive when I saw my drawing completed.

7. To perfect the sport of jogging, develop good breathing habits.

8. It's the final two minutes; my eyes are glaring at the scoreboard.

9. This is the worse course I've taken.

10. Sarah's cold is getting worst.

11. Unlike many other children, her home life was good.

12. State law requires that restaurant personnel serve food with a sanitation certificate.

13. It looks like they will be married in June.

Making Your Writing Concrete and Specific

General words name broad classes of things, such as **job, car,** or **person.** Such terms usually need to be clarified by more *specific* ones:

job = senior accountant for Rockford Press

car = red, four-door, Ford Escort station wagon

person = male Caucasian, with red hair, blue eyes (and so on)

The more specific your words, the sharper your meaning:

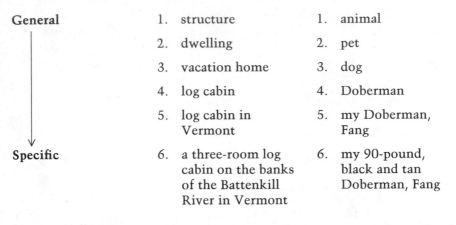

General		
	1. structure	1. animal
	2. dwelling	2. pet
	3. vacation home	3. dog
	4. log cabin	4. Doberman
	5. log cabin in Vermont	5. my Doberman, Fang
Specific	6. a three-room log cabin on the banks of the Battenkill River in Vermont	6. my 90-pound, black and tan Doberman, Fang

Notice how the picture becomes more vivid as we move to lower levels of generality. A word such as **pain** is general—it only **tells;** a phrase such as **a throbbing in my temples** is more specific—it *shows.* Readers know less than you do about your subject and viewpoint; to understand your way of seeing and your exact meaning, they need specifics.

Abstract words name qualities, concepts, or feelings (**beauty, luxury, depression**) whose exact meaning has to be nailed down by *concrete* words—words that name things we can know through our five senses:

a beautiful view = snowcapped mountains, a wilderness lake, pink granite ledge, and 90-foot blue spruce trees

a luxury condominium = redwood hot tub, hand-painted Mexican tile counters, floor-to-ceiling glass walls, oriental rugs

a depressed person = suicidal urge, feeling of worthlessness, no hope for improvement, insomnia

A word such as **terrible** is abstract —it only **tells.** Instead of telling that yesterday's weather was terrible, **show** how it was terrible:

> Yesterday was another of those terrible January days, with a gray sky, freezing rain, icy winds, and not one ray of sunshine.

Just as your subject must be limited enough to be treated in one paragraph, your discussion must be concrete and specific enough to provide clear and convincing support. Let's say that your topic statement is this one:

> Pedestrians crossing the street in front of my house place their lives in danger.

In supporting your main point you need to *show* with concrete and specific examples. Don't say merely:

> For example, a **person** was **injured** there by a **vehicle recently.**

The boldfaced words only tell; they don't show. Readers won't know what you mean. Instead, you might write:

> My Uncle Albert was hit by a speeding garbage truck last Tuesday and had his leg broken.

Choose specific words that say *exactly* what you mean. Don't write **thing** when you mean **problem, pencil,** or **gift.** Revise she is a swell person to she is kind, loving, and generous. Instead of evaluating a coworker as **nice, great,** or **terrific,** use terms that are more concrete, such as **reliable, skillful,** and **competent** or **dishonest, irritable,** and **awkward**—further clarified by examples (**never late for work,** and the like). Words such as **great** reveal your attitude but nothing about the person.

Keep in mind that *general* and *specific* are relative terms. Thus, **football player** is more specific than **athlete** but more general than **quarterback,** which in turn is more general than **San Francisco quarterback, Joe Montana.** The more you move from a general class to a particular member of that class, the more specific you become.

> teacher → college professor → brilliant sociology professor → Dr. Ramrod, with the photographic memory

Your level of generality for any message depends on your purpose and audience.

In some instances, of course, you may wish to generalize for the sake of diplomacy. Instead of writing **Bill, Mary, and Sam have been tying up the office phones with personal calls,** you might prefer to generalize: **Some employees have been tying up.** . . . The second version allows you to get your message across without pointing the finger.

Most good writing has both general and specific information. The more general material is in the topic statement and sometimes in the conclusion because these parts, respectively, set the paragraph's direction and summarize its content. Informative writing invariably has a balance of *telling* and *showing.* Abstract and general expressions tell, and concrete and specific expressions show. But if the telling or showing is too abstract or general, the writing will be useless. Consider these expressions:

Meaningless abstraction	Professor Able's office is a sight to behold. [*What does "a sight to behold" mean?*]
Meaningless generalization	Pollution is affecting our environment. [*What kind of pollution? What kind of effect? What part of our environment?*]

Neither statement gives any useful information. Here are more concrete and specific versions:

Informative abstraction	Professor Able's office looks like a dump.
Informative generalization	Industrial emissions are causing lakes to die.

Now, the telling in these statements needs clarification through concrete and specific showing:

Concrete showing	The office has a floor strewn with books, a desk buried beneath a mountain of uncorrected papers, and ashtrays overflowing with ripe cigar butts.
Specific showing	Sulfur dioxide emissions from coal-burning plants combine with atmospheric water to produce sulfuric acid. The resultant "acid rain" increases the acidity of lakes until they no longer can support life.

The showing should be as concrete and specific as necessary to make the point. Consider this general point:

Telling   A 55-mile-per-hour speed limit makes highways
                        safer.

Here is a general explanation of the point:

General   In 1972, thousands of people were killed or
                        injured on America's highways. Many families
                        had at least one relative who was a casualty. After
                        the speed limit was lowered to 55 miles per hour
                        in 1973, the death toll began to drop.

Although the explanation offers some information, it would be more effective if amplified with solid numbers and statistics that get the original point across.

Specific   In 1972, 56,000 people died on America's
                        highways; 200,000 were injured; 15,000 children
                        were orphaned. In that year, if you were a
                        member of a family of five, chances are that
                        someone related to you by blood or law was killed
                        or injured in an auto accident. After the speed
                        limit was lowered to 55 miles per hour in 1973,
                        the death toll dropped steadily to 41,000 deaths
                        in 1975.

Concrete and specific expressions are not only more informative; they are more convincing as well.

Application 9–3

In each set of terms, identify the most abstract or general and the most concrete or specific. Be prepared to give reasons for your choices.

1. a presidential candidate, a U.S. senator, Edward Kennedy, a politician

2. a favorite spot, a beautiful place, an island in the Bahamas, a hideaway

3. woman, surgeon, person, professional, individual

4. an awful person, a cruel and dishonest person, a nasty person

5. a competitor, a downhill racer, an athlete, a skier, a talented amateur

6. violence, assassination, terrorism, political action

Making the Tone Appropriate

Your tone is your personal mark—the personality that takes shape between the lines. The tone you create in any writing depends on (1) the distance you impose between yourself and the reader, and (2) the attitude you show toward the subject. Assume that a friend is going to take over a job you've held. You've decided to write your friend instructions for parts of the job. Here is your first sentence:

> Now that you've arrived in the glamorous world of office work, put on your track shoes; this is no ordinary clerical job.

What is the tone in that sentence? First, we notice that the writer imposes little distance between himself and the reader (he uses the direct address, **you,** and the humorous suggestion to **put on your track shoes**). And the ironic use of **glamorous** suggests that the writer means just the opposite, that the job holds little glamour.

For a different reader (let's say the recipient of a company training manual) the writer would have chosen some other way to open:

> As an office assistant with this company, you will spend little of your day seated at your desk.

The tone now is serious, no longer intimate, and the writer expresses no distinct attitude toward the job. For yet another audience (say, those who will read a company pamphlet for all new secretaries), the writer again might have altered his tone:

> Office assistants in our company are responsible for duties that extend far beyond desk work.

Here, the businesslike, impersonal tone imposes even more distance between writer and audience, especially through the shift from second- to third-person address.

Your tone changes in response to the situation and the audience, even if the subject remains the same. Letters to your professor, your grandmother, and your friend, each about a disputed grade, would have noticeably different tones:

1. Dear Professor Snapjaws:
    I am convinced that my failing grade in calculus did not reflect a fair evaluation of my work over the semester . . . [*a formal tone*]

2. Dear Grandma,
    Thanks for your letter. I'm doing well in school, except for the failing grade I unjustly received in calculus . . . [*semiformal tone*]

3. Dear Fred,
    Boy, have I been shafted! That old turkey, Snapjaws, gave me an F in calculus . . . [*informal tone*]

In each version the writer expresses disapproval. But as the distance between himself and his audience decreases, his tone becomes more informal: (1) **did not reflect a fair evaluation**; (2) **I unjustly received**; (3) **Have I been shafted!** The writer adjusts his tone to suit the audience. Also, he uses tone to control the distance from his audience. Clearly the intimate tone and attitude of outrage in the letter to Fred would be inappropriate for the letter to Professor Snapjaws, where the writer settles for firm disapproval. So too would the attitude of polite disapproval in the letter to Grandma be inappropriate for the letter to Fred or the professor.

ESTABLISH AN APPROPRIATE DISTANCE

We already know how tone works in speaking. When you meet someone, you might respond in any of several ways, each creating a tone that defines your relationship.

Honored to make your acquaintance. [*formal tone—greatest distance*]

How do you do? [*formal*]

Nice to meet you. [*semiformal—medium distance*]

Hello. [*semiformal*]

Hi. [*informal—least distance*]

Hey. [*informal*]

What's happening? [*informal*]

Your greeting is based on how much distance you decide is appropriate; and, in turn, the greeting determines how you come across. Each of these responses is appropriate in specific situations, inappropriate in others. **What's happening?** might be okay when you meet a fellow student, but not the college president. Just as different types of dress fit different situations (cut-offs for the beach, a suit for a job interview), so also do different tones of writing and speaking.

To decide on an appropriate distance from which to address a particular audience, follow these guidelines:

- Use a formal or semiformal tone in writing for superiors, professionals, or academics (depending on what you think the reader expects).

- Use a semiformal or informal tone in essays and letters (depending on how close you feel to your reader).

- Use an informal tone when you want your writing to be conversational—to close the distance between you and your reader.

Whichever tone you decide on, be consistent throughout your message.

Inconsistent tone	My dorm room isn't fit for a pig [*too informal*]; it is ungraciously unattractive [*too formal*].
Revised	My dilapidated dorm room is unfit to live in.

In general, lean toward an informal tone without falling into slang. Make your writing conversational by following these suggestions:

1. Keep the language simple.
2. Use an occasional contraction.
3. Address readers directly, when appropriate.
4. Don't be afraid to use **I**, when appropriate.
5. Prefer active to passive voice.

Keep the Language Simple   Say it in plain English. Try not to use a three-syllable word when one syllable will do. Trade for less:

utilize	= use
approximately	= about

to be cognizant	= to know
to endeavor	= to try
to secure employment	= to find a job
demonstrate	= show
determine	= find
multiplicity of	= many
effectuate	= do
terminate	= end
component	= part
endeavor	= effort

Count the syllables. Trim whenever you can. But, most important, choose words that you hear and use in everyday speaking—words that are universally familiar.

Don't write **I deem** when you mean **I think**, or **Keep me apprised** instead of **Keep me informed**, or **I concur** instead of **I agree**, or **securing employment** instead of **finding a job**, or **it is cost prohibitive** instead of **we can't afford it**. Experiments have shown that readers have to spend extra time on passages with unfamiliar or less familiar words. Don't write like the author of a report from the Federal Aviation Administration who suggested that manufacturers of the DC-10 be directed to **re-evaluate the design of the entire pylon assembly to minimize design factors which are resulting in sensitive and/or critical maintenance and inspection procedures** (25 words, 50 syllables). Here is a plain-English translation: **Redesign the pylons so that they are easier to maintain and inspect** (12 words, 19 syllables). Here is another case of inflated language:

Inflated	Upgrade your present employment situation. [*5 words, 12 syllables*]
Revised	Get a better job. [*4 words, 5 syllables*]

These are examples of the worst kind of puffery: too many words, and words bigger than needed. Here are more:

Inflated	I suggest that you reduce the number of cigarettes that you smoke per day.
Revised	Smoke less.

Inflated	I am thoroughly convinced that Sam is a trustworthy individual.
Revised	I trust Sam.
Inflated	Make an improvement in the clerical situation.
Revised	Hire more secretaries. *or* Hire better secretaries. (*Inflated language also can be ambiguous!*)

Of course, now and then the bigger word can serve best—if it expresses your exact meaning. Don't substitute **end** for **terminate** if you're referring to something with an established limit.

Correct	Our lease terminates this month.

Also, if one bigger word can replace a handful of simpler words and can sharpen your meaning, use the bigger word.

Weak	Six loops around the outside edges of the dome tent are needed for the pegs to fit into.
Informative and precise	Six loops around the dome tent's **perimeter accommodate** the pegs.
Weak	Upper management has **taken over for themselves** our authority as decision makers.
Informative and precise	Upper management has **usurped** our authority as decision makers.
Weak	Sexist language **contributes to the ongoing prevalence of** gender stereotypes.
Forceful and precise	Sexist language **perpetuates** gender stereotypes.

Never seek simplicity at the cost of clarity; make every word count. Use the fancy word *only* when your meaning and your audience demand it.

Use an Occasional Contraction   Every now and then, use a contraction to loosen up the tone. Balance an **I am** with an **I'm,** a **you are** with a **you're,** an **it is** with an **it's,** and so on (as we've done throughout this book).

Be careful, however, not to overuse contractions.

| Excessive contractions | It's a shame that Clementine's been crying since she's learned her date'll be late because his tire's flat and his wallet's lost. |

Generally, use contractions only with pronouns—not with nouns or proper nouns (names). Otherwise, the constructions are awkward or ambiguous.

Awkward contractions	Barbara'll be here soon.
	She could've come earlier.
	Health's important.
	Love'll make you happy.
Ambiguous contractions	The dog's barking.
	Bill's skiing.
	The baby's crying.

These ambiguous contractions can easily be confused with possessive constructions (page 560).

ADDRESS READERS DIRECTLY

Use the personal pronouns **you** and **your** generously to create contact with your reader. Otherwise, your writing sounds impersonal.

| Impersonal tone | A writer should use **you** and **your** generously to create contact with his or her readers. |

Notice how distance *and* words increase. Direct address creates a more personal tone.

| Impersonal tone | Students at our college will find the faculty always willing to help. |
| Personal tone | As a student at our college, **you** will find the faculty always willing to help. |

Research shows that readers relate better to something addressed to them directly.

Caution: Use **you** and **your** only to correspond *directly* with the reader, as in a letter, memo, instructions, or some form of advice, encouragement, or persuasion. By using **you** and **your** when your subject and purpose call for first or third person, you might write something wordy and awkward such as this:

Wordy and awkward	When **you** are in northern Ontario, **you** can see wilderness lakes everywhere around **you**.
Appropriate	Wilderness lakes are everywhere in Northern Ontario.

Use *I* and *we* When Appropriate   Don't disappear behind your writing. Use **I** when referring to yourself.

Distant	This writer would like a refund.
Revised	I would like a refund.
Distant	The fear was awful until the police arrived.
Revised	I was terrified until the police arrived.

Avoid, of course, opening too many sentences with **I** by combining ideas and shifting word order (page 184).

Prefer the Active Voice   Because the active voice is more direct and economical than the passive, it generally creates a more intimate and less formal tone. Review pages 168–171 for the use of active and passive voice.

EXPRESS A CLEAR AND APPROPRIATE ATTITUDE

Another problem with tone occurs when you suggest an unclear or inappropriate attitude toward the subject. Let readers know where you stand. Don't force them to translate. Say **I enjoyed the course** instead of **My attitude toward the course was one of high approval**. Say **Let's liven up our dull relationship** instead of **We should inject some rejuvenation into our lifeless and dull liaison**.

Don't be afraid to inject personal commentary when it's called for. Consider how the message below increases in force and effectiveness with the boldfaced commentary:

In 1972, 56,000 people died on America's highways; 200,000 were injured; 15,000 children were orphaned. In that year, if you were a member of a family of five, chances are that someone related to you, by blood or law, was killed or injured by **one of the most** violent forms of self-elimination ever devised by humanity—an auto accident.

If, however, your job is to report objectively, try to suppress any bias you might have; do not volunteer your attitude. Biased people make judgments without examining the facts. Even controversial subjects deserve objective treatment.

Imagine you are a reporter for your campus newspaper. You've been sent to investigate the causes of a confrontation between female faculty and the administration. Your initial report, written for tomorrow's edition, is intended simply to describe what happened. Here is how an unbiased description might read:

> At 10:00 A.M. on Wednesday, October 24, 80 women faculty members set up picket lines around the college's administration building, bringing business to a halt. The group issued a formal protest, claiming that their working conditions were repressive, their salary scale unfair, and their promotional opportunities limited. The women demanded affirmative action, insisting that the college's hiring and promotional policies and wage scales be revised. The demonstration ended when Glenn Tarullo, vice-president in charge of personnel, promised to appoint a committee to investigate the group's claims and to correct any inequities.

Notice the absence of implied judgments; the facts are presented objectively. A less impartial version, from a protester's point of view, might read like this:

> Last Wednesday, sisters struck another blow against male supremacy when 80 women faculty members paralyzed the college's repressive and sexist administration for more than six hours. The timely and articulate protest was aimed against degrading working conditions, unfair salary scales, and lack of promotional opportunities for women. Stunned administrators watched helplessly as the group organized their picket lines, determined to continue their protest until their demands for equal rights were met. An embarrassed vice-president quickly agreed to study the group's demands and to revise the college's discriminatory policies. The success of this long-overdue confrontation serves as an inspiration to oppressed women employees everywhere.

Notice how judgmental words (**male supremacy, degrading, paralyzed, articulate, stunned, discriminatory**) express the writer's attitude even though it's not called for. In contrast to this bias, the following version patronizingly defends the status quo:

> Our administration building was the scene of an amusing battle of the sexes last Wednesday, when a group of irate faculty feminists, 80 strong, set up picket lines for six hours. The protest was lodged against supposed inequities in hiring, wages, working conditions, and promotion for women faculty at our college. The libbers threatened to continue their protest until their demands for "equal rights" were met. A bemused vice-president responded to this carnival demonstration with patience and dignity, assuring the militants that their claims and demands—however inaccurate and immoderate—would receive just consideration.

Again, loaded words and superlatives slant the tone. Let your facts speak for themselves.

Writing teacher Marshall Kremers reminds us that being unbiased, of course, doesn't mean burying your head—and your values—in the sand.* Remaining "neutral" about something you know to be wrong or dangerous is unethical. You have an ethical responsibility to weigh the facts and to make your views known. If, for instance, you conclude that the college protest was clearly justified, don't hesitate to say so.

AVOID SEXIST USAGE

The way we use language reflects the way we think about ourselves. And so what are people supposed to think when **man** and **mankind** is used to stand for all humanity? Doesn't someone seem to be missing? For some earlier generations, this was a popular expression: **Behind every successful man stands a good woman.** What's the message here?

Even less blatant forms of English usage can create the impression that ours is a "man's world." For instance, whenever **he, his,** or **him** is used for referring to members of either sex, anybody can "realize **his** dreams" but not "**her** dreams."

Sexist usage	Anyone can make **his** fortune in Australia.
	Even a brilliant scholar has to admit **he** knows little.

Usage that gives people in general a male identity allows no room for females. In fact, females become virtually invisible in a world of **policemen, congressmen, firemen, foremen, selectmen, and aldermen.**

---

*See *IEEE Transactions on Professional Communication* 32.2 (1989):58–61.

Sexist usage refers to doctors, lawyers, and other professionals as **he** or **him** while referring to nurses, secretaries, and homemakers as **she** or **her**. In this traditional stereotype, males do the jobs that really matter, whereas females serve only as support and decoration. And when the odd pretenders do invade traditional "male" roles, we might express our surprise at their boldness by calling them **female executives** or **female sportscasters** or **female surgeons** or **female architects**. Likewise, to register our contempt for wimpy males who have settled for "female" roles, we refer to **male secretaries** or **male nurses** or **male flight attendants** or **male models**.

In the biased reality of sexist usage, the title **Mr.** protects the privacy of a male who might be married or unmarried, whereas **Mrs.** and **Miss** announce a female's marital status to the world. Moreover, an unmarried male is fondly referred to as a **bachelor**, although his female counterpart is stigmatized as an **old maid** or a **spinster**. And what unmarried female wouldn't want to be lucky enough to marry and become **the little woman?**

Besides being misleading and demeaning, sexist usage is offensive. Instead of bringing writer and readers closer together, sexist usage severs any human connection our writing might otherwise achieve.

To eliminate sexism from your writing, follow these guidelines:

- Use neutral expressions:

chair, or **chairperson**	rather than	chairman
businessperson	rather than	businesswoman
supervisor	rather than	· foreman
police officer	rather than	policeman
letter carrier	rather than	postman
homemaker	rather than	housewife
humanity	rather than	mankind
human history	rather than	man's history

- Rephrase to eliminate the pronoun, if you can do so without changing your original meaning.

Sexist   A writer will succeed if **he** revises.

Revised   A writer who revises succeeds.

- Use plural forms. Instead of **Each doctor . . . he**, use **All doctors . . . they** (but *not* **Each doctor . . . they**).

  Sexist   A writer will succeed if **he** revises.

  Revised   Writers will succeed if **they** revise. (but *not* A writer will succeed if **they** revise.)

  Note: When using a plural form, don't create an error in pronoun-referent agreement by having the *plural* pronoun **they** or **their** refer to a *singular* referent, as in "**Each writer** should do **their** best."

- When possible use **you**: "**You** will succeed if **you** revise." But use this form *only* when you are addressing someone directly. (See pages 209–210 for further discussion.)

- Use occasional pairings (**him or her, she or he, his or hers, he/ she**): "A writer will succeed if **she or he** revises."

  Note: Overuse of such pairings can be awkward. A writer should do **his or her** best to make sure that **she or he** connects with **his or her** readers.

- Use feminine and masculine pronouns alternately: "An effective writer always focuses on **her** audience. The writer strives to connect with all **his** readers."

- Drop diminutive endings such as **-ess** and **-ette** used to denote females (**poetess, drum majorette, actress**, etc.). Such endings seem to perpetuate an image of **the little woman**.

- Use **Ms.** instead of **Mrs.** or **Miss**, unless you know that the person prefers one of the traditional titles.

Not only do the words you choose reveal your way of seeing, but they also influence your reader's way of seeing. Sexist language carries built-in judgments, and, as the renowned linguist S. I. Hayakawa reminds us: "Judgment stops thought." In the world defined by sexist language, everyone remains frozen in her and his place.

Application 9–4

Rewrite these statements in plain English, with special attention to tone.

1. This writer desires to be considered for a position with your company.

2. My attitude toward your behavior is one of disapproval.

3. Please refund my full purchase expenditure in view of the fact that this radio is defective.

4. I can wish you no better luck than that you find this job to be as enjoyable as I have.

5. Prior to this time I have never failed an exam.

6. In relation to your job, I would like to say that we can no longer offer you employment.

7. A good writer is cognizant of how to utilize grammar in correct fashion.

8. Replacement of the weak battery should be effectuated.

9. Considering the length of the present school day, it is my opinion that the day is excessive lengthwise for most elementary pupils.

10. Make an improvement in your studying situation.

Application 9–5

In this letter, a student has written to the registrar, asking that his deadline for paying tuition be extended and explaining why he needs the extra time. Rewrite the letter in plain English.

Dear Mr. Jones:

Pursuant to your notice of September 6, advising me that my tuition was overdue, I regret to advise you that my tuition payment will be delayed until September 21, when my scholarship is received.

I humbly request you to be cognizant of the fact that this writer's tuition for all five prior semesters has been paid on time. At the present time, my first, and hopefully last, late payment is due to the fact that a computer breakdown in the NDEA offices has occasioned a delay in the processing of all scholarship renewal applications for a period of time roughly approximating two weeks. Enclosed please find a copy of a recent NDEA notice to this effect.

I am in hopes that you will be kind enough to grant me an extension of my tuition-due date for this brief period of time. Thanking you in anticipation of your kind cooperation, I remain

Gratefully yours,
Charles Smith
Student

Application 9–6

A version of this letter was published in a local newspaper. Rewrite it in plain English.

> In the absence of definitive studies regarding the optimum length of the school day, I can only state my personal opinion based upon observations made by me and upon teacher observations that have been conveyed to me. Considering the length of the present school day, it is my opinion that the school day is excessive lengthwise for most elementary pupils, certainly for almost all of the primary children.
>
> To find the answer to the problem requires consideration of two ways in which the problem may be viewed. One way focuses upon the needs of the children, while the other focuses upon logistics, scheduling, transportation, and other limits imposed by the educational system. If it is necessary to prioritize these two ideas, it would seem most reasonable to give the first consideration to the primary and fundamental reason for the very existence of the system itself, i.e., to meet the educational needs of the children the system is trying to serve.

Application 9–7

Rewrite these statements to eliminate sexist expressions—without altering the meaning.

1. Each student should select his courses early.
2. An employee in our organization can be sure he will be treated fairly.
3. Almost every child dreams of being a fireman.
4. The average man is a good citizen.
5. The future of mankind is uncertain.

6. Being a stewardess is not as glamorous as it may seem.

7. Everyone has the right to his opinion.

8. Every married surgeon depends on his spouse for emotional support.

9. Our female carpenter is also a poetess.

10. Dr. Marcia White is not only a female professor, but also chairman of the English department.

Application 9–8

Find a piece of writing that expresses a sexist bias. Rewrite one or more paragraphs to eliminate sexist usage without altering the original meaning. Attach a copy of your original to your rewrite, and be prepared to discuss the rewrite in class.

Find a piece of writing that refers to both sexes without lapsing into sexist usage, and bring it to class for analysis and discussion.

Application 9–9

How would you respond to someone who claimed that our concern with sexist language is just another fad? Working in small groups, brainstorm for material, and then compose a paragraph that supports your group's viewpoint convincingly. Begin your paragraph with a clear topic statement.

Each group can then discuss its paragraph with the whole class.

Automated Aids for Revising

Many of the strategies in Chapters 8 and 9 could be executed rapidly with word-processing software. By using the *global search-and-replace function* in some programs, you can command the computer to search for ambiguous pronoun references, overuse of passive voice, **to be** verbs, **There** and **It** sentence openers, negative constructions, clutter words, needless prefatory expressions and qualifiers, sexist language, and so on. With an on-line dictionary or thesaurus, you can check definitions or see a list of synonyms for a word you have used in your writing.

But despite the increasing sophistication of style checkers, diction checkers, and other such editing aids, automation never can eliminate the writer's burden of *choice*. None of the "rules" or advice offered here applies universally. Our language confronts us with almost infinite choices that cannot be programmed into a computer. Ultimately it is the informed writer's sensitivity to meaning, emphasis, and tone—the human contact—that determines the success or failure of any message.

SECTION THREE

ESSAYS FOR VARIOUS GOALS

Introduction

Earlier chapters have stressed the importance of identifying a *goal* and of refining the goal into a *purpose* (goal plus plan). This section will show you how to focus on your purpose more sharply to achieve a variety of writing goals.

Three Major Goals of Writing

The bulk of your writing in college and beyond can be categorized according to three major goals: *expressive*, *referential*, and *persuasive*. Let's consider each of these categories separately.

Expressive writing is mostly about *you*, the writer (your feelings, experiences, impressions, personality, and the like). Its goal is to help readers understand something about you or about your unique way of seeing things. Here are a few writing situations with an expressive goal:

You write to cheer up a sick friend with a tale about your latest blind date.

You write a Dear John (or Jane) letter.

You describe for your classmates a special relationship.

You write to your parents, explaining why you've been feeling down-in-the-dumps.

In each writing your goal is to share something about yourself with your audience.

Referential (or *explanatory*) *writing* is mostly about your view (your opinion, attitude, observation, or suggestion) on some *outside* subject. The goal is not so much to express emotions; it is to provide readers with information that explains your viewpoint or position. Most of your writing has a referential goal. Here are examples of referential writing situations:

> You write to describe the exterior of your dorm so that your parents can find it.
>
> You define *condominium* for your business law class.
>
> You report on the effects of budget cuts at your college for the campus newspaper.
>
> You write instructions for your classmates on how to obtain autographs of famous people by mail.
>
> You write an essay for your psychology professor on why people gossip.

The focus in each of these situations is not you or your reader, but rather on a subject that interests you both.

Persuasive writing is mostly about your *audience.* Beyond merely informing readers, your goal is to motivate them to change their thinking or take some action on a controversial issue. Persuasive writing is designed to appeal to the audience's reason, and sometimes to their emotions as well. Here are examples of persuasive-writing situations:

> You write an editorial for the campus newspaper, calling for a stricter alcohol policy in the dorms.
>
> You write a diplomatic note to your obnoxious neighbor, asking him to keep his dogs quiet.
>
> You write to ask a professor on sabbatical to reconsider the low grade you were given in history.
>
> You write to persuade citizens in your county to vote against a proposal for a toxic-waste dump.

The focus in each of these situations is on your reader's way of thinking.

These three categories (expressive, referential or explanatory, and persuasive) often overlap in your writing. In writing to *persuade* the dean to beef up campus security, you might discuss your personal fears (expressive goal) and explain how some students have been attacked (referential goal). But your *primary* goal will be persuasive. Most writing situations have *one* primary goal. And by keeping that goal sharply in focus, you can decide on the best strategies for getting the job done.

Major Development Strategies

A development strategy is simply a *plan* for achieving a goal. Specifically, it is a plan for coming up with the details, events, examples, explanations, and reasons that enable readers to grasp your exact meaning—a way of answering readers' questions. Depending on your writing situation, you can choose from four major strategies for developing a message: *description, narration, exposition,* and *argument.*

Description creates a word picture. It is either objective or subjective; that is, it provides a factual picture of something (referential goal), or it shares an impression or feeling (expressive goal). If your goal were to describe the geology of the Lady Evelyn Wilderness in northern Ontario for an environmental impact statement, you would use objective description. But if you wished to share with an interested friend your sensations while camping there, you would use subjective description.

Narration tells a story or depicts a series of related events, usually in chronological order. In essay writing, a narrative almost always makes a clear and definite point. Narration relies heavily on descriptive details to make the events vivid. If your goal were to tell about being stalked by a black bear while traveling through Ontario's Lady Evelyn Wilderness, you would use the strategy of narration.

Exposition is the commonest strategy for developing a message. Although exposition relies on description and, sometimes, narration, exposition does more than paint a picture or tell a story: this strategy explains the writer's viewpoint. Strategies of exposition can be divided into more specific plans: illustration, classification, process analysis, cause-effect analysis, comparison/contrast, and definition. For one paragraph or a whole essay, a writer decides on the strategy that best explains the main point. Although an essay often embodies some combination of these strategies, it usually will have one *primary* strategy. If your goal were to explain how sulfur dioxide pollution from industries in the Midwest threatens the waters of the Lady Evelyn Wilderness, you might use several expository strategies to make your point, but your primary strategy would be cause-effect analysis.

With *argument,* we strive to persuade readers that our stand on an issue is valid. Whereas the main point in exposition can be *shown* to be true or valid, the main point in an argument is debatable—capable of being argued by reasonable people on either side of the issue. Thus, if your goal were to persuade readers that logging companies should not be allowed to operate in the Lady Evelyn Wilderness, you would argue that logging would destroy this natural refuge. Opponents, however, might argue that logging would create jobs for local residents, thereby improving the economy. But neither side ever could *prove* that its position is the right one. The stronger argument, then, would be the one that makes the more convincing case. Although argumentation follows its own specified patterns of reasoning, it also relies on the strategies of description, narration, and exposition.

Just as writing may have overlapping goals, writing may employ overlapping strategies for development. Many of your essays, though, will employ one or another primary strategy; that is, a particular essay will be primarily descriptive, narrative, expository, or argumentative. The chapters in Section Three will help you spell out your purpose according to your goals and your strategies for achieving those goals. Sample essays and study questions precede the assignments. Careful analysis of these essays should help you compose your responses to the assignments. Some of these are professional essays; some are versions of essays by students. And, though not all of them can be considered "perfect," they do represent the kind of imaginative, engaging, and fluent responses that make writing make a difference. Each essay has been revised often enough to ensure worthwhile content, sensible arrangement, and a clear, readable style.

Note: Keep in mind that none of these development strategies is an end in itself. In other words, we don't write merely for the sake of contrasting or of discussing causes and effects. Instead, we contrast or discuss causes and effects because we've decided that this particular approach seems the best way to connect with readers on this particular topic. Each strategy is merely one way of looking at something—another option for approaching the countless writing situations we face throughout our lives and careers.

A Word About Structural Variations

Most sample essays in earlier chapters are basic examples of an introduction-body-conclusion structure: a one-paragraph introduction that leads into the thesis; several supporting paragraphs, each developed around a topic statement that treats one part of the thesis; and a one-paragraph conclusion that relates to the main point. But a quick glance at published writing—including these very paragraphs—shows that not all writing rigidly follows this one formula. Within this three-part structure are many variations. Some topics might call for several introductory paragraphs; a complicated supporting point may require that one topic statement serve two or more body paragraphs; some conclusions may take up more than one paragraph. On the other hand, you will often see single-sentence paragraphs opening, supporting, or closing an essay.

Furthermore, the thesis is not always the final sentence in the introduction. The thesis can be the first sentence of the essay, or it may be saved for the conclusion or not stated at all—*though it is always unmistakably implied.*

Sometimes the body paragraphs vary greatly in length or are interrupted by digressions (interpretations, personal remarks, flashbacks, and so on). This structure is acceptable if the connection between digressions and the main discussion is clear.

Still other essays have neither introductory nor concluding paragraphs. Instead, the opening or closing is incorporated into the main discussion.

Such choices about structural variation are all part of a writer's deliberate decisions—decisions that determine the ultimate quality of the message. But regardless of the type and extent of its variations, a good essay *always* reveals a distinct beginning, middle, and ending—and a clear line of thought.

Many of the essays in the following chapters embody one or more of these variations. Use them as inspiration for your own writing, whenever such variations can help sharpen your meaning.

10
Developing a Description

Because it creates a word picture—a clear image in readers' minds—description is the common denominator in all writing. Specifically, description answers these questions:

What is it?

What does it look like?

How could I recognize it?

What is it made of?

What does it do?

How does it work?

What is your impression of it?

How does it make you feel?

Although itself one of the four basic strategies for development (along with narration, exposition, and argument), description most often supports these other strategies by helping readers visualize details. Before discussing description as an exclusive strategy (*pure description*), let's consider its supporting role in writing developed through other strategies.

226

Description as a Support Strategy

Whether telling a story, explaining something, or arguing a point, writers rely on the *showing power* of description to enrich their discussions. Consider this topic statement about the physical complexities of New York City:

It is a miracle that New York works at all.

Now that we've been told, we need to be shown so that we can see for ourselves. The author enables us to share his impression of New York in this way:

[1]It is a miracle that New York works at all. [2]The whole thing is implausible. [3]Every time the residents brush their teeth, millions of gallons of water must be drawn from the Catskills and the hills of Westchester. [4]When a young man in Manhattan writes a letter to his girl in Brooklyn, the love message gets blown to her through a pneumatic tube—*pfft*—just like that. [5]The subterranean system of telephone cables, power lines, steam pipes, gas mains, and sewer pipes is reason enough to abandon the island to the gods and the weevils. [6]Every time an incision is made in the pavement, the noisy surgeons expose ganglia that are tangled beyond belief. [7]By rights New York should have destroyed itself long ago, from panic or fire or rioting or failure of some vital supply line in its circulatory system or from some deep labyrinthine short circuit. [8]Long ago the city should have experienced an insoluble traffic snarl at some impossible bottleneck. [9]It should have perished of hunger when food lines failed for a few days. [10]It should have been wiped out by a plague starting in its slums or carried in by ships' rats. [11]It should have been overwhelmed by the sea that licks at it on every side. [12]The workers in its myriad cells should have succumbed to nerves, from the fearful pall of smoke-fog that drifts over every few days from Jersey, blotting out all light at noon and leaving the high offices suspended, [people] groping and depressed, and the sense of world's end. [13]It should have been touched in the head by the August heat and gone off its rocker.

—E. B. White

To support his key term of *implausible*, White uses the primary development strategy of cause-and-effect analysis. But vivid description carries much of the burden here.

Because any subject can be viewed in countless ways, decisions about descriptive details must consider the writer's purpose and the reader's needs. The purpose of the paragraph above is not to describe

New York as a tourist brochure would; instead, it is to share the writer's dominant impression of the city as a huge, impossibly complex, living organism. He thus decides to communicate his impression through examples of the causes and effects of New York's problems— examples enriched and clarified by precise and vivid description.

White's paragraph has two types of descriptive details: (1) objective, which include precise images that a camera would record (people brushing their teeth, water flowing by the riversful), and (2) subjective, which include the vivid images that are filtered through the author's personal way of seeing ("incision," "ganglia," "myriad cells"). Objective details make the picture clear; subjective details make it vivid. The two types complement each other.

Finally, the level of details in White's paragraph provides enough solid images for the reader to understand the main point. Imagine if the paragraph had been developed at a higher level of generality:

Abstract and general	Concrete and specific
water must be drawn from great distances	millions of gallons of water must be drawn from the Catskills and the hills of Westchester [sentence 3]
the subterranean system of utilities	the subterranean system of telephone cables, power lines, steam pipes, gas mains, and sewer pipes [sentence 5]

To ensure coherence, White orders his details logically (in this case, from underground to ground level to sky). This spatial order creates a clear and distinct angle of vision, saving the major emphasis (the dehumanizing effect of this environmental chaos on the workers in skyscrapers) for last. The supporting description makes White's paragraph come to life for us.

Description as a Primary Strategy

So-called pure description does not mean describing merely for the sake of describing. Any pure description has one or both of these goals:

1. To provide factual information about something for someone who will use it, buy it, or assemble it, or who needs to know more about it for some good reason (objective description)

2.   To create a mood or impression in the reader's mind or to share a feeling (subjective description)

A strictly objective description has a referential goal. It includes facts about the thing itself, without the writer's personal comments:

Objective description   All day we had temperatures of 30 degrees F and heavy rains driven by winds of 35–45 mph.

This is the type of description commonly found in business and technical reports.

Subjective description has an expressive goal. It emphasizes the writer's impressions about the thing:

Subjective description   All day the weather was dismal.

Most of your own descriptions will include both observable facts and your personal impressions:

Combined description   The freezing rain and gale-force winds made our first day of vacation dismal.

For illustration, however, objective description and subjective description are treated separately in this chapter.

OBJECTIVE DESCRIPTION

Objective description is based purely on observable details: it is not colored by the writer's emotions or likes and dislikes. Objective description records *exactly* what the writer sees, which should be what anyone else would see from the writer's vantage point. Readers of an objective description expect only the facts. If your tape deck has been stolen, the police will need a description that includes the brand name, serial number, model, color, size, shape, identifying marks or scratches, and so on. For this audience, a subjective description (that the tape deck was a handsome addition to your car; that its sound quality was superb; that it made driving a pleasure) would be useless. These details describe only your feelings, not the object itself.

Here is a purely objective description:

Orienting sentence (1)   [1]The 2-acre site (lot 7) for my proposed log cabin is on the northern shore of Moosehead Lake, roughly 1000 feet east of the Seboomook

View from the water (2–5)

View from the shoreline (6–7)

Point camping area. [2]It is marked by a granite ledge, 30 feet long and 15 feet high. [3]The ledge faces due south and slopes gradually east. [4]A rock shoal along the westerly frontage extends about 30 feet from the shoreline. [5]On the easterly end of the frontage is a landing area on a small gravel beach immediately to the right of the ledge. [6]Lot boundaries are marked by yellow stakes a few feet from the shoreline. [7]Lot numbers are carved on yellow-marked trees adjacent to the yellow stakes.

This paragraph, written to help a soil engineer find the property by boat, answers these questions:

What is it?

What does it look like?

How could I recognize it?

The answers follow a spatial order, moving from whole to parts—the same order in which we would actually view the property.

Notice that the opening sentence is not a standard topic statement but a statement of fact. It does, however, provide an orientation, giving us a definite sense of what to expect in the discussion. Descriptions often have no topic statement, but they nonetheless begin with an orienting statement.

Because the writer's goal is referential, he includes only factual information, without personal impressions. Details are limited to the recognizable characteristics of the property. And because he simply wants to *introduce* the subject, he restricts his description to a brief but specific catalog of the lot's major features. For some other situation, the description naturally would be more specific. For instance, the soil engineer's report on his evaluation of the building site would be read by the health officials who approve building permits. That report would, therefore, carry details of this kind:

Hand-dug test holes revealed a well-draining, granular material, with a depth of at least 48 inches to bedrock.

The quantity of detail in a description is always keyed to the writer's purpose and the audience's needs.

Objective description serves many uses in college writing. In describing a lab experiment or a field trip or a fire hazard in the dorm, you would focus on the facts, not on your feelings.

In the workplace, you might use objective description to inform customers about a new product or service. If you apply for a business loan, the bank will require a description of the property or venture. As an architect or engineer you would describe your proposed building on paper before construction begins. As a medical professional, you would write detailed records of a patient's condition and treatment. Whenever readers need to visualize *the thing itself*, objective description is essential.

SUBJECTIVE DESCRIPTION

Strictly speaking, no useful description can be completely subjective; to get the picture, readers need at least some observable details. For our purposes, we can define subjective description as that which has objective details colored by personal impressions. The usual goal of subjective description is to create a mood or to share a feeling, as shown in the italicized expressions:

> One of my own favorite approaches to a rocky seacoast is by a rough path through an evergreen forest that has its own peculiar enchantment. It is usually an early morning tide that takes me along the forest path, so that the light is still pale and the fog drifts in from the sea beyond. *It is almost a ghost forest,* for among the living spruce and balsam are many dead trees—some still erect, some sagging earthward, some lying on the floor of the forest. All the trees, the living and the dead, are *clothed* with green and silver crusts of lichens. Tufts of the bearded lichen or old man's beard hang from the branches *like bits of sea mist* tangled there. Green woodland mosses and a *yielding carpet* of reindeer moss cover the ground. In the quiet of that place even the *voice of the surf* is reduced to a *whispered echo* and the sounds of the forest are but the *ghosts of sound*—the *faint sighing* of evergreen needles in the moving air; the creaks and heavier groans of half-fallen trees *resting against their neighbors* and rubbing bark against bark; the *light rattling fall* of a dead branch broken under the feet of a squirrel and sent bouncing and ricocheting earthward. [emphasis added]
>
> —Rachel L. Carson

This paragraph blends objective and subjective description to answer these questions:

Objective   What is it?

                       What does it look like?

What is it made of?

Subjective   What is your impression of it?

How does it make you feel?

The paragraph is developed to help us understand what the writer means by a forest with "its own peculiar enchantment." Concrete and specific details are those any reader could visualize:

the early morning light and fog

the many dead trees among the living ones

the lichens that coat the trees and hang from the branches

the mossy forest floor

the eerie sounds

But these details alone would not cause readers to share the writer's dominant impression of "peculiar enchantment." To create that special mood, the writer had to insert subjective details (in italics) as well. She had to filter the facts through her own feelings and impressions.

The observable details are arranged in the same order (general to specific) that we would follow in noticing things if we were in the writer's place: first location, then atmosphere, trees, algae on the trees, ground cover, sounds. Thus, we are able to perceive things in the same sequence as the writer perceived them.

Beyond creating a mood or sharing a feeling, subjective description can serve practical purposes. The following writer uses personal impressions to make a persuasive point.

> Close your eyes for a moment, and picture a professional baseball game. You probably see something like this: a hot summer afternoon, complete with sizzling bats, fans clad in the reds and yellows and pastels of summer, and short-sleeved vendors yelling "ICE CREAM HEEERE!" If you recall some recent World Series, though, you might envision a scene more like this: a c-c-cold starlit night highlighted by players in Thinsulate gloves and turtlenecks, fans in ski hats instead of baseball caps, and vendors hurriedly hawking coffee. This "football-like" image suggests that baseball season is just plain too long!
>
> —Mike Cabral

This paragraph creates contrasting moods in order to win readers' support for its conclusion—a subjective view addresses a practical matter.

Other such subjective appeals to readers' feelings can have persuasive value as well. A colorful description of your messy dorm or apartment might encourage fellow residents to clean up their act. Or a nauseating catalog of greasy food served in the college dining hall might move school officials to improve the menu. Even the most subjective writing can cause readers to see things as you do.

In this essay, a mixture of subjective and objective description introduces a new way of looking at beaches, both in and beyond summer:

Off-Season

I hate summer beaches. Ocean swimming is impossible; upon conquering a wave, I simply lose to the next, getting pushed back onto the hard-packed, abrasive sand. Booby traps of bottles, soda cans, toys, and rocks make walking hazardous. Heavy with the stench of suntan lotion, greasy French fries, dead fish, and sweat, the thick, searing air hangs motionless above the scorching sand. Blasting radios and growling beach buggies cut the slap-swoosh of the green-gray surf to a weak hiss. People devour a summer beach, gouging the sand with umbrella spikes and gripping it with oiled limbs, leaving only trampled debris at summer's end.

My interest in beaches begins, then, after the summer people leave. Gone are the trash and trappings. The winter wind is bitter but clean, fresh with the damp, earthy scent of cold seaweed. Only broken shells litter the sand, and nearer the water, ice-gray, surf-worn rocks rise like smooth serpents' backs. Wave upon wave, the bruise-colored sea thunders in, each rolling arc pouring ahead of the next, breaking into smaller and smaller waves, crawling up the beach.

Things endure but things change. Constant waves wash the face of the shore into roundness. Dunes fuse and slide apart, transformed into new mounds by the coarse wind. Erosion fences whistle and ripple and clack, protesting the sand shifting between the slats. No longer covered by sprawling sun worshippers, the beach forms a smooth slide of continent into ocean.

Waves naturally push and pull and wear things down. In time, the ocean will claim as its own the snack shack and the parking lots, the sea walls and the cottages. Walking the ocean's edge awakens a small fear that the waves might slither around my ankles and draw me into that icy foam. Paralyzed with cold, I will be worn and washed by the surf until I become just another part of the ever-shrinking beach.

So far, at least, I've been lucky: I walk winter beaches often and see nothing more sinister than gulls cracking crabs on the rocks.

But I still avoid the water's edge—beaches ravaged in summer might harbor a winter impulse for revenge.

—Pam Herbert

Vivid description is one of a writer's most powerful resources for creating real contact with readers.

GUIDELINES FOR DESCRIPTION

Whether paragraphs or essays, all descriptions are developed according to these guidelines:

1. *Although some descriptions have no topic (or thesis) statement, they always begin with some kind of orienting statement.* Objective descriptions in particular rarely call for a standard topic or thesis statement, because the goal of such descriptions is merely to catalog the details of a subject so that readers can visualize it.

2. *The choice of details in a description depends precisely on the writer's purpose and the reader's needs.* Brainstorming yields more details than a writer can use. Select only those that advance your meaning. Use objective details to provide a clear and exact picture and subjective details to convey a dominant impression.

3. *All details are at a level that is concrete and specific enough to convey an unmistakable picture.* Most often description works best at the lowest levels of abstraction and generality.

Vague	Exact
at high speed	80 miles an hour
a tiny office	an 8-by-12-foot office
some workers	the accounting staff
a high salary	$50,000 per year
impressive gas mileage	40 mpg, city; 50, highway

4. *The details are ordered in a clear sequence.* Descriptions generally follow a spatial or general-to-specific order—whichever parallels the angle of vision readers would have if viewing the item. Or the details are arranged according to the dominant impression desired.

Application 10–1

PARAGRAPH WARM-UP: OBJECTIVE DESCRIPTION

Assume that a close friend has been missing for two days. The police have been called in. Because you know this person well, the police have asked you for a written description. Write an *objective description* that would help the police identify this person. To create a clear picture, stick to details any observer could recognize. If possible, include one or more *unique* identifying features (scar, mannerisms, and so on). Leave out personal comments, and give only objective details. Refer to "Guidelines for Developing a Description," above. Use the paragraph on page 137 as a model.

Application 10–2

PARAGRAPH WARM-UP: SUBJECTIVE DESCRIPTION

Assume that your college newspaper runs a weekly column titled "Memorable Characters." You have been asked to submit a brief sketch of a person you find striking in some way. Create a word portrait of this person in one paragraph. Your description should focus on a dominant impression, blending objective details and subjective commentary. Be sure to focus on personal characteristics that support your dominant impression. Develop your description according to the guidelines above.

Application 10–3

ESSAY PRACTICE

Read this selection and answer the questions that follow it.

Cruelty at Tinker Creek

[1]A couple of summers ago I was walking along the edge of the island to see what I could see in the water, and mainly to scare frogs. Frogs have an inelegant way of taking off from invisible positions on the bank just ahead of your feet, in dire panic, emitting a froggy "Yike!" and splashing into the water. Incredibly, this amused me,

and incredibly, it amuses me still. As I walked along the grassy edge of the island, I got better and better at seeing frogs both in and out of the water. I learned to recognize, slowing down, the difference in texture of the light reflecting from mudbank, water, grass, or frog. Frogs were flying all around me. At the end of the island I noticed a small green frog. He was exactly half in and half out of the water, looking like a schematic diagram of an amphibian, and he didn't jump.

[2]He didn't jump; I crept closer. At last I knelt on the island's winter-killed grass, lost, dumbstruck, staring at the frog in the creek just four feet away. He was a very small frog with wide, dull eyes. And just as I looked at him, he slowly crumpled and began to sag. The spirit vanished from his eyes as if snuffed. His skin emptied and drooped; his very skull seemed to collapse and settle like a kicked tent. He was shrinking before my eyes like a deflating football. I watched the taut, glistening skin on his shoulders ruck, and rumple, and fall. Soon, part of his skin, formless as a pricked balloon, lay in floating folds like bright scum on top of the water; it was a monstrous and terrifying thing. I gaped bewildered, appalled. An oval shadow hung in the water behind the drained frog; then the shadow glided away. The frog skin bag started to sink.

[3]I had read about the giant water bug, but never seen one. "Giant water bug" is really the name of the creature, which is an enormous, heavy-bodied brown beetle. It eats insects, tadpoles, fish, and frogs. Its grasping forelegs are mighty and hooked inward. It seizes a victim with these legs, hugs it tight, and paralyzes it with enzymes injected during a vicious bite. That one bite is the only bite it ever takes. Through the puncture shoot the poisons that dissolve the victim's muscles and bones and organs—all but the skin—and through it the giant water bug sucks out the victim's body, reduced to a juice. This event is quite common in warm fresh water. The frog I saw was being sucked by a giant water bug. I had been kneeling on the island grass; when the unrecognizable flap of frog skin settled on the creek bottom, swaying, I stood up and brushed the knees of my pants. I couldn't catch my breath.

[4]Of course, many carnivorous animals devour their prey alive. The usual method seems to be to subdue the victim by drowning it or grasping it so it can't flee, then eating it whole or in a series of bloody bites. Frogs eat everything whole, stuffing prey into their mouths with their thumbs. People have seen frogs with their wide jaws so full of live dragonflies they couldn't close them. Ants don't even have to catch their prey: in the spring they swarm over newly hatched, featherless birds in the nest and eat them tiny bite by bite.

—Annie Dillard

Questions About Content

1. What is the implied thesis in this description? State it in your own words.

2. List five objective and five subjective details in the essay.

3. What is the dominant impression created by this description?

4. Name three features that make this essay interesting.

Questions About Organization

1. Is the introductory paragraph adequately developed? Explain.

2. Which paragraph has the most subjective description? Why are the other paragraphs more objective?

3. How does the writer order her details in the first two paragraphs? Trace the movement of the description.

4. Should the writer have explained about the beetle before describing the event? Why or why not?

5. Does each paragraph begin with an adequate orienting sentence? In your own words, state the main point of each paragraph.

6. Does the conclusion create a sense of completeness? Does it relate back to the introduction? Explain how it reinforces the implied thesis.

7. How does each paragraph deliver on the promise implied in its orienting sentence? Be specific.

8. What are four major devices that lend coherence to this selection?

Questions About Style

1. Identify one sentence that relies on subordination for combining related thoughts. How does this structure reinforce the meaning of the sentence?

2. Identify one sentence that relies on coordination for combining related thoughts. How does this structure reinforce the meaning of that sentence?

3. Which seems the most emphatic short sentence in the selection?

4. What is the writer's attitude toward what she witnessed? How do you know? What are the signals?

5. Describe the tone that grows from this essay. What kind of person does the author seem to be? How do you know?

RESPONDING TO YOUR READING

Explore your reactions to "Off-Season" (pages 233–234) by using the questions on page 93. Then respond with an essay of your own. Maybe you *love* beaches in summer and dislike them in winter. Or maybe the essay reminds you of some place of your own that changes with the seasons. Think of all the things you would like to say in reply to the essay, and then settle on the main thing you want to say.

Or perhaps you were struck more profoundly by something in Annie Dillard's essay (pages 235–236). If so, you might choose to respond to that one instead.

OPTIONS FOR ESSAY WRITING

1. In an essay for your classmates, describe a memorable scene— something that left a deep impression. Like Annie Dillard, blend objective and subjective details to convey a dominant impression. For precision and vividness, make your details specific and concrete.

2. In an essay for your classmates, describe a place that is special. Give a clear picture of both the place and your feelings about it. Be sure that your audience comes to understand why the place is special.

3. Do you have a hero or villain? Describe this person in an essay for your classmates. Provide enough descriptive details for your audience to understand why you admire or despise this person. Focus on a dominant impression and on at least *three* characteristics that support your impression. To provide the intimate details that will make your description vivid, choose someone about whom you know a good deal.

4. Describe for your classmates an automobile. It can be a luxuriously appointed or high-performance dream car or the basic transportation you drive to school. Give your audience the feel of the car, its "personality." Make them feel as if they are riding in it with you.

5. Describe what you like or dislike about your neighborhood.

6. Describe yourself to someone who doesn't know you. Choose at least three features that give the most accurate picture of who you are.

7. Describe a place that frightens you. Allow readers to share your fright.

8. What do you expect from your old age? Picture yourself as a senior citizen, and describe a day in your life.

11
Developing
a Narrative

Narration That Merely Reports • Narration That Makes a Point
• Guidelines for Narration • Applications

Like description, narration creates a word picture. But description tells about things as they *appear* (in space), whereas narration tells about events as they *happen* (in time). Of course, narration relies on descriptive details to make the story vivid. But the main function of narration is to enable readers to follow events by answering these questions:

What happened?

Who was involved?

When did it happen?

Where did it happen?

Why did it happen?

Narration sometimes answers these questions as well:

What were your impressions of it?

How did it make you feel?

Narration can play a number of roles: in a novel or fictional story, it stimulates our imagination and entertains us; in a newspaper story, it reports newsworthy events objectively; in essays, it makes a definite

240

point. Our interest here, however, is not in stories for entertainment; instead, we will discuss narration designed merely to report and narration designed to make a point.

Narration That Merely Reports

Some narratives simply give a picture of what happened, without stating—or even implying—any particular viewpoint. Some newspaper stories or courtroom testimonies offer only the bare facts. Because its goal is simply to re-create the events, this objective reporting does not answer these questions:

What were your impressions of it?

How did it make you feel?

In this paragraph the writer's job is simply to describe the events without inserting personal impressions:

The climactic scene (1)	[1]Two [suspects] hobbled into Federal Court in Brooklyn on crutches yesterday, each with a leg missing and each charged with smuggling cocaine and marijuana stored in the hollowed-out parts of
A related detail (2)	their confiscated artificial limbs. [2]A third suspect, a . . . woman, was also accused of taking part in the smuggling of $1 million worth of cocaine
Background (3–9)	from Bogota to Kennedy International Airport. [3]Acting on confidential information, customs agents took the three into custody Monday night. [4]The agents took one of the suspects, William Ochoa, 25 years old, to St. Vincent's Hospital in Manhattan, where physicians removed his plastic leg. [5]Inside, they said, they found one kilo (2.2 pounds) of cocaine wrapped in plastic bags. [6]The suspect told them he had lost his leg during a guerilla uprising in Colombia two years ago. [7]Agents said they found six ounces of marijuana in the artifical right limb worn by Jaime Zapata-Reyes, another suspect. [8]The woman, identified as Mrs. Lenore Jaramillo, 34, was allegedly found to be wearing three girdles, each concealing quantities of plastic-wrapped cocaine totaling one kilo. [9]Agents reported that each suspect had more
Conclusion (10–11)	than $400 and return tickets to Bogota. [10]United

> States Magistrate Vincent A. Catoggio held each in $100,000 bail. [11]Expressing concern over the missing artificial limbs, which had been described as damaged, he directed that customs agents return them in good condition. . . .
>
> —*The New York Times*

This paragraph implies no main point—no insertion of the writer's feelings or impressions. Because the focus is on a bizarre smuggling practice, we are simply given the details that clarify the opening (and climactic) scene of smugglers hobbling into court. Explanations of how the smugglers were caught are left out, because they are not relevant to this story.

To attract readers' interest, the writer juggles the sequence of events. The first two sentences place us at the story's climax. Then the background details follow strict chronological order so that we can keep track of events leading to the courtroom scene. To help us follow the story, the author consistently uses past tense and third-person point of view.

Narrative reports serve many purposes. In college, you might report on experiments or investigations in chemistry, biology, or psychology. Or you might retrace the events leading up to the American Revolution or the 1929 stock market crash. In the workplace, you might report on the events that led up to an accident on the assembly line. Or you might write daily accounts of your crew's progress on a construction project. Whenever readers need to understand *what happened*, narrative reporting is essential.

Narration That Makes a Point

Many of your narratives will be designed to make or support some definite viewpoint or thesis. When you recount last night's date, your purpose usually is to explain some viewpoint: that some people can be fickle, that first dates can be disastrous, or the like. Narratives of this type focus on some aspect of the subject that deserves our attention. In this story of a scene witnessed from a commuter train, our attention is focused on how urban dwellers can become desensitized to tragedy.

Orienting sentence

> [1]One afternoon in late August, as the summer's sun streamed into the car and made little jumping shadows on the windows, I sat gazing out at the tenement-dwellers, who were themselves looking out of their windows from the

gray crumbling buildings along the tracks of upper Manhattan. [2]As we crossed into the Bronx, the train unexpectedly slowed down for a few miles. [3]Suddenly from out of my window I saw a large crowd near the tracks, held back by two policemen. [4]Then, on the other side, from my window, I saw a sight I would never be able to forget: a little boy almost severed in halves, lying at an incredible angle near the track. [5]The ground was covered with blood, and the boy's eyes were opened wide, strained and disbelieving in his sudden oblivion. [6]A policeman stood next to him, his arms folded, staring straight at the windows of our train. [7]In the orange glow of late afternoon, the policeman, the crowd, the corpse of the boy were for a brief moment immobile, motionless, a small tableau to violence and death in the city. [8]Behind me, in the next row of seats, was a game of bridge. [9]I heard one of the four men say as he looked out at the sight, "God, that's horrible." [10] Another said in a whisper, "Terrible, terrible." [11]There was a momentary silence, punctuated only by the clicking of the wheels on the track. [12]Then, after a pause, I heard the first man say: "Two hearts."

—Willie Morris

In this narrative, the author filters the events through his own feelings. Although the awful facts of this story are colored only slightly by the author's own impressions (sentences 4, 5, and 7), the point implied is all too clear. Sometimes, narration can be the best form of *showing*.

We are kept on track in the paragraph by the author's consistent use of past tense and first-person point of view (the author tells of *his* experience). An alternative point of view for narration is the third person (telling of someone else's experience). Whichever point of view you select, be consistent; avoid shifting from one to another.

Narratives can also serve a persuasive purpose, by causing readers to change their attitudes or take some sort of action. You might tell about a boating accident as a way of encouraging voters' support for tougher boating laws. On the job, you might recount the details of a disruptive conflict among employees as a way of persuading your employer to finance stress-management workshops. By telling the story, you can help readers see things your way.

This narrative helps persuade us not to smoke by telling what it's like for a young person to confront the possibility of early death.

I entered college at 17 and began taking classes with some 25-
and 30-year-old students. Such an age difference made me feel much
luckier than these older people. What were they doing in a freshman
class, anyway? Compared to them, I had unlimited time to
succeed—or so I thought. Soon after my eighteenth birthday, the
horrid piece of lung tissue I coughed into the sink gave a whole new
meaning to my notion of "youth." Five years of inhaling hot smoke,
carbon monoxide, nicotine, and tobacco pesticides had finally
produced enough coughing and sickness to terrify me. "Oh, my god,
I'm going to die young; I'm going to die before all those 30-year-
olds." For years, I had heard my mother tell me that I was
committing suicide on the installment plan. Now I seemed to be
running out of installments.

—Chris Adey

By letting the story make the point, Chris's narrative seems far more
persuasive than the usual sermons that begin with something like,
"Smoking is bad for you."

The viewpoint in a narrative might be expressed as a topic or thesis statement at the beginning or end of the story. Or, as in the two
narratives above, the main point might not be stated at all, but only
implied by the story. Many stories from the Bible make a definite point
without ever stating it directly. But even when its point is saved for last
or just implied, the story almost always opens with some statement that
orients readers to the events.

The following narrative, "Back At the Ranch," recalls how a
dreadful moment during the writer's adolescence changed his own perception of "manhood."

Back At the Ranch

A young boy molts. Tender skin falls off, or gets scraped off,
and is replaced by a tougher, more permanent crust. The transition
happens in moments, in events. All of a sudden, something is gone
and something else is in its place. I made a change like that standing
in the back of a pick-up truck when I was 15.

It was 1967 and I had a summer job at a camp in Wyoming. It
was beautiful there, high-pasture country with a postcard view of
the Tetons. As an apprentice counselor I straddled the worlds of
boys and men, breathing the high air, watching over kids, hanging
out with cowboys. The cowboys wrangled the horses for the camp
and were mostly an itinerant group, living in summer cabins below
the barn, and they tolerated my loitering down there. I hitched up
my jeans just like them, braided my lasso like them, smoked and
cursed and slouched like them.

On the day it happened, I was standing with a group of cowboys by the ranch office. We heard the sound of a big engine coming in the long driveway, and after a while a red Corvette Sting Ray convertible, of all things, motored up in front of us. Conversation stopped. In the driver's seat was a hippie. His hair fell straight down his back and a bandanna was tied around his head. His style may have been standard for somewhere, but not for Jackson, Wyo.

The guy was decked out with beads and earrings and dressed in fantastic colors, and next to him his girlfriend, just as exotic, with perfect blond hair, looked up at us over little square glasses with a distracted, angelic expression. All in a red Corvette.

I was fascinated, mesmerized. I looked around me with a big grin and realized that I was alone in this feeling. The cowboys all had hard stares, cold eyes. I adjusted, a traitor to myself, and blanked out my expression in kind.

The hippie opened up a big smile, and said: "I went to camp here when I was a kid . . . came by to say hi. Is Weenie around?"

In that moment, Weenie, the owner of the place, having heard the throb of the engine, appeared in the ranch office door and walked toward us with a bowlegged stride, his big belt buckle coming first. He walked right up to the driver and looked down on him.

"Get out." Weenie didn't say hi. "Get out of here now."

"What? Wait a minute. I came to say hi. I went to camp here. I just came to say hi."

"Get the hell off this ranch. *Now.*" And staring at the hippie, Weenie kicked some dust up on the side of the Corvette.

"What's wrong with you, man?"

"You're what's wrong with me, son."

I noticed the cowboys were nodding. I nodded. Weenie's right. The guy should leave. He doesn't belong here.

"But you sent me a Christmas card!" By this time, the hippie had choked up a little. "I don't believe it. You sent me a goddamn Christmas card!"

The group of us closed in a little around the car. We-don't-like-that-kind-of-talk-from-a-hippie was the feeling I was getting. Thumbs came out of belt-loops. Jaws began to work.

"Looks like the little girlie's cryin'," said one of the cowboys, a tough one named Hondu. He spoke with his lips turned down on one side as if he was mouthing a cigarette. "Maybe so," said another, with mock consideration.

The notion rested in the air peacefully for a moment, then, in a sudden whipping motion, Hondu's jackknife was out, open and raised. With his other hand, he reached down and grabbed a fat bunch of the hippie's hair and pulled it toward him. Smiling grimly, he hacked it off and held it up for us to see.

During this, I looked down at the hippie's face, which was lifted up and sideways in such a way that he was looking right at me. Involuntarily, my head tilted just like his and we froze like that for a second.

"There now, that's better, ain't it?" asked Hondu.

The hippie, stunned, turned to his girlfriend, whose eyes and mouth had been wide open as long as he had been sitting there. Then he turned back to us, his face contorted, helpless. And then he went wild. He threw open his door and tried to jump up from the seat, but forgot that his seat belt was fastened and it held him in place. He struggled against it, screaming, swinging his arms like a bar fighter trying to shrug off his buddies restraining him. It was funny. Like a cartoon.

I looked around. We were all laughing. Our group closed up a little more, and came toward the car. The air bristled. He was the one who started the trouble. Well, he would get what he was looking for, all right.

The hippie stopped struggling, threw the Vette into gear, and fishtailed in the dust. We all jumped out of the way, but the open door of the car bumped into Weenie's favorite dog, a Rhodesian Ridgeback, an inside-out-looking animal that gave a wild yelp and ran straight into a willow thicket. We could hear his yips over the sound of the big engine as the hippie gunned it and took off.

That settled it. The hippie hit the dog.

Without hesitation, we jumped into one of the trucks. Rifles were drawn from the rack in the cab. Other weapons were thrown up into the bed of the pickup. I was standing there and caught one.

We took off, and because the rough road slowed down the Corvette, we were gaining. I was filled with a terrible, frightening righteousness. I was holding a rifle, chasing a man and a woman with a rifle in my hand. I looked around at my partners in the truck, and the air came out of me. We meant harm. We didn't care. I wondered who I was exactly. I needed to know. And in that moment, it happened: I switched sides and never said a word about it.

We hit the asphalt road and floored it, but we couldn't catch the Corvette. No way. The smoke from its exhaust settled around us like fog in the valley.

Still, 23 years later, I can see the two of us clearly, chosen by the same moment. Memory cuts back and forth between our faces. The wind pulls tears from the hippie's eyes; his long hair waves behind him in his fiery convertible rocketing down Route 191 under the Tetons. I with my short hair stand in the back of a pickup truck watching after him, chasing after him, following, facing the same wind.

– Jay Allison

What is the implied thesis in this essay? Can you sum up the thesis in your own words?

Sometimes a narrative can be a good way of recording our confusion or ambivalence about something. Some experiences or events might leave us with all kinds of conflicting feelings that are impossible to sort out. At times such as these, we simply *don't know* how we feel about what has happened. But even though we can't distill one dominant impression from the experience, we know the story deserves telling. The next narrative, "A Funeral in Manitoba," records several impressions simultaneously; in the events she witnesses, the author sees all at once comedy, sadness, grotesque preoccupation with funeral rituals, but a shared sense of faith and respect, as well.

A Funeral in Manitoba

When Nick Wiebe, the undertaker, arrives with the body, the lobby is jammed and a small respectful crowd is gathered in the yard. Pulling the casket on a dolly, Nick elbows his way through the mob and clears a path to the main aisle; the crowd reforms like an honor guard on either side. Word of the deceased's arrival crackles through the congregation; heads turn and crane to catch a glimpse. The dead man's relatives march down the aisle in a procession and take their seats at the front; heads turn slowly to follow them. Nick trundles the casket down the aisle, places it in the center of a circle of observers, and opens it.

The funeral is very cheerful. It's an old-fashioned service, mostly in German. The church is stark and bare and the hymns are droned unaccompanied. The young minister wears a black suit and a black silk shirt with no collar. He is flanked by the church deacons who, seated all in a row like six ravens, lead the singing. The sermon is simple and quietly spoken. The minister describes the dead man floating in an azure sky surrounded by a joyful host of departed friends and relatives. He speaks with such calm reassurance and such conviction that on this sunny summer afternoon he almost compels belief in a radiant eternal life. Death is the beginning, not the end; the funeral is a celebration. The crux of the service is the obituary. Read by the minister, it is a lengthy, detailed account of the dead man's accomplishments, his baptism and marriage, the highlights to his career, the strengths of his character, his love for his family and for God, and his last thoughts before he died; it includes a history of his last illness, minutely chronicling the time, nature, and extent of all his operations as the agony of the cancer took hold. Crude and direct, the obituary is very powerful; for a few moments it gives the dead man mythic stature. Lying up there in his coffin, he is the focus of all eyes and his character is the subject of all thoughts; the church becomes a theatre for the tiny human drama of which he is the star.

The service is very long, over an hour. The air in the church becomes foetid, and people begin to fan themselves with their hymn books, waving them like so many small white wings. At the end everyone files out past the open coffin; the line winds round and round the church and reaches down into the basement where people have been listening on the intercom. The corpse looks very yellow and waxy. Turning back towards the congregation, I can see that people's glistening faces are beatific; it's been a good service.

Funerals are Winkler's most popular mass entertainment. They are advertised all over southern Manitoba on radio CFAM, a Mennonite station partly owned by the Kroekers which specializes in religious broadcasts, classical music, and commercials. Hundreds of people come 30 and 40 miles to attend the funeral of someone they didn't know. Most funerals are spectaculars requiring a cast of thousands, and the lunch of coffee and buns served in the basement later parallels the parable of the loaves and the fishes. Winkler shuts up tight during a funeral; an eerie silence descends on the town and the streets are deserted. The only clue to everyone's whereabouts is the mass of cars around the church. A particularly grotesque suicide or a gruesome accident will draw an especially big crowd.

"I had a young couple once who were killed in a car accident shortly after they were married," says Nick Wiebe. "We laid her out in her wedding dress. It was very sad. I figure between 4,000 and 5,000 people went through the funeral home on the weekend, just to look. They made a complete shambles of the place."

An especially long and impressive funeral is a symbol of community status. "I remember when a minister died," smiles Nick. "The funeral lasted three hours. Thirteen ministers spoke. They went on so long it got dark. We ran into a blizzard on our way to the cemetery and had to turn back. On Sunday we had another service at the little country church by the cemetery. That service lasted three hours. It got so dark by the time we buried him we had to turn on the lights of the hearse to light the grave."

—Heather Robertson

Although it is never stated, Robertson's implied viewpoint might be summed up like this: *This kind of ritual is in one way amusing, but in another way touching as well.* On the one hand, we get the impression of a carnival atmosphere, of funerals as "spectaculars requiring a cast of thousands." But beyond its appeal as "mass entertainment," the ritual suggests a deeper meaning: "Crude and direct, the obituary is very powerful; for a few moments it gives the dead man mythic stature." The narrator invites us to discover the significance of the event for ourselves. Can you find other phrases that reveal the narrator's mixed feelings of condescension and respect and empathy?

Guidelines for Narration

As paragraphs or essays, all narratives are developed according to these guidelines:

1. *Whether stated or implied, the viewpoint (or main point) is clearly conveyed by the narrative details.* When the main point is stated, the topic or thesis statement is often at the end of the narrative. (A narrative that simply reports, of course, has no main point.) The narrative always begins with a clear orienting statement that places readers at the center of the action. By helping us analyze and evaluate an experience, complex narratives such as "Back At the Ranch" or "A Funeral in Manitoba" make some point about a larger issue.

2. *The choice of details in a narrative depends specifically on the writer's purpose and the reader's needs.* Because your brainstorming is likely to yield more details than you can use, select only those that directly advance your meaning. Focus on the important details, but don't leave out the lesser details that hold the story together. Whenever appropriate, filter the facts through your own impressions.

3. *All details are at a level that is concrete and specific enough to convey a clear picture of what happened.* Narration is most effective at the lowest levels of abstraction and generality. Whenever you can, show people talking.

4. *The details are ordered in a clear sequence.* Chronological ordering often works best in a narrative, because it enables readers to follow the events as they occurred. But for special emphasis, the sequence can sometimes be revised (as in the paragraph from Willie Morris, pages 242–243).

5. *The coherence of a narrative depends mostly on the writer's use of consistent tense and point of view and on the use of transitions as time and sequence markers.* Instead of past tense, you might use present tense, to create a greater sense of

immediacy, making readers feel like actual participants (as in "A Funeral in Manitoba"). Also, decide whether you are writing from the point of view of a spectator (as in "A Funeral in Manitoba") or a participant (as in "Fallen Arches," pages 251–252), and stick to that one point of view. Review pages 144–146 for use of transitions.

Application 11–1

PARAGRAPH WARM-UPS: NARRATION THAT SIMPLY REPORTS

1. Think of an event you've witnessed that would interest your classmates. Using the paragraph on page 241 as a model, write an objective narrative reporting the story. Begin with an orienting sentence that places readers at the center of the action.

2. Assume that you have recently witnessed an event or accident in which someone has been accused of an offense. Because you are an objective witness, the authorities have asked you to write a short report, telling *exactly* what you saw. Your report will be used as evidence. Tell what happened without injecting personal impressions or interpretations.

Application 11–2

PARAGRAPH WARM-UPS: NARRATION THAT MAKES A POINT

1. Using George Orwell's paragraph on page 139 as a model, write a narrative about something you did that you instantly regretted. Allow your readers to *see* the event and to *share* your immediate feelings. If you decide not to state your point directly, be sure it is implied by the details of the story.

2. Tell about a recent experience or incident you witnessed that left a strong impression on you. Write for your classmates, and be sure to include the facts of the incident as well as your emotional reaction to it. In other words, give your audience enough details so that they will understand your reaction. Use Willie Morris's or Chris Adey's paragraph as a model, letting the details of the story imply your main point.

Application 11–3

ESSAY PRACTICE

Read this narrative essay and answer the questions that follow it.

Fallen Arches

[1]As my battered blue Ford pulled up alongside the golden arches, I did not pause to wonder why I was one of the many teenagers employed here. I sensed that there would be plenty of chances in the course of my eight-hour day to ponder why after a year and a half I was still working as a McDonald's crew person.

[2]On a normal eleven-to-seven shift, I would have anticipated both a lunch rush (an overflow of customers and not enough crew people) and a dinner rush. But realizing that this was a beautiful September Saturday, I knew there would only be one big rush, starting at eleven and finally ending at seven. "I should feel privileged," I thought, "after all, they only schedule the best workers to come in for the busiest part of the day." But somehow I didn't feel any better.

[3]Approaching the store by shuffling through endless Big Mac boxes and shake cups strewn about the parking lot, I caught a glimpse of my clean green image, reflected in McDonald's newly washed glass door. My creased green pants, baggy green shirt, and freshly white working shoes complemented my hair, which was neatly bundled up in my neat little green cap. My name tag, neatly secured in the upper right corner of my blouse, carried the slogan, "We do it all for you." I knew that all this mirror image of mine lacked was a neat, plastic smile.

[4]Opening the door, I entered a room filled with identically dressed crew people waiting on customers, sweeping floors, cleaning tables, emptying trash cans, doling out fresh hot french fries, toasting bakery fresh buns, and cooking 100 percent pure-beef hamburgers almost as quickly as the customers could stuff them down. All this to the tune of various buzzers signaling the happy workers to follow various procedures. The 12 hamburger patties lying on the grill had a buzzer sound exactly 20 seconds after being carefully laid on the hottest part of the grill. This buzzer prompted Mike, our "meatman," to sear in the juices (fat) of each individual meat patty. Forty seconds later, Mike turned the meat patties at the prodding of a second buzzer, and forty seconds and another buzzer after that Mike removed the meat from the grill that was set exactly 350 degrees F. Mike always moved quickly and efficiently. He was a human robot, capable of cooking $700 worth of food for

McDonald's in one hour. And of that $700, Mike would receive approximately $4.00.

⁵My appraisal of this scene was soon interrupted, however, when I heard a customer bellowing to the whole store that his hamburger had catsup and mustard on it, and that he had specifically told the counter person he did not like mustard. I didn't need to listen any further. The number-one rule at McDonald's is that the customer is always right. The crew person is always mistaken, and it is the job of the manager to soothe the temper of the dissatisfied customer. Soon the bellowing customer would receive a new hamburger with catsup only, and a "Be Our Guest" card entitling him "to one free hamburger and french fries." The customer would then walk away feeling satisfied, and the server at the counter, temporarily embarrassed, would then begin to scurry again.

⁶Realizing that it was near eleven, I started my walk toward the time clock, when I was confronted by an assistant manager, Ken. "How much money are you going to pull in this hour, Julie? The record for the highest window server is $272, but I'm sure that if you really try you can break it today." Remaining silent, I looked up into his serious, neat green eyes, listened to the click of the time clock signaling 11:00 A.M., and punched my time card, ready, I thought, to begin work. But then I hesitated. As if by instinct alone, I turned around, reached again for my card, and punched it out for the last time.

—Julie Morgan

Questions About Content

1. What is the double meaning implied in the title?

2. Why is there no thesis statement in the introduction?

3. Name three features that makes this essay interesting.

4. How does the introduction attract readers' attention?

5. What specific readers' questions are answered in the body section?

6. The closing sentence nails down, without directly stating it, the main point of the story. Express the point in your own words.

Questions About Organization

1. In a brief outline, list the major events in chronological order.

2. List five transitions and connectors that serve as time and space locators.

Questions About Style

1. What is the outstanding stylistic feature in this essay? Give an example.

2. Explain why the writer decides to use "plastic smile" instead of "friendly" or "pleasant" smile (paragraph 3); "bellowing" instead of "screaming" or "complaining" (paragraph 5); "serious" instead of "sincere" or "sparkling" (paragraph 6). Are these the most precise words to convey her meaning? At least two other words in this essay reinforce the writer's meaning. Identify them and discuss their specific roles. Why does she repeat "neat" so often?

3. The tone of this essay can be called *ironic* (the writer feels superior to her subject and shows contempt for it by saying one thing while clearly meaning another). Identify the most vivid words and phrases that create the ironic tone.

4. Are tone and details appropriate for the audience (the writer's classmates)? Explain.

RESPONDING TO YOUR READING

1. Explore your reactions to "A Funeral in Manitoba" (pages 247–248) by using the questions on page 93. Then respond with your own narrative essay. You might share with readers some ritual or ceremony in your family or community, a ritual that you consider particularly meaningful or meaningless. Or you might want to tell about a ceremony you attended that changed your way of thinking or feeling about something. Or you might tell about an initiation ceremony for some organization.

   Perhaps you will want your narrative to show that the ceremony or ritual has a place in human experience, or is merely silly or destructive. Or perhaps your viewpoint will be less definite, and you will want to show how the event left you feeling confused or ambivalent. You might then let readers discover for themselves the significance of the event.

   Whether you settle on one definite impression about the event ("This is dumb" or "This is important" or some such) or are left struggling with conflicting impressions, be sure your narrative states or clearly implies a viewpoint.

2. Sometimes we all make judgments that seem to outsiders (and maybe even to ourselves!) split-second decisions—actually based on earlier events.

Write a narrative essay to a stipulated audience (classmates, close friend, parent, employer) telling of the events that led up to a decision you've made. Be sure that your treatment of the story (details, tone) is appropriate to the situation, audience, and purpose. Specific topics might include these decisions: to quit school, to hitchhike to Florida, to buy something extravagant, to do something dangerous, to run away from something, to challenge somebody, or to take a stand on an issue. Your goal could be to entertain a friendly reader or to placate an angry one. Be sure to identify your goal beforehand.

Your story should have a point. Describe the events in enough detail for readers to understand how you arrived at your decision. Include both your physical and your psychological sensations. To increase interest, begin with the action, saving the main point for last. Or, without stating the viewpoint directly, simply imply it in the narrative, as the writer of "Fallen Arches" did.

To avoid gaps in your narrative and to improve readability and coherence, limit the time of your story to a few hours or to no more than a day or two. For concreteness, try to show people talking.

3. "Back At the Ranch" (pages 244–247) proves that an essay about "What I Did Last Summer" can be much more than a tired list of worn-out images and travel clichés—that telling our own story *can* make a difference.

    Explore your reactions to this essay by using the page 93 questions. Then respond with your own narrative about an event that has made a difference in your life. Work to recapture for us the force of the event and its impact on you. Tell us all about what happened, but be sure to let us know what *meaning* the event ultimately had for you.

OPTIONS FOR ESSAY WRITING

1. Assume that you are applying for your first professional job after college. Respond to the following request from the job application:

    Each of us has been confronted by an "impossible situation"—a job that appeared too big to complete, a situation that seemed too awkward to handle, or a problem that felt too complex to deal with. Describe such a situation and how you dealt with it. Your narrative should make a point about the situation, problem solving, or yourself.

2. Use Norman Mailer's essay (page 116) as a model for a narrative/descriptive essay about an unforgettable event.

3. Tell about the most disillusioning experience of your life and how it has affected you.

4. Tell about the event that has caused you the greatest guilt and how you have dealt with that guilt.

12

Explaining Through Examples: Illustration

Examples are among the most powerful tools for explaining what you mean. We can see how examples work by looking at this next example. Assume that you've expressed this viewpoint:

Topic or thesis statement   Commercial television is not all bad.

You can anticipate that your readers will respond with questions such as these:

Readers' questions   What makes you think so?

Can you give me examples I can grasp?

Your readers, in other words, expect definite and specific instances of what they could accept as "good commercial television." Examples give the evidence that enables readers to understand and accept your viewpoint.

Uses and Types of Examples

The backbone of explanation, examples are concrete and specific instances of a writer's main point. The best way to explain what you mean by an "inspiring teacher" is to use one of your professors as an

256

example. You might illustrate this professor's qualities by describing several of her teaching strategies. Or you might give an extended example (say, how she helped you develop confidence). Either way, you have made the abstract notion "inspiring teacher" concrete and thus understandable—you have made your meaning clear. (Notice how the main point in this paragraph is clarified by the professor example.)

In your school and workplace writing, you will use examples time and time again. For a psychology course, you might give examples of paranoid behavior among world leaders; for an ecology course, of tree species threatened by acid rain—and so on. In the workplace, you might give examples of how the software developed by your company can be used for medical diagnosis, of how your community can provide a favorable economic climate for new industry, or the like. Whenever readers need evidence to understand or accept an assertion, examples are essential.

Examples do more than clarify meaning. They also make writing more interesting and convincing. Here is a paragraph without examples.

> [1]The irony of the emphasis being placed on careers is that nothing is more valuable for anyone who has had a professional or vocational education than to be able to deal with abstractions or complexities, or to feel comfortable with subtleties of thought or language, or to think sequentially. [2]People who have such skills will have a major advantage in just about any career. [3]In all these respects, the liberal arts have much to offer. [4]Just in terms of career preparation, therefore, a student is shortchanging himself or herself by shortcutting the humanities.

The writer of this paragraph fails to persuade us that a liberal arts education is vital, because the paragraph never gets below the highest level of generality—all *telling*, no *showing*. Sentences 2 and 3 provide no information to clarify and support the opening and closing points. Any reader will be left with unanswered questions.

> What do you mean by "abstractions or complexities," "subtleties of thought or language," or "to think sequentially"?

> How, exactly, do students "shortchange" themselves by shortcutting the humanities?

> Can you show me how a liberal arts education is useful in one's career?

Here is a version of the same paragraph, this time developed with examples (in italics) that answer readers' questions:

Main point (1)	[1]The irony of the emphasis being placed on careers is that nothing is more valuable for anyone who has had a professional or vocational education than to be able to deal with abstractions or complexities, or to feel comfortable with subtleties of thought or language, or to think
Examples (2–5)	sequentially. [2]*The doctor* who knows only disease is at a disadvantage alongside the doctor who knows at least as much about people as [he or she] does about pathological organisms. [3]*The lawyer* who argues in court from a narrow legal base is no match for the lawyer who can connect legal precedents to historical experience and who employs wide-ranging intellectual resources. [4]*The business executive* whose competence in general management is bolstered by an artistic ability to deal with people is of prime value to [her] company. [5]For *the technologist*, the engineering
Summary of examples (6) **Concluding point (7)**	of consent can be just as important as the engineering of moving parts. [6]In all these respects, the liberal arts have much to offer. [7]Just in terms of career preparation, therefore, a student is shortchanging himself by shortcutting the humanities. [*emphasis added*]

—Norman Cousins

The first version only *tells*, whereas the second *shows* as well. The examples convince us that the author has a valid point.

In developing his paragraph, the author had to answer questions of his own:

How much should I say?

Which details will best clarify my meaning?

How can I be sure that I don't say too much?

By anticipating readers' questions about his main point, the writer was able to put himself in their place. From this perspective he could decide on kinds and number of examples. He chose examples from four major fields (medicine, law, business, and technology), deciding that these four would be enough to get his point across. Additional (or less familiar) examples might only have confused or overwhelmed readers. Seeing things from a reader's perspective is a writer's best guidance for developing any type of message.

In contrast to the humanities paragraph, with its series of brief examples, here is a paragraph developed through an extended example:

Main point (1)
Extended example of the problem (2–6)

[1]This seems to be an era of gratuitous inventions and negative improvements. [2]Consider the beer can. [3]It was beautiful—as beautiful as the clothespin, as inevitable as the wine bottle, as dignified and reassuring as the fire hydrant. [4]A tranquil cylinder of delightfully resonant metal, it could be opened in an instant, requiring only the application of a hand gadget freely dispensed by any grocer. [5]Who can forget the small, symmetrical thrill of these two triangular punctures, the dainty *pfff*, the little crest of suds that foamed eagerly in the exultation of release? [6]Now we are given, instead, a top beetling with an ugly, shmoo-shaped "tab," which, after fiercely resisting the tugging, bleeding fingers of the thirsty [person], threatens [the] lips with a dangerous and hideous hole. [7]However, we have discovered a way to thwart Progress, usually so unthwartable. [8]*Turn the beer can upside down and open the bottom.* [9]The bottom is still the way the top used to be. [10]True, this operation gives the beer an unsettling jolt, and the sight of a consistently inverted beer can might make people edgy, not to say queasy. [11]But the latter difficulty could be eliminated if manufacturers would design cans that looked the same whichever end was up, like playing cards. [12]What we need is Progress with an escape hatch.

Extended example of the solution (8–11)

Conclusion (12)

—John Updike

To support his main point about "gratuitous inventions and negative improvements," the author selects the beer can as a familiar example. His purpose, however, is not only to point out the problem but to offer a solution, as well. Thus the two extended examples follow a logical order: from *problem* to *solution*.

A narrative also can serve as an extended example. The sample paragraph on page 141 uses a brief narrative to illustrate the point that television is a potent brainwashing medium.

Good examples have persuasive value; they give readers something to hold on to, a way of understanding even the most surprising or unlikely assertion. This essay relies on well-chosen examples to justify a new way of looking at old junk—to explain why the writer "saves" things she no longer needs.

My Time Capsule

I always seem to be searching for the right change at checkout counters. The situation is familiar enough: my purchase totals something that involves a few extra pennies, so I open my little brown purse and begin digging for the correct coins. After a few minutes of rummaging through assorted junk, I come up red-faced and empty-handed. But despite my repeated frustrations, I just can't bring myself to clean that purse. I guess I hang on to things I don't need because some of my worst junk holds vivid memories. If someone were to find the purse, they would have a record of my recent life—a kind of time capsule.

For instance, in my purse is an old car key. It belonged to my '73 Chevy, a car that rarely started on cold mornings. I still remember the hours I spent huddled on that frosty front seat, flicking the ignition key on and off, pumping the accelerator, and muttering various profanities every time the engine refused to turn over. Even though I junked the car last year, I still (Who knows why?) keep the key in my so-called change purse.

Whenever I dig for coins, I always encounter the torn half-ticket I've been saving for several years, a ticket to the Broadway musical *The King and I*. The famous Yul Brynner was outstanding in his vintage role as the King of Siam. Unfortunately, though, I had to miss a good part of the show simply because I needed to use the bathroom at the same time as half the audience. And much of what I did see was obscured by the green, porcupine hairdo on the guy in front of me. From my view behind Mr. Porcupine, the actors looked like they were in the woods. But because of Yul, I guess, I keep my ticket stub—in my purse, of course.

Somewhere near the key and the ticket sits another artifact: the coat button that came undone earlier this year (the same button I always initially mistake for a coin). The button helps me remember the day I wore not only a turtleneck sweater, but also two scarves for one of last winter's coldest days. Like a fool, I tried tying my coat collar around what had now become a 20-inch neck. Naturally, the button popped off, and naturally, it got thrown into my purse.

For weeks I've been buying "micro-rays-of-hope" toward millionaire-hood in the state's lottery game. I can't resist playing my usual six numbers on Wednesdays and Saturdays—even though I always lose. *Not winning* poses no real problem for me, but kissing my obsolete ticket good-bye does. Somehow the act of throwing away even a losing ticket symbolizes admitting defeat. It means the state's racket has caught another sucker. It means my latest tangible flash of financial hope must sit among the soggy potato skins in my garbage pail. So I "temporarily" save my defunct tickets by folding them neatly away in my purse. Every time I see them, I'm reminded of the many times I COULD have become a millionaire.

I'm convinced that the passing of time is directly related to the bloatedness of my change purse because it's forever expanding. In fact, if I opened it right now, I'd find many more memories than the few I've mentioned. I'd see the semi-wrapped sourball I almost ate, until I realized it was lime green. I'd find the three unmated earrings, each with its own life history. I'd rediscover the safety pin that once saved me from awful embarrassment. And my old pen cap (minus the pen), a golf tee, a packet of sugar, and a few expired coupons would all be in there, all with legends of their own.

Even though I'm a slow learner, I know now that metal money belongs not in a purse but in a piggy bank. I'll never have to worry about a coin in my time capsule again—unless, of course, it's my old Susan B. Anthony quarter. But that's another story.

—Gina Ciolfi

Ciolfi challenges our assumptions about the value of junk-filled purses by giving us a catalog of her buried treasures. Her explanation relies on an engaging array of extended examples, followed by a series of brief examples (next-to-last paragraph).

Guidelines for Using Examples

All illustrations, whether paragraphs or essays, are developed according to these guidelines:

1. *All examples serve the writer's purpose and the readers' needs.* An effective example fits the point it is designed to illustrate. Also, the example is familiar and forceful enough for readers to recognize and remember.

2. *The example is always more specific and concrete than the point it illustrates.* Most vivid examples are at the lowest level of generality and abstraction.

3. *Examples in a series are arranged in an accessible order.* If your illustration is a narrative or some historical catalog, the examples are ordered chronologically. Otherwise, a "least-to-most" (least-to-most-dramatic or important or useful, and so on) order works well. Placing the most striking example last ensures greatest effect.

4. *Effective writers know "how much is enough."* Overexplaining is a good way to insult a reader's intelligence.

Application 12–1

PARAGRAPH WARM-UP: EXPLAINING THROUGH ILLUSTRATION

Assume your campus newspaper is inviting contributions for a new section called "Insights," a weekly collection of one-paragraph essays by students. This new section has two goals:

1. to provide a forum for fresh points of view
2. to raise readers' consciousness, helping them think more incisively about the world

Each paragraph in this section should be designed to share a specific insight the writer has gained by close observation of campus life, American values, habits, or the like. Using the paragraph by Cousins or Updike as a model, write such a paragraph for the newspaper.

Application 12–2

ESSAY PRACTICE

The following essay appeared in *Newsweek* magazine. Read this essay, and answer the questions that follow it. Then select one of the essay assignments.

A Case of "Severe Bias"

[1]This is who I am not. I am not a crack addict. I am not a welfare mother. I am not illiterate. I am not a prostitute. I have never been in jail. My children are not in gangs. My husband doesn't beat me. My home is not a tenement. None of these things defines who I am, nor do they describe the other black people I've known and worked with and loved and befriended over these 40 years of my life.

[2]Nor does it describe most of black America, period.

[3]Yet in the eyes of the American news media, this is what black America is: poor, criminal, addicted and dysfunctional. Indeed, media coverage of black America is so one-sided, so imbalanced that

the most victimized and hurting segment of the black community—
a small segment, at best—is presented not as the exception but as
the norm. It is an insidious practice, all the uglier for its blatancy.

⁴In recent months, oftentimes in this very magazine, I have
observed a steady offering of media reports on crack babies, gang
warfare, violent youth, poverty and homelessness—and in most
cases, the people featured in the photos and stories were black. At
the same time, articles that discuss other aspects of American life—
from home buying to medicine to technology to nutrition—rarely, if
ever, show blacks playing a positive role, or for that matter, any role
at all.

⁵Day after day, week after week, this message—that black
America is dysfunctional and unwhole—gets transmitted across the
American landscape. Sadly, as a result, America never learns the
truth about what is actually a wonderful, vibrant, creative
community of people.

⁶Most black Americans are *not* poor. Most black teenagers are
not crack addicts. Most black mothers are *not* on welfare. Indeed, in
sheer numbers, more *white* Americans are poor and on welfare than
are black. Yet one never would deduce that by watching television or
reading American newspapers and magazines.

⁷Why does the American media insist on playing this myopic,
inaccurate picture game? In this game, white America is always
whole and lovely and healthy while black America is usually sick
and pathetic and deficient. Rarely, indeed, is black America ever
depicted in the media as functional and self-sufficient. The free
press, indeed, as the main interpreter of American culture and
American experience, holds the mirror on American reality—so
much so that what the media says is *is*, even if it's not that way at
all. The media is guilty of a severe bias and the problem screams out
for correction. It is worse than simply lazy journalism, which is bad
enough; it is inaccurate journalism.

⁸For black Americans like myself, this isn't just an issue of
vanity—of wanting to be seen in a good light. Nor is it a matter of
closing one's eyes to the very real problems of the urban
underclass—which undeniably is disproportionately black. To be
sure, problems besetting the black underclass deserve the utmost
attention of the media, as well as the understanding and concern of
the rest of American society.

⁹But if their problems consistently are presented as the *only*
reality for blacks, any other experience known to the black
community ceases to have validity, or to be real. In this scenario,
millions of blacks are relegated to a sort of twilight zone, where who
we are and what we are isn't based on fact but on image and
perception. That's what it feels like to be a black American whose

lifestyle is outside of the aberrant behavior that the media presents as the norm.

[10]For many of us, life is a curious series of encounters with white people who want to know why we are "different" from other blacks—when, in fact, most of us are only "different" from the now common negative images of black life. So pervasive are these images that they aren't just perceived as the norm, they're *accepted* as the norm.

[11]I am reminded, for example, of the controversial Spike Lee film, "Do the Right Thing," and the criticism by some movie reviewers that the film's ghetto neighborhood isn't populated by addicts and drug pushers—and thus is not a true depiction.

[12]In fact, millions of black Americans live in neighborhoods where the most common sights are children playing and couples walking their dogs. In my own inner-city neighborhood in Denver—an area that the local press consistently describes as "gang territory"—I have yet to see a recognizable "gang" member or any "gang" activity (drug dealing or drive-by shootings), nor have I been the victim of "gang violence."

[13]Yet to students of American culture—in the case of Spike Lee's film, the movie reviewers—a black, inner-city neighborhood can only be one thing to be real: drug-infested and dysfunctioning. Is this my ego talking? In part, yes. For the millions of black people like myself—ordinary, hard-working, law-abiding, tax-paying Americans—the media's blindness to the fact that we even exist, let alone to our contributions to American society, is a bitter cup to drink. And as self-reliant as most black Americans are—because we've had to be self-reliant—even the strongest among us still crave affirmation.

[14]I want that. I want it for my children. I want it for all the beautiful, healthy, funny, smart black Americans I have known and loved over the years.

[15]And I want it for the rest of America, too.

[16]I want America to know us—all of us—for who we really are. To see us in all of our complexity, our subtleness, our artfulness, our enterprise, our specialness, our loveliness, our American-ness. That is the real portrait of black America—that we're strong people, surviving people, capable people. That may be the best-kept secret in America. If so, it's time to let the truth be known.

—Patricia Raybon

Questions About Content

1. Where is the thesis? Why does it come at that point in the essay? Is this an effective placement of the thesis? Explain.

2. Is this essay convincing? Does it adequately support the thesis? Explain.

3. Identify one paragraph developed through an extended example and one through a series of brief examples.

4. Should the examples be more specific? Why, or why not?

Questions About Organization

1. Is Raybon's opening effective? Explain.

2. Are the two single-sentence paragraphs appropriate? Explain.

3. Is this essay organized to provide the best emphasis? Explain.

Questions About Style

1. Name an outstanding style feature of this essay. Explain, and give examples.

2. How would you characterize the tone of this essay? Is it appropriate for the audience and purpose? Explain, and give examples.

RESPONDING TO YOUR READING

1. Explore your reactions to "My Time Capsule" (pages 260–261) by using the questions on page 93. Then respond with an essay of your own, relying on examples to support your viewpoint.

   You might show readers the worth you perceive in things that seem unimportant to most people. Maybe you keep some childhood toys, or clothes that no longer fit, or "junk" that holds special meaning for you only.

   Or you might challenge readers' assumptions by asserting a surprising or unorthodox viewpoint: that some "natural" foods can be hazardous, that television game shows can be truly educational, that "growing up" is something to be dreaded, that exercise can be bad for health, or that so-called advances in medical science or electronics make us worse off.

   Or maybe you want to talk about examples of things that make you angry or sad or happy or frightened, or things too many of us take for granted. Whatever your topic, be sure your examples illustrate and explain a definite viewpoint.

2. Explore your reactions to "A Case of Severe Bias" by using the questions on page 93. Then respond with an essay of your own, using powerful examples to make your point.

Perhaps someone has misjudged or stereotyped you or a group you belong to. If so, set the record straight in a forceful essay to a specified audience. Or perhaps you can think of other types of media messages that seem to present a distorted or inaccurate view (say, certain commercials or sports reporting or war movies, and so on). For instance, do certain movies or TV programs give the wrong message? Give your readers examples they can recognize and remember.

OPTIONS FOR ESSAY WRITING

1. Write a human interest article for your campus newspaper in which you discuss some feature of our society that you find humorous, depressing, contemptible, or admirable. Subjects might include our eating habits, our consumer habits, our suburban living habits, our idea of a vacation, the cars we drive, how we show our patriotism, how we exercise, how we follow fads, how we dress, how we ignore the elderly, how we exploit minorities, how we create heroes, how we exercise our freedom of speech, or our obsession with gadgets. Provide at least three well-developed examples to support your thesis.

2. What pleases or disappoints you most about college life? Illustrate the causes to your parents (or some other specific audience) with at least three examples.

3. Suppose you were a filmmaker for a group that wanted to explain American life as honestly as possible to a small nation whose people know little about us. Your assignment is to make three five-minute movies, each about a feature of American life, the three together intended to give a typical view of America. What would be the subjects of your three segments? Indicate why you chose each subject. Write a description of each movie.

4. Assume that, as a freshman, you've been assigned a faculty adviser, a caring sociology professor who likes to know as much as possible about his advisees. He asks each student to write an essay on this topic:

    Is your hometown (city, section of a city) a good or bad place for a young adult to live?

    Notice that the professor has not asked you to write about yourself directly (as you might in a personal narrative); rather, she has solicited your judgment. Support your response with specific and concrete examples that will convince the reader of your sound judgment.

5. "Clothes make the person." Assess the validity of this statement, supporting your thesis with examples.

6. What makes a good friend? Cite examples to back up your thesis.

7. What would you take with you in a catastrophe? Give detailed examples, and explain your choices.

8. Pierre, a French teenager who plans to attend an American university, has asked what the typical American college student is like. He has inquired about interests, values, leisure activities, attitudes, and tastes. Selecting several characteristics *you* think typify American college students, write a response to Pierre.

9. How are groups of people (women, minorities, young or old people) stereotyped by the media? Select a group, and give detailed examples of their portrayal by the media.

10. Assume you have been commissioned to write a magazine article predicting how something in society will have changed by the year 2010. Focus on *one* area (life-styles, science, education, transportation, space travel, medicine, politics, the environment, our diet, or something else), and describe how that area will differ in 2010.

11. Besides your family, who or what has influenced you most? Give specific examples to show how you have been influenced.

12. Serials and series have become a very popular type of television program. Weekly or daily shows such as "Days of Our Lives," "Twin Peaks," "Northern Exposure," and "General Hospital" attract faithful viewers who enjoy episodes in the lives of a group of fictional characters.

    Select a series that you particularly enjoyed at some time during the last few years, and write an essay in which you discuss the elements in the show that made it interesting or appealing.

    If you are that rare individual who never tuned in regularly to a series, write about the appeal of some other leisure activity you enjoyed while others were watching television.

13. Americans generally consider themselves thrifty and efficient. Yet wastefulness is rampant in the American life-style: machines are built to be obsolete within five years; usable clothes are discarded; disposable items clog our landfills; energy and natural resources are wasted.

    Are the above statements justified? If so, what do they tell us about ourselves? Explain and defend your answer, using examples from your reading, study, or observation.

13

Explaining Parts and Categories: Division and Classification

Combined Strategies • Using Division
• Guidelines for Division • Using Classification
• Guidelines for Classification • Applications

Sometimes we divide one thing into parts to make sense of it; at other times we group an assortment of things into categories to sort them out. Division and classification are the two strategies for sorting things out. Although these two activities often go hand-in-hand, each serves a distinct purpose. *Division* deals with *one* thing. Its purpose is to separate that thing into parts, pieces, sections, or categories (say, a paragraph or essay divided into introduction, body, and conclusion). *Classification* has to do with an *assortment* of things that have some similarities. Its purpose is to group these things systematically (say, a record collection sorted into categories—jazz, rock, country and western, classical, and pop).

We use division and classification almost every day. Assume that you are shopping for a refrigerator. If you are mechanically inclined, you will probably begin by thinking about the major parts that make up a refrigerator: storage compartment, cooling element, motor, insulation, and exterior casing. With individual parts identified, you can now ask questions about them to determine the efficiency or quality of each part in different kinds of refrigerators. You have divided the refrigerator into its components.

You then shop at five stores and come home with a list of 20 refrigerators that seem to be built from high-quality parts. You now try to make sense out of your list by grouping items according to selected characteristics. First, you divide your list into three classes according to size in cubic feet of capacity: small refrigerators, middle-sized refrigerators, and large refrigerators. But size is not the only criterion. You want economy, too, and so you group the refrigerators according to cost. Or you might classify them according to color, weight, energy efficiency, and so on, depending on your purpose. Here is how division and classification are related:

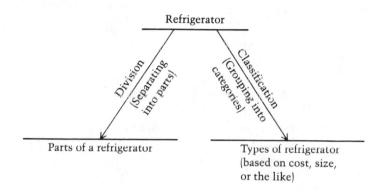

These two ways of sorting also can be used for more abstract things. You might divide a day into daytime and nighttime or into morning, afternoon, and evening. Or, for other purposes, you may want to classify days, sorting them as good days and bad days, or profitable days and unprofitable days, and so on.

Whether you choose to apply division or classification can depend on your purpose. An architect called upon to design a library will think almost entirely of division. Once she has defined the large enclosed area that is needed, she must identify the parts into which that space must be divided: the reference area, reading areas, storage areas, checkout facilities, and office space. In some kinds of libraries she might consider providing space for special groups of users (such as reading areas for children). In very large libraries she might need to carry the division further into specialized kinds of space (such as highly secure areas for rare manuscripts or special collections, or areas with special acoustic provisions for listening to recorded materials). But however simple or complex her problem, she is thinking now only about the appropriate division of *space*. She does not have to worry about how the library will classify its books and other material.

But classification is one of the library staff's main problems. The purpose of a library is not only to store books and other forms of information, but above all to make the information retrievable. In order for us to find a book or item, the thousands or millions of books stored in the library must be arranged in logical categories. That arrangement becomes possible only if the books are carefully classified.

Combined Strategies

Taken from a university's *Career Handbook*, this essay incorporates both classification and division as ways of explaining the major career specialties in computer science.

Computer Scientists: A Classification

Computer scientists deal with the software (programming) end of computer technology. They hold B.S. degrees from accredited schools, with majors in software engineering or computer science. The curriculum focuses on the logic and language of programming, and, briefly, on the hardware of the machine. (Programming is the process of instructing computers to perform various applications. A program defines in complete and minute detail just what the computer is to do in particular circumstances.)

Computer scientists play major roles in science, government, and business. Their programs might be used for guiding satellites, developing federal and state budgets, controlling inventories, making and confirming reservations, or grading examinations— among countless other uses. This broad demand for programs creates a diversity of job opportunities. The major specialties within computer science can be grouped into three categories: systems programming, applications programming, and systems analysis.

Systems programmers write programs that run the computer equipment itself. These programs act as an interface (connector) between the machines and the users' programs. Examples of systems programs include those that control the computer's operating system, monitor, printer, and interpreter. Much systems programming is done in machine language (using a binary-number system: 0's and 1's).

The job of the applications programmer overlaps with that of the systems programmer in that both entail the same type of programming logic, but for different purposes and in different codes (languages). Applications programs put the computer to work on specific jobs such as keeping track of accounts in banks and insurance companies. These programs act as an interface between the systems program and the user. Applications programs usually are written in high-level languages (COBOL, Pascal, BASIC, FORTRAN, etc.).

Systems analysts are the organizers. They monitor the systems and applications programs, and are responsible for eliminating any bugs (program failures). Instead of actually writing the programs, systems analysts update those written by systems programmers, as required. They may also analyze an organization's particular needs, and write specifications for a computer system. These specifications are then given to a programmer. Systems analysts require several years of experience as programmers.

In any role, computer scientists are responsible for analyzing a problem, and then reducing it to the sequence of small, deliberate steps the computer can use to solve the problem.

—Armand Dumont

This essayist groups the career specialties into three individual categories and, in the final paragraph, divides the collective specialties into the major tasks they have in common. Whenever readers need help sorting things out, division and classification are indispensable.

Using Division

As a development strategy, division answers these questions for readers:

What are its parts?

What is it made of?

In this paragraph, the author uses division to explain his view of the ideal education.

Lead-in to main point (1–3)	[1]It is perhaps idle to wonder what, from my present point of view, would have been an ideal education. [2]If I could provide such a curriculum for my children they, in their turn, might find it all a bore. [3]But the fantasy of what I would have liked to learn as a child may be revealing, since I feel unequipped by education for problems that lie outside the cloistered, literary domain in
Main point (4)	which I am competent and at home. [4]Looking back, then, I would have arranged for myself to be taught survival techniques for both natural and

Parts of the "ideal education" (5)

urban wildernesses. [5]I would want to have been instructed in self-hypnosis, in aikido (the esoteric and purely self-defensive style of judo), in elementary medicine, in sexual hygiene, in vegetable gardening, in astronomy, navigation, and sailing; in cookery and clothesmaking, in metalwork and carpentry, in drawing and painting, in printing and typography, in botany and biology, in optics and acoustics, in semantics and psychology, in mysticism and yoga, in electronics and mathematical fantasy, in drama and dancing, in singing and in playing an instrument by ear; in wandering, in advanced daydreaming, in prestidigitation, in techniques of escape from bondage, in disguise, in conversation with birds and beasts, in ventriloquism, in French and German conversation, in planetary history, in **Most important part** morphology,* and in Classical Chinese. [6]Actually, **(6)** the main thing left out of my education was a proper love for my own body, because one feared to cherish anything so obviously mortal and prone to sickness.

—Alan Watts

Moving on from a topic statement that *tells*, the author *shows* by dividing the *ideal education* into specific kinds of instruction. In developing his message, the author followed the guidelines listed here.

Guidelines for Division

1. *The division is applied to a singular subject.* Only one thing at a time can be divided (*ideal education;* not *ideal education and ideal career*).

2. *The division is consistent with the writer's purpose.* The author could have divided education in countless ways: into primary, secondary, and higher education; into vocational and liberal education; into social sciences, humanities, sciences, and mathematics—and so on. But his purpose was to explain a view that goes beyond traditional categories. And we are given the "parts" of an education that we may not yet have considered.

---

*The structure of organisms.

3. *The division is complete in serving the writer's purpose.* Only 100 percent of something can be divided, and the parts, in turn, should add up to 100 percent. If a part is omitted, the writer should say so (*"some* of the parts of an ideal education"). For his purposes, the author above includes all the parts.

4. *The subject is subdivided as far as needed to make the point.* The author's first division is into survival techniques for (a) natural and (b) urban wildernesses. He then subdivides each of these into the specific parts listed in sentences 5 and 6. If he had stopped after the first division, he would not have made his point.

5. *The division follows a logical order.* In sentence 5 the parts of an ideal education range from practical to recreational to intellectual skills. In sentence 6 the most important part is saved for last—to provide emphasis.

Using Classification

Whereas division identifies the parts of one thing, classification sorts a group of related things into categories, thereby answering the readers' question:

In what categories do *X*, *Y*, and *Z* belong?

You ask this same question in looking through the college catalog for courses that fulfill specific requirements.

The next paragraph uses classification to explain how television commercials distort and degrade the image of American women. (Both men and women are mentioned in the topic statement because this paragraph is part of an essay discussing images of men as well as of women. One main idea can serve more than one paragraph.)

Main point (1)   ¹In the guise of what they consider comedy, the producers of television commercials have created a loathsome gallery of men and women patterned, presumably, on Mr. and Mrs. America.

Supporting point (2)   ²Women liberationists have a major target in the commercial image of women flashed hourly and daily to the vast majority. ³There are, indeed, only

Categories of women in television commercials (3)   four kinds of females in this relentless sales procession: the gorgeous teen-age swinger with bouncing locks; the young mother teaching her

Supporting point and lead-in to final classification (4–5)

Categories of women not shown in commercials (6)

baby girl the right soap for skin care; the middle-aged housewife with a voice like a power saw; and the old lady with dentures and irregularity. [4]All these women, to be sure, exist. [5]But between the swinging sex object and the constipated granny there are millions of females never shown in commercials. [6]These are—married or single—intelligent, sensitive women who bring charm to their homes, who work at jobs as well as lend grace to their marriage, who support themselves, who have talents or hobbies or commitments, or who are skilled at their professions.

—Marya Mannes

In developing her message, the author followed guidelines that govern any classification.

Guidelines for Classification

1. *The classification is applied to a plural subject.* Here, the subject is American women.

2. *The basis of the classification is consistent with the writer's purpose.* To make her point, this author used two bases: first, she classified women by their roles in television commercials; next, by the many other actual roles that women fill. For a different purpose, she might have classified women by occupation or level of education or political persuasion, and so on.

3. *The classification is complete (according to its basis).* Because television commercials only pretend to provide enough role categories to account for all women, the author completes the classification with her own categories in sentence 6.

4. *The categories are arranged in logical order.* The advertisers' categories move from youth to old age. The author's categories come last, to provide the best emphasis for her point.

5. *The categories do not overlap.* If the author had added the category of *mindless female* to the four stereotypes that she identifies in television commercials, her classification would overlap, because all four categories could be included in the stereotype *mindless female*.

As further illustration of overlapping categories, suppose a supermarket classified its meats as *pork*, *beef*, *ham*, and *lamb*. This classification would overlap because ham is a product of pork meat rather than an exclusive category.

Application 13–1

PARAGRAPH WARM-UPS: DIVISION

1. Assume that your social life is less than desirable because you are new in town, are shy, and haven't met many people. You decide to contact a dating service for professional help in meeting a companion. Among the forms you are given to complete is this statement: "In one paragraph, describe the qualities you desire in an ideal companion." Write the paragraph according to the "Guidelines for Division" on page 272.

2. Using the paragraph on pages 271–272 as a model, write a paragraph for the college curriculum committee, explaining your idea of an ideal education.

Application 13–2

PARAGRAPH WARM-UP OR ESSAY PRACTICE: CLASSIFICATION

As a work-study student, you are helping prepare the orientation for next year's incoming freshmen. Your supervisor asks you to write a paragraph (or essay, if your instructor requires) outlining the jobs available to graduates in your major. Your piece will be published in a career pamphlet for new students. Write the piece. (You may need to do some library research for this assignment. A good source would be *The Occupational Outlook Handbook*.)

Application 13–3

ESSAY PRACTICE

Read this essay, and answer the questions that follow it. Then select one of the essay assignments.

Friends, Good Friends—and Such Good Friends

Women are friends, I once would have said, when they   1
totally love and support and trust each other, and bare to each
other the secrets of their souls, and run—no questions asked—
to help each other, and tell harsh truths to each other (no, you
can't wear that dress unless you lose ten pounds first) when
harsh truths must be told.

Women are friends, I once would have said, when they   2
share the same affection for Ingmar Bergman, plus train rides,
cats, warm rain, charades, Camus, and hate with equal ardor
Newark and Brussels sprouts and Lawrence Welk and camping.

In other words, I once would have said that a friend is a   3
friend all the way, but now I believe that's a narrow point of
view. For the friendships I have and the friendships I see are
conducted at many levels of intensity, serve many different
functions, meet different needs and range from those as all-the-
way as the friendship of the soul sisters mentioned above to
that of the most nonchalant and casual playmates.

Consider these varieties of friendship: 4

1. Convenience friends. These are the women with   5
whom, if our paths weren't crossing all the time, we'd have no
particular reason to be friends: a next-door neighbor, a woman
in our car pool, the mother of one of our children's closest
friends or maybe some mommy with whom we serve juice and
cookies each week at the Glenwood Co-op Nursery.

Convenience friends are convenient indeed. They'll lend   6
us their cups and silverware for a party. They'll drive our kids
to soccer when we're sick. They'll take us to pick up our car
when we need a lift to the garage. They'll even take our cats
when we go on vacation. As we will for them.

But we don't, with convenience friends, ever come too   7
close or tell too much; we maintain our public face and
emotional distance. "Which means," says Elaine, "that I'll talk
about being overweight but not about being depressed. Which
means I'll admit being mad but not blind with rage. Which
means I might say that we're pinched this month but never
that I'm worried sick over money."

But which doesn't mean that there isn't sufficient value to   8
be found in these friendships of mutual aid, in convenience
friends.

2. Special-interest friends. These friendships aren't   9
intimate, and they needn't involve kids or silverware or cats.
Their value lies in some interest jointly shared. And so we may

have an office friend or a yoga friend or a tennis friend or a friend from the Women's Democratic Club.

"I've got one woman friend," says Joyce, "who likes, as I do, to take psychology courses. Which makes it nice for me— and nice for her. It's fun to go with someone you know and it's fun to discuss what you've learned, driving back from the classes." And for the most part, she says, that's all they discuss.   10

"I'd say that what we're doing is *doing* together, not being together," Suzanne says of her Tuesday-doubles friends. "It's mainly a tennis relationship, but we play together well. And I guess we all need to have a couple of playmates."   11

I agree.   12

My playmate is a shopping friend, a woman of marvelous taste, a woman who knows exactly *where* to buy *what*, and furthermore is a woman who always knows beyond a doubt what one ought to be buying. I don't have the time to keep up with what's new in eyeshadow, hemlines and shoes and whether the smock look is in or finished already. But since (oh, shame!) I care a lot about eyeshadow, hemlines and shoes, and since I don't *want* to wear smocks if the smock look is finished, I'm very glad to have a shopping friend.   13

3. Historical friends. We all have a friend who knew us when . . . maybe way back in Miss Meltzer's second grade, when our family lived in that three-room flat in Brooklyn, when our dad was out of work for seven months, when our brother Allie got in that fight where they had to call the police, when our sister married the endodontist from Yonkers and when, the morning after we lost our virginity, she was the first, the only, friend we told.   14

The years have gone by and we've gone separate ways and we've little in common now, but we're still an intimate part of each other's past. And so whenever we go to Detroit we always go to visit this friend of our girlhood. Who knows how we looked before our teeth were straightened. Who knows how we talked before our voice got un-Brooklyned. Who knows what we ate before we learned about artichokes. And who, by her presence, puts us in touch with an earlier part of ourself, a part of ourself it's important never to lose.   15

"What this friend means to me and what I mean to her," says Grace, "is having a sister without sibling rivalry. We know the texture of each other's lives. She remembers my grandmother's cabbage soup. I remember the way her uncle played the piano. There's simply no other friend who remembers those things."   16

4. Crossroads friends. Like historical friends, our   17

crossroads friends are important for *what was*—for the
friendship we shared at a crucial, now past, time of life. A
time, perhaps, when we roomed in college together; or worked
as eager young singles in the Big City together; or went
together, as my friend Elizabeth and I did through pregnancy,
birth and that scary first year of new motherhood.

Crossroads friends forge powerful links, links strong   18
enough to endure with not much more contact than once-a-
year letters at Christmas. And out of respect for those
crossroads years, for those dramas and dreams we once shared,
we will always be friends.

5. Cross-generational friends. Historical friends and   19
crossroads friends seem to maintain a special kind of
intimacy—dormant but always ready to be revived—and
though we may rarely meet, whenever we do connect, it's
personal and intense. Another kind of intimacy exists in the
friendships that form across generations in what one woman
calls her daughter-mother and her mother-daughter
relationships.

Evelyn's friend is her mother's age—"but I share so much   20
more than I ever could with my mother"—a woman she talks
to of music, of books and of life. "What I get from her is the
benefit of her experience. What she gets—and enjoys—from
me is a youthful perspective. It's a pleasure for both of us."

I have in my own life a precious friend, a woman of 65   21
who has lived very hard, who is wise, who listens well; who has
been where I am and can help me understand it; and who
represents not only an ultimate ideal mother to me but also the
person I'd like to be when I grow up.

In our daughter role we tend to do more than our share of   22
self-revelation; in our mother role we tend to receive what's
revealed. It's another kind of pleasure—playing wise mother to
a questing younger person. It's another very lovely kind of
friendship.

6. Part-of-a-couple friends. Some of the women we call   23
our friends we never see alone—we see them as part of a
couple at couples' parties. And though we share interests in
many things and respect each other's views, we aren't moved to
deepen the relationship. Whatever the reason, a lack of time
or—and this is more likely—a lack of chemistry, our
friendship remains in the context of a group. But the fact that
our feeling on seeing each other is always, "I'm *so* glad she's
here" and the fact that we spend half the evening talking
together says that this too, in its own way, counts as a
friendship.

(Other part-of-a-couple friends are the friends that came   24
with the marriage, and some of these are friends we could live
without. But sometimes, alas, she married our husband's best
friend; and sometimes, alas, she *is* our husband's best friend.
And so we find ourself dealing with her, somewhat against our
will, in a spirit of what I'll call *reluctant* friendship.)

7. Men who are friends. I wanted to write just of women   25
friends, but the women I've talked to won't let me—they say I
must mention man-woman friendships too. For these
friendships can be just as close and as dear as those that we
form with women. Listen to Lucy's description of one such
friendship:

"We've found we have things to talk about that are   26
different from what he talks about with my husband and
different from what I talk about with his wife. So sometimes
we call on the phone or meet for lunch. There are similar
intellectual interests—we always pass on to each other the
books that we love—but there's also something tender and
caring too."

In a couple of crises, Lucy says, "he offered himself, for   27
talking and for helping. And when someone died in his family
he wanted me there. The sexual, flirty part of our friendship is
very small, but *some*—just enough to make it fun and
different." She thinks—and I agree—that the sexual part,
though small is always *some*, is always there when a man and a
woman are friends.

It's only in the past few years that I've made friends with   28
men, in the sense of a friendship that's *mine*, not just part of
two couples. And achieving with them the ease and the trust
I've found with women friends has value indeed. Under the
dryer at home last week, putting on mascara and rouge, I
comfortably sat and talked with a fellow named Peter. Peter, I
finally decided, could handle the shock of me minus mascara
under the dryer. Because we care for each other. Because we're
friends.

8. There are medium friends, and pretty friends, and very   29
good friends indeed, and these friendships are defined by their
level of intimacy. And what we'll reveal at each of these levels
of intimacy is calibrated with care. We might tell a medium
friend, for example, that yesterday we had a fight with our
husband. And we might tell a pretty good friend that this fight
with our husband made us so mad that we slept on the couch.
And we might tell a very good friend that the reason we got so
mad in that fight that we slept on the couch had something to
do with that girl who works in his office. But it's only to our

very best friends that we're willing to tell all, to tell what's going on with that girl in his office.

The best of friends, I still believe, totally love and support and trust each other, and bare to each other the secrets of their souls, and run—no questions asked—to help each other, and tell harsh truths to each other when they must be told.   30

But we needn't agree about everything (only 12-year-old girl friends agree about *everything*) to tolerate each other's point of view. To accept without judgment. To give and to take without ever keeping score. And to *be* there, as I am for them and as they are for me, to comfort our sorrows, to celebrate our joys.   31

—Judith Viorst

Questions About Content

1. Is the title effective? Explain.

2. Where is the thesis? Is it effective? Why?

3. How many bases can you identify in the above classification? Are these bases consistent with the writer's purpose? Explain.

4. What specific reader questions are answered in the body?

Questions About Organization

1. How many paragraphs make up the introduction? Is the introduction effective? Explain.

2. Does the arrangement of supporting paragraphs provide the best emphasis for the thesis? Explain.

3. Are the many short paragraphs appropriate to the writer's purpose? Explain. What effect do these short paragraphs have on the readers?

4. Is the conclusion effective? Explain.

Questions About Style

1. What is an outstanding style feature of this essay? Give examples.

2. Characterize the tone of this essay. Identify four expressions contributing to that tone.

3. Are the sentence fragments acceptable and effective here? (See page 537.)

RESPONDING TO YOUR READING

Explore your reactions to Viorst's "Friends, Good Friends—and Such Good Friends" by using the questions on page 93. Then respond with an essay of your own that uses classification to support some particular point about different types of friends in your life. Or instead you might write about different types of dates you've had. Whether your approach is humorous or serious, be sure your classification supports a definite viewpoint.

OPTIONS FOR ESSAY WRITING

1. Differences among members are the details that make any group of people interesting. Male college freshmen may be sorted into categories according to majors, socioeconomic backgrounds, political preferences, racial backgrounds, religious backgrounds, driving habits, attitudes toward studies, attitudes toward marriage, styles of dress, or countless other characteristics. We could do the same for any other group: teachers, parents, employers, athletes, people we see at the beach. Your basis for sorting will depend on the point you want to make about the group.

    Identify a group that you find interesting. Sort that group into at least three categories. Write for your classmates, and make sure your classification has a point. (Review "Guidelines for Classification" on pages 274–275 for a discussion of the features that make a classification effective.)

2. Television seems to invade every part of our lives. It can influence our buying habits, our political views, our literacy, and our attitudes about sex, marriage, family, and violence. Identify a group of commercials, sitcoms, talk shows, sports shows, or the like that have a bad (or good) influence on viewers. Sort the group according to a clear basis, using at least three categories for your classification.

14

Explaining Each Step or Stage: Process Analysis

Explaining How to Do Something • Guidelines for Instructions
• Explaining How Something Happens • Applications

People and things interact in different ways to produce different results. Each interaction is a process. In the manufacturing process, people interact with machines and materials to produce finished goods. In the natural process, earth, air, sunlight, and water interact to produce plant life. In a chemical process, air and fuel interact in an engine's carburetor to produce a combustible vapor. Most process analyses you will write in college and afterward are designed to answer one of these two questions for readers:

How do I do it?

How does it happen?

In school you might give instructions to a classmate for dissecting a frog or solving a physics problem. At work you might tell a colleague or customer how to achieve a result: how to analyze a soil sample; how to program a computer; how to swing a golf club.

Besides showing how to do something, you often have to explain how things happen: how the United States became involved in World

War I; how a digital computer works; how economic inflation occurs. The type of explanation will depend on your writing situation.

Explaining How to Do Something

Almost anyone with a responsible job writes instructions. And everyone reads some sort of instructions. The new employee needs instructions for operating the office machines; the employee going on vacation writes instructions for the person filling in. An owner of a new car reads the manual for service and operating instructions. Readers of instructions have these questions:

How do I do it?

Why do I do it?

What materials or equipment will I need?

Where do I begin?

What do I do next?

Are there any precautions?

Instructions *emphasize the reader's role*, explaining each step in enough detail for readers to complete the task safely and efficiently. Here is a paragraph of instructions aimed at inexperienced joggers:

Main point (1) **First step (2)**	[1]Most jogging injuries occur when inexperienced runners begin too quickly. [2]Before taking a step, spend at least ten minutes stretching and warming up, using any exercises
Supporting detail (3)	you find most comfortable. [3](After your first week, consult a jogging book for specialized
Second step (4) **Supporting detail (5)**	exercises.) [4]When you've completed your warm-up, set a brisk pace walking. [5]Exaggerate the distance between steps, taking long strides and
Transitional sentence (6) **Third step (7–8)**	swinging your arms briskly and loosely. [6]After roughly 100 yards of this pace, you should feel ready to jog. [7]Immediately break into a very slow trot: lean your torso forward and let one foot fall in front of the other (one foot barely leaving the ground while the other is on the pavement). [8]Maintain the slowest pace possible, just above a
Precaution (9–10)	walk. [9]*Do not bolt like a sprinter!* [10]The biggest mistake is to start fast and injure yourself.

Supporting details
(11–15)

[11]While jogging, relax your body. [12]Keep your shoulders straight and your head up, and enjoy the scenery—after all, it is one of the joys of jogging. [13]Keep your arms low and slightly bent at your sides. [14]Move your legs freely from the hips in an action that is easy, not forced. [15]Make your feet perform a heel-to-toe action: land on the heel; rock forward; take off from the toe.

In developing this message, the writer followed guidelines that govern all instructions.

Guidelines for Instructions

1. *The instructions are informed.* The instruction writer has to know the process, down to the smallest detail. Unless you have performed the task, do not try to write instructions for it.

2. *The instructions are complete but not excessive.* The material answers all questions a reader has about how to carry out the procedure. Each step is spelled out *and* clarified by precautions, supporting points, and details as needed.

    It is easy to assume that other people know more than they really do about a procedure, especially when you can perform the task almost automatically. Think about when someone was teaching you to drive a car; or perhaps you have tried to teach someone else. When you write instructions, remember that the reader knows less than you. On the one hand, you need to include enough details for your reader to understand and perform the task successfully. On the other hand, you should omit general information that the average reader can be expected to know. Excessive details get in the way.

    The jogging instructions are clear and uncluttered because the writer has assessed correctly the general reader's needs. Terms such as *long stride, torso,* and *sprinter* should be clear to the general reader without definitions or illustrations. In contrast, *a slow trot* is explained in detail, because different readers might have differing interpretations of this term. When in doubt about the need for details, you are safer to overexplain than to underexplain.

3. *The instructions are logically organized.* Instructions are almost always arranged in chronological order, with warnings and precautions inserted for specific steps.

4. *The instructions are immediately readable.* Instructions must be understood upon *first* reading, because readers usually take immediate action. Because they emphasize the *reader's role,* instructions are written in the *second person,* as direct address.

    All steps are in the *active voice* ("move your legs" versus "your legs should be moved") and the *imperative mood* ("rock forward" versus "you should rock forward"). In this way, each step begins with an *action verb (lean, relax, keep)* that gives an immediate signal about the specific actions to be taken.

    Generally, sentences are shorter in instructions than in other kinds of writing: use one sentence for one step, so that readers can perform one step at a time.

    Finally, transitional expressions *(while, after, next)* improve readability by marking time and sequence.

Explaining How Something Happens

When you explain how steps lead to completion of a process, you answer these readers' questions:

How does it happen? (or, How is it made?)

When and where does it happen?

What happens first, next, and so on?

What is the result?

In an essay exam you may have to explain how salt water can be converted to fresh water, or how a color television image is transmitted. Colleagues and clients need to know such things as how stock and bond prices are governed, how your bank reviews a mortgage application, how your town decided on its zoning laws, and so on. This type of explanation *emphasizes the process itself*—instead of the reader's or writer's role—as shown here.

Main point (1–3)
                    [1]The most alarming of all man's assaults upon the environment is the contamination of air, earth, rivers, and sea with dangerous and even lethal materials. [2]This pollution is for the most part irrecoverable; the chain of evil it initiates not only in the world that must support life but in living tissues is for the most part irreversible. [3]In this now universal contamination of the environ-

Details of the process and its results (4–6)

ment, chemicals are the sinister and little-recognized partners of radiation in changing the very nature of the world—the very nature of its life. [4]Strontium 90, released through nuclear explosions into the air, comes to earth in rain or drifts down as fallout, lodges in soil, enters into the grass or wheat or corn grown there, and in time takes up its abode in the bones of a human being, there to remain until his [or her] death. [5]Similarly, chemicals sprayed on croplands or forests or gardens lie long in soil, entering into living organisms, passing from one to the other in a chain of poisoning and death. [6]Or they pass mysteriously by underground streams until they emerge and, through the alchemy of air and sunlight, combine into new forms that kill vegetation, sicken cattle, and work unknown harm on those who drink from once pure wells.

Conclusion (7)

[7]As Albert Schweitzer has said, "Man can hardly even recognize the devils of his own creation."

—Rachel Carson

Rachel Carson's explanation is effective because its level of detail suits her purpose and her audience's needs. The paragraph is part of a book for general readers; therefore, the author needed to decide how specific she should be to get her point across. Without the clarifying details, the paragraph would have been too vague—only telling, not showing. But even more specific and technical details, such as chemical formulas or the half-life of strontium, would have confused the audience. The author knew that, as nonspecialists, we would use her information simply for a broad understanding of dangers to our environment. Her goal was to make us aware of the problems, not to write a textbook on chemical pollution. Of course, for an audience of chemistry or ecology majors, she would have included more technical details. In various writing situations, your subject, purpose, and audience will differ; therefore, paragraphs will vary in their mixture of general and specific.

Like a set of instructions, an explanation of how something happens must be factual and objective as well as clear and detailed enough to allow readers to follow the process step by step. Because this type of analysis emphasizes the process itself, rather than the reader's role, it is written in the third person.

Much of your writing in college term papers and essay exams is designed to explain how things happen. Your audience is the professor, who is evaluating what you have learned. Because this informed reader knows *more* than you do about the subject, you often need to discuss only the main points, omitting some details.

But explaining how something happens for readers who know *less* than you is the real challenge. Here you have to translate specialized information for people who are neither willing nor able to fill in the blank spots; thus, you become the teacher, and uninformed readers become the students.

Application 14–1

PARAGRAPH WARM-UP: GIVING INSTRUCTIONS

Choose some activity you perform well. Think of a situation requiring you to write instructions for that activity. Single out a major step within the process (such as pitching a baseball or adjusting ski bindings for safe release). Provide enough details for the reader to perform that step safely and efficiently.

Application 14–2

PARAGRAPH WARM-UP: EXPLAINING HOW SOMETHING HAPPENS

Select a simple but specialized process that you understand well (how gum disease develops, how the heart pumps blood, how steel is made, how electricity is generated, how a corporation is formed, how a verdict is appealed to a higher court, and so on). Write a paragraph giving an uninformed classmate a general but clear understanding of the process.

Application 14–3

ESSAY PRACTICE: GIVING INSTRUCTIONS

Read this essay, and answer the questions following it. Then select one of the essay assignments.

The writer of these instructions is a counselor at the North American Survival School, which offers courses ranging from mountaineering to desert survival. Besides being a certified Emergency Medical Technician, this writer has extensive experience hiking and camping in snake country. The school is preparing a survival manual for distribution to all its students. This writer's contribution is a set of instructions on dealing with snakebites. Many of the readers will have no experience with snakes (or first aid), and so the writer decides to keep things short and simple, for quick, easy reading as needed.

How to Deal with Snakebites

[1]Too often, a pleasant weekend outdoors can become a nightmare. Every year, thousands of Americans are injured— sometimes fatally—by poisonous snakebites. Less than 1 one percent of poisonous snakebites are fatal. But many of the injuries and virtually all fatalities can be avoided as long as you are alert and cautious and follow a few simple instructions.

[2]First, remember that although most snakes can bite, in the United States only rattlesnakes, copperheads, coral snakes, and water moccasins are poisonous. All these snakes are most dangerous in early spring, when venom sacs are full from winter hibernation. Rattlers are found in most of the United States, while copperheads are only in the East. Coral snakes range throughout the South, while water moccasins live in Southern lowlands and swampy areas. You might disturb one of these snakes by pushing over a log or stone, walking through tall grass, stumbling over one sunning on a rock, or bumping into one while swimming. You could even wake up after a cold night to find one sharing your tent or sleeping bag. Always be alert.

[3]Some simple precautions can help you avoid snakebites. Since most bites occur around the ankles, wear long, thick pants and high boots of heavy rubber or leather. Also, watch where you walk, swim, or sleep. As you walk, watch where you put your feet, and be especially careful climbing over fallen trees or stone walls. In moccasin country, swim only where the water is moving and the shoreline is free of heavy vegetation. If you cannot sleep in a closed tent with a snakeproof floor, place your sleeping bag on a high, dry, open spot, and keep it zipped tightly. When you do encounter a snake, stop dead! Then move backwards *very* slowly, making no moves that will frighten the snake. Above all, carry a snakebite kit in your pack, just in case the precautions fail.

[4]A poisonous snakebite is easy enough to recognize. Within minutes the wound will swell and turn bright red. You will feel a throbbing pain that radiates from the bite. The swelling, redness, and pain will spread gradually and steadily. You may experience nausea and/or hot flashes. In any case, if you are not sure whether the bite is poisonous, play it safe and treat it as if it were poisonous.

⁵If you have been bitten, *do nothing that could hasten the spread of the poison.* Above all, don't panic. Resist the temptation to walk, run, or move quickly. And stay away from stimulants such as coffee, tea, cola, alcohol, or aspirin. In fact, avoid ingesting anything except perhaps for a few sips of water. Begin by taking a minute to think calmly about what you *should* do.

⁶To ensure your safety, follow these suggestions. Remain calm and move as little as possible. Keep the wound lower than the rest of your body so that the poison will remain localized. Have companions get you to a hospital as quickly as possible, without causing you needless exertion. If the hospital is more than an hour away, you might apply an icepack to retard the spread of the poison, or a tourniquet (snugly enough to stop venous flow but not so tight as to stop arterial flow—and loosened briefly every five minutes). If you have no snakebite kit, you might cut a small X about ¼ inch deep at the point of greatest swelling on the wound to suck out and spit out some poison. Perform this last procedure *only* if you have no oral cuts or injuries and there is no chance of getting medical treatment for several hours.

⁷By taking precautions and remaining alert, you should not have to fear snakebites. But if you are bitten, your best bet is to remain calm.

—Frank White

Questions About Content

1. Is there a thesis sentence? If so, where?

2. What opening strategy is used to create interest?

3. Is the first body paragraph necessary? Explain.

4. Is the information adequate and appropriate for the stated audience and purpose? Explain.

5. What specific readers' questions are answered in the body?

Questions About Organization

1. What is the order of the body paragraphs? Is this the most effective order? Explain.

2. Is the conclusion adequate and appropriate? Explain.

Questions About Style

1. What is the outstanding stylistic feature of this piece?

2. Is the tone of these instructions too "bossy"? Explain.

ESSAY ASSIGNMENT

Assume a specific situation and audience (like those for snakebite procedures), and write instructions for one of the following procedures, or for anything that you can do well (no recipes, please). Be sure you know the process down to the smallest detail. Narrow your subject (perhaps to one complex activity within a longer procedure) so you can cover it fully. Avoid day-to-day procedures that college readers would already know (brushing teeth, washing hair, and other such elementary activities). Here are some possibilities:

how to portage a canoe

how to care for a down sleeping bag

how to avoid hypothermia

how to select a used car

how to snowplow on skis

how to jump-start a car

how to housebreak a puppy

how to survive the first semester in college

how to overcome insomnia

how to apply the Heimlich Maneuver

how to sprout new plants from clippings

how to defend oneself from a mugger

how to study for finals

how to deal with sexual harassment

Application 14–4

ESSAY PRACTICE: EXPLAINING HOW SOMETHING HAPPENS

This essay, written by a biology major for a pamphlet on environmental pollution, is aimed at an uninformed audience. Read it, and answer the study questions that follow. Then select one of the essay assignments.

How Acid Rain Develops, Spreads, and Destroys

[1]Acid rain is environmentally damaging rainfall that occurs after fossil fuels burn and release nitrogen and sulfur oxides into the atmosphere. Acid rain, simply stated, increases the acidity level of waterways, because these nitrogen and sulfur oxides combine with the normal moisture in the air. The resulting rainfall is far more acidic than normal rainfall. Acid rain is a silent threat because its effects, although slow, are cumulative. This analysis explains the cause, the distribution cycle, and the effects of acid rain.

[2]Most research shows that power plants burning oil or coal are the primary cause of acid rain. Fossil fuels contain a number of elements that are released during combustion. Two of these, sulfur oxide and nitrogen oxide, combine with normal moisture to produce sulfuric acid and nitric acid. The released gases undergo a chemical change as they combine with atmospheric ozone and water vapor. The resulting rain or snowfall is more acid than normal precipitation.

[3]Acid level is measured by pH readings. The pH scale runs from 0 through 14; a pH of 7 is considered neutral. (Distilled water has a pH of 7.) Numbers above 7 indicate increasing degrees of alkalinity. (Household ammonia has a pH of 11.) Numbers below 7 indicate increasing acidity. Movement in either direction on the pH scale, however, means multiplying by 10. Lemon juice, which has a pH value of 2, is 10 times more acidic than apples, which have a pH of 3, and 1000 times more acidic than carrots, which have a pH of 5.

[4]Because of carbon dioxide (an acid substance) normally present in air, unaffected rainfall has a pH of 5.6. At this time, the pH of precipitation in the northeastern United States and Canada is between 4.5 and 4. In Massachusetts, rain and snowfall have an average pH reading of 4.1. A pH reading below 5 is considered to be abnormally acidic, and therefore a threat to aquatic populations.

[5]Although it might seem that areas containing power plants would be most severely affected, acid rain can in fact travel thousands of miles from its source. Stack gases escape and drift with the wind currents. The sulfur and nitrogen oxides are thus able to travel great distances before they return to earth as acid rain.

[6]For an average of two to five days after emission, the gases follow the prevailing winds far from the point of origin. Estimates show that about 50 percent of the acid rain that affects Canada originates in the United States; at the same time, 15 to 25 percent of the U.S. acid rain problem has its origin in Canada.

[7]The tendency of stack gases to drift makes acid rain a widespread problem. More than 200 lakes in the Adirondacks,

hundreds of miles from any industrial center, are unable to support life because their water has become so acidic.

[8]Acid rain causes extensive damage wherever it falls. It erodes various types of building rock, such as limestone, marble, and mortar, which are gradually eaten away by the constant bathing in acid. Damage to buildings, houses, monuments, statues, and cars is widespread and costly. Some priceless monuments and carvings have already been destroyed, and even trees of some varieties are dying in large numbers.

[9]More important, however, is acid rain damage to waterways in the affected areas. Because of its high acidity, acid rain dramatically lowers the pH in lakes and streams. Although its effect is not immediate, acid rain can eventually make a waterway so acidic it dies. In areas with natural acid-buffering elements such as limestone, the dilute acid has less effect. The northeastern United States and Canada, however, lack this natural protection, and so are continually vulnerable.

[10]The pH level in an affected waterway drops so low that some species cease to reproduce. In fact, a pH level of 5.1 to 5.4 means that fisheries are threatened; once a waterway reaches a pH level of 4.5, no fish reproduction occurs. Because each creature is part of the overall food chain, loss of one element in the chain disrupts the whole cycle.

[11]In the northeastern United States and Canada, the problem of excess acidity is compounded by the runoff from acid snow. During the cold winter months, acid snow sits with little melting, so that by spring thaw, the acid released is greatly concentrated. Aluminum and other heavy metals normally present in soil are also released by acid rain and runoff. These toxic substances leach into waterways in heavy concentrations, affecting fish in all stages of development.

—Bill Kelly

Questions About Content

1. Is the title too long? Explain.

2. Is the information appropriate for the intended audience (uninformed readers)? Explain.

3. What specific readers' questions are answered in the body?

Questions About Organization

1. Are the body paragraphs arranged in the best order for readers to follow the process? Explain.

2. What is the purpose of so many short paragraphs?

3. Why does this essay have no specific conclusion?

Questions About Style

1. What is the outstanding style feature of this essay? Give an example.

2. Give one example of each of the following sentence constructions, and explain briefly how each reinforces the writer's meaning: passive construction, subordination, short sentence.

ESSAY ASSIGNMENT

Select a specialized process that you understand well (from your major or an area of interest) and explain that process to uninformed readers. Choose a process that has several distinct steps. Write so that members of your composition class will gain detailed understanding. Topics might include these:

how the body metabolizes alcohol

how industrial pollution is killing our lakes

how economic inflation occurs

how a lake or pond becomes a swamp

how a volcanic eruption occurs

how cigarettes cause heart and lung disease

how exposure to the sun causes skin cancer

Don't merely generalize. Get down to specifics.

15

Explaining Why It Happened or What Will Happen: Cause-and-Effect Analysis

Whereas a process analysis explains *how* something is done or how something works, a cause-and-effect analysis explains *why* something happened or what happens as a result of something.

We use cause-and-effect analysis daily. If you awoke this morning with a sore shoulder (effect), you might recall exerting yourself yesterday at the college Frisbee olympics (cause). In turn, you may take aspirin, hoping for relief (effect). If the aspirin works, it will have *caused* you to feel better. But some causes and effects are not so easy to identify, because their relationships are more complex. Consider these cause-and-effect statements:

    [*cause*]   [*effect*]
1. I tripped over a chair and broke my nose.

    [*effect*]   [*cause*]
2. I never studied because I slept too much.

One might argue that other causes or effects could be identified for each of the statements above.

294

[effect]   [cause]
I tripped over the chair because the lights in my apartment were out.

[effect]   [cause]
The lights were out because the power had been shut off.

[effect]   [cause]
The power was shut off because my roommate forgot to pay the electric bill.

or

[cause]   [effect]
Because I slept too much, my grades were awful.

[effect]   [effect]
Because my grades were awful, I hated college.

[effect]   [effect]
Because I hated college, I dropped out.

[cause]   [effect]
Because I dropped out of college, I lost my scholarship.

As we analyze a situation, some effects can, in turn, become causes of other effects, or vice versa. As our reasoning proceeds in the examples above, the causes or effects become more *distant*. The *immediate* cause of 1, however—the one most closely related to the effect—is that the writer tripped over the chair. Likewise, the *immediate* effect of 2 is that the writer did no studying. Thus, even with apparently simple events, the challenge in a causal analysis is to distinguish between *immediate* causes or effects and *distant* ones. And when we set out to explain cause-and-effect relationships, we need to make our reasoning clear to readers. Otherwise, we might confuse readers with such illogical statements:

[cause]   [effect]
Because my roommate forgot to pay the electric bill, I broke my nose.

[effect]   [cause]
I lost my scholarship because I slept too much.

To understand the writer's meaning, readers need a step-by-step breakdown of the process.

A writer must also distinguish among *probable*, *possible*, and *definite* causes. Sometimes a definite cause can be identified easily ("The engine is overheating because of a faulty radiator cap"); but, most often, a good deal of searching and thought are needed to isolate a specific cause. Suppose that you want to answer this question: "Why are there no children's day-care facilities on our state college campus?" A brainstorming session might yield this list of possible causes:

lack of need among students

lack of interest among students, faculty, and staff

high cost of liability insurance

lack of space and facilities on campus

lack of trained personnel

prohibition by state law

lack of legislative funding for such a project

You proceed with interviews, questionnaires, and research into state laws, insurance rates, and availability of personnel. You begin to rule out some items, and others appear as probable causes. Specifically, you find a need among students, high campus interest, an abundance of qualified people for staffing, and no evidence of state laws prohibiting such a project. Three probable causes remain: lack of funding, high insurance rates, and lack of space. Further inquiry shows that lack of funding and high insurance rates *are* issues. These causes, however, could be eliminated through new sources of revenue: charging a fee for each child, soliciting donations, diverting funds from other campus organizations, and so on. Finally, after carefully examining available campus space and after consulting with school officials, you arrive at one definite cause: lack of space and facilities.*

Early in your analysis you might have based your conclusions hastily on insufficient evidence (say, an opinion expressed in a newspaper editorial that the campus was apathetic). Now you can base your conclusions on solid, factual evidence. You have moved from a wide range of possible causes to a narrower range of probable causes, then to a definite cause. Anything but the simplest effect is likely to have more than one cause. By narrowing the field, you can focus on the real issues.

The fact that one event occurs just before another is no proof that the first caused the second. You might have walked under a ladder in the hallway an hour before flunking your chemistry exam—but you

---

*Of course, one could argue that the lack of space and facilities is somehow related to the problem of funding. And the fact that the college is unable to find funds or space may be related to the fact that students' need is not sufficiently acute, or interest sufficient, to exert real pressure. Lack of space and facilities, however, come out as the *immediate* cause.

would not be able to argue convincingly that the one event had caused the other.

Cause-and-effect analysis serves countless uses in college writing. In a research paper, you might explore the causes of the Israeli-Palestinian conflict or the effects of stress on college students or the prime causes of small-business failure. In a report for the Dean of Students, you might explain the causes of students' disinterest in campus activities or the effect of a ban on smoking in public buildings.

In your workplace problem solving, you might analyze the high rates of absenteeism among your company's employees or the causes of low morale. You might explore the cause(s) of a decrease in company profits or the malfunction of a piece of equipment. Perhaps local citizens will need to know how air quality will be affected by your power plant's proposed change from coal to oil. Or perhaps you will need to predict for assembly line workers the effects of robotics technology on their jobs within ten years. Whenever readers want to understand why something happened or what will happen next, cause-and-effect analysis is essential.

For all its *practical* value, cause-effect analysis can make a *personal* difference, as well. In this next essay, Al Andrade remembers the cause of a turning point in his own awareness.

The Old Guy

The workout was progressing as it usually does. My father and I took turns grunting the weights up and down off our chests. Our pectorals, shoulders, and arms were shaking. Throughout the one-hour session, we encouraged and coached one another. Fortunately, weight lifting demands short breaks after every set. Without these breaks, our workout might last only two minutes. The time spent preparing for the next set (or recovering from the last one) is important, not because I'm lazy, but because it gives me a chance to catch up on things with Dad. Since we don't get to see each other very often, the latest news, gossip, and philosophies get aired in the weight room.

While I was changing the weight on the barbell for our next set, Dad was hanging around the exercise room. We'd been talking about the possibility of building an apartment on the lot next door. This discussion led to one about real estate, which led to one about the stock market, which led to one about his retirement. Lately, Dad has been complaining about his company's lousy retirement plan. I figured he was just a practical guy planning for a more comfortable retirement. Then he looked up from behind the squat rack and said, "You know, Al, if I'm lucky, I only have 20 or 25 years left, and I don't want to be eating dog food when I retire." I snickered at the dog food remark. He's always overstating things for emphasis. The other part of his remark—the part about having only 20 or 25 years left—also seemed a bit melodramatic. At first, Dad's comment rolled off me like a bead of sweat, until I began doing some personal arithmetic of my own.

Our workout moved from the bench press to the chinning bar. I went first. Then I watched while Dad strained to pull himself up for the tenth repetition. "Not bad for an old guy," he said after he jumped down off the bar. I looked at him and thought he really wasn't bad. (For an old guy.) Aside from a minor middle-aged belly, he is more powerful now than ever. He routinely dead lifts 450 pounds. And even with a bad shoulder, Dad can still bench press over 250 pounds. Not bad for an old guy is right. (Or a young guy, for that matter.) This time, however, the reference to his age wasn't as easy for me to shrug off.

No longer concentrating on the weights, I thought about aging. The thought of Dad aging didn't overly distress me. I mean, the man was healthy, strong, and sweating just a few feet away. But then I pictured myself getting old, considering what I'll be doing and saying in 25 years. Would I be grousing about retirement plans? Would I be working out twice as hard with the notion that I might live a little longer?

Most likely I'd be doing the same things Dad is doing now. A 45-year-old family man counting the years he has left. I'd be a man who's too busy making a living to ever make enough money. Instead of counting up the years, I'd be counting them down: 10 years before my retirement, 15 years before I won't be penalized for withdrawing money from my I.R.A., and 2 years before my son's twenty-fifth birthday. The cycle will be complete. I will replace my father, and a son will replace me.

I understand how "life goes on" and how "we're not getting any younger." But now I worried about the inevitability of middle age. I couldn't help putting myself in the old guy's place—of retirement worries and declining chin-ups. Twenty-three-year-old people aren't supposed to worry about retirement, or even middle age. Brilliant careers and healthy, productive lives lie ahead for us, right? We've got everything to look forward to. We think about raising families, achieving goals, and becoming a success, not about our own mortality. But we all eventually reach a time when thoughts of our own old age and death become an everyday reality.

Dad wrapped his hands around the chinning bar for his last set. He struggled to get six repetitions this time. I jabbed him from behind and jokingly scolded "What's the matter with you?" He turned, and shook his finger at me, and said, "We'll see what you can do at 45 years old." I told him I could wait.

—Al Andrade

Using vivid description and narration, Andrade shows us what happened and why it happened. As readers we are allowed to experience that inevitable moment when a young person first confronts the reality of aging. Andrade gives us no explicit thesis. But what thesis does his essay seem to imply? Can you express his implied thesis in one sentence?

Reasoning from Effect to Cause

By reasoning from effect to cause, you answer these readers' questions:

Why did it happen?

What caused it?

Here is an effect-to-cause paragraph:

Effect (main point) (1)	[1]In the right situation, a perfectly sane
Distant cause and examples (2)	person can hallucinate. [2]It is most likely to happen when [he or she] is in a place that provides little stimulation to [the] senses, such as a barren, unbroken landscape or a quiet, dimly lit room.
Examples (3–4)	[3]Hallucinations are an occupational hazard of truck drivers, radar scanners, and pilots. [4]These occupations have in common long periods of monotony: lengthy stretches of straight highway, the regular rhythms of radar patterns, the droning
Evidence (5)	hum of engines. [5]A. L. Mosely of the Harvard School of Public Health found that every one of 33 long-distance truck drivers he surveyed could recall having at least one hallucination.
Immediate cause (6–7)	[6]Monotony means that the brain gets fewer sensory messages from the outside. [7]As external stimulation drops off, the brain responds more to messages from inside itself.

—Daniel Goleman

Guidelines for Effect-to-Cause Analysis

In developing the paragraph above, the author followed guidelines that govern any causal analysis.

1. *The support shows that the cause fits the effect.* To clarify his main point, the author shows varied examples of "right"

situations and of "sane" persons. Research evidence from Harvard is included to provide convincing support.

2. *The links between effect and cause are clear.* The author's reasoning goes like this:

> [*distant cause*]   [*immediate cause*]   [*effect*]
> nonstimulating places   →   monotony   →   hallucination

The distant cause is discussed first so that the immediate cause will make sense. Because readers need to see connections, the author had to organize his paragraph carefully.

Reasoning from Cause to Effect

When you reason from cause to effect, you answer these readers' questions:

What are its effects?

What will happen if it is done?

A cause-effect analysis must distinguish between ultimate (or distant) and immediate effects or among possible, probable, and definite effects. Here is a cause-to-effect paragraph:

> [1]What has the telephone done to us, or for us, in the hundred years of its existence? [2]A few effects suggest themselves at once. [3]It has saved lives by getting rapid word of illness, injury, or famine from remote places. [4]By joining with the elevator to make possible the multistory residence or office building, it has made possible—for better or worse—the modern city. [5]By bringing about a quantum leap in the speed and ease with which information moves from place to place, it has greatly accelerated the rate of scientific and technological change and growth in industry. [6]Beyond doubt it has crippled if not killed the ancient art of letter writing. [7]It has made living alone possible for persons with normal social impulses; by so doing, it has played a role in one of the greatest social changes of this century, the breakup of the multigenerational household. [8]It has made the waging of war chillingly more efficient than formerly. [9]Perhaps (though not probably) it has prevented wars that might have arisen out of international misunderstanding caused by written

communications. [10]Or perhaps—again not probably—by magnifying and extending irrational personal conflicts based on voice contact, it has caused wars. [11]Certainly it has extended the scope of human conflicts, since it impartially disseminates the useful knowledge of scientists and the babble of bores, the affection of the affectionate and the malice of the malicious.

—John Brooks

Guidelines for Cause-to-Effect Analysis

The paragraph above conforms to the guidelines for any causal analysis:

1. *The support shows that the effects fit the cause.* To clarify and support his main point, the author shows the telephone's effects on familiar aspects of modern life. Because his purpose is to discuss effects in general (not only *positive* effects), the author balances his development with both positive and negative effects.

2. *The links between cause and effects are clear.* The reasoning goes like this:

   [*cause*]   [*immediate effect*]   [*ultimate effects*]
   telephone → created rapid communication → saved lives, led to the
                                                 modern city, and so on

   [*cause*]   [*immediate effect*]   [*ultimate effect*]
   telephone → enabled people to live alone → led to breakup of multi-
                                                 generational household

Without the link provided by the immediate effects, the ultimate effects would make no sense to readers:

   The telephone has saved lives. [*Why?*]

   It has made possible the modern city. [*Why?*]

   It perhaps has caused wars. [*Why?*]

For further linking, the paragraph groups *definite effects* (3–8), and then *possible effects* (9–10), with a conclusion that ties the discussion together.

Application 15–1

PARAGRAPH WARM-UP: FROM EFFECT TO CAUSE

Identify a problem that affects you, your community, family, school, dorm, or other group ("The library is an awful place to study because————"). You might wish to phrase your topic statement as a question. In a paragraph, analyze the causes of this problem. Choose a subject you know about or one you can research to get the facts. Identify clearly the situation, the audience, and your purpose. Here are some possible subjects:

why I did poorly in a course

why a friendship was destroyed

why I am so deeply in debt

why I quit my job

Application 15–2

PARAGRAPH WARM-UP: FROM CAUSE TO EFFECT

Think of a major change you have made or would like to make in your life (moving off campus, changing majors, studying more seriously, or the like). Write a paragraph discussing the effects of this change, for a stipulated audience and purpose.

As an alternate assignment, discuss the good or bad effects of a recent friendship or relationship. Write directly to the person affected.

Application 15–3

ESSAY PRACTICE: ANALYZING CAUSES

After reading this essay, answer the study questions. Then select one of the essay assignments.

Fear of Dearth

[1]I hate jogging. Every dawn as I thud around New York City's Central Park reservoir, I am reminded of how much I hate it. It's so tedious. Some claim jogging is thought-conducive; others insist the

scenery relieves the monotony. For me, the pace is wrong for contemplation of either ideas or vistas. While jogging, all I can think about is jogging—or nothing. One advantage of jogging around a reservoir is that there's no dry shortcut home.

[2]From the listless look of some fellow trotters, I gather I am not alone in my unenthusiasm: Bill-paying, it seems, would be about as diverting. Nonetheless, we continue to jog; more, we continue to *choose* to jog. From a practically infinite array of opportunities, we select one that we don't enjoy and can't wait to have done with. Why?

[3]For any trend, there are as many reasons as there are participants. This person runs to lower [her] blood pressure. That person runs to escape the telephone or a cranky spouse or a filthy household. Another person runs to avoid doing anything else, to dodge a decision about how to lead his life or a realization that his life is leading nowhere. Each of us has [her] own carrot and stick. In my case, the stick is my slackening physical condition, which keeps me from beating opponents at tennis whom I overwhelmed two years ago. My carrot is to win.

[4]Beyond these disparate reasons, however, lies a deeper cause. It is no accident that now, in the last third of the 20th century, personal fitness and health have suddenly become a popular obsession. True, modern [people] like to feel good, but that hardly distinguishes [us] from [our] predecessors.

[5]With zany myopia, economists like to claim that the deeper cause of everything is economic. Delightfully, there seems no marketplace explanation for jogging. True, jogging is cheap, but then not jogging is cheaper. And the scant and skimpy equipment which jogging demands must make it a marketer's least favored form of recreation.

[6]Some scout-masterish philosophers argue that the appeal of jogging and other body-maintenance programs is the discipline they afford. We live in a world in which individuals have fewer and fewer obligations. The work week has shrunk. Weekend worship is less compulsory. Technology gives us more free time. Satisfactorily filling free time requires imagination and effort. Freedom is a wide and risky river; it can drown the person who does not know how to swim across it. The more obligations one takes on, the more time one occupies, the less threat freedom poses. Jogging can become an instant obligation. For a portion of his day, the jogger is not his own [person]; he is obedient to a regimen he has accepted.

[7]Theologists may take the argument one step further. It is our modern irreligion, our lack of confidence in any hereafter, that makes us anxious to stretch our mortal stay as long as possible. We run, as the saying goes, for our lives, hounded by the suspicion that these are the only lives we are likely to enjoy.

[8]All of these theorists seem to me more or less right. As the growth of cults and charismatic religions and the resurgence of enthusiasm for the military draft suggest, we do crave commitment. And who can doubt, watching so many middle-aged and older persons torturing themselves in the name of fitness, that we are unreconciled to death, more so perhaps than any generation in modern memory?

[9]But I have a hunch there's a further explanation of our obsession with exercise. I suspect that what motivates us even more than a fear of death is a fear of dearth. Our era is the first to anticipate the eventual depletion of all natural resources. We see wilderness shrinking; rivers losing their capacity to sustain life; the air, even the stratosphere, being loaded with potentially deadly junk. We see the irreplaceable being squandered, and in the depths of our consciousness we are fearful that we are creating an uninhabitable world. We feel more or less helpless and yet, at the same time, desirous to protect what resources we can. We recycle soda bottles and restore old buildings and protect our nearest natural resource— our physical health—in the almost superstitious hope that such small gestures will help save an earth that we are blighting. Jogging becomes a sort of penance for our sins of gluttony, greed, and waste. Like a hairshirt or a bed of nails, the more one hates it, the more virtuous it makes one feel.

[10]That is why *we* jog. Why *I* jog is to win at tennis.

—Carrl Tucker

Questions About Content

1. Is the title appropriate for this essay? Explain.

2. In your own words, restate the main point (or thesis) of the essay in a complete sentence.

3. Why would readers find the content of this essay interesting?

4. Is this essay convincing? Explain.

5. What specific readers' questions are answered in the body?

Questions About Organization

1. Why do you suppose the writer used two paragraphs for his introduction? Explain the function of each.

2. What combination of opening strategies is used in the introduction?

3. Are the body paragraphs arranged in an order (such as general-to-specific) that emphasizes the thesis? If so, what is that order?

4. In a brief outline, list the major topic of each body paragraph.

5. Underline each topic statement. Does each paragraph have a topic statement?

6. Which topic statement in the body serves four individual paragraphs? Is this an effective arrangement? Explain.

7. The body paragraphs vary greatly in length; is this variation justified? Explain.

8. Which two reasons, among those offered to explain the jogging craze, does the author find least credible? Why are these reasons discussed at that place in the essay?

9. Is the brief, two-sentence conclusion effective? Explain.

Questions About Style

1. Identify one sentence that relies on subordination for combining related thoughts. Explain why this structure reinforces the meaning of that sentence.

2. Identify one sentence that relies on coordination for combining related thoughts. How does this coordinate structure reinforce the meaning of that sentence?

3. What is the most notable feature of sentence style throughout this essay? Comment on the effectiveness of this feature.

4. In the second sentence, is *thud* the best word the writer could have chosen? Explain.

5. Characterize the tone of Tucker's essay. Explain briefly how word choice and sentence structure contribute to this tone.

Note: The introduction to Section Three mentions that many published essays break the mold of the "formula essay." Tucker's essay is a good example of structural variation. After reviewing pages 224–225, reread Tucker's essay to identify specific ways (not covered in the questions above) in which he has broken the mold. Try to incorporate some of these variations into your own essay. At this stage of your writing, you should be ready to take some chances!

RESPONDING TO YOUR READING

1. Explore your reactions to "Fear of Dearth" by using the questions on page 93. Then respond with an essay of your own, analyzing a cause or causes.

You might write about some activity or behavior (harmful or beneficial, pleasurable or painful) that takes up much of your (and other people's) time. Beginning with that as an effect, analyze its cause(s). Like Tucker, you might want to generalize (as justified by your experience and observation) about why that activity has become so popular. Here are activities or behaviors whose causes you could analyze:

- Why do I (or we) spend so much time watching football games (or some other sport)?

- Why am I so obsessed with exercise, fashion, or diet?

- Why am I a soap opera fan?

- Why are we such party animals?

Be sure that your analysis supports a definite thesis about the cause(s) of the thing. Feel free to inject some humor.

2.   Explore your reactions to "The Old Guy" (pages 297–298) by using the page 93 questions. Then respond with an essay about something that worries or scares you, something you usually try not to think about. Maybe it's a person or a place, a situation or an event. Maybe, as with Andrade, it's something about growing up. Or maybe you worry about having to face some kind of change or about losing something or about having to confront something you've preferred to ignore or deny.

Analyze the cause(s) of your feelings in enough detail so that we can stand in your place. Show us what is happening and why it's happening and what it means for you. Be sure your analysis supports a definite thesis—whether you state the thesis or merely imply it.

OPTIONS FOR ESSAY WRITING

1.   Write an essay on the causes of human cruelty.

2.   Why are many Americans afraid of old age?

3.   Think about people you know who enjoy (or dislike) their work. What do you think explains that enjoyment (or dislike)?

4.   Why do people gossip? What human need does gossip satisfy, and how? Be sure that your essay makes some definite point about human nature.

5.   Most young people do not need to be told to enjoy life. They do. Personal growth and social experiences provide teenagers with

what adults often label as the "best years of one's life." For some teenagers, however, problems are overwhelming; recent statistics show an alarming increase in teenage suicide. What do you think are some major causes of teenage suicide? Explain in an essay.

Application 15–4

ESSAY PRACTICE: ANALYZING EFFECTS

In this essay, the writer shows that a type of weather can dramatically exemplify how our lives are ruled by forces beyond our control. Read the essay carefully, and answer the questions that follow. Then select one of the essay assignments.

*Close to the Edge**

[1]There is something uneasy in the Los Angeles air this afternoon, some unnatural stillness, some tension. What it means is that tonight a Santa Ana will begin to blow, a hot wind from the northeast whining down through the Cajon and San Gorgonio Passes, blowing up sandstorms out along Route 66, drying the hills and the nerves to the flash point. For a few days now we will see smoke back in the canyons, and hear sirens in the night. I have neither heard nor read that a Santa Ana is due, but I know it, and almost everyone I have seen today knows it too. We know it because we feel it. The baby frets. The maid sulks. I rekindle a waning argument with the telephone company, then cut my losses and lie down, given over to whatever it is in the air. To live with the Santa Ana is to accept, consciously or unconsciously, a deeply mechanistic† view of human behavior.

[2]I recall being told, when I first moved to Los Angeles and was living on an isolated beach, that the Indians would throw themselves into the sea when the bad wind blew. I could see why. The Pacific turned ominously glossy during a Santa Ana period, and one woke in the night troubled not only by the peacocks screaming in the olive trees but by the eerie absence of surf. The heat was surreal. The sky had a yellow cast, the kind of light sometimes called "earthquake weather." My only neighbor would not come out of her house for days, and there were no lights at night, and her husband roamed the place with a machete. One day he would tell me that he had heard a trespasser, the next a rattlesnake.

---

*Title added.

†*Mechanistic:* having purely physical or biological causes.

³"On nights like that," Raymond Chandler once wrote about
the Santa Ana, "every booze party ends in a fight. Meek little wives
feel the edge of the carving knife and study their husbands' necks.
Anything can happen." That was the kind of wind it was. I did not
know then that there was any basis for the effect it had on all of us,
but it turns out to be another of those cases in which science bears
out folk wisdom. The Santa Ana, which is named for one of the
canyons it rushes through, is a *foehn* wind, like the *foehn* of Austria
and Switzerland and the *hamsin* of Israel. There are a number of
persistent malevolent winds, perhaps the best known of which are
the *mistral* of France and the Mediterranean *sirocco*, but a *foehn*
wind has distinct characteristics: it occurs on the leeward slope of a
mountain range and, although the air begins as a cold mass, it is
warmed as it comes down the mountain and appears finally as a hot
dry wind. Whenever and wherever a *foehn* blows, doctors hear about
headaches and nausea and allergies, about "nervousness," about
"depression." In Los Angeles some teachers do not attempt to
conduct formal classes during a Santa Ana, because the children
become unmanageable. In Switzerland the suicide rate goes up
during the *foehn*, and in the courts of some Swiss cantons the wind
is considered a mitigating circumstance for crime. Surgeons are said
to watch the wind because the blood does not clot normally during a
foehn. A few years ago an Israeli physicist discovered that not only
during such winds, but for the ten or twelve hours which precede
them, the air carries an unusually high ratio of positive to negative
ions. No one seems to know exactly why that should be; some talk
about friction, others suggest solar disturbances. In any case, the
positive ions are there, and what an excess of positive ions does, in
the simplest terms, is make people unhappy. One cannot get much
more mechanistic than that.

⁴Easterners commonly complain that there is no "weather" at
all in Southern California, that the days and the seasons slip by
relentlessly, numbingly bland. That is quite misleading. In fact the
climate is characterized by infrequent but violent extremes: two
periods of torrential subtropical rains which continue for weeks and
wash out the hills and send subdivisions sliding toward the sea;
about twenty scattered days a year of the Santa Ana, which, with its
incendiary dryness, invariably means fire. At the first prediction of a
Santa Ana, the Forest Service flies men and equipment from
northern California into the Southern forests, and the Los Angeles
Fire Department cancels its ordinary non-firefighting routines. The
Santa Ana caused Malibu to burn the way it did in 1956, and Bel Air
in 1961, and Santa Barbara in 1964. In the winter of 1966–1967
eleven men were killed fighting a Santa Ana fire that spread through
the San Gabriel mountains.

⁵Just to watch the front-page news out of Los Angeles during a Santa Ana is to get very close to what it is about the place. The longest single Santa Ana period in recent years was in 1957, and it lasted not the usual three or four days but fourteen days, from November 21 until December 4. On the first day 25,000 acres of the San Gabriel mountains were burning, with gusts reaching 100 miles an hour. In town, the wind reached Force 12, or hurricane force, on the Beaufort Scale; oil derricks were toppled and people ordered off the downtown streets to avoid injury from flying objects. On November 22 the fire in the San Gabriels was out of control. On November 24 six people were killed in automobile accidents, and by the end of the week the Los Angeles *Times* was keeping a box score of traffic deaths. On November 26 a prominent Pasadena attorney, depressed about money, shot and killed his wife, their two sons, and himself. On November 27 a South Gate divorcee, twenty-two, was murdered and thrown from a moving car. On November 30 the San Gabriel fire was still out of control, and the wind in town was blowing eighty miles an hour. On the first day of December four people died violently, and on the third the wind began to break.

⁶It is hard for people who have not lived in Los Angeles to realize how radically the Santa Ana figures in the local imagination. The city burning is Los Angeles's deepest image of itself: Nathaniel West perceived that, in *The Day of the Locust*; and at the time of the 1965 Watts riots what struck the imagination most indelibly was the fires. For days one could drive the Harbor Freeway and see the city on fire, just as we had always known it would be in the end. Los Angeles weather is the weather of catastrophe, of apocalypse, and, just as the reliably long and bitter winters of New England determine the way life is lived there, so the violence and the unpredictability of the Santa Ana affect the entire quality of life in Los Angeles, accentuate its impermanence, its unreliability. The wind shows us how close to the edge we are.

—Joan Didion

Questions About the Content

1. Is the title effective? Explain briefly.

2. In your own words, restate the main point of the essay in a complete sentence.

3. Does the thesis statement clearly express the writer's attitude toward the wind? If so, how would you characterize her attitude?

4. Is Didion's essay credible? Are you convinced that this writer knows what she is talking about? Explain.

5. Identify three statements of opinion and three statements of fact.

6. Does the essay have informative value? Explain.

7. What did you like or dislike about Didion's essay? Make your answer as specific as possible.

Questions About Organization

1. In Didion's introduction identify (a) two sentences that provide background and (b) two sentences that create suspense.

2. Which order (general-to-specific, chronological, and so on) do the combined body paragraphs follow?

3. Identify four devices that increase the coherence of Didion's essay, and give examples of each.

4. Explain the purpose served by the mention of New England weather in the conclusion.

5. Does Didion's conclusion sum up the main points, or does it interpret and evaluate material in the body? Explain your answer.

Questions About Style

1. Identify one sentence in Didion's essay that relies on subordination as a method of combining three or more related ideas. Be prepared to explain why subordination was the appropriate method for combining these ideas. (Refer to pages 167–168 and 184–187.)

   Example

   What it means is that tonight a Santa Ana will begin to blow, a hot wind from the northeast whining down through the Cajon and San Gorgonio Passes, blowing up sandstorms along Route 66, drying the hills and the nerves to the flash point.

2. Identify one sentence that relies on coordination for combining three or more related thoughts. Be prepared to explain why coordination was the appropriate method for combining these ideas. (Refer to pages 166–167 and 184–187.)

   Example

   My only neighbor would not come out of her house for days, and there were no lights at night, and her husband roamed the place with a machete.

3. Identify two short sentences that provide dramatic emphasis for an important point.

    Example

    That was the kind of wind it was.

4. Briefly characterize the *tone* that emanates from Didion's essay. Be as specific as possible. (Refer to pages 204–210.)

5. Give examples of the details that do the *showing:*

    - Details that help us see.

    Example

    The maid sulks.

    - Details that help us feel.

    Example

    Some unnatural stillness.

    - Details that help us hear.

    Example

    A hot wind from the northeast whining down.

    - Details that a camera would record.

    Example

    The sky had a yellow cast.

    - Numerical details.

    Example

    On the first day, 25,000 acres of the San Gabriel mountains were burning.

RESPONDING TO YOUR READING

Explore your reactions to "Close to the Edge" by using the questions on page 93. Then respond with your own essay, analyzing the effects of a place, an event, or a relationship.

You might trace the effects in your life from having a specific friend or belonging to a specific family or group. Or you might explain the effects on your family, school, or community of a tragic event (such as a suicide) or a fortunate one (say, a financial windfall). Or you might want to show how the socioeconomic atmosphere of your hometown or neighborhood or family has affected the person you've become. Or you might explain how the weather, landscape, or geography of your area affect people's values and behavior and life-style.

On any topic, be sure your discussion supports a definite viewpoint about the effects of something.

OPTIONS FOR ESSAY WRITING

1. Explain the effects of a major decision you or your family has made. How has the decision changed your life?

2. Analyze the effect computers have had on your generation.

3. Analyze the effect of a significant event in your life (death of a loved one, inheriting money, serious illness, divorce, moving a great distance, or the like).

4. Analyze how coming to college has affected a relationship in your life.

16

Explaining Similarities or Differences: Comparison and Contrast

Developing a Comparison • Developing a Contrast
• Developing a Combined Comparison and Contrast
• Guidelines for Comparison and Contrast
• A Special Kind of Comparison: Analogy
• Guidelines for Analogies • Applications

Comparison explains how things are similar; *contrast* explains how they are different. We use comparison and contrast (sometimes just called *comparison*) to evaluate things or to shed light on their relationship.

Whenever we set out to evaluate something by measuring it against something else, we confront this question:

Is *X* better than *Y*?

To reach a judgment about the relative merit or significance of *X* and *Y*, we examine them side by side. We might compare two (or more) cars, computers, business machines, political candidates, college courses, careers, or the like. In Chapter 1 (pages 16–17), Shirley Haley evaluates her parents' life-style by contrasting it with the life-style she envisions for herself. To evaluate recent economic progress by American women and minorities, we can compare numbers from two or three earlier decades with today's numbers: How much larger is the percentage of women who now have college degrees or high-income jobs? In each comparison, one item provides a basis for evaluating the other.

A second kind of comparison helps readers understand one thing in terms of another by answering this question:

What in *X* can shed light on *Y*?

To explain effects of the American high-fat diet on heart disease and cancer, we can compare disease rates in Japan (with its low-fat diet) with rates in our country. To reveal the danger posed by advocates of white supremacy, or of racial hatred in general, we can compare today's attitudes and behavior with those in Nazi Germany a half-century ago. When the two items are examined side by side, one helps illuminate the other.

In short, we compare and contrast whenever similarities and differences can help us explore and explain something, as in the next essay. Here, the writer weighs the relative merits of two names to show readers that one name is better than the other.

"Campus Center" Versus "Student Union"

We refer to the building that houses the core of student activities at our school as the "Campus Center." Is this an accurate description of the space which provides the nucleus of university life?

Until about four years ago, the building was known as the "Student Union," a term appropriate to the place where students socialize, plan events, and debate issues. "A rose by any other name. . . ." you may be thinking. But to rechristen the building the "Student Union" would be in the best interest of our students.

"Campus Center" assigns no real meaning to the hub of so much student activity. The phrase calls to mind passive things: the large-screen television set and the couch potatoes who watch it all day, the video arcade, the billiard room—people just hanging around. "Campus Center" . . . repeat it a few times, and it sounds almost militaristic, controlled by forces reminiscent of some sort of police state—perhaps the headquarters for Orwell's Thought Police. The architect of this university has already done what he could to make it resemble a missile-launching site, and so why throw around labels that further the effect?

"Student Union," on the other hand, carries active connotations, sounding as if people *do* things there. "Student Union" points to the meaningful student organizations housed in the building. When we think "Student Union," we think student action: the Student Senate, the Program Council, WUSM Radio, the Women's Center, the Black Coalition, and so on. Whereas "Campus Center" is a value-neutral term that seems to connote the apathy that student organizers so often condemn, "Student Union" reminds us of our unity and alliance as a decisive force within the University. The "Student Union" belongs to us. The "Campus Center" belongs to someone else.

To revive the use of "Student Union" would be easy enough. We would merely be reversing a change made once before. Our newspapers and radio station have the tools to put "Student Union" back into our campus vocabulary. If we use the term in conversation, in announcements, on memos and posters, we might be surprised at how quickly our peers pick it up and pass it on. Instead of focusing on the building as a place for hanging around, the name would focus on the ideals embodied in the building and its organized student activities. "Student Union" reminds us that we as students have a say in what goes on.

—Lois Shea

Whenever readers need to know about similarities and differences, comparison and contrast are essential.

Developing a Comparison

A comparison is designed to answer this readers' question:

How are X and Y similar or alike?

The writer of this paragraph compares *drug habits* among people of all times and places to those among people of modern times:

Paragraph 1

Main point (1)	[1]All the natural narcotics, stimulants, relaxants, and hallucinants known to the modern botanist and pharmacologist were discovered by primitive [people] and have been in use from time
Historical similarity to modern habits (2–3)	immemorial.[2] One of the first things that *Homo sapiens* did with his newly developed rationality and self-consciousness was to set them to work finding out ways to bypass analytical thinking and to transcend or, in extreme cases, temporarily obliterate the isolating awareness of the self. [3]Trying all things that grew in the field or forest, they held fast to that which, in this context, seemed good—everything, that is to say, that would change the quality of consciousness, would

Religious similarity to modern habits (4–5)

make it different, no matter how, from everyday feeling, perceiving, and thinking. [4]Among the Hindus, rhythmic breathing and mental concentration have, to some extent, taken the place of mind-transforming drugs used elsewhere. [5]But even in the land of yoga, even among the religious and even for specifically religious purposes, *Cannabis indica* (marijuana) has been freely used to supplement the effects of spiritual exercises.

Modern continuation of habit (6–7)

[6]The habit of taking vacations from the more-or-less purgatorial world, which we have created for ourselves, is universal. [7]Moralists may denounce it; but, in the teeth of disapproving talk and repressive legislation, the habit persists, and mind-transforming drugs are everywhere available.

Concluding point based on comparisons above (8)

[8]The Marxian formula, "Religion is the opium of the people," is reversible, and one can say, with even more truth, that "Opium is the religion of the people."

—Aldous Huxley

Developing a Contrast

A contrast is designed to answer this readers' question:

How are X and Y different?

This paragraph contrasts the *beliefs* of Satanism with those of Christianity:

Paragraph 2

Main point (1)
First difference (2–3)

[1]The Satanic belief system, not surprisingly, is the antithesis of Christianity. [2]Their theory of the universe, their cosmology, is based upon the notion that the desired end state is a return to a pagan awareness of their humanity. [3]This is in sharp contrast to the transcendental goals of traditional Christianity.

Second difference (4)

[4]The power associated with the pantheon of gods is also reversed: Satan's power is waxing (increasing); God's, if he still lives, waning.

Third difference (5–8)

[5]The myths of the Satanic church purport to tell the true story of the rise of Christianity and the fall of paganism, and there is

a reversal here too. [6]Christ is depicted as an early "con man" who tricked an anxious and powerless group of individuals into believing a lie. [7]He is typified as "pallid incompetence hanging on a tree." [8]Satanic novices are taught that early church fathers deliberately picked on those aspects of human desire that were most natural and made them sins, in order to use the inevitable transgressions as a means of controlling the populace, promising them salvation in return for obedience.

Final—and major—difference (9–10)

[9]And finally, their substantive belief, the very delimitation of what is sacred and what is profane, is the antithesis of Christian belief. [10]The Satanist is taught to "be natural; to revel in pleasure and in self-gratification; to emphasize indulgence and power in this life."

—Edward J. Moody

Developing a Combined Comparison and Contrast

A combined comparison and contrast is designed to answer this readers' question:

How are X and Y both similar and different?

This paragraph first contrasts *education* with *training* and, second, compares how each serves important needs of society:

Paragraph 3

Main point (1)

[1]To understand the nature of the liberal arts college and its function in our society, it is important to understand the difference between *education* and *training*.

Difference of purpose (2)

How "trained" people serve society (3–5)

[2]Training is intended primarily for the service of society; education is primarily for the individual. [3]Society needs doctors, lawyers, engineers, teachers to perform specific tasks necessary to its operation, just as it needs carpenters and plumbers and stenographers. [4]Training supplies the immediate and specific needs of society so that the work of the world may continue. [5]And these needs, our training centers—the professional and trade schools—fill.

Similarity of effects
(6)

How "educated"
people serve society
(7–11)

Conclusion (12)

[6]But although education is for the improvement of the individual, it also serves society by providing a leavening of men and women of understanding, of perception and wisdom. [7]They are our intellectual leaders, the critics of our culture, the defenders of our free traditions, the instigators of our progress. [8]They serve society by examining its function, appraising its needs, and criticizing its direction. [9]They may be earning their livings by practicing one of the professions, or in pursuing a trade, or by engaging in business enterprise. [10]They may be rich or poor. [11]They may occupy positions of power and prestige, or they may be engaged in some humble employment. [12]Without them, however, society either disintegrates or else becomes an anthill.

—Harry Kemelman

Guidelines for Comparison and Contrast

Paragraphs 1, 2, and 3 are all developed according to these guidelines:

1. *Only items in the same general class can be compared or contrasted.* The items must be related in some way: dogs and cats, but not dogs and trees; men and women, but not women and bicycles; apples and oranges, but not apples and elephants. Items with nothing in common provide no logical basis for comparison or contrast.

2. *The comparison rests on a clear and definite basis: costs, uses, benefits, appearance, results, or the like.* Paragraph 1 compares people of all times for their drug habits; paragraph 2 compares Satanism and Christianity for their primary beliefs; Paragraph 3 compares education and training by their function in our society.

3. *A comparison or contrast shows likenesses or differences in order to make a point.* Depending on your purpose, your main point may be that X is better than Y, as useful as Y, or the like. The paragraphs above, respectively, show (a) that drug habits throughout history have not changed, (b) that Satanism is the exact opposite of Christianity, and (c) that education and training are different in their purpose but both necessary to society.

4. *Both parts of the comparison or contrast receive equal treatment.* Points discussed for one item also are discussed (or

implied) for the other, generally in the same order. Paragraphs 2 and 3 offer *observable* contrasts, giving roughly equal space to each item. In Paragraph 1, modern drug use habits (although briefly mentioned) is the other item in the comparison, an item suggested throughout the discussion, and one whose details readers easily can intuit from their own general knowledge. Paragraph 1, then, offers an *implied* comparison.

5. *The comparison or contrast is supported and clarified through examples.* Similarities and differences are shown through concrete, specific, and relevant examples.

6. *A comparison or contrast follows either a block pattern or a point-by-point pattern.* In the *block pattern,* first one item is discussed fully, then the next, as in Paragraph 3: "trained" people in the first block; "educated" people in the second. A block pattern is preferable when the overall picture is more important than the individual points.

    In the *point-by-point pattern,* one point about both items is discussed, then the next point, and so on, as in Paragraph 2: the first difference between Satanism and Christianity is in their respective cosmologies; the second is in their view of God's power; the third, in their myths about the rise of Christianity, and so on. A point-by-point pattern is preferable when specific points might be hard to remember unless placed side by side.

Block pattern	Point-by-point pattern

Item *A*
  first point
  second point
  third point, etc.
	first point of *A*/first point of *B*, etc.

Item *B*
  first point
  second point
  third point, etc.
	second point of *A*/second point of *B*, etc.

A Special Kind of Comparison: Analogy

Ordinary comparison shows similarities between two things of the *same class* (two teachers, two styles of dress, two political philosophies). Analogy, on the other hand, shows similarities between two things of *different classes* (writing and skiing, freshman registration and a merry-go-round, a dorm room and a junkyard). By using one item to clarify another, analogy answers this readers' question:

Can you explain X by comparing it to something I already know?

Analogies are good for emphasizing a point (*Some rain is now as acidic as vinegar*). But they are especially useful in translating something abstract, complex, or unfamiliar, as long as the easier subject is broadly familiar to readers. To translate how power dissipation in a resistor (as it restricts current flow) produces heat, you might use a kitchen toaster as an analogy. To understand that the toaster coil serves as a resistor, however (so that it can toast bread), readers would have to be familiar with toasters in general. Analogy therefore calls for particularly careful analyses of audience.

Besides naming things vividly, analogies help *explain* things. The following extended analogy from the *Congressional Research Report* helps us understand an unfamiliar technical concept (dangerous levels of a toxic chemical) by comparing it to something more familiar (a human hair).

Analogy   A dioxin concentration of 500 parts per trillion is
                       lethal to guinea pigs. One part per trillion is
                       roughly equal to the thickness of a human hair
                       compared to the distance across the United States.

Two common ways of using analogies are illustrated below (with each approach labeled for later reference).

ANALOGIES TO SOMETHING CONCRETE

As we discussed on pages 200–203, abstract ideas become clear through concrete support. A well-chosen analogy is an excellent way to provide a concrete comparison.

[*abstract*]   [*concrete*]
Maintaining a love relationship is like tending a garden.

[*abstract*]   [*concrete*]
Being illiterate is like being in prison.

Of course, these analogies would require a fully developed paragraph to make their meaning clear.

Here is a paragraph (part of the selection on pages 98–99) that explains an abstract concept (appreciation of the simple things all around us) through comparison with a concrete experience (finding a penny):

Paragraph 1

Main point (1–2)

Supporting points (3–4)

Analogy to a common event (with related examples) (5–7)

Concluding point drawn from the analogy (8–9)

¹I've been thinking about seeing. ²There are lots of things to see, unwrapped gifts and free surprises. ³The world is fairly studded and strewn with pennies cast broadside from a generous hand. ⁴But—and this is the point—who gets excited by a mere penny? ⁵If you follow one arrow, if you crouch motionless on a bank to watch a tremulous ripple thrill on the water and are rewarded by the sight of a muskrat paddling from its den, will you count that sight a chip of copper only, and go your rueful way? ⁶It is dire poverty indeed when a man is so malnourished and fatigued that he won't stoop to pick up a penny. ⁷But if you cultivate a healthy poverty and simplicity, so that finding a penny will literally make your day, then, since the world is in fact planted in pennies, you have with your poverty bought a lifetime of days. ⁸It is that simple. ⁹What you see is what you get.

—Annie Dillard

ANALOGIES TO SOMETHING FAMILIAR

Unfamiliar or complex things often can be understood through analogy to familiar things.

[unfamiliar]   [familiar]
Meditating is like diving into a clear, deep lake.

[unfamiliar]   [familiar]
The lungs of a heavy smoker look like charred meat.

[complex]   [easier]
A computer's memory is structured like post office mailboxes.

[complex]   [easier]
Punctuation marks work like road signs and traffic signals.

Here is a paragraph that helps us understand something unfamiliar (what an editor does to a manuscript) through a comparison to something familiar (what a mechanic does to a car):

Paragraph 2

Main point (about unfamiliar process) (1)

[1]Having a manuscript under Ross's scrutiny was like putting your car in the hands of a skilled mechanic, not an automotive engineer with a bachelor of science degree, but a guy who knows what makes a motor go, and sputter, and wheeze, and sometimes come to a dead stop; a man with an ear for the faintest body squeak as well

Clarifying details of the unfamiliar process (2)

as the loudest engine rattle. [2]When you first gazed, appalled, upon an uncorrected proof of one of your stories or articles, each margin had a thicket of queries and complaints—one writer got

Details of the familiar process (3–5)

a hundred and forty-four on one profile. [3]It was as though you beheld the works of your car spread all over the garage floor, and the job of getting the thing together again and making it work seemed impossible. [4]Then you realized that Ross was trying to make your Model T or old Stutz Bearcat into a Cadillac or Rolls-Royce. [5]He was at work with the tools of his unflagging perfectionism, and, after an exchange of growls or snarls, you set to work to join him in his enterprise.

—James Thurber

Guidelines for Analogies

Paragraphs 1 and 2 are both developed according to these guidelines:

1. *The two subjects of the analogy are never of the same class or type.* If the paired subjects in the preceding paragraphs shared the same class (for example, if *editors and manuscripts* were paired, respectively, with *English teachers and student essays* instead of *mechanics and cars*), we would have ordinary comparison, not analogy.

2. *One of the subjects is used only to explain the other.* Analogy makes one item clear by using another. Unlike ordinary comparison, where *both* subjects are of equal interest, analogy has *one* subject of primary interest. In Paragraphs 1 and 2 we are

interested in *finding pennies* or in *automobile repair* only to the extent that these subjects clarify the primary subjects.

3. *The easier subject must be one that is broadly familiar to readers.* If readers do not understand the secondary subject, then the analogy is worthless. An analogy between *computer memory* and *mailboxes in a post office* would be lost on anyone who has never seen the inside of a typical post office. Likewise, an analogy between *punctuation marks* and *traffic signals* would be meaningless to persons newly arrived from an underdeveloped country that has no traffic signals. Analogy calls for careful analysis of the audience.

4. *An analogy is designed to support a specific main point.* The analogy itself has no value unless it supports and clarifies a main point.

5. *An analogy cannot serve as proof of anything.* Analogies provide new insights and perspectives only. They don't prove anything, because no two subjects are identical in all respects. The analogies in Paragraphs 1 and 2 merely show that the two subjects are alike in a way that clarifies each main point.

Application 16–1

PARAGRAPH WARM-UP: COMPARISON/CONTRAST

Using comparison or contrast (or both), write a paragraph discussing the likenesses or differences between two people, animals, attitudes, activities, places, or things. Identify clearly the situation, the audience, and your purpose.

Here are some possible subjects:

two places I know well

two memorable teaching styles (good or bad)

two friends' attitudes toward work

two similar consumer items

two pets I've had

the benefits of two kinds of exercise

two ways of spending a summer

Application 16–2

PARAGRAPH WARM-UP: ANALOGY

1. We often ignore or take for granted many beautiful or important things around us. Using Annie Dillard's paragraph (page 321) as a model, develop an analogy to share with a stipulated audience an insight you've had about something special. (The paragraph you wrote for Application 7–9 might serve as a starting point here.)

2. Using analogy, develop a paragraph explaining something abstract, complex, or unfamiliar by comparing it to something concrete, simpler, or familiar. ("Writing is like . . . "; "Love is like . . . "; "Meditating is like . . ."; "Osmosis works like . . . "). Identify a specific audience and purpose.

Application 16–3

ESSAY PRACTICE

After reading this essay, answer the study questions. Then select one of the essay assignments.

Meaningful Relationships

[1] I heard of a man and woman recently who had fallen in love. "Hopelessly in Love" was the woman's antique phrase for it. I hadn't realized people still did that sort of thing jointly. Nowadays the fashion is to fall in love with yourself, and falling in love with a second party seems to be generally regarded as bad form.

[2] It may be, of course, that many people are still doing it, but simply not admitting it publicly, perhaps on the assumption that it is a shameful act, as adultery used to be. Nowadays people discuss their adultery with strangers at parties and on airplanes, and not long ago I saw a married couple chatting about theirs on television, the way people used to discuss their car-repair problems. A possible explanation, I suppose, is that, in an age when the fashion is to be in love with yourself, confessing to being in love with somebody else is an admission of unfaithfulness to one's beloved. The truth is probably more complicated.

[3] Consider, for example, the situation of Ed and Jane, a hypothetical modern couple who see each other across a crowded room, feel inexplicable sensations not reducible to computer printouts and make human contact. After conventional preliminary

events, they will naturally want to express what exists between them. Jane may announce that they "relate" beautifully. Ed may boast about how gratifyingly they "communicate." The beauty of their "relating" and the gratifications of their "communicating" may induce them to "establish a relationship." Why it is always a "relationship" they establish, and never a "communicationship," I don't know, but "relationship" is the universally approved term. On days when things go badly, they do not have a lovers' quarrel. Instead, Jane says that Ed is not "relating" and Ed says that Jane is not "communicating." On days when things go well they boast about how "fulfilling" their "relationship" is. Ed and Jane do not dream of living happily ever after. They are more like the Bell telephone system. They aspire to heavy communicating in a fulfilling relationship.

⁴In fact, they are probably afraid of falling in love; and if, in spite of everything, they nevertheless do fall in love, they are too embarrassed to tell anybody. Why? One reason is that it is such an out of date thing to do. Falling in love is not scientific. It cannot be described in the brain-numbing jargon of sociology. It can only be described in the words of song writers. People in Cole Porter's antique old songs were always falling in love, and worse, talking about romance. Romance! Astaire and Rogers in a penthouse, and other such musty stuff. We have moved on to Mick Jagger, to John Lennon, who urged everybody to do it in the road instead of in the penthouse.

⁵Falling in love is archaic, like cookouts and tailfins on your Plymouth. Communicating, relating, experiencing fulfilling relationships—these are what up-to-date boys and girls engage in. When disaster strikes, it is not "the end of a love affair" to make them blue, but "the destruction of our relationship" to make them yearn for new "therapeutic experience."

⁶This grotesque terminology in which Americans now discuss what used to be called affairs of the heart is curious not only for its comic pseudoscientific sound, but also for the coolness with which it treats a passion formerly associated with heat. It takes a very cool pair of cats to talk about the grandest of passions as though it were only an exercise in sociology. Imagine Dante filling pages about the satisfactory nature of communicating with Beatrice, or Juliet raving on through five acts about her fulfilling relationship with Romeo.

⁷The way people talk, of course, reflects the way they think, and this avoidance of the language of love probably reflects a wish to avoid the consuming single-minded commitment to love to which the old words led, often no doubt to the dismay of people who uttered them. Why in our time we should tread so gingerly to avoid commitment to love to the second party is the subject for a monograph. Perhaps it comes from a fear of living too fully, perhaps

from the current cultural fashion conditioning us to believe that whatever interferes with self-love will lead to psychic headache.

[8]Whatever the explanation, it is a bleak era for love, which makes it a time of dull joys, small-bore agonies and thin passions. "I could not love thee, dear, so much, lov'd I not honor more," the poet once could write. Today he could only say, "I could not have so fulfilling a relationship with thee, dear, had I not an even more highly intensified mental set as regards the absurd and widely discredited concept known as honor."

—Russell Baker

Questions About Content

1. Is the title appropriate? Explain.

2. How does this writer limit the broad subject "romantic love" to a manageable subject for an essay?

3. In your own words, restate the point of the comparison in a complete sentence.

4. List three reasons readers would find the content of this essay interesting.

5. Is this essay convincing? Explain.

Questions About Organization

1. Does this comparison follow the block pattern or the point-by-point pattern? Comment on the effectiveness of the pattern.

2. One subject of the comparison is discussed much more extensively than the other. Given that both parts of a comparison should receive equal treatment, is this imbalance justified? Explain.

3. In a brief outline, list the major topic of each body paragraph.

4. Which are the two most concrete paragraphs in the essay? Briefly explain their function. Why are they placed there in the essay?

5. Which topic sentence in the body serves two individual paragraphs? Is this an effective structure? Explain.

6. The body paragraphs vary greatly in length; is this variation justified? Explain.

7. Could there be other paragraph divisions for this essay? If so, give examples.

Questions About Style

1. Identify two analogies, and explain how they help make the point.

2. How do you interpret "small-bore agonies" in the final paragraph? How does this phrase reinforce the essay's primary meaning?

3. What is the outstanding stylistic feature of this essay? Give examples.

4. Characterize the tone. Give examples of word choice and sentence structure that contribute to the tone.

RESPONDING TO YOUR READING

1. Explore your reactions to *"Campus Center" Versus "Student Union"* by using the questions on page 93. Then respond with your own essay, comparing or contrasting two or more related items to help readers understand your preference.

    You might focus on a school-related topic, as in comparing your high school and college writing classes; or living in a dorm versus living in a fraternity or sorority; or living on campus versus commuting. Or you might compare the positions of two political candidates on local, state, or federal aid to education. Or you might compare two word processing systems.

    If you work part time, you might focus on a work-related topic, as in comparing two job procedures, two locations for a company branch, or two brands of machinery or equipment.

    Be sure your comparison supports a definite viewpoint and rests on a clear basis: costs, uses, benefits, appearance, or the like.

2. After reading "Meaningful Relationships," compose an essay addressing this question: Besides the way people talk about it, in what way has America's perception of romantic love changed over the past couple of decades? By drawing your own comparison, explain why this change has been for better or for worse. For specific examples, you might wish to compare the portrayal of love in older versus recent movies, commercials, magazines, or songs. Or perhaps you could interview parents or grandparents. Be sure your comparison supports a definite point and rests on a clear basis: courtship rituals, premarital relationships, husband-and-wife roles, or the like.

OPTIONS FOR ESSAY WRITING

1. Football, baseball, and basketball were all invented in America, and each has been called "The American Sport." What features do all three sports have in common that reflect distinctively American values, interests, and character?

2. If you had your high school years to relive, what would you do differently?

3. During your years in school, you've had much experience with both good teaching and bad teaching. Based on your experiences, what special qualities are necessary for good teaching? Use a series of contrasts to make your point.

4. Some people use labels (*straight, gay, freak, redneck, hick, nerd,* and the like) to categorize other people. The problem with such labels is that they are stereotypes. It's easy to say that John is a "typical jock" and thereby to ignore his complexity. Think of some label that someone might apply to you, and, through contrast, show how that label would be unfair and inaccurate.

5. Compose an essay on this point: "To some, money is a means; to others, an end."

17
Explaining the Exact Meaning: Definition

All successful writing shares one feature—*clarity*. Clear writing begins with clear thinking; clear thinking begins with an understanding of what all the terms mean. Therefore, clear writing begins with careful definition that both reader and writer understand.

Words can have two kinds of meaning: *denotative* and *connotative*. The denotations of words are the meanings in a dictionary. A word's denotation means the same thing to everyone. The denotation of *apple* is *the firm, rounded, edible fruit of the apple tree.* But words have connotations as well, overtones or suggestions beyond their dictionary meanings. A word can have different connotations for different people. Thus, *apple* might connote *Adam and Eve, apple pie, Johnny Appleseed, apple polisher, good health*, and so on. Denotative definition, then, answers these readers' questions.

What is it?

What is its dictionary meaning?

Connotative definition answers this question:

What does it mean or suggest to you?

329

For an illustration of the differences between denotative and connotative definitions, consider the word *survival*, defined in the dictionary as *the act of remaining alive.* In the next paragraph, the writer finds this denotative definition inadequate to make his point. He therefore provides his own connotative definition:

Main point (1)	[1]The question of the age, we like to think, is one of survival, and that is true, but not in the way we ordinarily mean it. [2]The survival we ordinarily mean is a narrow and nervous one: simply the continuation in their present forms, of the isolated lives we lead. [3]But there is little doubt that most of us *will* survive as we are, for we are clearly prepared to accept whatever is necessary to do so: the deaths of millions of others, wars waged in our name, a police state at home. [4]Like the Germans who accepted the Fascists, or the French citizens who collaborated with the Germans, we, too, will be able to carry on "business as usual," just as we do now. [5]Our actual crisis of survival lies elsewhere, in the moral realm we so carefully ignore, for it is there that our lives are at stake.
Denotative definition (2)	
Cause-effect (3)	
Examples (4)	
Connotative definition (5)	

—Peter Marin

By showing what he *doesn't* mean by *survival*, the author helps us understand what he *does* mean in the final sentence. This technique is called *definition by negation.* We will see definition by negation again, along with other techniques, in the samples that follow.

Using Denotative Definitions

We use denotative definitions for two purposes: (1) to explain a term that is specialized or unfamiliar to our readers, and (2) to explain our exact definition of a word that has more than one meaning.

Most fields have their own specialized terms. Engineers, architects, and builders talk about *prestressed concrete, tolerances,* or *trusses;* psychologists and police officers refer to *sociopathic behavior* or *paranoia;* lawyers and real estate brokers discuss *liens, easements,* and *escrow accounts.* For readers outside the field, these terms must be defined.

Sometimes a term will be unfamiliar to some readers because it is new or no longer in use (*future shock, meltdown,* and *sexism*) or a slang word (*bad, heavy, freak, mad money*).

Once a term such as *paranoia* or *mad money* has been defined, its meaning is not likely to change in another context. And it is easy enough to figure out that technical terms should be defined for nonspecialist readers who have no idea what *prestressed concrete* or *escrow account* means. Some readers, though, are unaware that more familiar terms such as *guarantee, disability insurance, liability, lease,* or *mortgage* take on very specialized meanings in some contexts. What *guarantee* means in one situation is not necessarily what it means in another. Denotative definition then becomes crucial to full understanding by all parties.

CHOOSING THE LEVEL OF DETAIL

How much detail will a reader need to understand a term or a concept? Sometimes you can make your meaning clear with a synonym (a term with a similar meaning). Sometimes you will need a sentence. And often, you will need an entire paragraph—or an essay.

Using Synonyms to Define   Often, you can clarify the meaning of an unfamiliar word by using a more familiar synonym:

> To *waffle* means to be evasive and misleading.

> After the yacht race, the crew came ashore in a *dinghy* (small rowboat).

> The *leaching field* (sievelike drainage area) needs 15 inches of crushed stone.

The definition of *leaching field* would be adequate in a report to a client whose house you are building. But in a town report titled "Groundwater Contamination from Leaching Fields" written for your local board of health, you would need an expanded definition.

Note: Be sure that the synonym clarifies your meaning instead of obscuring it. Don't say:

> A *tumor* is a neoplasm.

Do say:

> A *tumor* is a growth of bodily cells that occurs independently of surrounding tissue and serves no useful function.

Using Sentence Definitions   To be clear, a definition often requires more than a synonym. A sentence definition (which may be stated in more than one sentence) follows a fixed pattern: (1) the name of the term to be defined, (2) the class to which the item belongs, and (3) the features that make the item different from all others in its class. This is the pattern used in dictionaries.

Term	Class	Distinguishing features
polygraph	a measuring instrument	that records changes in pulse, blood pressure, and respiration, and is used in lie detection
carburetor	a mixing device	in gasoline engines that blends air and fuel into a vapor for combustion within the cylinders
transit	a surveying instrument	that measures horizontal and vertical angles
diabetes	a metabolic disease	caused by a disorder of the pituitary or pancreas and characterized by excessive urination, persistent thirst, and inability to metabolize sugar
brief	a legal document	containing all the facts and points of law pertinent to a case and filed by an attorney before arguing the case in court
stress	an applied force	that tends to strain or deform a body

In their presentation, these elements are combined into one or more complete sentences:

Diabetes is a metabolic disease caused by a disorder of the pituitary or pancreas and characterized by excessive urination, persistent thirst, and inability to metabolize sugar.

Sentence definition is especially useful if you need to stipulate your precise definition for a term that has several possible meanings. In construction, banking, or real estate, *qualified buyer* can have different meanings for different readers, as can *remedial student* in education.

GUIDELINES FOR SENTENCE DEFINITIONS

1. *Classify the term precisely.* The narrower your class, the clearer your meaning. *Transit* is classified as a surveying instrument, not as a *thing* or as an *instrument. Stress* is classified as *an applied force;* to say that stress "is what . . ." or "takes place when . . ." is incorrect—these are not words of classification. Diabetes is classified as a *metabolic disease,* not as a *medical term.*

2. *Differentiate the term accurately.* Separate the expression from every other item in the same class. If the distinguishing features are too broad, they will apply to more than this one item. A definition of *brief* as *a legal document used in court* fails to differentiate *brief* from all other legal documents (wills, affidavits, and the like). Conversely, a definition of *carburetor* as *a mixing device* used in automobile engines is too narrow, because it ignores the carburetor's use in all other gasoline engines.

3. *Avoid circular definitions.* Do not repeat, as part of the distinguishing feature, the word you are defining. To say that *stress is an applied force that places stress on a body* is to give a circular definition.

EXPANDED DEFINITIONS

The sentence definition of carburetor on page 332 is adequate for a general reader who simply needs to know what a carburetor is. An instruction manual for mechanics, however, would define *carburetor* in much greater detail; these readers need to know how a carburetor works, how it is made, and what conditions cause it to operate correctly. Your choice of synonym definition, sentence definition, or expanded definition depends on the amount of information your readers need—and that, in turn, depends on why they need it.

As illustration of how the level of detail in a definition is keyed to the needs of the audience, consider this sentence definition:

> It [paranoia] refers to a psychosis based on a delusionary premise of self-referred persecution or grandeur (e.g., "The Knights of Columbus control the world and are out to get me" . . .), and supported by a complex, rigorously logical system that interprets all or nearly all sense impressions as evidence for that premise.

This definition is part of an article published in *Harper's,* a magazine with general readership. We can easily see that the audience will require a more detailed definition of this specialized term. Here is the expanded version:

Main point (1)	[1]Paranoia is a word on everyone's lips, but only among mental-health professionals has it
Sentence definition (2)	acquired a tolerably specific meaning. [2]It refers to a psychosis based on a delusionary premise of self-referred persecution or grandeur (e.g., "The Knights of Columbus control the world and are out to get me" . . .), and supported by a complex, rigorously logical system that interprets all or nearly all sense impressions as evidence for that
Effect-cause (3)	premise. [3]The traditional psychiatric view is that paranoia is an extreme measure for the defense of the integrity of the personality against
Process analysis (4)	annihilating guilt. [4]The paranoid (so goes the theory) thrusts his guilt outside himself by denying his hostile or erotic impulses and projecting them onto other people or onto the
Cause-effect (5-7)	whole universe. [5]Disintegration is avoided, but at high cost; the paranoid view of reality can make everyday life terrifying and social intercourse problematical. [6]And paranoia is tiring. [7]It requires exhausting mental effort to construct trains of thought demonstrating that random events or details "prove" a wholly unconnected premise.
Contrast (8)	[8]Some paranoids hallucinate, but hallucination is by no means obligatory; paranoia is an interpretive, not a perceptual, dysfunction.

—Hendrik Hertzberg and David C. K. McClelland

General readers are much more likely to understand this expanded definition than the sentence definition alone.

As we have seen in earlier sections, synonyms and sentence definitions are part of most writing. But, in turn, expanded definition relies on the various strategies for development discussed in those earlier sections. The specific strategies you choose for expanding a definition will depend on your subject, purpose, and audience needs.

Strategies for development are not rigid, prescribed forms into which you must bend and squeeze your writing; rather, they are the channels of logical thought and clear expression. Thus, the writers of the selection above, defining *paranoia*, combine those development patterns most likely to answer the questions they can anticipate from readers:

What causes paranoia? [*effect-cause*]

How does it happen? [*process analysis*]

What are the effects of paranoia? [*cause-effect*]

How is paranoia different from other mental illnesses? [*contrast*]

Notice how the following definition uses various development strategies to clarify the meaning of a slang term that is no longer in common use:

Main point (1)

Contrast and division (2)

Division (3)

Cause-effect (sentence definition) (4)

Cause-effect as analogy (5)

[1]During my teen years I never left the house on my Saturday night dates without my mother slipping me a few extra dollars—mad money, it was called. [2]I'll explain what it was for the benefit of the new generation in which people just sleep with each other: the fellow was supposed to bring me home, lead me safely through the asphalt jungle, protect me from slithering snakes, rapists, and the like. [3]But my mother and I knew young men were apt to drink too much, to slosh down so many rye-and-gingers that some hero might well lead me in front of an oncoming bus, smash his daddy's car into Tiffany's window or, less gallantly, throw up on my dress. [4]Mad money was for getting home on your own, no matter what form of insanity your date happened to evidence. [5]Mad money was also a wallflower's rope ladder; if a guy you came with suddenly fancied someone else, well, you didn't have to stay there and suffer; you could go home.

—Anne Roiphe

Here again the writer combines development strategies that answer readers' questions about her main point:

Why does this generation not worry about *mad money*? [*contrast*]

What behavior did a young woman expect (or dread) from a date? [*division*]

What was mad money for? [*cause-effect*]

This expanded definition, from an auto insurance policy, defines *damages for bodily injury to others*, a phrase that could have many possible meanings:

Main point (1)

[1]Under this coverage, we will pay damages to people injured or killed by your auto in

Sentence definition (2)	Massachusetts accidents. [2]Damages are the amount an injured person is legally entitled to collect through a court judgment or settlement.
Cause-effect (3–6)	[3]We will pay only if you or someone else using your auto with your consent is legally responsible for the accident. [4]The most we will pay for injuries to any one person as a result of any one accident is $5,000. [5]The most we will pay for injuries to two or more people as a result of any one accident is a total of $10,000. [6]This is the most we will pay as the result of a single accident no matter how many autos or premiums are
Negation (7)	shown on the Coverage Selections page. [7]We will *not* pay: for injuries to guest occupants of your auto; for accidents outside of Massachusetts or in places in Massachusetts where the public has no right of access; for injuries to any employees of the legally responsible person if they are entitled to Massachusetts workers' compensation benefits.

This definition is designed to answer two basic questions:

Under what conditions will the insurer pay damages?

Under what conditions will the insurer not pay?

Thus the development patterns of *cause-effect* and *negation* (showing what something *isn't*) most logically serve the purpose of this definition.

Using Connotative Definitions

A denotative definition can take us only so far. It cannot communicate the special meaning a writer may intend. In such cases, connotative definitions explain *exactly* what we mean. Connotative definitions explain terms that hold personal meanings for the writer beyond their mere dictionary definitions. Because they introduce readers to the writer's complex, private associations, connotative definitions almost always call for expanded treatment.

In the next paragraph, the denotative definition of *house (a struc-*

ture serving as a dwelling) is replaced by a more personal, artistic, and spiritual definition:

Main point (1)*
Analogies (2-4)

[1]What is a house? [2]A house is a human circumstance in Nature, like a tree or the rocks of the hills; a good house is a technical performance where form and function are made one; a house is integral to its site, a grace, not a disgrace, to its environment, suited to elevate the life of its individual inhabitants; a house is therefore integral with the nature of the methods and materials used to build it. [3]A house to be a good home has throughout what is most needed in American life today—integrity. [4]Integrity, once there, enables those who live in that house to take spiritual root and grow.

— Frank Lloyd Wright

For other people, *house* might connote a place to live, something to buy and sell, or peace and security. But to this great architect, *house* takes on a special meaning, one that he explains through a series of analogies.

Application 17-1

Adequate formal sentence definitions require precise classification and detailed differentiation. Tell whether you think each of these definitions is adequate for a general reader. Rewrite those that seem inadequate. If necessary, consult dictionaries and specialized encyclopedias. Discuss your revision in class.

1. A bicycle is a vehicle with two wheels.

2. A transistor is a device used in transistorized electronic equipment.

3. Surfing is when one rides a wave to shore while standing on a board specifically designed for buoyancy and balance.

4. Bubonic plague is caused by an organism known as *Pasteurella pestis.*

5. Mace is a chemical aerosol spray used by the police.

---

*A question is a good beginning for an expanded definition.

6. A Geiger counter measures radioactivity.

7. A cactus is a succulent.

8. In law, an indictment is a criminal charge against a defendant.

9. A prune is a kind of plum.

10. Friction is a force between two bodies.

11. Luffing is what happens when one sails into the wind.

12. A frame is an important part of a bicycle.

13. *Hypoglycemia* is a medical term.

14. An hourglass is a device used for measuring intervals of time.

15. A computer is a machine that handles information with amazing speed.

16. A Ferrari is the best car in the world.

17. To meditate is to exercise mental faculties in thought.

Application 17–2

PARAGRAPH WARM-UP: DENOTATIVE DEFINITION

Using denotative definition, write a paragraph explaining the meaning of a term that is specialized, new, or otherwise unfamiliar to your reader. List in the margin the strategies for expansion you've used. Begin your paragraph with a formal sentence definition (term-class-differentiation). Select a term from one of the lists below, from your major (defined for a nonmajor), or from your daily conversation with peers (defined for an elderly person).

Identify clearly the situation, the audience, and your purpose.

Specialized terms	Slang terms
summons	jock
generator	Yuppie
dewpoint	nerd
capitalism	turkey
salt marsh	groupie

economic recession	fox
microprocessor	to break
water table	boss
T-square	getting it together
editorial	awesome
fashion	macho

Application 17–3

PARAGRAPH WARM-UP; CONNOTATIVE DEFINITION

Using connotative definition, write a paragraph explaining the special meaning or associations that a term holds for you. Select a term from the list below, or provide one of your own. List in the margin the expansion strategies you've used. Identify clearly the situation, the audience, and your purpose.

patriotism	education	freedom
trust	marriage	courage
friendship	God	peace
progress	guilt	morality
beauty	the perfect date	happiness
adult	sex appeal	fear

Application 17–4

ESSAY ANALYSIS AND PRACTICE

After reading this essay, answer the study questions. Then select one of the essay assignments.

The Belated Father

[1]There is a small clipping, no more than 2 square inches, that has been in my file marked "Fathers" since last fall. It's a simple

story about a judge in western Massachusetts who, when confronted with a 15-year-old kid in trouble, made an unusual judgment. He sentenced the father to 30 days of dinner at home.

[2]There are some other things in the folder. One is a letter to an advice column from a woman whose husband has never kissed their baby son because he said, "I felt funny kissing a guy." Behind that letter is a statistic: "Ten percent of the children in this country live in fatherless homes."

[3]There is also a quote from a novel about the children of the sixties, written by Stephen Koch. It says, "Who among those fiery sons, with their vague and blasted eyes, really connected with his father; who even knew, let alone admired, what the father did in that invisible city of his? Fatherhood meant delivering, or not delivering, checks. It meant not being around, or being unwelcome when around. It meant either shouting or that soul-crushing silence most deeply installed in the soul of any red-blooded American boy: Dad mute behind his newspaper."

[4]I wish there were something else in the file folder, some story, some role model you could applaud.

[5]There are so many young fathers who don't want to be like their own dads. They feel awkward when they find themselves alone with their fathers today. They flip through their own mental files on the subject. There is Father Knows Best and Father Knows Nothing, Father as Pal, and Father as Trans-parent. There is even an occasional full-time father—who trips in all the pitfalls of full-time mothers.

[6]None of these will do. They don't fit. They don't feel right. So these sons are trying to devise their own role models, to be their own first generation. They are becoming—what shall we call them?—working fathers.

[7]Margaret Mead has written that "human fatherhood is a social invention." Maybe so. But they are re-inventing it. They want to be involved in the full range of their children's lives, to know which days the kids have to wear sneakers for gym and which kid would starve before he'd eat cauliflower.

[8]They are learning to deal with kids when they are crying or dirty or hungry. As one father said, "When I was a kid, my father would play ball with me, but the minute I hurt my knee, we'd both call for my mother. I don't want to divide my kids like that."

[9]He wants the kind of relationship that is only woven in the intimacy of daily, time-consuming routines during which you "learn" what they call intuition—the second sense that tells you one kid is worried and another is sad, and the difference between a cry that is tired and one that is hungry or hurt. These fathers don't want to be Sunday events.

[10]On the other hand, they have new guilts. They feel guilty if they miss the school play and guilty if they are tired or out of town. They can't push it down justifying their absence with the need to Make It, or with the notion that children are women's work.

[11]They wonder: "Can I be a successful worker and a successful father?" Their bosses are usually men of their father's generation whose offices are geared to full-time mothers and absent fathers. If they refuse overtime will they get ahead? What if they can't travel their way to a better job?

[12]At the office they suddenly find themselves wondering, Did the babysitter show? I wonder if the bully in the playground is bothering Bobby again? Finally they wonder whether they have enough energy left over from working and fathering for their own lives and plans and marriages.

[13]And when they describe all this, all this that is so new to them, they notice their wives quietly smiling. These fathers you see, are becoming—well, how should we put it? Like us.

—Ellen Goodman

Questions About Content

1. Does the title adequately forecast what is to follow? Explain.

2. Does this essay have a thesis statement? If so, where is it?

3. Why will readers find the content of this essay interesting?

4. Is this expanded definition primarily denotative or connotative? Explain.

5. What is the primary expansion strategy in this definition? Explain.

6. Which paragraph is developed through negation?

7. What is the major development strategy in paragraphs 7–12?

Questions About Organization

1. How many paragraphs make up the introduction? What is the major development strategy in the introduction? Is this strategy effective? Explain.

2. Is the one-sentence paragraph (4) effective? What role does it serve?

3. What role does paragraph 6 serve?

4. Trace the line of thought in this essay. Is this the most effective order? Explain.

5. Does the conclusion relate back to the introduction and the thesis? Explain.

6. Are most paragraphs too short? Explain.

Questions About Style

1. What are the two most notable stylistic features in this essay?

2. Identify the major devices that increase coherence.

3. The writer sometimes uses sentence fragments. Where are they? Are they effective? Explain.

4. What is the author's attitude toward her subject? Identify four terms conveying that attitude.

5. Identify four concrete and specific images that make the essay vivid.

RESPONDING TO YOUR READING

Along with changing times come changes in our way of seeing. Some terms that held meanings for us two or three years ago may have acquired radically different meanings by now. If we once defined *success* narrowly as social status and income bracket, we might now define it in broader words: leading the kind of life that puts us in close touch with ourselves and the world around us, or some such. In similar ways, the meanings of many other terms (*education, friendship, freedom, maturity, self-fulfillment, pain, love, home, family, career, patriotism*) may have changed for us. Although some terms take on more positive meanings, others acquire more negative ones. The meaning of *marriage* will depend on whether the person defining it has witnessed (or experienced) marriages that have been happy and constructive or bitter and destructive. And quite often an entire society's definition of something changes, *marriage* being a good example.

Your assignment is to identify something that has changed in meaning, either for you individually or for our society as a whole. Discuss both the traditional and the new meanings (choosing a serious, ironic, or humorous point of view) in such a way that your definition makes a specific point or commentary, either stated or implied, about society's values or your own. Use Goodman's essay as a model.

OPTIONS FOR ESSAY WRITING

1. Write an expanded definition of "The American Dream"—what this expression means to you or how its meaning has changed for you.

2. Write an expanded definition of *man* or *woman* based on images created by a magazine *(Playboy, Esquire, Cosmopolitan, Ms.)* or by television commercials.

18

Developing a Persuasive Argument

Anticipating Audience Resistance • Having a Debatable Point
• Supporting Your Claim • Appealing to Reason
• Recognizing Illogical Reasoning • Appealing to Emotion
• Applications

Many earlier essays in this book can be called "persuasive"—to the extent that they move readers to agree with particular viewpoints such as these:

- that media reports on African-Americans often are biased (page 262)

- that the "wifely" stereotype persists in today's generation (94)

- that the weather can influence human behavior (307)

- that many of today's young fathers seek real involvement as parents (339)

Although these essays employ various development strategies (illustration, cause-effect, and so on), their underlying goal is to persuade readers to see things the writer's way. Once they have sufficiently enlightened their readers, these writers can expect little disagreement.

But sometimes we write for the *primary* goal of persuasion; we decide to take a stand on an issue about which people always disagree—

no matter how enlightened they become. All kinds of issues routinely provoke argument: about whether something is true or false or good or bad, about what caused something, about what should be done. Examples: *Has television produced a generation of couch potatoes? Do the risks of nuclear power outweigh its advantages? Should your school require athletes to have good grades? Should your dorm be coed? Does your close friend really have an alcohol problem?* In their answers to questions such as these, people disagree. And so we write in hopes of winning readers over to our side.

In a free society, controversy is expressed everywhere. And whatever your stand on any controversy, you can expect some readers to disagree—no matter how long and how brilliantly you argue. But even though you won't change *everyone's* mind, a persuasive argument is bound to influence *some people.* No matter how controversial the issue, your argument still can make a difference.

Anticipating Audience Resistance

Argument focuses on its audience. It may ask them to accept an opinion or to support a position or to take action or to change their behavior. But because it calls for varying degrees of involvement, an argument provokes *resistance* from its readers.

Persuading an audience to accept a conflicting point of view might well be the ultimate measure of a writer's skill. People rarely change their minds—without good reason. When you challenge someone's stand on an issue, or try to change people's behavior, you can expect your audience to react defensively, with questions such as these:

Why should I even read this?

Why should I change my mind?

How can I be sure you are right?

Can you prove it?

How do you know?

Why should I do it?

Says who?

Your problem is getting readers to admit you might be *right*, which means, of course, they will also have to admit they might be *wrong*.

And the size of your problem depends ultimately on who your readers are, what you want them to do, and how strongly they identify with their position. (People who are undecided are easier to persuade than those whose "minds are made up.") The bigger the readers' stake in the issue, the more personal their involvement, the more resistance you can expect. To overcome this resistance, you have to put yourself in your audience's position—you have to see things *their* way before you argue for *your* way. Before you can make readers budge even an inch, before you can create contact, you have to make them realize that your position is worth considering.

Making a good argument requires that you bring together all the strategies and resources you've acquired so far, along with features specific to argumentative writing:

1. a main point or claim that the audience finds debatable

2. convincing support for the claim

3. appeals to the audience's reason

4. appeals to the audience's emotions (as appropriate)

5. a clear and unmistakable line of thought

The final test of any argument is whether its *audience* finds it convincing.

Having a Debatable Point

The main point in an argument must be debatable (something open to dispute, something that can be viewed from more than one angle). Mere statements of fact are not debatable:

Facts
Several nearly disastrous accidents have occurred recently in nuclear power plants.

Women outlive men.

Economic policies of the Bush administration have led to cuts in student loan programs.

More than 50 percent of traffic deaths are alcohol related.

Because these statements can be verified (shown to be true—at least with enough certainty so that most people would agree), they cannot be debated. Nor can matters of taste or personal opinion be debated:

Statements of personal taste or opinion

I love oatmeal.

Salmon is my favorite fish.

Catholics are holier than Baptists.

George Bush's speaking style puts me to sleep.

I hate the taste of garlic.

Likes or dislikes are not issues to be argued; the fact of your preference in such matters already is established. Questions of taste or personal opinion never can be resolved, because they rest on no objective reasons.

Even many main points that call for expository development are not debatable (for most audiences). Consider these topic or thesis statements:

Viewpoints that can be verified

During the last decade, the Moral Majority has gained political influence.

Many of today's music videos demean women or advocate sexual violence.

Competition for good jobs in the 90s will be stiffer than ever.

Police roadblocks help deter drunk driving.

Too many young people are dying because of alcohol abuse.

The truth or validity of these viewpoints can be proved. And once the facts are established, the audience has no choice but to say, "Yes, it's true."

What, then, is a debatable point? It is one that cannot be proved true, but only more or less probable. For example, few readers would debate the notion that electronic games have altered the play habits of millions of American children. But some readers would debate the notion that electronic games are dominating children's lives. Some other debatable points:

Debatable points

The political activities of the Moral Majority violate the constitutional separation of church and state.

> Music videos that demean women or advocate sexual violence should be censored.
>
> Schools should place more emphasis on competition.
>
> Police roadblocks are a justifiable deterrent against drunk driving.
>
> Our state should raise the drinking age to 21.

No amount of reasoning by any expert and no supporting statistics can *prove* the rightness or wrongness of these claims. But even though controversial issues never can be resolved, writers can argue (more or less persuasively) for one side or the other. And—unlike points expressing personal opinion or taste—the validity of an arguable assertion can be measured by the quality of support the writer presents. How does the assertion hold up against *opposing* assertions? In argument, we try to decide on the better approach. The winning argument is the one that presents the best case.

Always state your arguable point directly and clearly as a thesis. Although other development strategies (especially description and narration) sometimes allow the thesis merely to be implied, argumentative writing almost never does. Let readers know exactly where you stand.

The following essay presents the debatable assertion that electronic games are bad for children. As you read this essay, think about the ways our writer supports his claim. Is the support persuasive? Why, or why not?

No, You Can't Have Nintendo

My wife and I are the kind of mean parents whom kids grumble about on the playground. We're among that ever-shrinking group of parents known as Nintendo holdouts. We refuse to buy a Nintendo set. (Nintendo, for those of you who have been living in a cave for the past few years, is something that you hook up to your TV set that enables you to play various games on your home screen.) Around Christmastime, my son made a wish list, and I noticed that Nintendo was No. 1. I said, "You know you're not going to get Nintendo." He said, "I know I'm not going to get it from *you*. But I might get it from *him*." Alas, Santa, too, let him down.

I've heard parents' rationalizations about the games: "They're good for hand-eye coordination." (So is playing ball.) "It's something kids can do without an adult watching." (So is—dare I say that word?—READING.) "While he's playing at the screen, I can relax for a few minutes." (Who among us hasn't used the electronic babysitter from time to time? But "a few minutes"? Who are we kidding?)

I don't think that playing a video game now and then is really harmful to children. But the children I know are so obsessed with these games that they have prompted at least one second-grade teacher (my son's) to ban the word Nintendo from the classroom. When I asked my 7-year-old if the teacher wouldn't let the kids talk about the games because that's all they were *talking* about, he said, "No. That's all we were *thinking* about."

Our society is already so computerized and dehumanized that kids don't need one more reason to avoid playing outside or going for a walk or talking with a friend. I'd still feel this way even if there were nothing intrinsically wrong with games whose objectives are to kill and destroy.

I know, I know. There are games other than those like Rampage, Robocop, Motor Cross Maniacs, Bionic Commando, Dr. Doom's Revenge, Guerrilla War and Super Street Fighter. But aren't the violent games the ones the kids love to play for hours? And hours. And hours. My son told me he likes the "killing games" the best, hasn't had much experience with "sports games," and likes "learning games" the least because they are "too easy." (Manufacturers take note.) My 5-year-old daughter told me she enjoyed playing Duck Hunt at a friend's house. The beauty of this game is that even very young players can have the fun of vicariously shooting animals. And then there's the game with my favorite title—an obvious attempt to combine a graceful sport with exciting action: Skate or Die.

Some might try to convince us that these violent electronic games are good for a child's self-esteem and development. For years psychologists have been telling us how important fairy tales are to help children work out their fears and fantasies about good and evil, life and death. Maybe electronic games are just a modern way of doing this. Maybe, but. . . .

Maybe, but I don't remember kids reading and rereading "Hansel and Gretel" instead of playing outdoors when I was a kid. I don't remember hearing about children stealing money so they could buy copies of "Little Red Riding Hood." I don't remember many of my childhood friends skipping school so they could stay home and read "The Tortoise and the Hare." But this is what's going on with video and computer games.

The January [1990] issue of the *Journal of the American Academy of Child and Adolescent Psychiatry* (foreboding enough title for you?) featured an article entitled "Pathological Preoccupation with Video Games." The author believes that some game manufacturers try to develop programs that "deliberately promote habituation," and the goal of some of the people who make up these games is "to induce an altered level of concentration and focus of attention in the gamester."

If you have children, or know any, doesn't this "altered level of concentration and focus" sound familiar? If not, try talking to a child while he is staring at that screen, pushing buttons. He won't hear you unless the words you happen to be saying are, "I just bought a new game for you."

In case you couldn't tell, I'm worried that electronic games are dominating children's lives. There are games that simulate sports like baseball and basketball, and that's all some kids know about the sports. Someday soon, a young couple will take their children to their first baseball game and hear the kids exclaim. "This is great. It's almost like the *real baseball* we play on our home screen." When I took my son to a recent Lakers basketball game, the thing that seemed to excite him most (in addition to the self-flushing urinal) was a video game in the lobby. You see, if a kid didn't want to be bored watching some of the greatest athletes in the world play, he could just put a quarter in the machine and watch lifeless electronic images instead.

My son's teacher was right. Kids do play and talk about these games too much. They even have books and magazines that kids can study and classes so they can get better at the games. And that's what's got me worried. I'm just concerned that this activity is so absorbing, kids are going to grow up thinking that the first people to fly that airplane at Kitty Hawk were the Super Mario Brothers.

I don't like to discourage children from doing something they're good at; in this case, I must. And believe me, my desire to see them play the games less does not diminish how impressed I am by their skill—they seem to be getting better and better at these games at a younger and younger age. If you believe in evolution, you have to assume that right now DNA is coming together in new ways to create a "Nintendo gene" in our children which they'll pass along to their children. So, our grandchildren will be *born* with the ability to play electronic games. And, about the "Nintendo gene": I've got a feeling it's going to be dominant.

—Lloyd Garver

To support his claim, Garver offers powerful examples of various types of "video domination." Can you identify all his examples? (Try underlining them.) Why do you suppose Garver delays his thesis until paragraph 10? Is this an effective strategy here? Explain.

Supporting Your Claim

In Chapter 6, we saw that any credible assertion rests on opinions derived from facts. But facts out of context can be interpreted in various ways. To ensure that your argument is legitimate, offer convincing reasons, choose reliable sources of information, distinguish objective from subjective evidence, and avoid drawing specious conclusions.

OFFERING CONVINCING REASONS

Any argument is only as convincing as the *reasons* that support it. No matter how "right" you think you are, you have to make your readers agree. And before readers will change their minds, they need to know *why*. They expect you to complete a version of this statement

My position is _____ because _____.

Your reasons follow the "because."

To admit you are *right*, opponents also have to admit they are *wrong*—something few of us are likely to do without pretty good reasons.

Arguing effectively, however, doesn't simply mean unloading on your reader every reason you can think of. Use only those reasons likely to move your specific audience. Assume, for instance, that all students living on your campus have a meal plan with a 15-meal requirement (for weekdays), costing $1800 yearly. You belong to a group trying to reduce the required meals to 10 weekly. Before seeking students' support and lobbying the administration, your group constructs a list of reasons supporting its position. A quick brainstorming session produces this list:

The number of required weekday meals should be reduced to ten per week because:

1. Many students dislike the food.

2. Some students with only afternoon classes like to sleep late, and should not have to rush to beat the 9:00 A.M. breakfast deadline.

3. The cafeteria atmosphere is too noisy, impersonal, and dreary.

4. The food selection is too limited.

5. The price of a yearly meal ticket has risen unfairly and is now more than 5 percent higher than last year's price.

Reviewing this list, you quickly spot a flaw: all these reasons rest almost entirely on *subjective* grounds, on matters of personal taste or opinion. For every reader who dislikes the food or sleeps late, there probably is one who likes the food or rises early—and so on. None of your intended audience (students, administrators) is likely to judge these reasons as very significant.

If you want your reasons to be judged significant, base them on *objective* evidence and on goals and values you and your readers *share*.

Offer Objective Evidence   Evidence is any information that supports your claim. Evidence is objective when it can be verified (shown to be factual) by everyone involved. Common types of objective evidence include statistics, examples, and expert testimony.

Statistics can be highly persuasive. Whenever you have statistics that are relevant to your argument, use them:

> Roughly 30 percent of the 500 students we surveyed in the cafeteria eat only two meals per day.

Any statistics you present have to be accurate and easy for the audience to understand and verify. Always cite your sources.

Examples show specific instances of your point, and they help audiences *visualize* the idea or concept. For instance, the best way to explain what you mean by "wasteful" is to show "waste" occurring:

> From 20 to 25 percent of the food prepared is never eaten.

> Each dorm suite has its own kitchen, but these are hardly being used.

Good examples have persuasive force; they give readers something to hold onto, a way of understanding even the most surprising or unlikely claim. Always use examples your audience can identify with.

Expert testimony lends authority and credibility to any claim. Almost any reader likes to know what the experts have to say:

> Food service directors from three local colleges point out that their schools' optional meal plans have been highly successful.

To be credible, however, an expert has to be unbiased and considered reliable by the audience.

Appeal to Shared Goals and Values   Although objective evidence can be persuasive, evidence alone isn't always enough to change a reader's mind. Audiences expect a writer to share their goals and values. If you hope to make contact, you have to identify at least one goal you and your audience have in common: "What do we both want most?" In the meal plan issue, for example, we can assume that everyone is primarily concerned with eliminating wasteful practices. And so your argument should appeal to such a goal:

> These changes in the meal plan would eliminate waste of food, labor, and money.

Audiences in various situations have various goals (job security, being appreciated, a sense of belonging, safety, prosperity, excitement, or whatever). Be sure your argument takes a common, central goal into account.

Our goals are shaped by certain values (friendship, loyalty, honesty, equality, fairness, and so on).* Make sure your argument appeals to the values you and your audience share. In the meal plan case, *fairness* seems as if it would be an important value:

> No one should have to pay for meals she or he doesn't eat.

If you hope to be persuasive, give readers reasons *that have real meaning for them.*

Here is how your group's final list of reasons might read:

> The number of required weekday meals should be reduced to ten per week because:

1. No one should have to pay for meals she or he doesn't eat.

2. Roughly 30 percent of the 500 students we surveyed in the cafeteria eat only two meals per day

3. From 20 to 25 percent of the food prepared is never eaten—a waste of food, labor, and money.

4. Each dorm suite has its own kitchen, but these are hardly being used.

5. Between kitchen suites and local restaurants, students only on the Monday-through-Friday plan do survive on weekends. Why couldn't they survive just as well during the week?

6. Food service directors from three local colleges point out that their schools' optional meal plans have been highly successful.

---

*From Milton Rokeach, *The Nature of Human Values.* New York: Free Press, 1973: 57–58.

Any reasonable audience should find this argument compelling: each reason is based on a verifiable fact or (as in item 1) good sense. Although these reasons might not move all members of the audience to support your cause, readers will have to admit that your argument is sound; they will understand *why* you've taken your stand.

Always place yourself in the audience's position. Think about reasons *they* will find important—reasons that might very well differ from those *you* find important.

CHOOSING RELIABLE SOURCES

Whether your reasons come from reading, observing, listening, or experiencing, make sure that each source is reputable, authoritative, and objective. Assume that you have set out to support the claim that employees at the fireworks factory where you work part-time should practice Transcendental Meditation to relieve stress. To convince your supervisors and co-workers, you will need to provide (among other things) evidence that meditation has therapeutic benefits for those suffering stress. For part of your supporting evidence you decide to cite outside sources (such as articles and books), to interview some practitioners of meditation, and to cite your own experience.

You can expect claims in a professional journal, such as *The New England Journal of Medicine*, to have bases in scientific fact. Also, a reputable magazine such as *Scientific American* is a dependable source of evidence or of informed opinion. On the other hand, you might wisely suspect the claims in supermarket scandal sheets or movie magazines. Even claims in monthly digests, which offer simplistic, reductive, and mostly undocumented "wisdom" to mass reading audiences, should be taken lightly.

You would need to make sure that you interview only people who have practiced meditation for a long time. Anyone practicing for only a few weeks could not be expected to assess bodily changes reliably. And you would need to interview a representative sample of people who have practiced for a long time: people of both sexes, different ages, different life-styles before they began meditating, and so on.

Your own experience often is an inadequate base for generalizing. You cannot tell whether your experience is in fact representative, regardless of how long you may have practiced meditation. Interpret your experience only within the broader context of your collected evidence.

What kinds of good reasons does Garver's essay (page 348) offer to support his claim? Can you identify specific evidence and appeals (Garver's audience is made up largely of parents. Would the same reasons work for a younger audience? Why, or why not?)

DISTINGUISHING OBJECTIVE FROM SUBJECTIVE EVIDENCE

Objective evidence consists of facts or good sense. It can stand up under testing, because it is verifiable. Subjective evidence consists of opinion. It may collapse under testing unless the opinion is expert, authoritative, and unbiased.

Base your conclusions on objective evidence. Early in your research you might read an article making positive claims about the effects of Transcendental Meditation; however, the article provides no data on measurements of pulse, blood pressure, or metabolic rates. Although your own experience and opinion might fully agree with the author's, you should not hastily conclude that meditation is beneficial to everyone. So far you have only two opinions—yours and the author's—without any scientific support (such as tests of a cross section under controlled conditions). Conclusions now would rest on subjective evidence. Only after a full survey of reliable sources can you decide which conclusions are supported by the bulk of your evidence.

AVOIDING SPECIOUS CONCLUSIONS

Specious conclusions are deceptive, because they seem correct at first glance but are not so when scrutinized. Conclusions based on subjective evidence are often specious, as are sweeping generalities. Conclusions that have been derived speciously fail to stand up under testing. Assume that you are an educational consultant. Your community has asked you to analyze the accuracy of I.Q. testing as a measure of intelligence and as a predictor of students' performance. Reviewing your collected evidence, you find a positive correlation between low I.Q. scores and low achievers, and vice versa. You then verify your own statistics by examining a solid cross section of reliable sources. You might now feel justified in concluding that I.Q. tests do measure intelligence and predict performance accurately. This conclusion might be specious, however, unless you could show that:

1. Neither parents nor teachers nor the children tested had seen individual test scores and had thus been able to develop biased attitudes.

2. Children tested in all I.Q. categories had later been exposed to an identical curriculum at an identical pace. In other words, they were not channeled into programs on the basis of their scores.

Your total data could be interpreted only within the context of these two variables.

Even objective evidence can be used to support specious conclusions, unless such evidence is interpreted precisely, objectively, and within a context that accounts for major variables. Later in this chapter we will discuss the specific kinds of logical fallacies that can make conclusions specious.

Appealing to Reason

Keep in mind that argument is not separate and different from other types of writing discussed earlier in the book. In argument we always rely on some combination of description, narration, and exposition. Many persuasive arguments, however, are built around one or both of these reasoning patterns: *induction* (reasoning from specific evidence to a general conclusion) and *deduction* (applying a proven generalization to a specific case). But before looking at inductive and deductive strategies separately, let's consider how they work together to create sound logic.

Just about any daily decision (including the ones you're asked to make in this book) is the product of inductive or deductive reasoning, or both. Suppose that on registration day you learn you've been assigned to Math 101 with Professor Digit. You immediately decide to request a transfer to some other section. Let's trace the reasoning that led to your decision.

First, you reasoned inductively, from this specific evidence to a generalization:

- *Fact:* Your older brother, a good mathematician and a serious student, received a *D* from Professor Digit two years ago, even though you saw your brother slaving over his math assignments night after night.

- *Fact:* Sixty percent of Professor Digit's students receive a *D* or *F*.

- *Fact:* Professor Digit often remarks, in class, that he despises teaching "dull-witted freshmen."

- *Fact:* Two friends, both good students, failed Professor Digit's course. Each repeated the course with a different instructor: one received a *B +*, one a *B*.

- *Fact:* About one-third of Professor Digit's students drop his course after receiving their first grade.

Based on this evidence, you reached this generalization:

Professor Digit seems to grade his students unfairly.

By reviewing and compiling the evidence, you were able to arrive at an *informed opinion* (a probability, not a fact). You arrived there by *inductive reasoning*. Armed with this generalization, in turn, you were able to use *deductive reasoning* to reach a conclusion:

Generalization	Professor Digit seems to grade his students unfairly.
Specific instance	I am one of Professor Digit's students.
Conclusion	I am likely to be graded unfairly.

Based on this conclusion, you decided to request a transfer to some other section.

We use induction and deduction repeatedly, often unconsciously. Specific facts, statistics, observations, and experiences lead us inductively to generalizations such as these:

Pre-med majors must compete for the highest grades.

Politicians can't always be trusted.

Big cities can be dangerous.

A college degree alone does not ensure success.

This college has a fine reputation.

On the other hand, deductive reasoning leads us from generalizations to specific instances to conclusions.

Generalization	Big cities can be dangerous.
Specific instance	New York is a big city.
Conclusion	New York can be dangerous.

Generalization	Pre-med majors must compete for the highest grades.
Specific instance	Brigitte will be a pre-med major next year.
Conclusion	Brigitte will have to compete for the highest grades.

When we write to convince others that our reasoning is sound, we need to use these processes deliberately and consciously—and to be careful about how sweepingly we state our generalizations.

USING INDUCTION

We use induction in two situations: to move from various items of specific evidence to some related generalization, and to establish the cause or causes of something. Assume that you've been dating someone for a while, but in the last week you've made these observations:

> Eloise hasn't returned my phone calls in a week.
>
> She always wants to go home early.
>
> She yawns a lot when we're together.
>
> She talks to everyone but me at parties.
>
> She does anything to avoid being alone with me.

Based on this evidence, you reason inductively to the generalization:

> Eloise is losing interest in me.

The same kind of reasoning establishes the possible or probable causes of Eloise's aloofness. As you reflect on the relationship, you recall a number of inconsiderate things you've done recently:

> I've been awfully short-tempered lately.
>
> I forgot all about her birthday last week.
>
> I'm usually late for our dates.
>
> A few times, I've made wisecracks about her creepy friends.
>
> In planning a date, I never ask for her opinion.

Thus, you conclude that your own inconsiderate behavior probably has caused your relationship with Eloise to suffer (unless, of course, Eloise has mono or you have developed bad breath).

Induction is a good way to establish probability, arrive at generalizations. Although generalizations aren't *proof* of anything, the better your evidence, the more likely it is that your generalizations are accurate. Avoid basing a generalization on too little evidence. That Eloise yawns a lot would not be sufficient basis for you to conclude that she's losing interest in you. (Maybe she's ill or just chronically tired!) Be sure readers can follow your line of reasoning and can see how your evidence adds up to your generalization as the logical sum of collected evidence. Otherwise, your assertions will seem unreasonable. If Eloise had yawned during only one evening, that fact alone would not support the hasty generalization that your relationship is on the rocks. Provide enough facts, examples, statistics, and informed opinions to make your assertions believable.

As an illustration of inductive reasoning, consider this passage from a 1963 letter by Martin Luther King, Jr., to white clergymen after he was jailed for organizing a demonstration in Birmingham, Alabama.

A key statistic (1)
An informed opinion (2)

Acknowledgment of opposing views (3)
Examples (4)

[1]We have waited for more than 340 years for our constitutional and God-given rights. [2]The nations of Asia and Africa are moving with jetlike speed toward gaining political independence, but we still creep at horse-and-buggy pace toward gaining a cup of coffee at a lunch counter. [3]Perhaps it is easy for those who have never felt the stinging darts of segregation to say, "Wait." [4]But when you have seen vicious mobs lynch your mothers and fathers at will and drown your sisters and brothers at whim; when you have seen hate-filled policemen curse, kick, and even kill your black brothers and sisters; when you have seen the vast majority of your twenty million Negro brothers smothering in an airtight cage of poverty in the midst of an affluent society; when you suddenly find your tongue twisted and your speech stammering as you seek to explain to your six-year-old daughter why she can't go to the public amusement park that has just been advertised on television, and see tears welling up in her eyes when she is told that Funtown is closed to colored children, and see ominous clouds of inferiority beginning to form in her little mental sky, and see her beginning to distort her personality by developing an unconscious bitterness toward white people; when you have to concoct an answer for a five-year-old son who is asking, "Daddy, why do white people treat colored people so mean?"; when you take a cross-country drive and find it necessary to sleep night after night in the uncomfortable corners of your automobile because no motel will accept you; when you are humiliated day in and day out by nagging signs reading "white" and "colored"; when your first name becomes "nigger," your middle name becomes "boy" (however old you are) and your last name becomes "john," and your

wife and mother are never given the respected title "Mrs."; when you are harried by day and haunted by night by the fact that you are a Negro, living constantly at tiptoe stance, never quite knowing what to expect next, and are plagued with inner fears and outer resentments; when you are forever fighting a degenerating sense of "nobodiness"—then you will understand why we find it difficult to wait. ⁵There comes a time when the cup of endurance runs over, and [people] are no longer willing to be plunged into the abyss of despair. ⁶I hope, sirs, you can understand our legitimate and unavoidable impatience.

A generalization from specifics (5)

Main point as a direct appeal(6)

—Martin Luther King, Jr.,

This argument is intended to make Dr. King's readers see things from his point of view. Notice how the inductive argument is organized: sentence 4 carries the burden of support for Dr. King's stand. And the support itself is organized for greatest effect on the audience, with examples that progress from the injustice he has witnessed to the injustice he and his family have suffered to the humiliation he feels. Not only does he provide ample evidence to support his closing generalization (African-Americans have reason to be impatient), but his evidence also adds up logically—and leads dramatically—to his conclusion.

Remember that an argument is only as strong as the objective evidence that supports it. Although the strength of a writer's conviction is important, the evidence is more so. It takes more than determination alone to change people's minds; it takes solid evidence and sound reasoning as well.

USING DEDUCTION

You reason deductively when you use generalizations to arrive at specific conclusions. Once the generalization "African Americans have legitimate cause for impatience" is established *inductively* (and accepted), one can argue deductively:

Generalization	African Americans have legitimate cause for impatience.
Specific instance	Mr. Smith is African American.
Conclusion	Mr. Smith has legitimate cause for impatience.

The conclusion is valid because the generalization is accepted and the specific instance is a fact. Both these conditions *must* exist in order for the conclusion to be sound.

Deductive reasoning applies to specific situations generalizations that are accepted as valid:

Generalization	Students who are required to pay for meals they don't eat are treated unfairly.
Specific instance	Many students at our college are required to pay for meals they don't eat.
Conclusion	Many students at our college are treated unfairly.

Here is how you might use deductive reasoning daily:

If you know that Professor Jones gives no make-up exams, and you sleep through her final, then you can expect to flunk her course.

If you know that Batmobiles need frequent repairs, and you buy a Batmobile, then you can expect to spend many hours repairing your car.

The soundness of deductive reasoning can be measured by sketching an argument in the form of a *syllogism*, the basic pattern of deductive arguments. Any syllogism has three parts: a major premise, a minor premise, and a conclusion—as shown here:

Major premise	All humans are mortal.
Minor premise	John is human.
Conclusion	John is mortal.

If readers accept both premises, they have no choice but to accept your conclusion. For the conclusion to be valid, the major premise must state an accepted generalization, and the minor premise must state a factual instance of that generalization. And the conclusion must express the same degree of certainty as the premises (that is, if a "usually" appears in a premise, it must appear in the conclusion as well). Also, the syllogism must be stated correctly, the minor premise linking its subject with the subject of the major premise; otherwise, the syllogism is faulty, like this:

A faulty syllogism	All human beings are mortal.

John is mortal. [*Minor premise is incorrectly stated; many creatures are mortal, but not human.*]

John is a human being.

Each premise in a syllogism is usually derived from inductive reasoning. Because every human being we've known so far has been mortal, we can reasonably conclude that *all* human beings are mortal. And once we've thoroughly examined and studied John and decided that he is a human being, we can put the two premises together to arrive at the conclusion that John is mortal.

Illogical deductive arguments usually result from a faulty major premise (or generalization). You usually can verify a minor premise easily (merely by observing John, to determine if he is a human being). But the major premise is a generalization; unless you have enough inductive evidence, your generalization can be faulty. How much evidence is *enough?* Let your good judgment tell you. Base your premise on *reasonable* evidence, so that your generalization reflects reality as most people would know it. Avoid unreasonable premises such as these:

Faulty generalizations   All men are male chauvinists.

Cats are sneaky and mean.

School is boring.

Men with long hair are drug addicts.

People can't be trusted.

Frailty, thy name is woman.

Notice the problem when one such generalization serves as the major premise in an argument:

Major premise   People can't be trusted.

Minor premise   My mother is a person.

Conclusion   My mother can't be trusted.

In many deductive arguments, the generalizations are not stated directly; instead they are implied, or understood:

Joe is harming his health with cigarettes. [*Implied generalization: Cigarette smoking harms health.*]

Sally's low verbal scores on her college entrance exam suggest that she will need remedial help in composition. [*Implied generalization: Students with low verbal scores need extra help in composition.*]

Here's what happens to the conclusion when the unstated generalization is faulty:

Dr. Jones is a college professor, and so she must be absent-minded. [*Implied generalization: All college professors are absent-minded.*]

Martha is a feminist, and so she must hate men. [*All feminists hate men.*]

He's our president, and so what he says must be true. [*Presidents are never mistaken or dishonest.*]

In addition to incorrect or unsupported generalizations, another danger in deductive arguments is the *overstated generalization;* that is, making a limited generalization apply to all cases. Be sure to modify your assertions with qualifying words such as *usually, often, sometimes,* and *some,* instead of absolute words such as *always, all, never,* and *nobody.* Notice how these generalizations are overstated:

All Dobermans are vicious.

Politicians never keep their promises.

Rephrase these to make them reasonable and realistic:

Some Dobermans are vicious.

Politicians seldom keep their promises.

And when you apply these generalizations, remember that the conclusion that follows must also be qualified.

This paragraph illustrates a deductive argument.

These ought to be the best of times for the human mind, but it is not so. All sorts of things seem to be turning out wrong, and the century seems to be slipping through our fingers here at the end, with almost all promises unfulfilled. I cannot begin to guess at all the causes of our cultural sadness, not even the most important ones, but I can think of one thing that is wrong with us and eats away at us: we do not know enough about ourselves. We are ignorant about how we work, about where we fit in, and most of all about the enormous, imponderable system of life in which we are embedded as working parts. We do not really understand nature, at all. We have come a long way indeed, but just enough to become conscious of our ignorance. It is not so bad a thing to be totally ignorant; the hard thing is to be partway along toward real knowledge, far enough to be aware of being ignorant. It is embarrassing and depressing, and it is one of our troubles today.

—Lewis Thomas

The deductive argument runs like this:

Implied generalization   People who don't know enough about themselves are in a sad state of mind.

Specific instance   We don't know enough about ourselves.

Conclusion   Therefore, we are in a sad state of mind.

The argument is valid because it meets these criteria:

- The major premise is acceptable.

- The minor premise is verifiable.

- The argument is not overstated. Notice the limiting words:

    all sorts of things [*not* all things]

    almost all promises [*not* all promises]

    one thing that is wrong [*not* everything]

    one of our troubles [*not* all of our troubles]

- The author limits his argument to *one* instance or problem ("we do not know enough about ourselves").

Recognizing Illogical Reasoning

Whether you argue inductively or deductively, beware of the kinds of illogical reasoning called *fallacies* (assertions and statements derived from faulty logic). Because they reveal flaws in your thinking, fallacies weaken your case. By recognizing the most common fallacies, you should be able to avoid them.

MAKING FAULTY GENERALIZATIONS

As we have seen, induction *leads* to a generalization, but deduction *proceeds from* a generalization. And because we all love to generalize, we have to be particularly wary of making two kinds of major errors. Generalizations can be faulty for two reasons:

1. Because they are hasty (based on insufficient or irrelevant evidence), as we have seen in the section on inductive reasoning.

2. Because they are far too broad and sweeping. Something true in one case need not be true in all cases.

How true are these generalizations?

> Blondes have more fun.
>
> Television is worthless.
>
> Humanities majors do not get good jobs.
>
> Money buys happiness.

A common version of faulty generalization is *stereotyping*, the simplistic and trite assignment of characteristics to groups.

> All politicians are crooks.
>
> Southern cops are brutal.
>
> The French are hot-tempered.
>
> The Irish are big drinkers.
>
> Elderly people are senile.
>
> Women cry easily

BEGGING THE QUESTION

You beg the question when you assume that a debatable premise (or premises) underlying your assertion has already been supported convincingly. In other words, you are "begging" readers to accept your premise before you have shown it to be reasonable, as in these examples:

> Useless subjects like composition should not be required.
>
> Voters should reject Candidate *X*'s unfair accusation.
>
> Books like *X* and *Y*, which destroy the morals of our children, should be banned from our libraries.

Such arguments assume in one of their premises what the arguer is supposed to be proving. If a subject is useless, obviously it should not be required. But that it *is* useless is precisely what has to be established. Likewise, Candidate *X*'s accusations have to be proved unfair, and books such as *X* and *Y* have to be proved corrupting. In each of these cases, the arguer is "begging the question" by asking for the desired conclusion without the effort of supporting it by reasoning. Any sound argument is based on valid premises.

AVOIDING THE QUESTION

As we will see in the next section, some appeals to emotions, of course, are legitimate (pity, fear, and the like). But you avoid the question when you distract readers from the real issue with material that is irrelevant or that obscures the issue by making an irrational appeal to emotions.

An appeal to pity

He should not be punished for his assault conviction because as a child he was beaten severely by his parents. [*Has no legal bearing on the real issue: his crime.*]

An appeal to fear

If we outlaw guns, only outlaws will have guns. [*Ignores the question of the deaths and injuries caused by guns.*]

An appeal to normalcy

She is the best person for the teaching job because she is happily married and has two lovely children. [*Has nothing to do with the real issue: her qualifications as a teacher.*]

An appeal to flattery

A person with your sophistication surely will agree that marriage is outmoded. [*Has nothing to do with the conclusion that remains to be verified.*]

An appeal to authority or patriotism

Uncle Sam stands behind savings bonds. [*Ignores the question of whether savings bonds are a good investment: Although they are safe, they often pay lower interest than do some other investments.*]

Snob appeal (persuading readers to accept your assertion because they want to be identified with respected, heroic, or notable people)

A real man knows that *Musk* cologne is the best. [*Has nothing to do with the issue of individual preference or quality.*]

As any intelligent person knows, Candidate A will make a good president. [*Has nothing to do with the candidate's qualifications.*]

Joe Namath makes his popcorn in a *Butter Upper*, and so it must be the best corn popper. [*Has nothing to do with the quality of the item.*]

USING THE BANDWAGON APPROACH

The bandwagon approach gets readers to agree by claiming that everyone else agrees. It urges readers to follow the crowd and thereby avoids the real issue.

No one in our sorority would date men from that fraternity.

Everyone has tried marijuana at least once.

More Cadillac owners are switching to Continentals than ever before. [*Of course, if the numbers provided real evidence, the assertion would be legitimate.*]

ATTACKING YOUR OPPONENT

Another way to ignore the real question is by attacking your opponent through name-calling or derogatory statements about his or her character *(ad hominem argument)*:

The effete intellectual snobs in academia have no right to criticize our increase in nuclear weapons. [*Calling people names does not discredit their argument.*]

He was once convicted for perjury, and so why should we believe what he says? [*How do we know that he hasn't since been honest?*]

College students are too immature to know what they want, and so why should they have a say in the college curriculum? [*College students often are young but not necessarily immature.*]

USING FAULTY CAUSAL ARGUMENT

As we have seen on pages 294–297, a cause can have more than one effect, and vice versa. A faulty causal argument oversimplifies an otherwise complex cause-and-effect relationship:

> Running improves health. [*Ignores the fact that many runners develop injuries, and that some even drop dead while running.*]

> Albert receives good grades because he is brilliant. [*In fact, although Albert may be bright, he also studies a lot and takes easy courses.*]

Another instance of faulty causal argument is assigning the wrong cause or ignoring other causes:

> My girlfriend is depressed because she really can't stand me any more but is afraid to tell me. [*Maybe she's depressed because she failed an exam, or because she had an argument with a close friend, or because a relative is ill.*]

Another mistake is to suggest a causal relationship that doesn't exist simply because one event follows another (*post hoc fallacy*):

> Manfred had a nervous breakdown after taking calculus. [*Actually, Manfred had suffered from serious emotional problems since the death of his family in a fire.*]

Yet another version of faulty causal arguing is *rationalization*, a way of denying the real reasons for our failures:

> I flunked math because the teacher was awful and the book was boring. [*Not because I never studied!*]

> Because I became a father at 19, I was never able to go to college. [*Not because I was too lazy to spend my evenings doing anything but watching television!*]

IMPOSING THE EITHER-OR FALLACY

The either-or fallacy occurs when a writer reduces a complex issue to only two extreme positions or sides—black or white—even though other choices exist.

> Teachers are either boring or eccentric. [*Leaves out many other possibilities.*]

We have the choice between polluting our atmosphere or living without energy. [*Leaves out the possibility of generating clean energy.*]

Marry me, or I'll kill myself.

Like all other appeals to emotion instead of reason, this kind of argument may influence some readers for a while but certainly will crumble when scrutinized.

Appealing to Emotion

Accompanied by a logical argument, an appeal to emotion can be a good way of reaching readers. But such an appeal must address the audience's sense of justice, their desire for self-improvement, their sense of dignity, or their sense of humor—*not* their prejudices, their vanity, their insecurities, or their blind faith. In short, emotional appeals are legitimate to the extent that they appeal to our virtues, not our weaknesses. While an appeal to emotion can strengthen an argument, it *cannot* substitute for an appeal to reason.

A writer makes an effective emotional appeal in four common ways: by showing empathy, by acknowledging opposing views, by maintaining a moderate tone, and by inserting humor where appropriate. Each of these approaches is discussed below.

SHOWING EMPATHY

To show empathy is to identify with the reader's feelings, to express genuine interest in the reader's best interest. Consider the lack of empathy in this paragraph:

> Dear Buck,
>
> After a good deal of thought I've decided to write to you about your weight problem. Let's face it: you're much too fat. Last week's shopping trip convinced me of that. Remember the bathing suit you liked, the one that came only in smaller sizes? If you lost weight, you might be able to fit into those kinds of suits. In addition to helping you look attractive, the loss of 30 or 40 pounds of ugly fat would improve your health. All you have to do is exercise more and eat less. I know it will work. Give me a call if you need any more help or suggestions.

Although this writer makes the problem vivid to his reader and supports his assertions, this argument is almost certain to fail. The writer's superior attitude can't help but alienate the reader. Here is a revised version, now with a distinct expression of empathy.

> Dear Buck,
>
> Remember that great bathing suit we saw in Stuart's the other day, the one you thought would be perfect for the beach party but that didn't come in your size? Because the party is still 3 weeks away, why not begin dieting and exercising so you can buy the suit? I know that losing weight is awfully hard, because I've had to struggle with that problem myself. Buck, you're one of my best friends, and you can count on me for support. A little effort on your part could make a big difference in your life.

The tone of this version communicates the writer's genuine interest in Buck's welfare—and feelings. Without taking a superior position, the writer manages to appeal to Buck's desire for self-improvement. Empathy is especially important in an argument encouraging some specific action on the reader's part.

ACKNOWLEDGING OPPOSING VIEWS

Because an argument addresses readers on the opposing side, you must do everything possible to get them over to your side. *Before* arguing your case, show respect for your readers by acknowledging the merit in their position, as the writer of this passage does:

Orienting statement (1–3)	[1]Well, the moon was there. [2]The moment there was a chance to get on it, someone was bound to try. [3]The process was accelerated by national rivalries, but it would have happened even if the U.S. or the Soviet Union alone had had
Acknowledgment of opposing view (4–5)	a monopoly on rocketry. [4]For any great country has a supply of brave and spirited [people] who would have been ready for any adventure technology might give them. [5]That is grand: it makes one proud of belonging to the same
Writer's argument (6–9)	species. [6]But there is something else that is perhaps not so grand, that is unarguable and also sinister. [7]That is—there is no known example in which technology has been stopped being pushed to the limit. [8]Technology has its own inner dynamic. [9]When it was possible that technology

> could bring off a moon landing, then it was
> certain that sooner or later, the landing would be
> brought off—however much it cost in human
> lives, dollars, rubles, social effort.
>
> —C. P. Snow

This writer takes a controversial position on an event that is almost sacred in American history. But by showing respect for the popular view, he decreases readers' resistance to his own position. Your acknowledgment of opposing views shows that you understand that no arguable position can be *proved* correct. Readers respect fairness.

MAINTAINING A MODERATE TONE

Another way to connect with readers is through a moderate and balanced tone. People are more likely to listen to you if they like you! Resist the temptation to overstate your case to make your point. Stay away from emotionally loaded words that boil up in the heat of argument. This writer is unlikely to win converts:

> Scientists are the culprits responsible for the rape of our
> environment. Although we never see these beady-eyed, amoral
> eggheads actually destroying our world, they are busy in their
> laboratories dreaming up new ways for industrialists and developers
> to ravage the landscape, pollute the air, and turn all our rivers, lakes,
> and oceans into stinking sewers. How anybody with a conscience or
> a sense of decency would become a scientist is beyond me.

Granted, this piece is forceful and sincere and does suggest the legitimate point that scientists share responsibility—but the writer doesn't seem very likable. The paragraph is more an attack than an argument. Besides generalizing recklessly and providing no evidence for his assertions, the writer uses emotionally loaded words (*eggheads, stinking sewers*) that overstate his position. A good argument appeals to *reason*, not just *emotion*. The tone of overstatement here surely will make readers skeptical. Always avoid extreme positions.

Here is another version of the paragraph above. Because the main point is controversial, this writer understates it, thus making his argument more convincing:

> [1]It might seem unfair to lay the blame for impending
> environmental disaster at the doorstep of the scientists. [2]Granted,
> the rape of the environment has been carried out, not by scientists,
> but by profiteering industrialists and myopic developers, with the

eager support of a burgeoning population greedy to consume more than nature can provide and to waste more than nature can clear away. [3]But to absolve the scientific community from complicity in the matter is quite simply to ignore that science has been the only natural philosophy the western world has known since the age of Newton. [4]It is to ignore the key question: who provided us with the image of nature that invited the rape, and with the sensibility that licensed it? [5]It is not, after all, the normal thing for people to ruin their environment. [6]It is extraordinary and requires extraordinary incitement.

—Theodore Roszak

Notice how the argument begins by acknowledging the opposing view (sentences 1–2). The tone is firm yet reasonable. When the writer points the blame at scientists, in sentences 3–4, he offers evidence.

The writer softens his tone while making his point by using a rhetorical question in sentence 4. *Rhetorical questions* are really statements in the form of questions; because the answer is obvious, readers can be expected to provide it for themselves. Used sensibly, a rhetorical question can be a good way of impelling readers to confront the issue (as the question in sentence 2 of the letter to Buck, page 370) without offending them.

When you use rhetorical questions, do so with caution. They can easily alienate readers, especially if the issue is personal:

> Your constant tardiness is an inconvenience to everyone. It's impossible to rely on a person who is never on time. Do you know how many times I've waited in crummy weather for you to pick me up? What about all the appointments I've been late for? Or how about all the other social functions we haven't "quite" made it to on time? It's annoying to everyone when you're always late.

Notice how the aggressive tone of this piece is heightened because of the rhetorical questions. The writer seems to be throwing his friend's bad habit into his face. Such a tone only makes readers defensive.

How big is the problem, and how forceful should you be? Some strong issues may *deserve* the emotional emphasis created by rhetorical questions. This is another kind of decision you need to make continually about your audience and purpose. Notice how this paragraph combines the force of rhetorical questions with a touch of humor.

> I was pleased to have a glimpse of you last night as you honked your horn and whizzed by me (am I right?) at about 100 miles per

hour. Perhaps I'm straining the bonds of our friendship, but here goes. Why do you drive so fast? Don't you have any regard for others? Isn't the world moving fast enough already? I know: You're suicidal—right? Often the ones hurt because of people like you are innocent bystanders: children, senior citizens, little dogs, kitty cats. Is there anything on this list that you do slow down for? And how about yourself? Suppose you wrecked your car and yourself as well. Have you ever thought about being hospitalized for the rest of your life? How about death? That's pretty final. Come on: slow down and live; enjoy the world around you; get a less powerful car; take the bus; ride a bike; walk; call me—I'll give you a ride. Next time you drive by me, I hope to see something more than a flash of light.

Rhetorical questions seem appropriate here because the drastic situation called for drastic persuasive measures. Notice also the short sentences for emphasis.

INSERTING HUMOR WHERE APPROPRIATE

In some situations, your raising an issue—no matter how legitimate— is likely to make your reader defensive. Sometimes a bit of humor can rescue an argument that might otherwise cause hard feelings. In the next paragraph, the writer wanted to call attention to his roommate's sloppiness. With such a delicate issue, the writer decided to add some humor and exaggeration to his argument.

Jack,

If you never see me alive again, my body will be at the bottom of your dirty clothes pile that rises like a great mountain in the center of our room. How did I end up there? Well, while doing my math I ran out of paper and set out for my desk to get a few pieces— despite the risk I knew I was taking. I was met by a 6-foot wall of dirty laundry. You know how small our room is; I could not circumnavigate the pile. I thought I'd better write this note before going to the janitor's room for a shovel to dig my way through to my desk. The going will be tough and I doubt I'll survive. If the hard work doesn't kill me, the toxic fumes will. Three years from now, when you finally decide to do your wash, just hang my body up as a reminder to stash your dirty clothes in your closet where they will be out of sight and out of smell.

Your dead roommate

Of course, humor sometimes works and occasionally doesn't. Always anticipate how your audience will react; otherwise, humor can backfire.

What determines whether your argument creates contact with readers is *how* you say what you have to say. Different purposes and audiences invariably call for different tones—a major decision in persuasive writing.

Make your tone moderate but not voiceless. Readers need to sense a real person behind the words. In the following essay, Laurie Simoneau asks dorm students and parents to support a request for thermostats in each dorm room. As you read the essay, think about how the support, the appeals, and the tone combine for a persuasive argument.

The Sweatbox and the Icebox: Dorm Students Need Thermostats

It's 9 A.M. I peel my sweat-soaked body off the soggy sheet and turn off my alarm. I wipe my moist forehead and chin with a tissue and lick my parched lips. Even though my window is wide open, the heat repels the cold November air. After showering I study my cracked lips and dry, blotchy skin. Infuriated, I dress and head for class.

Upstairs, my friend Lisa crawls out of bed at the sound of her own alarm. She shivers—despite the flannel pajamas, sweatshirt, and wool socks she put on last night in a vain attempt to retain body heat. Her window is shut tight, and so is her heating vent. Lisa complains often to the Housing Office, but her room still freezes.

Within days, the Student Health Office is overrun by sniffling, hacking, sneezing, retching students who must each day either leave the dorms in a sweat, only to face harsh November winds, or who freeze all night long, take hot morning showers, then freeze again until they reach the warmth of the classroom. And these aren't isolated cases: I've surveyed all students in my dorm, and 80 percent complained about room temperatures.

The extreme temperatures of many dorm rooms are hurting students' health and performance. They are getting sick. They are unable to study in the discomfort of their own rooms. They sleep poorly, and they are furious.

The problem has an obvious cause: among the eight rooms in each suite are only two thermostats. And so the occupants of these two rooms adjust the heat to a temperature they find comfortable. As a result, rooms at other points on the heating pipe receive too little or too much heat. The logical solution: install thermostats in the remaining six rooms of every suite.

The cost of dorm housing more than doubles the cost of tuition (for state residents). Students choose dorms over off-campus housing because of the "positive living-learning environment" promised in the college brochures. But many of us, I think, would now scoff at the mention of such a promise. What these sweating, shivering, sniffling, hacking, sneezing, retching students request is a comfortable room temperature *throughout* the dorms. What they need are thermostats.

I ask all students and parents involved to please phone or write the Housing Office (555-1515) to voice your complaint and your request. With your support we can create the "positive living-learning environment" all residential students desire and deserve.

—Laurie Simoneau

In addition to presenting objective evidence (examples, etc.), Laurie writes in a forceful tone. Is such a tone appropriate here? Why, or why not?

Application 18–1

Which of these statements are debatable? Be prepared to give the reasons for your choices. (Review pages 346–350.)

1. Grades are an aid to education.
2. Forty percent of incoming freshmen at our school never graduate.
3. Physically and psychically, women are superior to men.
4. Pets should not be allowed on our campus.
5. Computer courses are boring.
6. Every student should be required to become computer literate.
7. The computer revolution is transforming American business.
8. Computer prices are dropping by as much as 25 percent yearly.
9. French wines are better than domestic wines.
10. French wines generally are more subtle and complex than domestic wines.
11. French wines are overpriced.
12. College is not for everyone.

Application 18–2

Using your own subjects or those below, develop five arguable assertions. (Review pages 346–348.)

Examples

[*sex*] The sexual revolution has created more problems than it has solved.

[*a personal gripe*] The heavy remedial emphasis at our school causes many introductory courses to be substandard.

taxes	law	a classroom incident
sex	music	jobs
drugs	war	a personal gripe
pollution	dorm life	a suggestion for improving something

Application 18–3

The statements below are followed by false or improbable conclusions. What specific supporting evidence would be needed to justify each conclusion so that it is not a specious generalization? (First, you need to infer the missing generalization or premise; then you have to decide what evidence would be needed for the premise to be acceptable.) (Review pages 356–364.)

Example

Only 60 percent of incoming freshmen eventually graduate from this college. Therefore, the college is not doing its job.

To consider this conclusion valid, we would have to be shown that:

1. All freshmen want to attend college in the first place.
2. They are all capable of college-level work.
3. They did all assigned work promptly and responsibly.

1. Eighty percent of black voters in Alabama voted for George Blank as governor. Therefore, he is not a racist.

2. Fifty percent of last year's college graduates did not find the jobs they wanted. Therefore, college is a waste of time and money.

3. She never sees a doctor. Therefore, she must be healthy.

4. This house is expensive. Therefore, it must be well built.

5. Felix is flunking freshman composition. Therefore, he must be stupid.

6. My parents never argue. Therefore, they must be happily married.

7. Abner has never had an accident in two years of driving. Therefore, he must be a good driver.

Application 18–4

Select one of these general claims, and list five specific items that would inductively support each. (Review pages 356–360.)

Example

General claim	We have little cause to be optimistic about our global future.
Inductive support	1. Our environment is becoming more and more polluted.
	2. The nuclear arms race is intensifying.
	3. Energy shortages threaten the economic survival of industrialized countries.
	4. The earth's population will double in 35 years.
	5. Changing weather patterns threaten the world's agricultural production.

1. We have good cause to be optimistic about our global future.

2. College is not for everyone.

3. Grades are (an aid, a detriment) to education.

4. Our school (should, should not) drop student evaluation of teachers.

5. Television has made a (positive, negative) contribution to the education of the young in this country.

Application 18–5

PARAGRAPH WARM-UP: INDUCTIVE REASONING

Using Dr. King's paragraph (page 359) as a model, write a paragraph in which you use inductive reasoning to support a general conclusion about one of these subjects (after you have narrowed it) or about one of your own choice.

highway safety	minorities
a college core requirement	the legal drinking age
the changing role of women	credit cards

Identify your audience and purpose. Provide enough evidence so that readers can follow your chain of reasoning to your conclusion.

Application 18–6

Assume that someone recently has made a decision that you disagree with (say, the dean has imposed a curfew because of several assaults on campus, or a friend has decided to drop out of school). Write a letter to the specific person or group involved, arguing that the decision was unwise, unfair, or in some way harmful. Persuade the audience to change its mind. Provide enough evidence for your assertion, and use a tone that is diplomatic and reasonable. Reserve your main point for the end of your argument.

Application 18–7

One of these conclusions is valid. The others rely on implied generalizations that are faulty or overstated. Identify the errors and revise. (Review pages 360–365.)

1. Because Martha claims to be a feminist, she should support the Equal Rights Amendment.

2. Harold smokes marijuana, and so he is likely to develop lung cancer.

3. Hubert, a typical male, seems threatened by feminists.

4. Because John is now a suburbanite, he will probably become an alcoholic.

5. Because I'm a poor writer, my English instructor must think I'm stupid.

Application 18–8

PARAGRAPH WARM-UP: DEDUCTIVE REASONING

Select an accepted generalization from this list or use one of your own as the topic statement in a paragraph using deductive reasoning. (Review pages 360–364.)

- "Beauty is in the eye of the beholder."

- "That person is richest whose pleasures are the cheapest."

- Some teachers can have a great influence on a student's attitude toward a subject.

- A college degree doesn't guarantee career success.

Application 18–9

Assume that you have a younger brother, sister, or friend who is thinking about attending your college. Based on what you know about your reader's needs, write a letter that argues for or against attending.

Application 18–10

Identify the fallacy in each of these sentences, and revise the assertion to eliminate the error. (Review pages 364–369.)

Example

Faulty   Television is worthless. [*sweeping generalization*]

Revised   Commercial television offers too few programs of educational value.

1. Mary dropped out of school because Professor Quantum gave her an F in math.

2. Because our product is the best, it is worth the high price.

3. America—love it or leave it.

4. Three of my friends praise their Jettas, proving that Volkswagen makes the best car.

5. My grades last semester were poor because my exams were unfair.

6. Anyone who was expelled from Harvard for cheating could not be trusted as a president.

7. Until college students contribute to our society, they have no right to criticize our government.

8. Because he is a devout Christian, he will make a good doctor.

9. Anyone with common sense will vote for this candidate.

10. You should take up tennis; everyone else around here plays.

11. Poverty causes disease.

12. Convex running shoes caused Karl Crane to win the Boston Marathon.

Application 18–11

Revise this paragraph so that its tone is more moderate and reasonable, more like an intelligent argument than an attack. Feel free to add personal insights that might help the argument.

> People who argue that marijuana should remain outlawed are crazy. Beyond that, many of them are mere hypocrites—the boozers of our world who squander their salary in bars and come home to beat the wife and kids. Any intelligent person knows that alcohol burns out the brain, ruins the body, and destroys the personality. Marijuana is definitely safer; it leaves no hangover; it causes no physical damage or violent mood changes, as alcohol does; and it is not psychologically or physically addictive. Maybe if those redneck jerks who oppose marijuana would put down the beer cans and light a joint, the world would be a more peaceful place.

Application 18–12

After reading this paragraph, answer the questions that follow.

> [1]Responsible agronomists report that before the end of the year millions of people, if unaided, might starve to death. [2]Half a billion

deaths by starvation is not an uncommon estimate. [3]Even though the United States has done more than any other nation to feed the hungry, our relative affluence makes us morally vulnerable in the eyes of other nations and in our own eyes. [4]Garret Hardin, who has argued for a "lifeboat" ethic of survival (if you take all the passengers aboard, everybody drowns), admits that the decision not to feed all the hungry requires of us "a very hard psychological adjustment." [5]Indeed it would. [6]It has been estimated that the 3.5 million tons of fertilizer spread on American golf courses and lawns could provide up to 30 million tons of food in overseas agricultural production. [7]The nightmarish thought intrudes itself. [8]If we as a nation allow people to starve while we could, through some sacrifice, make more food available to them, what hope can any person have for the future of international relations? [9]If we cannot agree on this most basic of values—feed the hungry—what hopes for the future can we entertain? [10]Technology is imitable and nuclear weaponry certain to proliferate. [11]What appeals to trust and respect can be made if the most rudimentary of moral impulses—feed the hungry—is not strenuously incorporated into national policy?

—James R. Kelly

1. Is this argument inductive or deductive? Explain.

2. Does the author appeal to our emotions? If so, where and how?

3. In which sentences does he support his position with hard evidence?

4. Restate the main point as a declarative sentence. Is the point arguable? Explain.

5. Identify one short sentence that provides emphasis. Explain how it reinforces the author's position.

6. Are the rhetorical questions effective here? Explain.

Application 18-13

RESPONDING TO YOUR READING

Explore your reactions to "No, You Can't Have Nintendo" (pages 348–350) by using the page 93 questions. Then respond with an essay of your own. You might challenge Garver's view by pointing out the benefits of electronic games. Or you might support his view by pointing out other electronic forms of "contemporary domination" (say, televised sports, political advertising, product advertising, sit-com views of the world, violence toward women in television shows, and so on). Or you might take some middle position on the issue. Whatever your stance, be sure to support your view with clear, logical reasoning and solid evidence.

19

Composing Various Arguments

Shaping to Reveal Your Line of Thought
• Observing Audience Guidelines • Observing Ethics Guidelines
• Specific Goals of Argument • Applications

Persuasion, at best, is risky business, because no single approach is guaranteed to work. Your own approach will depend on the people involved, the relationships, and the topic. And if the audience is truly resistant, even the best arguments might fail. Although you have no way of predicting whether your efforts will succeed, the chances improve immensely when your argument is emphatic, engaging, and fair.

Shaping to Reveal Your Line of Thought

As you plan, draft, and revise your argument, give it a shape that emphasizes key material, a shape readers can recognize. Readers want to be able to follow your reasoning; they expect to *see* how you've arrived at your conclusions.

Like other writing for other aims, persuasive writing has an introduction, body, and conclusion. But within this familiar shape, your argument should do some special things as well.

Standard shape for an argument

Introduction (Attracts and Invites Your Readers and Provides a Forecast)

- Identify the issue clearly and immediately. Show the audience that your essay deserves their attention.

- Acknowledge the opposing viewpoint *accurately*, and concede its merit.

- Offer at least one point of your own that your audience can agree with.

- As you build to your thesis, offer *significant* background material so that your readers are fully prepared to understand your position.

- State a clear, concrete, and *definite* thesis. Never delay your thesis without good reason. (For now, you might list supporting points in your thesis statement.) Of course, if your thesis is highly controversial, you might want to delay it until you've had a chance to offer some convincing evidence.

- Do all these things in no more than a few paragraphs.

Body (Offers the Support and Refutation)

- Use reasons that rest on *impersonal* grounds of support.

- In one or more paragraphs *each*, organize your supporting points for best emphasis (from least to most important or dramatic or compelling, or vice versa). If you think your audience has little interest, begin with the more powerful material. Sometimes you can sandwich weaker points between stronger points. But if all your points are equally strong, begin with the most familiar and acceptable to your audience—to elicit some early agreement. In general, try to save the strongest points for last.

- Develop each supporting point with concrete, specific *details* (facts, examples, narratives, quotations, or other evidence that can be verified empirically or logically). Never be vague.

- Using transitions and other connectors, string your supporting points and their supporting evidence together to show a definite line of reasoning.

- In at least one separate paragraph, refute opposing arguments (including any anticipated readers' objections to your points)— unless you've done your refuting earlier or throughout.

Conclusion (Sums Up Your Case and Makes a Direct Appeal)

- Summarize your main points and your refutation, emphasizing your strongest material. (Keep things short and sweet.) Offer a view of the Big Picture.

- End by appealing directly to readers for a definite action (where appropriate).

- Let readers know what they should be doing or thinking or feeling after reading your argument.

The sample arguments in Applications 19–1 through 19–4 are each shaped around some version of this model. Virtually no argument, however, rigidly follows the order or specifications outlined here. Select whatever shape you find useful in your situation—as long as it reveals your line of thought.

By shaping your argument deliberately, you stand the best chance of moving your audience to accept or appreciate—or at least understand clearly—your way of seeing something controversial.

Observing Audience Guidelines

Whenever you set out to persuade, always keep in mind this one principle:

> If the argument doesn't work in the eyes of its audience, it doesn't work at all.

Readers expect to be able to *identify* with you and with what you're saying. If they can't agree that your argument has meaning for *them* personally, or if they decide they dislike you, readers will reject *anything* you say.

Connecting with an audience means being able to see things their way. The following guidelines can help you make that connection.

1. Spend a lot of time anticipating how your opponent (or readers) will react, and tailor your argument to address that reaction. If you expect an angry response, find ways to lessen the anger and to create contact.

2. *Never* misrepresent the opposition. A sure way to lose an argument is to make the opponent more of a "bad guy" or simpleton than the facts warrant. Be sure your interpretation of opposing viewpoints is in no way distorted.

3. Try to concede *something* to the opponent. Surely your opponents have at least one good reason for their position! Acknowledge the merits of their case *before* arguing for the superiority of your own. Try not to seem like a know-it-all.

4. Avoid extreme personas. *Persona* is the image or impression of a writer that comes through "between the lines." Be sure your persona comes across as *reasonable*—not fanatical. When we're feeling strongly *for* something, and our audience feels just as strongly *against* it, we tend to become angry or impatient or frustrated; sometimes the temptation to be righteous or indignant or downright hostile to opponents seems overpowering. Suppressing these impulses to "tell someone off" is crucial. People simply tune out people they don't like—no matter how good the argument. Make your persona likable. Admit the imperfections in your case. A little humility never hurts.

5. Find points of agreement with your audience. Get them to say yes early.

6. Try to anticipate the reader's biggest objection to your position, and address it in detail.

7. Use only your best material. Not all your material is likely to be of equal strength or of equal significance to your audience. Decide carefully which material—from your *audience's* view— best supports your case.

8. Make no claim unless you can support it with good reasons.

9. Never make a claim or ask for a response you know readers will reject outright. Ask for something your audience can live with.

The following persuasive letter observes the previous guidelines. Our writer, Brook Biddle, applied earlier to a state university for mid-year acceptance as a full-time transfer student. But, facing severe budget cuts, the university decided not to review any applications for mid-year transfer. And so Brook appeals his case directly to the University president.

As you read Brook's letter, think about the ways he makes a human connection and how he appeals to reason.

Dear President Mason:

As fall semester ends, I face bleak prospects: After three semesters of excellent work as a special student, I had planned to begin the new year fully enrolled at State U. Enter the budget cuts.

Having reached the credit limit for special students, I'm now looking at the end of my academic career for at least a semester, if not forever.

I realize that the budget cuts mandated drastic measures on your part. However, the decision not to review mid-year transfer applications may have already served its purpose. If so, might there be time to review those applications and admit the very best applicants on a space-available basis?

Of all the tough decisions you've had to make in this financial crisis, the decision not to review mid-year applications must have been one of the toughest. On one hand, you have a responsibility not to "water down" the education of those students already admitted. On the other hand, you have a responsibility toward students who have been working hard at junior colleges or as special students, all in hopes of being admitted this winter. It's not fair for the presently enrolled students to have their classes overcrowded by mid-year transfers, but then again, it's not fair for the transfer students to be denied a chance.

The legislature understandably needs to receive a loud and clear message that State U is struggling. And I see the danger of legislators interpreting transfer admissions as a sign of "business as usual"—a sign that State U has weathered these cuts and thus might be able to handle further cuts.

I don't envy your role in the decision process, and I'm in no position to fault your handling of the issue. Maybe this is just the kind of "blood" our legislature had to see.

Through state house demonstrations (of which I was a part), countless protest letters and phone calls, and political SOS's from higher education officials, we have implored the legislators to ease up. And they have been forced to listen. Almost as soon as they had announced the latest round of cuts, the legislature felt compelled to soften the blow by almost one-third. Maybe the university's political hardball helped.

But the point has now been made. State U has profited from its decision not to review mid-year applications, and there still may be time to counteract the losses.

Besides benefiting the students themselves, mid-year transfers would benefit the university. A transfer student occupying an otherwise empty seat costs State U no money; tuition dollars, in fact, bring money in. And assuming that only the best students are admitted, they enhance the entire student body.

Of course, some majors already are overcrowded, and so transfers would have to be admitted on a space-available basis. The Registrar assures me that he has worked with the admissions office in earlier years to fill last-minute spaces with transfers as late as mid-January. And the Admissions Director claims that his office's role in this process is "the easy part."

I realize that even the "easy part" might not be so easy at this late stage, but I would love to see the university give it a try.

Picture State U after the budget cuts, and what do you see? The football, basketball, and hockey teams are still playing. The radio station is still broadcasting.

What's missing from this picture? Students. A couple of dozen highly motivated transfer students. So what's the big deal? The university can get by without these students.

The big deal is that the university exists to educate. Without a football team you can still have a university. Without a track team, without a swimming pool, even without a radio station or newspaper you can still have a university. As long as teachers are teaching students, there is still a university. But take away the students, and what's the point? Students should come first, and they should go last.

Respectfully,

Christopher B. Biddle

Christopher B. Biddle

Befitting the relationship with his reader, Brook's tone is forceful but respectful and *reasonable*. Brook is careful to ask for nothing the reader would consider extreme or outrageous. Instead of special consideration for himself only ("Make an exception for me") he asks that *all* transfer applications be reviewed ("Give us all a fair chance"). And by citing the views of other university officials, Brook shows he has done his homework on this issue.

Observing Ethics Guidelines

We argue to change readers' thinking, but not "to win" at any cost. An effective argument is not necessarily an *ethical* argument. For instance, advertisers effectively advance an implied argument that goes something like this: "Our product is just what you need!" Some of their more specific claims: "Our artificial sweetener is made of proteins that occur naturally in the human body [amino acids]" or "Our potato chips contain no cholesterol." Such claims are technically accurate, but misleading: amino acids in artificial sweetners can alter body chemistry to cause headaches, seizures, and possibly brain tumors; potato chips are loaded with saturated fat—from which the liver produces cholesterol. While the advertiser's claims may be factual, these facts are incomplete, and they imply misleading conclusions. Can you think of other examples from advertising or politics?

Whether such miscommunication occurs deliberately or through neglect, a message is unethical when it prevents readers from making their best decision. To be ethical, writing must meet standards of honesty, fairness, and concern for everyone involved.*

To help ensure that whatever you write is ethical, ask yourself these questions:

- Do I avoid exaggeration, understatement, sugarcoating, or any distortion that leaves readers at a disadvantage?

- Do I really know what I'm talking about—or am I "faking it"?

- Am I being honest and fair with everyone involved?

- Am I reasonably sure that what I'm saying harms or endangers no one?

- Do I give readers all the understanding and information they need for making an informed decision?

- Do I give readers a clear view of *both* sides of the argument?

- Do I make readers aware of alternatives to my position, if there are any?

- Do I give full credit to all sources of ideas and information?

---

*This list was largely adapted from Stephen H. Unger, *Controlling Technology: Ethics and the Responsible Engineer.* New York: Holt, 1982: 39–46; Richard L. Johannesen, *Ethics in Human Communication,* 2nd Edition. Prospect Heights, Illinois: Waveland, 1983: 21–22; George Yoos, "A Revision of the Concept of Ethical Appeal," *Philosophy and Rhetoric* 12 (Winter 1979): 41–58.

When we argue, we often are tempted to emphasize anything that advances our case and to ignore anything that impedes it. But readers always expect fair treatment. Don't let them down by merely doing "whatever it takes" to be persuasive.

Specific Goals of Argument

We argue so that readers will see things our way. In this sense, all arguments share a goal. But arguments can differ considerably in their intended effect on readers—in what they ask readers to do. The goal of an argument might be to influence readers' opinions, seek readers' support, propose some action, or change readers' behavior. Let's look more closely at different arguments that seek different levels of involvement from readers.

ARGUING TO INFLUENCE READERS' OPINIONS

An argument intended to change an opinion is aimed for minimal involvement from its readers. Maybe you want readers to agree that specific books and films should be censored, that women should be subject to military draft, that grades are a detriment to education, that yuppies are ruining city neighborhoods. Or maybe you seek agreement on the reverse of any of these positions. The specific goal behind any such argument is merely to get readers to change their thinking, to say "I agree."

ARGUING TO ENLIST READERS' SUPPORT

In seeking readers' support for our argument, we ask readers not only to agree with a position but to take a stand as well. Maybe you want readers to vote for a candidate, reject a plan for fluoridating the public water supply, lobby for additional computer equipment at your school, or help enforce dorm or library "quiet" rules. The goal in this kind of argument is to get readers actively involved, to get them to ask "How can I help?"

MAKING A PROPOSAL

The world is full of problems to solve. And *proposals* are designed precisely to solve problems. The type of proposal we examine here typically asks readers to take some form of direct action (to improve dorm security, fund a new campus organization, or improve working conditions). But before readers can be persuaded to *act*, they have to agree that the problem is worth their attention. And once they've agreed, readers need a definite plan for solving the problem. A proposal writer's job, specifically, is to satisfy these four criteria:

1. spell out the problem (and its causes) in enough detail to convince readers of its importance

2. point out the benefits of solving the problem

3. offer a realistic solution

4. urge the reader to act on the proposed solution

Proposal writers have to think very carefully about *exactly* what they want their readers to do. This kind of argument seeks to get readers to say "Let's do it."

ARGUING TO CHANGE READERS' BEHAVIOR

Persuading readers to change their behavior is perhaps the biggest challenge in argument. Maybe you want your boss to treat employees more fairly, or a friend to be less competitive, or a teacher to be more supportive in the classroom. Whatever your goal, readers are bound to take your argument personally. And the more personal the issue—the more readers are asked to do—the greater resistance you can expect. This kind of argument is especially difficult because it is more personal than a proposal. With it we try to get readers to say, "I was wrong. From now on, I'll do it differently."

SAMPLE ARGUMENTS

The four essays shown in Applications 19–1 through 19–4, respectively, are addressed to readers who have an increasing stake or involvement in the issue. By reading and comparing these essays, you will get a good sense of how writers in various argumentative situations can reveal persuasively *their* way of seeing.

Application 19–1

ESSAY PRACTICE: ARGUING TO INFLUENCE READERS' OPINION

The writer of this essay argues that traditional city neighborhoods are losing their character as they are transformed into suburb-like havens for affluent young professionals. Read the essay, and answer the

questions that follow. Then (as your instructor requests) select one of
the essay assignments.

The Evils of Gentrification

[1]As a child, I always dreamed of living in a big city. It didn't
matter which, so long as it had more people than I could possibly
know and more places than I could ever visit. In the small
Midwestern suburb where I grew up, I knew every face, building,
and street sign by heart. A single city neighborhood seemed to
possess more diversity, excitement, and character than all the
shopping malls, manicured lawns, and clean suburban streets I had
ever seen. I was eager to leave those clean streets behind.

[2]But now I find that the very presence of people like myself—
men and women between the ages of 18 and 34 who are choosing to
stay single and childless—is changing the face of American cities,
making them oddly like the suburbs where we grew up. We have
altered the landscape to suit our needs. Our socioeconomic status
has given us the power to spend, and thus, the power to transform
neighborhoods once defined by racial and ethnic characteristics. The
blacks and the Jews and the Irish have dispersed; we, the baby boom
kids, have taken their place.

[3]This process has been given the rather awkward title of
"gentrification," but I would prefer to leave that term in the hands
of the sociologists who coined it. No single word can describe a
phenomenon that forces the neighborhood dry cleaner to close his
doors and brings in a $1-a-scoop ice cream store to take his place.
That is what happened on Columbus Avenue in New York City, the
"New Town" lakefront neighborhood in Chicago, the Montrose
section of Houston, the Capitol Hill neighborhood in Washington,
D.C., and the other areas where the young, affluent baby boom
spenders gather to live and consume.

[4]Nor can a sociological term match the experience of a walk
down the Main Streets of these new neighborhoods, all born within
the last decade. On New York's Columbus Avenue, young people
pack the sidewalks each night, eating $5 hamburgers at high-tech
restaurants and buying $15 glitter socks at new-wave boutiques. For
groceries they must walk 10 minutes to the nearest A&P; for a pair
of Keds sneakers or a haircut, they must go even farther. The barber
shop is gone, the shoe store is gone, the grocery is gone.

[5]The attraction of these new neighborhoods is simple: as young
people delay marriage and children, they more desperately need, and
thus seek, the company of others like themselves. The marketplace
understands that need and exploits it, which is why young people on
Capitol Hill are spending more than $500 a month for studio
apartments that only a few years ago cost half as much. In Chicago,

you could live in the Northwest Side's ethnic neighborhoods and pay next to nothing for rent—but where would you go to buy a half-pound of chocolate-chip cookies at midnight?

⁶And so we move into these tiny, overpriced apartments, driving out the poor, the middle class, and even the children, turning the neighborhood into the exclusive domain of the singles and the childless. As of 1980, Manhattan had a population-per-household of 1.96; that's the second lowest in the nation, right behind the Kalawao leper colony in Hawaii.

⁷It isn't merely those who decide to delay marriage and children who have prompted the change, but also the growing homosexual population that will remain permanently childless and affluent. Even in macho Houston, the gay population has come into the open as an economic force. Although the rest of Houston may look down its nose at the Montrose section's newfound gay chic, it can't help but appreciate the potent power of money to create a viable neighborhood.

⁸I say viable because many people defend this process of neighborhood transformation. They argue that the new stores and restaurants provide a city-to-city anchor for a nomadic society; one can move from Chicago to Boston and find a virtually identical neighborhood to live in. There's hardly a city left in America that doesn't have some sort of "gentrified" quarter—from San Francisco, where one might argue that the whole city has been transformed, to Washington, where changes are just beginning.

⁹I can't really argue with that defense. It is comforting to find good restaurants close by, nice stores, perhaps a theater showing a movie I want to see. But it also feels suspiciously like something I grew up with in that small Midwestern suburb: the shopping mall. A day spent in Chicago's New Town is not all that different from a day at the giant Woodfield Mall in the Chicago suburb of Schaumburg.

¹⁰So now, thanks to the sheer economic force of my generation, I don't have to move back to the suburbs. The suburbs have moved to me. I can walk out my door and find all the stores I want; I don't even have to drive. I can buy a baseball cap with horns on each side, a takeout container of homemade linguini with clam sauce, a greeting card that will make me seem quite clever. Everything I want is right in front of me—everything except the city of my childhood dreams.

—David Blum

Questions About Content

1. Does the writer acknowledge the opposing viewpoint? If so, where?

2. Does the writer concede anything to his opponents (give them credit for anything)? Explain.

3. Does the thesis grow out of sufficient background details? Explain.

4. Does the writer offer convincing reasons for his case? Explain.

5. Does the writer make too much of an emotional appeal? Explain.

Questions About Organization

1. Which strategy of expository development is used most here?

2. Trace the line of thought by summarizing the topic of each paragraph. Is the material arranged in the best order?

3. Why did the writer use a two-paragraph introduction? Explain.

Questions About Style

1. What is the notable style feature of this essay? Explain and illustrate.

2. How would you characterize the tone? Is it appropriate for the audience and purpose? Does the writer avoid any extreme personas? Explain.

RESPONDING TO YOUR READING

Explore your reactions to "The Evils of Gentrification" by using the questions on page 93. Then respond with your own essay arguing for or against a physical change (that has occurred or will occur) in some part of your environment.

The change might involve your community, your neighborhood, your school, some favorite hideaway, a place where you work, or the like. Perhaps your old high school is facing a proposed change from traditional classroom space to an "open concept" (various classes clustered around an open area, each class in a cubicle). Or perhaps your favorite lakeside retreat is now giving way to condominium development.

Be sure your essay has a discoverable thesis, and addresses a specific audience affected by the change in some way. Although this essay will make an emotional appeal, your argument should not rest solely on subjective grounds (how you *feel* about it), but also on factual details.

To organize this essay, use a comparison-contrast structure (pages 313–319).

OPTIONS FOR ESSAY WRITING

1. A few years ago, students at a leading university (call it Ivy University) voted in support of this position: that the school infirmary stockpile cyanide capsules to be made available to all personnel in the event of a global nuclear war. Argue for or against the position expressed by the students at Ivy University.

2. Argue for or against this assertion: Parents have the right to make major decisions in the lives of their teenagers.

3. Are grades an aid to education?

4. Sally and Sam have two children, ages 2 and 5. Sally, an attorney, is currently not working but has been offered an attractive full-time job. Sam believes Sally should not work until both children are in school. Should Sally take the job? Why, or why not?

5. In 1977, voters in Dade County, Florida, repealed an ordinance protecting homosexuals from discrimination in housing and employment. Defend or attack this public decision.

6. Should college scholarships be awarded for academic achievement or promise rather than for financial need?

7. Should books and films and music be censored?

8. Defend the "American Way of Life" to a person from another country (say, a foreign exchange student) who has criticized it as too commercial, hectic, and superficial.

9. Should women be drafted?

10. Imagine that you have just read this passage in a newspaper column:

Ten years ago, only about two-thirds as many Americans were graduating from college as now, and plenty of jobs were available requiring college degrees. Nowadays, by contrast, there are no longer enough upper-level jobs to absorb the flood of college graduates. We are producing an "overqualified" generation, some of whom must wind up in jobs not requiring higher education, or even in no jobs at all. The resulting personal frustration and social unrest are the fault of an overexpanded higher education system.

I am not arguing, however, that more young people should be denied the *chance* to go to college. Instead of reducing admissions, we should cut back on the awarding of degrees. In other words, we don't flunk enough students out; in fact, with grade inflation, we now flunk almost *nobody* out. If the lower third of each class were dropped after two years, the excess of degrees would vanish, with beneficial effects for the nation.

Respond to the passage. If you agree, offer further support; if you disagree, suggest an alternative, giving support for your idea.

11. We live in an imperfect world. Everywhere are problems to be solved. During your more than 12 years in school, you've undoubtedly developed legitimate gripes about the *quality* of American education. Based on your experiences *and* perceptions *and* research, think about one specific problem in American education, and argue for its solution. Remember, you are writing an argument, not an attack; your goal is not to offend but to persuade readers—to get them over to your way of seeing.

   After making sure that you have enough inductive evidence to support your main generalization, write an editorial essay for your campus newspaper: identify the problem; analyze its cause(s); and propose a solution. Possible topics:

   - too little (or too much) attention given to remedial students

   - too little (or too much) emphasis on *practical* education (career training)

   - too little (or too much) emphasis on competition

   - teachers' attitudes

   - parents' attitudes

   - students' attitudes

12. Should people be allowed to choose the sex of their child?

13. Should police force the homeless into shelters in cold weather?

14. Should minors who commit violent crimes be tried as adults and, in certain cases, be subject to the death penalty?

15. Should beauty pageants be outlawed?

Application 19–2

ESSAY PRACTICE: ARGUING TO ENLIST READERS' SUPPORT

This essayist argues that school athletes should meet minimal academic standards as a condition for participating in team sports.

Read the essay, and answer the questions that follow. Then (as your instructor requests) select one of the essay assignments.

Standards You Meet and Don't Duck

[1]I'm telling you about my son Mark, not because I want to embarrass him, but because I find it useful in discussing public-policy questions to ask what I would advocate if the people affected by my policy proposals were members of my own family.

[2]Mark, who is not quite 12, is a good kid: friendly, bright, a good athlete and (potentially) a very good student. But he has a tendency to be lazy about his studies.

[3]So at the beginning of the year, I issued an edict: He would perform acceptably well in school or he wouldn't be allowed to play organized sports outside school.

[4]He talked me into a modification: Rather than penalize him for last year's grades, earned before the new rule was announced, let him sign up for the Boys Club league now, and take him off the team if his mid-terms weren't up to par.

[5]Well, the mid-terms came out, and the basketball team is struggling along without the assistance of my son the shooting guard.

[6]All of which is a roundabout and perhaps too personal a way of saying my sentiments are with the Prince George's County (Md.) school officials. My suburban Washington neighbors, confronted with angry parents, disappointed students and decimated athletic teams, are under pressure to modify their new at-least-C-average-or-no-extracurriculars policy.

[7]I hope they will resist it. The new policy may not be perfect, but it reflects a proper sense of priorities, which is one of the things our children ought to be learning. It may turn out to be a very good thing for all concerned—including the 39 percent of the county's students who are temporarily ineligible for such outside activities as athletics, cheerleading, dramatics and band.

[8]I've heard the arguments on the other side, and while I don't dismiss them out of hand, they fall short of persuading me that the new standards are too tough or their application too rigid. I know that for some students, the extracurriculars are the only thing that keep school from being a complete downer. I know that some youngsters will be tempted to pass up Algebra II, chemistry and other tough courses in order to keep their extracurricular eligibility (weighted grade points could solve that problem). And I know that for students whose strengths are other than academic, success in music or drama or sports can be an important source of self-esteem.

[9]Still I support the C-average rule—partly because of my

assumption that it isn't all that tough a standard. We're not talking here about bell-shaped curves that automatically place some students above the median and some below it. I suspect that we're talking less about acceptable academic achievement than about acceptable levels of exertion. I find it hard to believe that Prince George's teachers will flunk kids who really do try: who pay attention in class, turn in all their work, seek special assistance when they need it and also bring athletic glory to their schools. (If it turns out that some youngsters are being penalized for inadequate gifts rather than insufficient effort, I'd support some modification of the rule.)

[10]The principal value of the new standard is that it helps the students, including those in the lower grades, to get their own priorities right: to understand that while outside activities can be an ego-boosting adjunct to classroom work, they cannot be a substitute for it. Even the truly gifted, whose nonacademic talents might earn them college scholarships or even professional careers, need as solid an academic footing as they can get.

[11]Pity, which is what we often feel for other people's children, says give the poor kids a break. Love, which is what we feel for our own, says let's help them get ready for real life—not by lowering the standards but by providing the resources to help them meet the standards. One principal who saw 38 percent of his students fall below the eligibility cutoff agrees. Said Thomas Kirby: "I don't see any point in having a kid who can bounce a basketball graduate from high school and not be able to read."

—William Raspberry

Questions About Content

1. Does the writer acknowledge the opposing viewpoint, and does he address his opponents' biggest objection to his position?

2. Where is the thesis? Is it easily found?

3. Does the writer offer sound reasons for his case? Explain.

4. Does the writer offer impersonal (as well as personal) support? Explain.

Questions About Organization

1. Is the introduction effective? Explain.

2. Does the writer place his strongest material near the beginning or the end of the essay? Is this placement wise?

3. How does the writer achieve coherence and smooth transitions between paragraphs?

Questions About Style

1. Comment on the sentence variety in this essay.

2. Does the writer avoid an extreme persona here (say, sounding like a righteous parent)? Explain.

3. Characterize the tone of the essay. Is it appropriate?

RESPONDING TO YOUR READING

Explore your reactions to "Standards You Meet and Don't Duck" by using the questions on page 93. Then respond with your own essay supporting or opposing the author's view. Your goal is to get readers involved.

Perhaps you will want to argue from the viewpoint of athletes who are affected by such grade standards. Or you might argue for some other school requirement, as in urging your old high school (or your college) to require an exit essay of its graduating seniors to ensure an acceptable level of literacy. Or maybe you feel that some other standard has been neglected or that some school requirements are unfair.

Whatever your position, be sure that your essay has a discoverable thesis and that you address a specific audience whose support you seek. In order to be persuasive, base your support not only on personal grounds (how you feel about it), but on impersonal grounds (verifiable evidence), as well.

OPTIONS FOR ESSAY WRITING

1. Write a response to the assertion that the liberal arts have become an unaffordable luxury. Be sure to consider the arguments for and against specialized vocational education versus a broadly humanistic—but less "practical"—education. What do you think?

2. Your college is thinking of abolishing core requirements. Write an essay to the dean in which you argue for or against this change.

3. Should freshman composition be required at your school? Support your position with a convincing argument addressed to the faculty senate.

4. Should your school (or institute) drop students' evaluations of

teachers? What are the pros and cons of students' evaluations? Write to the student and faculty senates.

5. Perhaps you belong to a fraternity, a sorority, or some other organized group. Identify an important decision your group has to make. Write an essay supporting your position on the issue to the group.

6. Your community is about to vote on whether to fluoridate its public water supply. Do some research, and write an editorial supporting your position on fluoridation. As an alternate assignment, take a stand on some other decision facing your community or family, and write an essay defending your position to a stipulated audience.

7. The Cultural Affairs Committee at your school has decided to sponsor a concert next fall, featuring some popular singer or musical group. Although the committee (mostly faculty) is aware that today's music reflects great diversity in personal taste and musical style, the committee members are uncertain about which performer or group would be a good choice for the event. In fact, most committee members admit to being ignorant of the characteristics that distinguish one performance or recording from another. To help in the decision, the committee has invited the student body to submit essays (not letters) arguing for a performer or group. Free tickets will be awarded to the writer of the best essay. Compose your response.

8. Should your school have an attendance policy? Or a plagiarism policy?

9. Should your school have a foreign language requirement?

10. Challenge an attitude or viewpoint that is widely held by your audience. Maybe you want to persuade your classmates that the time required to earn a Bachelor's degree should be extended to five years. Or maybe you want to claim that the campus police should (or should not) wear guns. Or maybe you want to ask students to support a 10 percent tuition increase in order to make more computers and software available.

      What kind of resistance can you anticipate? How will you connect with readers? How can you avoid outright rejection of your claim? What reasons will have meaning for your audience? What tone would be appropriate? Present your case in a persuasive argument.

Application 19–3

ESSAY PRACTICE: MAKING A PROPOSAL

This proposal addresses a fairly common problem: a large television set in the campus center is causing congestion and wasting students' time. One student decides to confront the problem by writing a proposal to the director of the campus center.

Read the proposal carefully, and answer the questions that follow. If your instructor so requests, select one of the essay assignments.

A Proposal for Better Use of the Television Set in the Campus Center

[1]Leaving the campus center yesterday for class, I found myself stuck in the daily pedestrian jam on the second-floor landing. People by the dozens had gathered on the stairway for their daily dose of "General Hospital." Fighting my way through the mesmerized bodies, I wondered about the appropriateness of the television set's location, and of the value of the shows aired on this set.

[2]Along with the recent upsurge of improvements at our school (in curriculum and standards), we should be considering ways to better use the campus center television. The tube plays relentlessly, offering soap operas and game shows to the addicts who block the stairway and main landing. Granted, television for students to enjoy between classes is a fine idea, but no student needs to attend college to watch soap operas. By moving the set and improving the programs, we could eliminate the congestion and enrich the learning experience.

[3]The television needs a better location: out of the way of people who don't care to watch it, and into a larger, more comfortable setting for those who do. Background noise in the present location makes the set barely audible; and the raised seating in front of the set places the viewers on exhibit to all who walk by. A far better location would be the back wall of the North Lounge, outside the Sunset Room—a large, quiet, and comfortable space. Various meetings sometimes held in this room could be moved instead to the browsing area of the library.

[4]More important than the set's location is the quality of its programs. Videotaped movies might be a good alternative to the shows now aired. Our audiovisual department has a rich collection of excellent movies and educational programs on tape. People could request the shows they would like to see, and a student committee could be responsible for printing showtime information.

[5]The set might also serve as a primary learning tool by allowing communications students to create their own shows. Our school has the videotaping and sound equipment and would need only a faculty adviser to supervise the project. Students from scriptwriting, drama, political science, and journalism classes (to name a few) could combine their talents, providing shows of interest to their peers. We now have a student news program that is aired evenings on a local channel, but many who live some distance off campus cannot receive this channel on their sets at home. Why not make the program accessible to students during the day, here on campus?

[6]With resources already in our possession, we can make a few changes that will benefit almost everyone. Beyond providing more efficient use of campus center space, these changes could really stimulate people's minds. I urge you to allow students and faculty to vote on the questions of moving the television set and improving its programs.

—Patricia Haith

Questions About Content

1. Where is the thesis? Is it easily found?

2. Does the proposal satisfy the four criteria outlined on page 391? Explain.

3. For her primary audience, does the writer offer the best reasons for her case? Explain.

4. For a different audience (say, students who avidly follow the soap operas), would the writer have to change her material at all? Explain.

5. Is this argument primarily inductive or deductive?

6. Does the writer establish agreement with the reader? If so, where?

Questions About Organization

1. Which expository strategy is used most in this essay?

2. Is the narrative introduction effective? Explain.

3. Is the conclusion effective? Explain.

Questions About Style

1. What are two outstanding features of style in this essay? Explain.

2. Is the tone of this essay appropriate for its audience and purpose? Explain.

3. Is the writer's voice likable? Explain.

OPTIONS FOR ESSAY WRITING

1. Identify a problem in your school, community, family, or job. Develop a proposal for solving the problem. Stipulate a definite audience for your proposal. Here are some possible subjects:

   - improving living conditions in your dorm

   - improving security in your dorm

   - creating a day-care center on campus

   - saving labor, materials, or money on the job

   - improving working conditions

   - eliminating a traffic hazard in your neighborhood

   - increasing tourist trade in your town

   - improving the services of your college library

   - finding ways for an organization to raise money

   - improving the food service on campus

   - establishing more equitable use of computer terminals on campus

   - improving faculty advisement of students

   Be sure to spell out the problem, explain the benefits of change, offer a realistic plan, and urge your readers to definite action. Think very carefully about *exactly* what you want your readers to do.

2. It is 1995. Research has shown that incidents of child abuse in America have increased sharply and steadily—at a much higher rate, in fact, than that of the child population itself. Because the courts have been ineffective in providing a deterrent, a growing number of citizens feel that the laws against child abuse should be revised.

A national organization calling itself Citizens for Children's Rights has been working for three years to create a strong political action group. In its view, child abuse originates with irresponsible, emotionally disturbed, or otherwise incompetent parents. The organization's position is that, for the sake of children, parenthood should be regulated. Specifically, its members propose the thesis that people should be licensed before they can be allowed to become parents. Here is the full text of the organization's argument, as published in paid newspaper ads throughout the nation:

Why Parenthood Should Require a License

Child abuse has become our national disgrace. In the past decade, its incidence has increased by an average 20 percent yearly. This year alone, over 500,000 children (fewer than 20 percent of *all* cases) will be the *reported* victims of physical, sexual, or emotional violence by one or both parents. And among the reported offenders, only 3 *percent* are ever convicted. Even more tragic, the pattern of violence is cyclical, with many abused children later becoming abusive parents themselves. To solve this shameful problem, some Americans propose stiffer penalties; others argue for increased supervision by social service agencies and for rehabilitation of abusive parents. But these solutions would treat the problem only *after* it has occurred—too late to offer any real protection for children. Our solution would require parents to become licensed *before* setting out to raise children.

If we grant that parenthood is a *profession* in its own right, then reasons for licensing its practice are obvious enough. Virtually all professions have formal procedures for certifying the competence of their practitioners. Certification is considered especially important for groups whose primary responsibility is human well-being. Physicians, nurses, psychologists, attorneys, and teachers (among others) are all required to satisfy minimal criteria for training, skill, and suitability for their roles. In exchange for the privilege of practicing in these professions, members are expected to assume a clearly defined set of responsibilities. Why, then, should the practice of parenthood be exempt from similar requirements? Specifically, why should some parents enjoy the privilege without assuming the responsibility? Parenthood, in fact, seems the least likely profession to tolerate incompetence.

To help eliminate criminal incompetence among parents, we propose this licensing procedure:

1. Parents who are too young, poor, or uneducated often resort to violence as a way of coping with the pressures of child rearing.

Therefore, all prospective parents should satisfy minimal requirements of age, income, and education.

2. All prospective parents should be required to attend classes on child care and development, and to pass an examination on the art of parenting.

3. To determine whether they are likely to be fit parents, all candidates should be tested psychologically (for emotional stability, mature judgment, and nonviolent traits). In questionable cases, investigation of one's mental health background may be necessary.

4. All applicants should be required to submit an essay explaining why they feel qualified to be good parents.

5. All applicants should be charged a fee (based on a percentage of their income) for the administration of this program.

Enforcement of a national licensing policy would be a fairly simple matter. Parents failing to become licensed would be taxed a percentage of their income or property for each child. The proceeds of this "tax" would be placed in a trust fund for the child—a fund administered by a government agency. For parents with lower incomes (who were otherwise qualified), proceeds from licensing fees would be contributed to enrich their family environment. For parents with no resources   and no prospects of any—the child would be placed with couples who are physically incapable of having children, but who satisfy all the requirements and could provide the love and nurturing a child is entitled to.

Although our proposed solution to the horror of child abuse may seem radical, it is realistic, and above all, most fair to the children. Many details remain to be worked out, but we ask for your agreement in principle. In a country that was founded on human rights, it is only reasonable that our children have the right to be born into an environment that is culturally enriching, financially sound, and emotionally secure. And this right should be mandated by law. We therefore urge all citizens to vote on Proposition 15.

—Citizens for Children's Rights

Assume that, through intensive lobbying, Citizens for Children's Rights has collected enough signatures to have its proposal placed on next month's ballot in your state as a referendum. And a recent survey shows that a majority of voters feel that the proposal should become law. You, however, belong to (choose one):

1. a group fully opposed to the above proposal (although not ready to offer an alternate solution, you are convinced that the proposal violates basic liberties)

2. a group wanting to offer an entirely different proposal

3. a group agreeing with *part* of the proposal, but finding it extreme, and wanting to offer a more balanced and reasonable version

In order to change public opinion, your group decides to take out its own full-page newspaper ad, and you are the one elected to write the position statement that expresses your group's argument. You will have to make a case for your position in the same way that the Citizens for Children's Rights have for theirs. Whatever position you choose, you will need to pick apart the assertions in the original proposal. For every point, you will need to identify an opposing point (the other side of the argument). And if you belong to group 2 or 3 above, you will need to offer alternatives, as well.

Application 19–4

ESSAY PRACTICE: CHANGING THE READER'S BEHAVIOR

This essay is in the form of a complaint letter written by an employee to her boss. It illustrates the challenge of trying to influence another person's behavior. Read it carefully, and answer the questions that follow. Then select one of the essay assignments.

Letter to the Boss

[1]For several months I have been hesitant to approach you about a problem that has caused me great uneasiness at work. More recently, however, I've found that several other employees are equally upset, and I feel, as one of your close friends, that I should explain what's wrong. With you as our boss, we all have an exceptional employer-employee relationship, and I'd hate to see one small problem upset it.

[2]John, when you have criticism about any one of us at work, you never seem to deal directly with that specific person. When the chefs were coming in late, you didn't confront them directly to express your displeasure; instead, you discussed it with the other employees. When you suspected Alan's honesty and integrity as a bartender, you came to me rather than to Alan. I learned yesterday from the coat-checker that you are unhappy with the [waitpersons] for laughing and joking too much. And these are just a few of many such incidents.

[3]I understand how difficult it is to approach a person with constructive criticism—in fact, it's taken me several months to mention this problem to you! Having been on the receiving end of grapevine gossip, though, I would accept the complaint much more gracefully if it came directly from you. Many of the employees are needlessly upset, and our increasing dissatisfaction harms the quality of our work.

[4]Because I've never been a supervisor, I can only imagine your difficulty. I'm sure your task is magnified because when you bought this restaurant last spring, we employees all knew one another, but you knew none of us. You've told me many times how important it is for you to be a friend to all of us, but sometimes friendship can stand in the way of communication.

[5]Our old boss used to deal with the problem of making constructive suggestions in this way: Every other Saturday evening we would have a meeting at which he would voice his suggestions and we would voice ours. This arrangement worked out well, because none of us felt singled out for criticism, and we all had the chance to discuss any problems openly.

[6]I value your friendship, and I hope you will accept this letter in the sincere spirit in which it's offered. I'm sure that with a couple of good conversations we can work things out.

—Marcia White

Questions About Content

1. Bracket all facts in this letter, and underline all statements of opinion (see Chapter 6). Are all opinions supported by facts? Explain.

2. Does the writer acknowledge the opposing viewpoint? Explain.

3. Is this letter likely to be convincing? Explain.

4. Does the writer admit the imperfections in her case? Explain.

Questions About Organization

1. Explain the function of the introductory paragraph. Is the writer guilty of "beating around the bush"? Explain.

2. Which body paragraphs are deductive? Which inductive?

3. Is the arrangement of the body paragraphs effective? Explain.

4. Is the final body paragraph too indirect? Explain.

5. Which is the most concrete paragraph? Explain its function.

6. Are the second and third body paragraphs necessary? Explain.

7. Is the conclusion effective? Explain.

Questions About Style

1. In the second and third body paragraphs, identify one example of coordination, and explain how this structure reinforces the writer's meaning.

2. Identify and give examples of one outstanding stylistic feature in this essay.

3. How would you characterize the tone? Is it appropriate for the situation, audience, and purpose? Identify three sentences that contribute to this tone.

4. Identify three sentences in which the writer expresses empathy with her reader.

5. Is the writer's voice likable? Explain.

OPTIONS FOR ESSAY WRITING

1. Everyone has habits that annoy others or are harmful in some way. Identify a bad habit of a friend, relative, co-worker, or someone you spend a lot of time with, and write an essay (as a letter) trying to persuade the person to break the habit. As additional encouragement, suggest specific actions that your reader might take to overcome the habit. (Stay away from the classic, cigarette smoking.)

   You're writing to someone close to you, and so, besides being concrete and direct, be diplomatic. Your primary goal here is not to "tell someone off" (much as you might like to!) but to help your friend change for the better. To make sure your reader confronts the problem, you need to be candid and outspoken. To be sure you don't lose a friend, you need to be patient, diplomatic, and supportive.

   Make careful decisions about *what* you say and *how* you say it. Say something nice once in a while, but be sincere (anybody can spot a phony). First, identify the problem clearly; then, point out the causes and the reasons for change; and finally, offer suggestions for change. Pay close attention to your tone. You want to sound like an honest friend, not a judge. Because you anticipate defensiveness on the part of your reader, decide on ways of getting your message across to overcome that defensiveness.

2. Think of a situation in which you recently encountered problems—in a job, in school, or as a consumer. Choose something about which you have a major complaint. Write an essay (as a letter) to the person in charge or otherwise responsible, laying out the issues and suggesting appropriate changes.

3. Someone close to you is trying to make an important decision and has asked your advice. Respond in a persuasive essay.

SECTION FOUR

RESEARCH
AND
CORRESPONDENCE

20

Developing a Research Report

We do research to get facts or expert opinions or to increase our understanding of issues. For example, we might want to know the price range of building lots on Boca Grande Island or the latest findings in AIDS research. Or we might want to know what experts are saying about the long-term effects of global warming. Or we might want to better understand the causes of the Israeli-Palestinian conflict or the role of the banking industry in rain forest destruction.

Research is not only a college skill, but a life skill, as well. For example, if you learn that your well water is contaminated with benzene, should you merely ask for your neighbor's opinion about the dangers, or should you track down the real answers for yourself?

In the workplace, *information* has become the ultimate commodity. And workplace professionals are expected to locate all kinds of information daily (How do we market this product? How do we avoid accidents like this one? How can we keep costs down? How can we attract dependable employees? Are we headed for a recession? and so on). We all need to know where and how to look for answers. And we need to know how to communicate our findings *on paper*.

Any kind of significant research is for some purpose: to answer a question, to make an evaluation, to establish a principle. We set out to discover whether diesel engines are efficient and dependable for a purpose: we're thinking about buying a car equipped with one; we're trying to decide whether to begin producing them; or the like. Research is the way to find your own answers, to submit your opinions to the test of fact, to reach the conclusion that has the greatest chance of being accurate. A research report records and discusses your findings. It provides the information that leads to an informed conclusion.

The Research Report Process*

A research report that *makes a difference* involves a lot more than cooking up any old thesis, collecting the first bunch of stuff you come across, and then blending in some juicy quotations and paraphrases that supposedly "prove" you've done the assigned work. Above all, research is a process of *problem solving.* And, as in any problem solving, we can't begin to solve the problem until we have clearly defined it.

Granted, there are certain procedures in the research process that follow a recognizable sequence:

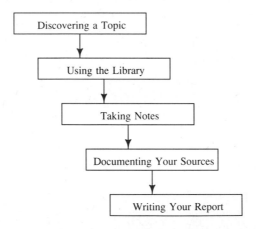

Later sections in this chapter treat these more "procedural" parts of the research process.

But research writing never is merely a "by-the-numbers" set of

---

*My thanks to SMU librarian Shaleen Barnes for inspiring this whole section.

procedures ("First, do this; then, do that"). Intertwined with each of the procedural parts are the "thinking" parts of the process, the many careful decisions that make a research report make a real difference:

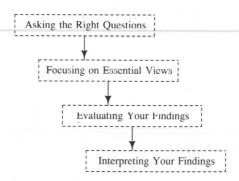

Let's consider more closely each "thinking" part of the research process.

ASKING THE RIGHT QUESTIONS

Any answers you uncover will be only as good as the questions you ask. Suppose, for instance, you've decided to research the 1989 Exxon Valdez oil spill in Alaska's Prince William Sound: The immediate problem was the tanker hitting the shoal. But what *specific* parts of the problem interest you? (The events that led up to the disaster? The ways it could have been avoided? Environmental effects? Economic effects? Or what?) Before you settle on a definite question, you need to navigate a long list of possible questions, some of which are shown in the Figure 20.1 tree chart.

Any *one* of the questions (or clusters of questions) from our tree chart could serve as the topic of a worthwhile research report on such a complex topic. By asking the right questions, you discover a focus and a topic that you can research in real depth—instead of settling for a superficial and simplistic approach to a complex issue. (Perhaps you can think of other questions we might add to our chart.)

FOCUSING ON ESSENTIAL VIEWPOINTS

Let's assume you've settled on this question for research: "Has the cleanup from the Exxon Valdez disaster been adequate?" To answer this

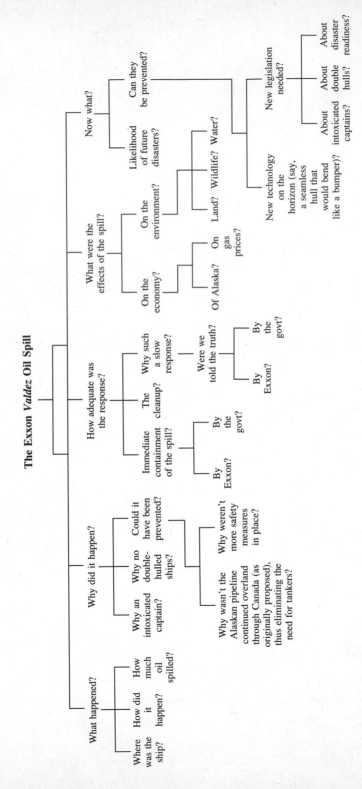

Figure 20.1   Some Questions for Researching a Topic

question fairly and accurately, you would have to consider all sides of the story:

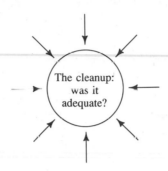

Here are some essential points of view on the cleanup:

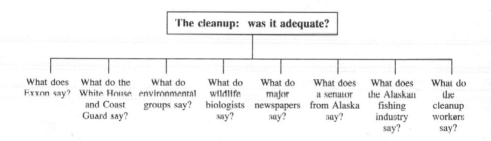

All these sources look at the one event from different points of view. And each viewpoint contributes to the whole picture. Remember that even "experts" sometimes can be mistaken. And so, to achieve your own, balanced viewpoint, you need to hear from a cross section of everyone involved.

EVALUATING YOUR FINDINGS

Once you have collected all the essential evidence about your topic, you need to decide how much of it is legitimate. Consider, for example, the fact that Exxon filed a $2 billion suit against the federal government, claiming the Coast Guard interfered with the cleanup by prohibiting early use of chemical dispersants. How would you evaluate Exxon's claim?

Questions for evaluating a particular finding

- Is this information accurate, reliable, and relatively unbiased?
- Can the claim be verified by the facts?
- Is all of it (or any of it) useful?
- Is this the whole story?
- Does something seem to be missing?
- Do I need more information?

Not all the material you collect will have equal value. Some might be distorted or incomplete or misleading. Don't base your own conclusions on faulty evidence. And don't merely emphasize findings that support your own biases or assumptions.

Remember that the purpose of research is not to prove the "rightness" of some assumption you might have had at the beginning; instead, you do research to find the *right* answers. And only when your research is near completion can you settle on a *definite* thesis—based on what the facts suggest.

INTERPRETING YOUR FINDINGS

Once you've decided which of your findings seem legitimate, you need to decide what this all means:

Questions for interpreting your findings

- What do all these facts or observations mean?
- Do any findings conflict?
- Are other interpretations possible?
- Should I reconsider the evidence?
- What are my conclusions?
- What, if anything, should be done?

Clearly, your interpretation should fit your evidence and should lead to an accurate conclusion—an overall judgment about what all your material means. (For example, "The cleanup has been woefully inadequate" or "The cleanup seems to have been thorough," etc.)

Sometimes your research will produce contradictory or indefinite conclusions. For example, some people argue that the crude oil remaining on Alaskan shores will be "scrubbed" clean over the years by the fierce winter tides—making any further cleanup unneccessary. Others charge that this view is an oil-company "cop-out." An accurate conclusion would have to come from your analyzing all views and deciding that one outweighs the others—or that only time will tell.

Never force a simplistic conclusion on a complex issue. For instance, maybe your thesis would have to be inconclusive, such as this one: "Although controversy continues over the adequacy of the cleanup, the upcoming winter seasons will tell whether Mother Nature has been able to finish the job." A wrong conclusion is far worse than no definite conclusion at all.

Discovering a Research Topic

Perhaps the crucial step in developing a research report is to decide on the right topic. Begin with a subject that has real meaning for you, and then decide on the specific question you want to ask about it. This chapter's opening pages showed how the subject of the Exxon Valdez oil spill might be approached. Now let's try another subject.

What would you like to know about? Let's say you're disturbed about all the chemicals used to preserve or enhance flavor and color in foods. Maybe this can be your subject: *food additives and preservatives.*

What specific part of this subject would you like to focus on? This will be your *topic*, and it will be phrased as a question. Suppose, for instance, you are majoring in elementary education and are especially interested in children's behavior. To identify the possible questions you might ask, you develop a tree chart (as on page 416), and finally you settle on this question: *What effects, if any, do food additives and preservatives have on children's behavior?*

Here is advice to help you avoid choosing the wrong kind of topic:

1. Avoid topics that are too broad. The topic "Do food additives and preservatives affect children?" would have to include information on children's growth and development, their intelligence, their susceptibility to diseases, and so on. A six- to twelve-page research report simply offers too little space to cover that broad a topic.

2. Avoid topics that limit you to a fixed viewpoint *before* you've done your research: "Which behavior disorders in children are caused by food additives and preservatives?" Presumably, you haven't yet established that such chemicals have *any* harmful effects (except perhaps from hearsay or from something you've read somewhere). Therefore, save any definite conclusions (along with your definite thesis) until you've had a chance to evaluate

your information. Your initial research is meant to find the facts, not to prove some point. *Allow your thesis to grow from your collected facts, instead of bending the facts to fit your thesis.*

3. Avoid topics that have been exhausted (abortion, capital punishment, life on Mars, the Bermuda Triangle)—unless, of course, you can approach such a topic in a fresh way, like this: "Could recent technological developments to help a fetus survive outside the womb cause the Supreme Court to reverse its 1972 ruling on abortion?" In other words, if the topic is a familiar one, try to answer a question that would offer readers a new perspective.

4. Avoid topics that can be summed up in an encyclopedia entry or in any one source: "The Life of Thoreau," "How to Cross-Country Ski," or "The History of Microwave Technology." From a different angle, of course, any of these areas might produce good topics: "Was Thoreau ever in love?"; "How do injury rates compare between cross-country and downhill skiing?"; "How safe are microwave ovens?" Research on the latter topics would yield material from which you could draw your *own* conclusions.

5. Avoid religious, moral, or emotional topics that offer no objective basis for informed conclusions: "Is euthanasia moral?"; "Will Jesus save the world?"; "Should prayer be allowed in public schools?" Any conclusions about these kinds of topics rest on personal opinion, not fact. Questions debated throughout the ages by philosophers, judges, and social thinkers are unlikely to be answered definitively in your research paper—or anywhere else, for that matter.

6. Avoid any topic that's chosen from desperation. Sometimes you won't be able to decide exactly what it is you want to know until you've visited the library a few times. If you can't find a definite topic this early, begin with a subject of general interest, and browse through the library sources to get ideas.

Far more important than the subject you choose is the *question* you decide to ask about it. Don't be surprised or discouraged if you spend many hours in search of the right question. The quality of your whole research project will depend on the quality of your decisions at this stage.

As soon as you have decided on a definite topic, you will want to make sure enough information is available from a sufficient variety of perspectives to provide you with an accurate and balanced view. To check for sources, you will need to know how to use the library.

Using the Library

Inexperienced researchers sometimes are confused about where to begin a search of the library. Here are the various options:

Where you begin your own search will depend on whether you seek background and basic facts or the very latest information. If you have some expertise in the topic, you might simply do a computerized search or browse through the specialized journals. But if you have only limited knowledge or if you need to focus your topic, you probably will want to begin with general reference sources.

REFERENCE WORKS

Reference works include encyclopedias, almanacs, handbooks, dictionaries, histories, and biographies. These are a good place to begin research, because they provide background information and bibliographies that can lead you to more specific information. The one drawback is that some reference books that have not been revised recently may be out of date. Always check the last copyright date.

Reference works are in a special section marked "Reference" —usually on the main floor of the building. All works will be indexed in the "Subject" card catalog, with a "Ref." designation immediately above the call number. Here is a partial list of reference works:

- *Cassell's Encyclopedia of World Literature*
- *Civil Engineering Handbook*

- *Dictionary of American Biography*
- *Encyclopaedia Britannica*
- *Encyclopedia of Food Technology*
- *Encyclopedia of the Social Sciences*
- *Fire Protection Handbook*
- *Handbook of Chemistry and Physics*
- *The Harper Encyclopedia of Science*
- *Information Please Almanac*
- *McGraw-Hill Encyclopedia of Science and Technology*
- *The New Dictionary and Handbook of Aerospace*
- *The New York Times Encyclopedic Almanac*
- *Oxford English Dictionary*
- *Paramedical Dictionary*
- *The Times Atlas of the World*
- *Who's Who in American Art*

Reference works are published for every discipline. If you were researching the effects of food additives, you would want to start with titles such as the *McGraw-Hill Encyclopedia of Food, Agriculture, and Nutrition* or the *RC Handbook of Food Additives*. Look for your subject in the card catalog, and then check for any subheadings such as "Handbooks, Manuals, etc." or "Dictionaries." These will be the books that get you started.

THE CARD CATALOG

In many libraries, every book, film, filmstrip, phonograph album, and tape is indexed in the card catalog under three separate designations: author, title, and subject. Thus you have at least three ways of locating whatever information you need.

Your library may place author, title, and subject cards in one alphabetical file or may provide individual catalogs labeled "Author," "Title," and "Subject." First decide whether you are looking for a specific title, one or more works written by a particular author, or material about a subject. Then check the arrangement of the card catalog to determine where to look.

Locating the Card   Say you are looking for a book on food technology by Norman W. Desrosier. If your library has a divided catalog, locate the *D* cards in the author section. If not, locate the *D* cards in the combined catalog. Flip through the cards in the drawer until you locate those listed under "Desrosier, Norman W." Figure 20.2 shows a typical author catalog card.

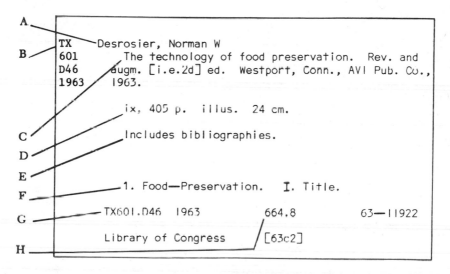

A.   The author's name, listed last name first. (On some cards the author's name is followed by his or her date of birth—and death, if he or she was deceased at the time of the book's last printing.)

B.   The call number. Each book has a different call number under the coding system by which books are classified. Books are arranged on the shelves in the order of their respective call numbers. This number is your key for locating the book.

C.   The title of one book written by this author, followed by the number of the edition, city of publication, publisher, and publication date.

D.   Technical information: This book has 9 chapters, 405 pages, illustrations, and is 24 centimeters high.

E.   Special information about the book: This book includes bibliographies listing related sources of information.

F.   Other headings under which this book is listed in the card catalog: In the subject section, the book is listed under "Food—Preservation"; it is also listed alphabetically by title.

G.   Library of Congress call number (the most commonly used).

H.   Dewey Decimal System call number (an alternative to the Library of Congress system).

Figure 20.2   A Catalog Card Classified by Author

As entry *F* on the author card indicates, you can find the same book listed alphabetically under its title, as shown in Figure 20.3. All other information is identical to that on the author card.

```
        The technology of food preservation.

TX      Desrosier, Norman W
601         The technology of food preservation.  Rev. and
D46         augm. [i.e.2d] ed.  Westport, Conn., AVI Pub. Co.,
1963        1963.

            ix, 405 p.  illus.  24 cm.

            Includes bibliographies.



            1. Food—Preservation.   I. Title.

            TX601.D46  1963           664.8              63—11922

            Library of Congress      [63c2]
```

Figure 20.3   A Catalog Card Classified by Title

If you know neither authors nor titles of books on a subject, turn to the subject listing. Figure 20.4 shows the card for the same book, found under the subject heading "Food—Preservation." Here again, all other items on the card remain the same.

Note: Some libraries now are storing all catalog information in computers. Instead of thumbing through cards in a drawer to find a publication, you simply type in the name of the author, title, or subject on the library's computer terminal. Ask a librarian for help.

Locating the Book on the Shelf   If your library has closed stacks, you fill out a call slip with book title, author, and call number. You then wait for a staff member to find your book. If the stacks are open, you find the book yourself. The call number is your key for locating the book. In the card catalog area, in stairways and elevators, and on doors to individual floors, you will see call number maps.

GUIDES TO LITERATURE

If you simply don't know which books, journals, indexes, and reference works are available for your topic, consult a guide to literature. For a

```
                Food - Preservation

TX      Desrosier, Norman W
601         The technology of food preservation.  Rev. and
D46         augm. [i.e.2d] ed.  Westport, Conn., AVI Pub. Co.,
1963        1963.

            ix, 405 p.  illus.  24 cm.

        Includes bibliographies.


        1. Food—Preservation.    I. Title.

        TX601.D46  1963              664.8              63—11922

        Library of Congress        [63c2]
```

Figure 20.4   A Catalog Card Classified by Subject

general listing of books in various disciplines, see Walford's *Guide to Reference Material* or *Sheehy's Guide to Reference Books.*

For sources in specific disciplines, consult specialized guides such as *The Encyclopedia of Business Information Sources* or *Sources of Information in the Social Sciences.* Ask your reference librarian about literature guides for your topic.

INDEXES

Indexes are lists of journal articles, magazine articles, newspaper articles, or books on particular subjects. Through various indexes you can locate the most recent information on your topic.

The most comprehensive index is *Readers' Guide to Periodical Literature,* which indexes articles from more than 150 popular magazines and journals. Because a new volume of the *Readers' Guide* is published every few weeks, you can locate articles less than one month old. The *Readers' Guide* indexes items alphabetically by subject, author, and book or film title. Figure 20.5 shows a section from one of its pages.

Locating the Entry   Assume you are researching the physiological effects of food additives and preservatives. As you turn to a recent issue of the *Readers' Guide,* you find many entries under the general heading "Food." Scanning the entries classified under "Food Additives," you spot an item that looks useful: "Food Additives and Hyperactive

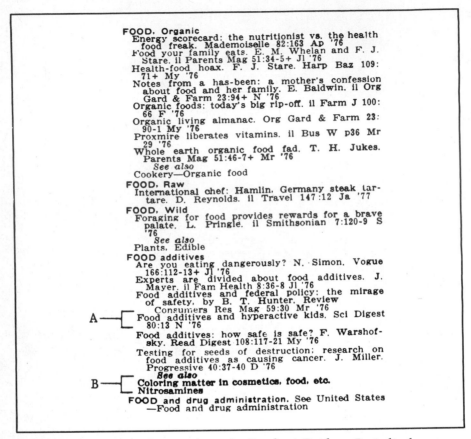

Figure 20.5   Section of a Page from the *Readers' Guide to Periodical Literature*

Kids''—item *A*. From that entry you gain this information: because the author's name is not given, the article probably was written by a writer on the magazine staff; the name of the periodical is *Science Digest* (abbreviations are explained in the opening pages of each *Readers' Guide*); the volume number is 80; the article is found on page 13 of the November 1976 issue. Item *B* refers to other headings under which you might find relevant articles.

Locating the Indexed Article   Each work listed in the card catalog is actually held by that library. Unless the item has been borrowed by someone else, you should locate it easily under its call number designation. Periodicals are more of a problem, however: not all works listed in periodical indexes are likely to be held by your library. The indexes list articles from hundreds of journals, newspapers, and magazines, but your library probably subscribes to a cross section only. If you find an index reference to an article not held by your library, ask your librarian to see if the article is available in nearby libraries or through an inter-library loan.

Consult the periodicals holdings list to determine which periodicals are held by your library. Copies are available in the area where indexes are shelved. Figure 20.6 shows a sample page from one library's list.

Earlier, you located an entry in the *Readers' Guide* titled "Food Additives and Hyperactive Kids," printed in *Science Digest.* Now, as you check the periodicals holdings list, you learn that your library subscribes to that journal (see item *A*). You also learn that all back issues to 1960 are recorded on microfilm.* Your article might not be recent enough to be found in the bound journal (many libraries keep only one year of back issues as bound copies). Ask your librarian to explain the use of microfilm files and readers.

If the article is in a very recent issue, look on the current periodical shelves, usually arranged alphabetically by title, to find your issue. In some libraries, older issues are bound together in hardcover bindings instead of being microfilmed.

In addition to indexes for popular and general periodicals, specialized indexes are available in nearly every discipline. A researcher in the business field might consult these indexes of specialized professional periodicals:

- *Business Periodicals Index*
- *Editor and Publisher Market Guide*
- *Editorial Research Report*
- *F and S Index of Corporations and Industries*
- *Predicasts*
- *Public Affairs Index*

Here are titles of indexes in other fields:

- *Agricultural Index*
- *Applied Science and Technology Index*

---

*To save space, many libraries subscribe to a microfilm service that photographs back issues of periodicals on microfilm.

-Q-

Quest   1973-

-R-

RN National Magazine for Nurses   Microfilm 1966-
RQ (ALA)   Microfilm 1970-
Ramparts (disc. micro. only)   Microfilm 1962-
                                     Sept. 1975
Readers Digest   Microfilm 1960-
Research in Education (ERIC)   1970-
Respiratory Care   1971-
Revista Rotaria (Spanish)   1970-
Revue d'Histoire Littéraire   1969-
    de la France
Rights   1971
Romanic Review   Microfilm 1960-
Rotarian   1974

-S-

Saturday Evening Post (micro. disc.)   Microfilm 1960-1969
                                        1971-
Saturday Review (Saturday Review World) Microfilm 1924-1972,
                                        1975
Saturday Review World (formerly: 1973-1974
    Saturday Review)
Scholastic Teacher (for microfilm   1972-
    see: Senior Scholastic)
School & Society (now: Intellect)   Microfilm 1960-1972
School Libraries (now: School Media   Microfilm 1951-1972
    Quarterly)
Science   Microfilm 1959-
Science Books   1970-1975
A——⌐ Science Digest   Microfilm 1960-
Science News   Microfilm 1960-
Scientific American   Microfilm 1929
Sea Change (Cape Cod Community
    College Literary Magazine)
Sea Frontiers (micro.)   Microfilm 1954-1975
Secretary   1973-
Senior Scholastic   Microfilm 1960-
Sewanee Review   Microfilm 1960-

Figure 20.6   A Page from a Library's Periodicals Holdings List

- *Biological Abstracts*
- *Chemical Abstracts*
- *Education Index*
- *The Energy Index*
- *Engineering Index*
- *Index Medicus*
- *International Nursing Index*
- *Psychological Abstracts*

Chapters in books or current essays about an artist, author, issue, region, figure, or other topic in humanities and social sciences may be part of larger collections. To find such material, consult the *Essay and General Literature Index.* Each year, the *Index* lists roughly 3500 essays and articles (by subject and author) that have been published in nearly 300 volumes of collected essays and miscellaneous works.

Two valuable sources for quickly building exhaustive bibliographies (lists of publications on your subject) are the *Science Citation Index* and its counterpart, the *Social Sciences Citation Index.* Book indexes, such as *Books in Print* or the *Cumulative Book Index,* list by author, title, or subject all books currently being published. (But keep in mind that a book usually is not current enough to offer the very latest information.) Newspaper indexes, such as *The New York Times Index* and the *Wall Street Journal Index,* are particularly useful for current topics.

Your library may have other indexes. Ask the reference librarian to help you identify appropriate indexes for your subject.

Having looked in the reference books that provide an overview of the psychological effects of food additives, you might now turn to *Psychological Abstracts* or *Index Medicus* for journal literature.

THE REFERENCE LIBRARIAN

The best source for help with library research is the reference librarian. This person's job—as the title implies—is to *refer* people to sources of information. Therefore, don't be afraid to ask for assistance. Even professional researchers sometimes need help. The reference librarian can save you hours of time by showing you how to use indexes or microfilm and microfiche readers, and how to locate reference books or bibliographies. Moreover, he or she can order items from other libraries (but this procedure takes time; be sure to plan ahead).

INDEXES TO FEDERAL GOVERNMENT PUBLICATIONS

The federal government publishes maps, periodicals, books, pamphlets, manuals, monographs, annual reports, research reports, and a remarkable array of other information. Kinds of information available to the public include presidential proclamations, congressional bills and reports, judiciary rulings, some reports from the Central Intelligence Agency, and publications from all other government agencies (Departments of Agriculture, Commerce, Transportation, and so on). Here is a brief sampling of the countless titles available in this gold mine of information:

Decisions of the Federal Trade Commission

Economic Report of the President

Effects of New York's Fiscal Crisis on Small Business

Journal of Research of the National Bureau of Standards

Major Oil and Gas Fields of the Free World

Siting Small Wind Turbines

Much of this information can be searched by computer as well as in printed volumes.

Your best bet for tapping this valuable but complex resource is to ask the librarian in charge of government documents for help. If your library does not own the publication you seek, it can be obtained through an interlibrary loan.

The three basic access tools for documents issued or published at government expense are these:

1. *The Monthly Catalog of the United States Government* is the major access to government publications and reports; it is indexed by author, subject, and title. The indexes provide you with the catalog entry number that leads you, in turn, to a complete citation for a work.

2. *Government Reports Announcements & Index* is a listing published every two weeks by the National Technical Information Service (NTIS), a branch of the U.S. Department of Commerce that serves as a clearinghouse for scientific and technical information—all stored in a computer database. The collection stores summaries of more than 1 million federally sponsored research reports published and patents issued since 1964. About 70,000 new summaries are added annually in 22

subject categories ranging from aeronautics to medicine and biology. Full copies of any of these summarized reports are available from NTIS.

3. *The American Statistics Index* is a yearly guide to statistical publications of the U.S. government. It is divided into two sections: *Index* and *Abstracts* (an index with summaries). The *Index* volume lists material by subject and provides geographic (federal, state, and so on), economic (income, occupation, and so on), and demographic (sex, marital status, race, and so on) breakdowns. The *Index* volume refers you to a number and entry in the *Abstracts* volume.

In addition to these three basic access tools, the government issues *Selected Government Publications*, a monthly list of roughly 150 titles (with descriptive abstracts). These titles range from highly general (*Questions About the Oceans*) to highly technical (*An Emission-Line Survey of the Milky Way*). Although this list may be of interest, it is by no means a refined research tool.

The government also publishes bibliographies on hundreds of subjects, ranging from "Accidents and Accident Prevention" to "Home Gardening of Fruits and Vegetables." Ask your librarian for information about such subject bibliographies.

COMPUTERIZED RETRIEVAL SYSTEMS

The Information Age has created the need for modern cataloging and research methods. In the United States alone, 35,000 to 45,000 books are published *each year*. Add to this number foreign publications and countless special interest magazines, journals, newspapers, films, recordings, and reports.

To help us quickly find what we need, more and more libraries offer computerized information services. If your library has an electronic card catalog, you can rapidly search the holdings to find specific works. Electronic retrieval services provide access to information far beyond everything held by your library. Much of today's information can be retrieved electronically from compact disks or from databases in mainframe computers. Electronic data retrieval is revolutionizing our way of doing research.

Databases on Compact Disks   A single laser-driven compact disk easily stores an entire encyclopedia. Using a computer, you can access even the smallest portion of that encyclopedia in just a few seconds. Instead of thumbing through printed reference books and indexes, you can now locate more and more basic resources on compact disks. The growing array of disk-based reference materials now includes electronic versions of *Books in Print* and *Ulrich's International Guide to Periodicals.*

One useful index stored on compact disk is InfoTrac™, an index to articles from 900 business, technical, and popular magazines and journals. InfoTrac is updated monthly. As in printed indexes, its entries are arranged by subject headings and subheadings. If, for instance, you type in the subject heading "food additives," the system will list dozens of entries. With a simple command, you can print out your own hard copy of the list.

Other databases on compact disk include the *Governmental Publications Index*™, a monthly listing of U.S. government publications, and LegalTrac™, a monthly listing of entries from 750 legal publications. Ask if your library subscribes to any of these disk-based indexing services.

Mainframe Databases   Many college libraries now subscribe to retrieval services that offer public access to more than 3000 individual databases stored on mainframe computers. At a terminal in a subscribing library, you can access information from countless indexes, journals, books, monographs, dissertations, and reports. Compared with databases on disks, mainframe databases usually include more specialized sources, and they can offer the most current entries—sometimes updated daily.

How Material Is Stored   In a bibliographic database system, entries for books, articles, and other publications are stored under headings for different fields (say, *Social Sciences*) and catalogued according to specific key words in the work itself (say, *food, additive, children,* and *behavior*). Even without knowing specific authors or titles, you can quickly see what's available on your topic by typing in the key words and having the computer respond with a listing of publications.

To illustrate how a typical database (or automated) search works, let's look at an example from Bibliographic Retrieval Services (BRS). This popular database service provides bibliographies and abstracts (brief summaries of the article or work) from a variety of fields in the life sciences, physical sciences, and business or social sciences. Here are just a few of the more than 50 BRS databases:

American Chemical Society Journals

Dissertation Abstracts

Harvard Business Review

International Pharmaceutical Abstracts

Military and Federal Specifications and Standards

Pollution Abstracts

Robotics Information Database

Many college libraries now subscribe to the BRS system.

A Sample Automated Search Assume you are continuing your research into the effects of food additives on children. You have done a brief search through the "manual" indexes and, for a comprehensive view, you decide on an automated search, using your library's BRS service. You ask a librarian for help, and the two of you sit at the terminal and begin.

After logging into the BRS system, you instruct the computer to search all the databases under the group headings "Life Sciences" and "Social Sciences," using the key words *food, additive, children,* and *behavior.* The computer responds with a listing of each database under "Life Sciences" and "Social Sciences" and the number of articles (containing the key words in each). For instance, the *Drug Information/ Alcohol Use–Abuse* database has no articles; *Medline* has nine; *International Pharmaceutical Abstracts* has one article; and so on. You notice that the *Psycinfo* Database (PSYC) lists 16 articles (since 1967). Because you are most interested in the psychological effects of additives (versus, say, the physiological effects), you instruct the computer to list the titles of all these articles. Here is the list (partial):

```
      1
TI THE FEINGOLD DIET: A CURRENT REAPPRAISAL

      2
TI FOOD ADDITIVES: THE CONTROVERSY CONTINUES
        [The list continues to number 16.]

      15
TI THE FUNCTIONAL RELATIONSHIP BETWEEN ARTIFICIAL
    FOOD COLORS AND HYPERACTIVITY

      16
TI HYPERKINESIS AND LEARNING DISABILITIES LINKED TO
    THE INGESTION OF ARTIFICIAL FOOD COLORS AND FLAVORS

    *END OF DOCUMENTS IN LIST
```

In this list are several titles of interest, but number 15 seems most relevant to your topic. You now instruct the computer to print the full bibliographic information (including the abstract) about this article.

The computer responds:

Accession number	AN 03410 64-2.
Author	AU ROSE-TERRY
Institution	IN NORTHERN ILLINOIS U.
Title	TI THE FUNCTIONAL RELATIONSHIP BETWEEN ARTIFICIAL FOOD COLORS AND HYPERACTIVITY
Source	SO JOURNAL OF APPLIED BEHAVIOR ANALYSIS 1978 WIN VOL 11(4) 439-446
Abstract	AB THE PRESENCE OF A FUNCTIONAL RELATIONSHIP BETWEEN THE INGESTION OF ARTIFICIAL FOOD COLORS AND AN INCREASE IN THE FREQUENCY AND/OR DURATION OF SELECTED BEHAVIORS THAT ARE REPRESENTATIVE OF THE HYPERACTIVE BEHAVIOR SYNDROME WAS EXPERIMENTALLY INVESTIGATED. TWO 8-YR-OLD FEMALES, WHO HAD BEEN ON B. F. FEINGOLD'S (1975-1976) K-P DIET FOR A MINIMUM OF 11 MONTHS, WERE THE SUBJECTS STUDIED. [The abstract continues.]

*END OF DOCUMENT

After reviewing the abstract, you decide it would be worthwhile to read the entire article, and so you make a note to check your library's holdings or to order a reprint or photocopy through the library's inter-library loan system. (Some reprints can be ordered directly through the computer terminal.) You turn again to the list of titles to see if any others seem promising.

Once you've searched the PSYC database to your satisfaction, you may decide to look at Medline or some other database on the list that was shown to have articles with your key words in the title.

Automated searches do, of course, offer advantages, including speed and timeliness. You can review 10 or 15 years' worth of indexed publications in minutes, and many systems provide abstracts (if requested) for a more detailed view of the publication. And for many current publications, the bibliographic information is available on a computer several weeks earlier than in bound indexes.

But automated searches have their limitations, as well. Few computerized bibliographies include works published before the mid-1960s; thus you would have to search manually, through bound indexes, for information published earlier. Also, when you do a manual (versus automated) search, you have the whole database (i.e., the bound volume itself) right in front of you, and as you flip pages and browse you often *randomly* discover useful titles. This kind of discovery is, of course, impossible with an automated search.

For any database search, remember that you almost always need to do a manual (random) search as well.

Note: An automated search through one of the popular database services typically costs about 30 dollars. But some libraries now offer all students one free search yearly. Other libraries will give search demonstrations to classes or large groups. Find out what your library offers. Any familiarity you can develop with this new information technology will be a real asset—whatever your career plans.

The On-Line Computer Library Center (OCLC)   You can speed up your research tremendously if a nearby library belongs to the On-Line Computer Library Center. The OCLC database, in Columbus, Ohio, has 8 million records with the same information found in a conventional card catalog. Using the library's computer terminal, you simply key in author, title, or subject. Within seconds, you get a listing of the publication you seek and information about where to find it—all at no charge. If your library doesn't have the publication, your librarian can activate the Interlibrary Loan System (ILS) The system forwards requests to libraries holding the material. Once a lender indicates (via its terminal) that it will supply the material, the system stops forwarding the request and notifies your librarian that the request has been filled. Your order will arrive at the library by mail in a week or two.

Finding Adequate Information Sources

As soon as you have a general sense of how to use your library, you'll want to make sure that enough information for your research topic is available. Do a quick search of the card catalog, reference books, and indexes. Compile a working bibliography of at least a dozen works. Maybe you won't use all this material, or maybe you'll need more later—but at least you now have a place to begin. Your bibliography will grow as you read about your subject. And many of the books you examine will have their own bibliographies, which in turn will lead you to additional sources.

For some topics, you will want to list *primary* as well as *secondary* information sources. Primary research is a first-hand study of the topic;

its sources are observation, questionnaires, interviews, inquiry letters, works of literature, or personal documents (letters, diaries, journals). If your topic is the love life of Thoreau, a good primary source will be his journals, poems, and letters. Secondary research is based on information and conclusions that other researchers—by their primary research—have compiled in books and articles. Whenever your topic permits, try to combine these approaches. Have a look for yourself.

Record all sources on notecards. Using a separate card for each source, record the complete bibliographic information, including the call number (see Figure 20.7). The information for this entry is identical to that which you will include in the bibliography (or "Works Cited") section of the final draft of your report. (See pages 480–482 for sample bibliography entries.)

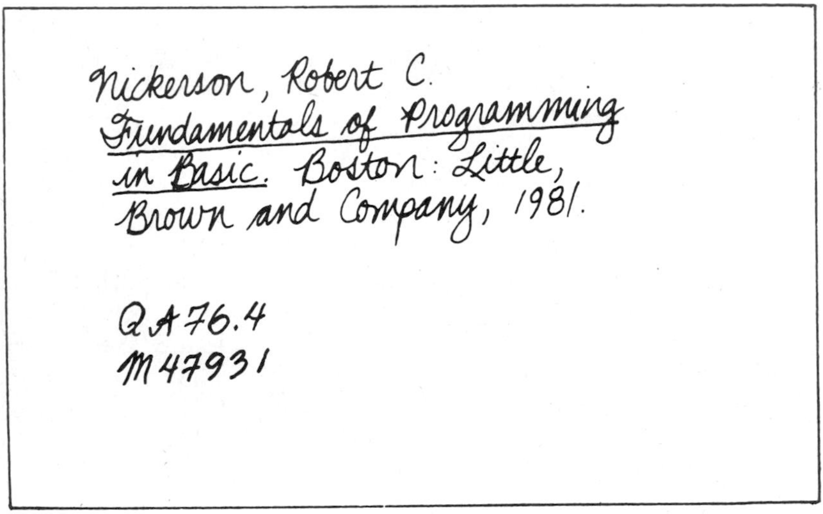

Nickerson, Robert C.
Fundamentals of Programming
in Basic. Boston: Little,
Brown and Company, 1981.

QA 76.4
M 47931

Figure 20.7   A Bibliography Card

Take the time to record the information for your working bibliography accurately. Doing so will save you from having to relocate a source at the last minute or having to eliminate one because you can't properly document it.

Taking Notes

Your finished report will be only as good as the notes you take. Using notecards is best, because they are easy to organize.

Use this procedure for taking notes:

1. Skim the entire book, chapter, article, or pamphlet.

2. Go back and decide which material is useful, accurate, reliable, and not overly biased. Use one card to record each separate item.

3. Decide how to record the item: as a quotation, a paraphrase, or a summary. In quoting, copy the statement word for word (see Figure 20.8). Place quotation marks around all directly quoted material, even a phrase or a word used in a special way.

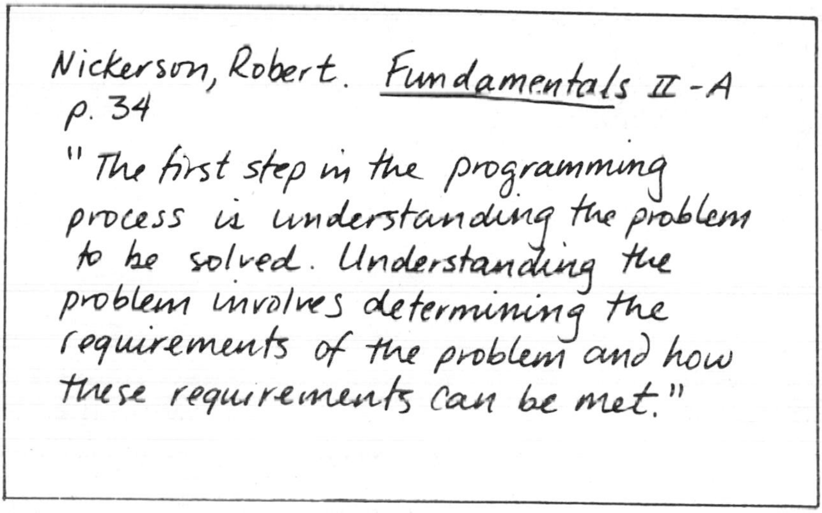

Nickerson, Robert. <u>Fundamentals</u> II -A
p. 34
" The first step in the programming process is understanding the problem to be solved. Understanding the problem involves determining the requirements of the problem and how these requirements can be met."

Figure 20.8   Sample Notecard for a Quotation

Otherwise, you could forget to give proper credit to the author and thereby face a charge of *plagiarism* (borrowing someone else's words without giving credit, intentionally *or* unintentionally). If you quote only sections of a sentence or paragraph, use an ellipsis—three dots (. . .) to indicate that words have been left out of a sentence (see the Appendix). If you leave out the last part of the sentence, the first part of the next sentence, or one or more whole sentences or paragraphs, use four dots (. . . .):

If you quote only sections . . . use an ellipsis. . . . If you leave. . . .

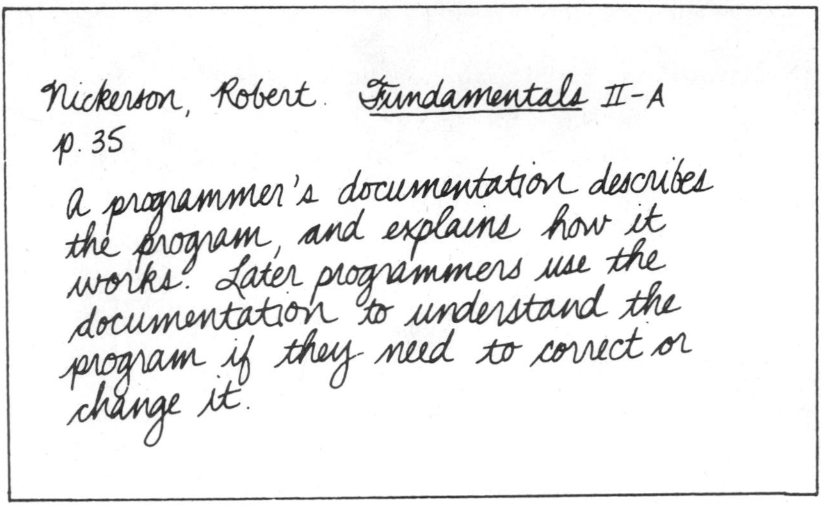

Nickerson, Robert. *Fundamentals* II-A
p. 35
a programmer's documentation describes
the program, and explains how it
works. Later programmers use the
documentation to understand the
program if they need to correct or
change it.

Figure 20.9   Sample Notecard for a Paraphrase

If you insert your own comments within the quotation, place brackets around them to distinguish your words from the author's (as discussed in the Appendix):

> "This job [aircraft ground controller] requires exhaustive attention."

Avoid using direct quotations too often, because your report then will be simply a collection of borrowed words. Instead, synthesize and condense information by paraphrasing and summarizing.

Figure 20.9 shows a paraphrased entry. The researcher condenses this original in her own words:

> Finally, the programming process is completed by bringing together all the material that describes the program. This is called *documenting* the program, and the result of this activity is the program's *documentation*. Included in the documentation are the program listing and a description of the input and output data. Documentation enables other programmers to understand how the program functions. Often it is necessary to return to the program after a time and to make corrections or changes. With adequate documentation, it is much easier to understand a program's operation.*

---

*This passage and those in Figures 20-7 and 20-8 are adapted from Robert C. Nickerson, *Fundamentals of Programming in BASIC* (Boston: Little, Brown, 1981).

Most of your notes will be paraphrased, but some notecards may have both paraphrases and direct quotations. Paraphrased material needs no quotation marks; however, it *must be documented* to indicate your debt to a source.

Be selective about what and how much you write in your notes. As you read, keep your original purpose in mind. Make notes of the main points related to your purpose, along with crucial statistics, figures, and other precise data and conclusions. Follow these guidelines:

1. Preserve the original message when quoting. Don't distort it by omitting vital information. Your aim is not to prove yourself correct but to uncover the facts. If the data disprove your view, do not ignore them.

2. When you get an idea of your own, write it on a notecard immediately. Keep a few cards handy to record observations, questions, or ideas as they come to mind.

Developing a Working Thesis and Outline

Don't expect to identify your thesis until you have evaluated and interpreted your findings (as discussed on pages 417–419). *How* you finally arrive at a thesis and outline is immaterial; *that* you arrive sooner or later is essential. To get there, use the following strategies—in whichever order works best for you.

Begin with a general view. Encyclopedias are a good place to find general information. Or you can read a book or pamphlet that offers a comprehensive view before you move to specialized articles in periodicals. Specialized dictionaries and newspaper or magazine articles also provide background. Ask your reference librarian to help you find sources.

Learn to skim. Open a book and look over the table of contents and the index. Check the introduction for an overview or thesis. In long articles, look for headings that may help you locate specific information. Short articles and pamphlets usually should be read fully.

To skim effectively, you have to concentrate. If you feel yourself drifting, take a break.

Be selective about note taking. Resist the temptation to copy or paraphrase every word. As you read, try to develop your own interpretation. Your finished report should be a combined product of your insights and collected facts you've woven together.

Remember that you are not merely collecting views, but screening and evaluating facts to answer a definite question—the question you formulated for your research topic in the first place. Your summary answer to that question will be your thesis, and it will be based on the most accurate and reliable information you have been able to find. On page 419 you phrased your topic as this question:

Research topic   *What effects, if any, do food additives and preservatives have on children's behavior?*

As you near completion of your research, you should be in a position to give at least a tentative answer to that question:

Tentative thesis   Some common food additives and preservatives play a definite role in childhood behavior disorders.

As your research proceeds, you might revise this tentative thesis any number of times. But at least for now, you have a working sense of direction.*

Now that you have identified a definite direction, you need a road map—a working outline. Perhaps your topic-as-question suggested its own rough outline earlier. However, you've probably had to do some reading first in order to assemble some sort of rough, working outline:

I.   The role of diet in behavior disorders
   A.   Children's sensitivity to small doses of chemicals
   B.   Abnormal behavior as an allergic response to some foods

II. Effects of specific additives and preservatives
   A.   On physical aggression
   B.   On classroom behavior
   C.   On scholastic performance
   D.   On peer socialization

III. Diet control in management of behavior disorders
   A.   Exclusion of flavoring and coloring substances
   B.   Exclusion of specific food preservatives and salicylates

Each of these parts, of course, can be divided into its own subparts as your research continues. By the time you compose your final outline (see the sample on pages 454–455), the shape of your report may have changed radically.

---

*In some cases, of course, your research will produce contradictory findings or indefinite conclusions, and so you might have to settle for an inconclusive thesis such as this one: *Although food additives are a suspected cause of childhood behavior disorders, the link has not yet been clearly established.* Be sure your interpretations and conclusions fit the best evidence you've collected. Never settle on a thesis that cannot be justified by the evidence.

Writing a First Draft

When you've collected your material, organized your notecards, and settled on a workable thesis, you are ready to write the first draft of your report.

Begin by revising your working outline. At this stage, try to develop a detailed formal outline, using at each level either topic phrases or full sentences. (A topic outline is shown on page 440, and a sentence outline on page 454.) Be consistent: use all phrases or all sentences.

A formal outline depends on logical notation and consistent format. *Notation* is the system of numbers and letters marking the logical divisions of your outline. *Format* is the arrangement of your material on the page (indention, spacing, and so on). Proper notation and format show the subordination of some parts of your topic to others. Be sure all sections and subsections are ordered, capitalized, lettered, numbered, punctuated, and indented to show how each part relates to other parts and to the whole. The general pattern of outline notation goes like this:

I.
    A.
        1.
        2.*
    B.
        1.
        2.
            a.
            b. (1)†
                (2)
    C.
II. etc.

(For a discussion of a sample formal outline, see page 452.)

When your outline is complete, check your tentative thesis to make sure no changes are needed there. The thesis should promise *exactly* what your report will deliver.

Now you can begin to write. To maintain control over the material, concentrate on only one section at a time. Students often find this

---

*Any division must yield at least two subparts. You could not logically divide "Types of Strip Mining" into "1. Contour Mining" without other subparts. If you can't divide your major topic into at least two subtopics, change your original heading.

†Further subdivisions can be carried as far as needed, as long as the notation for each level of division is individualized and consistent.

the most intimidating part of research: pulling together a large body of information in a report. Don't frantically throw everything on the page simply to get done. Remember that your final report will be the *only* concrete evidence of your labor.

Begin by classifying your notecards in groups according to the section of your outline to which each card is keyed. Next, find a flat surface. Take the notecards for your introduction and arrange them in order. Now, lay them out in rows, as you would lay out playing cards. Thus armed with your outline, your statement of purpose, your ordered notecards, and your expertise, you are ready to write your first section.

As you move from subsection to subsection, provide commentary and transitions, and document each source. When you complete your introductory section, proceed to the others, weaving ideas together by following the outline (and modifying as needed).

Documenting Your Sources

Most research draws on the information and ideas of others. Credit each source of direct quotations, paraphrases, and visuals (charts, graphs, tables). Proper documentation satisfies the professional requirements for ethics, efficiency, and authority.

Documentation is a matter of *ethics* in that the originator of an idea deserves to be acknowledged whenever that idea is mentioned. All published material is protected by copyright laws. Failure to acknowledge your source could make you liable to a charge of plagiarism, even if your omission was unintentional.

Documentation is also a matter of *efficiency*. It provides a chain through which our world's knowledge can be located. If you quote from a journal article, for instance, your reference will enable an interested reader to locate that source easily.

Finally, documentation is a matter of *authority*. In making any claim ("A Mercedes-Benz is a better car than a Ford"), you are liable to be challenged with "Says who?" Data on road tests, frequency of repairs, resale value, workmanship, and owners' comments can help validate your claim by showing that your opinion is based on *fact*. Your credibility increases in relation to the expert references supporting your claims. For a controversial subject, you may need to cite several authorities (instead of forcing a simplistic conclusion on your material), as in this example:

> Opinion is mixed as to whether a marketable quantity of oil exists under Georges Bank. Cape Cod geologist John Blocke feels that extensive reserves are unlikely ("Geologist Dampens Hopes" 3).

Oil geologist Donald Marshall doubts that oil in any quantity exists under Georges Bank ("Offshore Oil Drilling" 2). But the U.S. Interior Department claims that the Atlantic continental shelf may contain 5.5 billion barrels of oil (Kemprecos 8).

WHAT YOU SHOULD DOCUMENT

Document any source from which you have quoted words or borrowed facts and ideas that cannot be regarded as common knowledge (or general information) in that field. Common knowledge about a field can be found in any number of sources. In medicine it is common knowledge that foods high in fat can cause some types of cancer. Thus, in a research report on fatty diets and cancer, you probably would not need to document that fact. But you would document the results of tests on beta carotene and vitamin E as possible cancer preventives.

If your information can be found in only one specific source and not in various general reference sources, it should be documented. When in doubt, document the source.

HOW YOU SHOULD DOCUMENT

Documentation can follow any number of formats; however, the format recommended by the Modern Language Association is most often used in documenting freshman research papers. *The MLA Handbook for Writers of Research Papers* (1988) has replaced footnotes with in-text citations (also called parenthetical references). Instead of placing numbered footnotes (like this:[1]) in your text and listing source references at the bottom of the page or as endnotes, list your abbreviated references within the text, and then provide full documentation in a "Works Cited" section at the end of the report.* (The "Works Cited" section replaces the "Bibliography" section.) Let's look at a few examples.

An in-text, or parenthetical, citation usually includes the author's last name and the page cited, as in (Barrett 69). Here's how the citation would appear in the report:

> Recent evidence suggests that the advantages of automation clearly outweigh its disadvantages (Barrett 69).

Readers needing the full citation for Barrett can turn to "Works Cited," listed alphabetically by author, to get complete publishing information.

---

*Footnotes (and endnotes) are now used only when you wish to comment on or expand material in the text (as done here).

Keep parenthetical references brief. If you mention the author's name in your discussion, don't repeat it in the citation; simply provide the page reference:

> Barrett offers evidence that the advantages of automation clearly outweigh its disadvantages (69).

If the work is by a corporate author or if it is unsigned (that is, author unknown), use a shortened version of the title or corporate name in your citation, as in: ("Information Systems" 18). But make sure that shortened titles correspond with the complete entries in "Works Cited" ("Information Systems for Tomorrow's Office," *Fortune* 19 (Oct. 1982): 18).

Except for a direct quotation, an in-text citation should refer to no more than one paragraph. Sometimes you will have a paragraph in which all the data are yours except for the final two or three lines. Then, use a hinge sentence ("Jones has shown that peer approval is a primary need during adolescence.") to separate your own from borrowed information. Otherwise, a citation at the end of the paragraph might cause readers to conclude that the whole paragraph is borrowed.

Unless your instructor requests otherwise, use the following formats for references in your "Works-Cited" (or "Bibliography") section.

WORKS-CITED FORM FOR BOOKS

Any citation for a book should contain the following information (as applicable): author, title, editor or translator, edition, volume number, and facts about publication (city, publisher, date). (This information is found on a book's title and copyright pages.) Abbreviate publishers' names in your list of works cited, as in "Little" for Little, Brown and Company; "Knopf" for Alfred A. Knopf, Inc.; " GPO" for Government Printing Office; or "Yale UP" for Yale University Press.

Type the first line of the entry flush with the left margin. Indent the second and all subsequent lines five spaces. Double-space within each entry as well as between entries. Skip two horizontal spaces after any period* in an entry and one space after any comma or colon. Here are examples:

---

*Only those periods that separate different parts of an entry (say, author's name from the work's title) are followed by two spaces. Those periods that end an abbreviation within one part of an entry (say, "p. 24" or "Mary H. Jones") are followed by just one space.

Single Author

Kidder, Tracy. The Soul of a New Machine. Boston: Little,

  1981.

Two or Three Authors

Keck, Harvey, James Lott, and Roger Cayer. Principles of

  Geology. Chicago: Nashua, 1989.

More Than Three Authors

Fishberg, Richard H., et al. Cloud Formation. Montreal,

  Quebec: Loon, 1989.

Author(s) Not Named

The New Fisheries Directory. Boston: Smith-Lane, 1990.

Two Books with the Same Author

Lamont, John W. Biophysics. San Francisco: Phoenix,

  1982.

---. Diagnostic Techniques. New York: Radon, 1980.

When citing more than one work by an author, do not repeat the
author's name; simply type three hyphens followed by a period.

One or Two Editors

Kutash, Irwin L., and Louis B. Schlesinger, eds. Handbook

  on Stress and Anxiety. San Francisco: Jossey, 1980.

For three or more editors, name only the first, followed by "et al."

A Quotation of a Quotation

Ashburn, Thomas. Miracle Drugs. Washington, D.C.:

  Patriot Press, 1987, p. 84, as cited in Lester Furley,

  The Treatment of Rheumatoid Arthritis. New York:

  Holman, 1990.

When your author has quoted from another's work, refer to the original.

WORKS-CITED FORM FOR ARTICLES

A citation for an article should include this information (as applicable): author, title of article, title of periodical, volume or number or both, date, and page numbers for the entire article (not just the pages cited). List the information in the order given here, as in these examples:

A Magazine Article

```
Miller, J. A. "A Shared Chemistry for Brain and Body."

    Science News  19 Mar. 1981: 180-181.
```

If no author is given, list all other information. No punctuation separates the magazine title and date. Nor is the abbreviation *p.* or *pp.* used to designate page numbers.

An Article in a Journal with New Pagination in Each Issue

```
Thackman, John.  "Computer-Assisted Research."  American

    Librarian  51.1 (1990): 3-9.
```

Because each issue for that year will have page numbers beginning with 1, readers have to know the number of this issue. The "51" is the volume number, and the "1" is the issue number.

Omit "The" or any other introductory article from a journal or magazine title.

An Article in a Journal with Continuous Pagination

```
Barnstead, Marion H.  "The Writing Crisis."  Writing

    Theory 12 (1986): 415-33.
```

When page numbers continue from one issue to another for the whole year, readers do not need to know the issue number, because no other issue in that year will repeat the same page numbers.

A Newspaper Article

```
Schmidt, Hannah.  "The Nuclear Gamble."  Boston Times  15

    Mar. 1988, Western ed.: 4.
```

Omit any introductory article in the newspaper's name (not *The Boston Times*). If no author is given, list all other information. When a daily newspaper has more than one edition, cite the edition after the date. If the newspaper's name doesn't contain the city of publication, insert it, using brackets: *Sippican Sentinel* [Marion, Mass.].

WORKS-CITED FORM FOR OTHER KINDS OF MATERIALS

Encyclopedia, Dictionary, or Other Alphabetic Reference Work

```
"Hydraulics."  Technical Encyclopedia.  1981 ed.
```

If the entry is signed, begin with the author's name.

A Selection in an Anthology

```
Kafka, Franz.  "The Metamorphosis."  Introduction to
    Literature.  Ed. Roger Greene.  4th ed.  Boston:
    Appleby Publishers, 1990.  215-286.
```

The page numbers are for the one work cited in the anthology.

A Film

```
Nashville.  Dir. Robert Altman.  Universal, 1974.
```

A Radio or Television Program

```
The Wall Street Report.  PBS.  WGBH, Boston.  30 Jan. 1989.
```

An Interview

```
Cooper, John.  President, Datronics.  Personal Interview.
    Hyannis, Mass. 4 Dec. 1990.
```

A Lecture

```
Starkey, Harold.  "Enzyme Inhibitors."  Lecture given at
    Marshall College.  Rangeley, Minn., 15 Oct. 1990.
```

A Database Source

```
Calvin, Mary K.  "Nesting Habits of Sapsuckers."  Studies
    in Ornithology  15 (1982): 94-99; Baltimore, Md.:
```

```
Bioscience Retrieval Services, 1985, Accession No.

87649-35.
```

A Corporate or Government Report

```
The Presidential Task Force on Acid Rain.  The Role of Acid

Rain in Deforestation.  Washington, D.C.: GPO, 1985.
```

Cite other unpublished material (reports, dissertations, and so on) this way:

> Author (if known), Title (in quotes), Organization, date, page number(s).

In your "Works-Cited" section (which you can also title "Bibliography"), arrange the entries alphabetically by the author's last name. When the author's name is unknown, list the title alphabetically according to its first word (excluding *a*, *an*, and *the*). If a title begins with a digit ("5," "6," etc.), alphabetize the entry as if the digit were spelled out.

On pages 480–482, you will find a list of works cited by Shirley Haley in her research report.

Revising Your Research Report

After completing and documenting a first draft, rest for a day or two before returning to the report. Then use the Revision Checklist in Chapter 4, along with the following checklist, to evaluate the report for worthwhile content, sensible organization, and readable style.

RESEARCH REPORT CHECKLIST

(to be used with the Revision Checklist in Chapter 4)

Content

1. Does the report grow from a clear thesis?
2. Is the title accurate and unbiased?
3. Do the details show how you arrived at your conclusions?
4. Is the report based on credible sources and objective evidence? (See "Supporting Your Claim" in Chapter 18.)

5. Is the information complete?

6. Have you avoided drawing too much data from any one source?

7. Is your evidence free of weak spots?

8. Are all data clearly and fully interpreted?

9. Is all quoted material accurate?

10. Is the report free of excessively long quotations?

11. Can anything be cut?

12. Is anything missing?

13. Have you avoided forcing a conclusion on your material?

14. Are all sources documented?

15. Is the documentation complete and correct?

Organization

1. Does the introduction state clearly the purpose and thesis of the report?

2. Does the report itself follow the outline?

3. Is each paragraph focused on one main thought?

4. Do conclusions rest fully on the data discussed and interpreted?

5. Is your line of reasoning clear and easy to follow?

As time allows, keep revising until the research report represents your best effort.

A Sample Research Project

In the remainder of this chapter we trace one writer's decisions from the day her report was assigned until the day she submitted her final draft.

As soon as Shirley Haley learned that a research report was due in 6 weeks, she began to search for a worthwhile topic. Although Haley had many college friends who had adjusted to the hectic freshman pace, she knew others who were not doing so well: some had developed insomnia; others had gained or lost a good deal of weight; one friend was sleeping more than 12 hours a day. Other disorders ranged from compulsive eating and indigestion to chronic headaches and skin problems—all seemingly since the beginning of the semester. Haley wondered why, beyond the obvious pressures of college life, so many of her friends had become so unhealthy. She decided to search for answers.

A psychology major, Haley had recently read about *stress* in an introductory textbook. She wondered if there could be a connection between stress and the problems she was witnessing among her friends.

Haley was fortunate in being able to settle quickly on a topic that had real meaning for her and that was pretty well focused to begin with. But to come up with the right answers, she would have to ask all the right questions. Here is her tree chart:

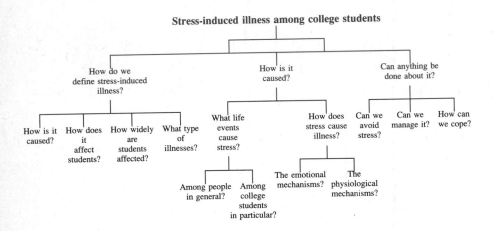

These questions gave Haley the kind of detailed perspective that would lend real direction to her research.

Once she knew the specific kinds of information she was looking for, Haley focused on the various viewpoints that would give her a balanced picture:

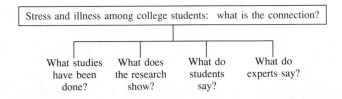

Now that she knew what questions to ask and from whom to get the answers, Haley was ready to do her research.

On her first trip to the library, Haley went straight to the *Readers' Guide to Periodical Literature;* because she had already read a description of stress in her psychology textbook, she felt no need to begin with such general reference works as encyclopedias and specialized dictionaries. In the most recent volume of the *Readers' Guide* was a sizable collection of articles under the heading "Stress." Haley also checked under the heading "College students"; there, under the subheading "Psychology," she found additional relevant titles. Then she checked through further volumes of the *Readers' Guide*, going back several years. Whenever she came across a promising title, she recorded the full citation on a bibliography card.

Next Haley searched through recent volumes of *Psychological Abstracts* (arranged like the *Readers' Guide*, but more specialized) for any studies that might have been done on stress and college students. Besides finding yet more titles in this index, she was able to look up and read abstracts of articles whose titles seemed promising. Under "Stress," she found an overwhelming number of titles—too many to follow up. But under "College Students," she found listings for some key articles that seemed to address her friends' health problems.

Now Haley checked her library's periodicals holdings list (see page 428) to determine which of these key articles were available in this library. Some, she found, were collected in bound volumes; others were on microfilm. With the help of a librarian, she learned how to locate and read articles on a microfilm reader. The librarian also assisted by ordering through interlibrary loan two articles not held in that library.

Then Haley proceeded to the card catalog, where she jotted down a few book titles and call numbers. Once in the stacks, she was able to browse through the books on the shelves. She also checked book and article titles in the "Selected Bibliography" section of her psychology textbook. Every time she discovered another promising source, she recorded the citation on a bibliography card.

Now that she had a good stock of sources, Haley began to skim the most promising works for key information. She was careful to evaluate each finding for accuracy, reliability, fairness, and completeness. Whenever she came across useful material, she recorded it on a notecard, being careful to indicate the source and page number(s) and to record quotations word for word. In her reading, she found a good body of information on stress management, and so she decided to structure her report in this way:

Problem → Causes and Effects → Solutions

After a long time reading and thinking about her findings, Haley settled on her overall interpretation—her judgment about the *meaning* of all this material. In this case, the evidence clearly pointed toward a definite conclusion: Stress was indeed a real factor in students' poor health. Now she could formulate a tentative thesis:

Stress is a definite cause of illness among college students.

Although Haley would later refine and expand her thesis, she had, for now, a good focal point for developing her report.

Haley continued to read, record information, outline, and organize her notecards. Finally, she decided she knew enough to write her first draft. Using the revision checklists, she reworked a first and then a second draft and completed the final draft that appears on the following pages. Read this final draft carefully, paying close attention to the writer's decisions that are discussed on the facing pages. (The numbers in the margins of the report refer to the points discussed on the facing pages.)

Discussion of the Sample Research Report

1. *Title page:* Most instructors expect students to prepare a title page for a research report. Many reports for government, business, and industry are prefaced by a title page with these standard items: report title, author's name, course or department, intended reader's name, and date of submission. Haley centers and spaces these items for visual appeal. The title page is not numbered.

2. *Outline* (on next two pages): You might be asked to submit your final outline with your report—either as a topic or a sentence outline. Haley prefaces her sentence outline with her thesis, so that readers can understand her plan at a glance. She divides her report into three major sections (The Problem, Specific Causes, and Possible Solutions) to reveal a clear and sensible line of thought. This shape is a version of effect-to-cause development (see pages 294–300).

   After each roman numeral is a sentence summarizing that major section. After each capital letter or number is a topic or orienting sentence coinciding with a paragraph or group of paragraphs in the report. Notice that each level of division in the outline yields at least *two* parts. Outline pages are not numbered, but the first page carries the heading "Outline."

1

Students Under Stress: College Can

Make You Sick

By

Shirley Haley

English 101, Section 1432

Professor Lannon

December 8, 1990

Outline

Thesis: Because of disruptive changes and pressures in
           their personal, social, and academic lives,
           college students are highly vulnerable to the
           physical effects of stress.

 I. The Problem: Stress is increasingly recognized as a
    definite cause of physical disorders.

    A. The mechanisms have been studied for years, but
       stress is still making us sick.

    B. Stress has a technical and a personal
       definition, and both are accurate.

    C. More and more of us suffer the physical effects
       of stress.

    D. College students are among the groups most
       affected.

 II. Specific Causes: Stress-induced illness is caused
     by a series of emotional responses that have
     physical consequences.

     A. Stress originates when the body works too hard to
        maintain equilibrium.

        1. If the alarm reaction persists, the body is
           forever ready for action.

        2. Psychosomatic illness is not imaginary.

B. A 1967 study showed a connection between the stress of common life events and illness.

C. Even a series of ordinary events in the lives of college students can cause dangerous levels of stress.

D. Various studies of college students confirm the stress-illness link.

III. <u>Possible Solutions</u>: Now that the problem is recognized, solutions are being found.

A. The effect stress has on us depends on how well we cope.

  1. We need both coping strategies and help from others.

  2. Without coping mechanisms, we are almost certain to be overwhelmed.

B. Students need to develop more realistic expectations of college life.

  1. College orientation should be more realistic.

  2. Stress-management courses should be offered by more colleges.

C. Some type of stress-management training should be available to every college student.

3

The Problem: Stress-Induced Illness

Excessive stress can cause physical illness. The mechanisms have been under study for years, but stress is still making us sick.

4

Some 60 years ago, the search began for a link between stress and illness. Walter Cannon identified the "fight or flight" response in 1929. Showing that emotional arousal causes physical reactions such as increased respiration and pulse rate and elevated blood pressure, Cannon laid the groundwork for stress research. In the 1930s Dr. Adolf Mayer, who began using charts of patients' life events to aid his medical

5

diagnoses, recorded "the changes of habit, of school entrances, graduations or changes, or failures; the various jobs . . . and other important events" (Dohrenwend and Dohrenwend 3). And Hans Selye in 1936 described the body's reaction to stress as "the syndrome

6

of just being sick" ("Stress Concept" 72).

Stress has a technical and a personal definition. Technically, stress is a response to life events that disrupt the physical being. In personal terms, stress is part of what happens when a person falls in or out of love,

7

receives good or bad news, drives a car, receives a traffic ticket, takes final exams, or graduates. All life experiences, good and bad, entail stress. In fact, some

3. *Headings and page numbering:* Haley uses section headings as signals to aid readability and help keep readers on track. This first page of the text is not numbered, but, as we will see, the second page is numbered "2."

4. *Background information:* Haley designs her first paragraph to grab our attention by showing immediately that stress makes us sick. She summarizes a half-century of stress research to emphasize that the whole stress issue is much more than a fad. Brief quotations from authorities lend credibility to Haley's opening sentence.

5. *Using quoted material:* Haley introduces brief quotes by naming the author and by combining the quotations with her own words to make complete sentences. No comma or other punctuation precedes these quotations, because they are phrased as part of Haley's sentences.

6. *Citing sources:* Haley cites each source in parentheses, inside the period, but outside any quotation marks. Because one of the authors cited in the first paragraph has more than one work listed in Haley's "Works-Cited" section, Haley is careful to list a shortened version of this work's title when she refers to that author.

7. *Defining the problem:* Observing a principle of all communication, Haley *defines* her subject before going on to discuss it. And she clarifies her definition with concrete examples of stressful situations. Haley is careful to point out that *some* stress can be beneficial, but that too much is destructive. She summarizes this distinction between levels of stress by quoting an authority.

2

degree of anxiety is a good motivator--we work better under stress. According to Dr. Kenneth Greenspan, director of the stress lab at New York Presbyterian Hospital, "as with a violin string, there is an optimal note: not all slack--not all taut" (Adler and Gosnell 107). But when we are too taut, our physical health is endangered.

More and more of us suffer physical effects of stress; we develop ulcers and colitis, fatigue and exhaustion, high blood pressure and headache. Among its dangers, stress probably makes us susceptible to infectious disease and cancer by inhibiting the activity of our "natural killer (NK) cells." These killer cells help the body fight off colds, flu, pneumonia, and other infections, and they destroy malignant cells. In a recent study, young adults who saw their lives as highly stressful showed decreased NK cell activity and a high rate of infectious illness (Bower 141).

Stress has its warning signs, cues to look for help before our bodies actually suffer some kind of breakdown. Among the commonest signs are an overpowering urge to cry or run away, persistent anxiety for no reason, insomnia, and a feeling of being "keyed up." (See Appendix A for a full list of signs.) Overeating and increased or excessive use of alcohol or drugs are often the result of

8. *Relating the material to the audience:* Readers always want to know what something means to *them personally;* Haley therefore includes a paragraph on the common effects and signs of stress. By helping her audience relate to the material early in the report, Haley stimulates our interest enough to make us want to keep reading.

9. *Referring to appendixes:* Haley refers us to an appendix at report's end for details that we might find useful but that would interrupt the flow of the report itself.

3

stress beyond endurance, an attempt to run away (Selye, Stress of Life 175).

10   Among the groups most confronted by changing events, and thus most affected by stress, are college students. In 1984 counselor Fred B. Newton at Kansas State University tried to develop a general character profile of students, to assess counseling needs. He found major problems to be worry, stress, and anxiety; 76 percent of students surveyed described the college environment as negative or, at best, neutral, "a hassle," "a runaround"; and the most important need was for warm, accepting relationships (542-543).

11   For many students the battle with stress begins early. Even before graduating high school they might face the pressure of being admitted to the college of their choice. Or they might come from affluent, successful families and feel they have to measure up to parents' achievements and expectations. Or they might struggle to keep up with successful brothers or sisters. "Second-rate doesn't rate at all in a majority of the households from which these [students] come--and they know it" (Brooks 613). The actual transition from high school to college creates more stress as students leave a friendly and familiar environment for one that seems impersonal and demanding, academically and socially (Compas 243).

10. *Thesis paragraphs:* Now that Haley has given us background
     information on stress in general and sparked our personal
     interest, she can focus specifically on stress in the lives of college
     students. Haley designs this paragraph and the next to lead into
     her thesis (top of page "4").

11. *Citing sources:* Because Haley has mentioned the author's name
     in her paragraph, she merely lists the page numbers in her
     parenthetical citation.

4

Such disruptive changes and pressures in their personal, social, and academic lives make students vulnerable to the physical effects of stress.

Specific Causes of Stress-Induced Illness

12 Stress originates when the body works too hard to maintain the equilibrium necessary for a healthy life. Any disruptive stimulus or demand, good or bad, sets off an adjustment that allows the body to regain its equilibrium. When a stimulus sets off this adjustment, when an "alarm reaction" puts the body "on alert," adrenaline rushes out to prepare the body for action: blood pressure rises to increase blood flow to muscles; digestion temporarily shuts down; blood sugar rises to increase energy; perspiration increases; and other physical changes occur, to prepare the body for "fight or flight" (Selye, "Stress Concept" 76).

13 If the alert is never over, if the alarm reaction persists, the body is forever ready for action. That is when stress is a problem. We can run away from a speeding car bearing down on us as we cross the street, and when the danger passes, the stress is over. But we can't run away from some inner threat, such as adjusting to college life, or the pressure to study and achieve good grades. And as the stress endures, the adjustment weakens, unable to maintain the equilibrium necessary for good health.

12. *Tracing the causes:* Before Haley covers the disruptive situations that cause stress, she spends three paragraphs explaining how the body reacts to such situations. This background is essential to our understanding of the connection Haley later makes between life events and illness.

13. *Interpreting research findings:* This paragraph shows us that Haley is *interpreting* her material, not merely giving us a collection of findings to sort out for ourselves.

5

Psychosomatic illness is not imaginary; it is real disease that can be diagnosed and treated. But the cause of psychosomatic illness is unmanaged stress. Until the stress is controlled, the disease can't be cured. Because of previous illness or heredity, one organ or system (heart, digestive system, skin) in a person's body tends to be most vulnerable. This part of the body is like the weak link in a chain; no matter what pulls the chain, good or bad, the chain breaks (Selye, "Stress Concept" 77).

14

A connection between the stress of common life events and illness was demonstrated in a 1967 study. First, researchers assigned point values to 43 specific life events (divorce, illness, marriage, loss of a job). After collecting health histories, the researchers asked their subjects to total the points for recent events in their lives. (The scale ranged from 100 points for the death of a spouse to 11 for a traffic violation--see Appendix B for a full listing.) Comparing the health histories to point totals, the researchers discovered that any group of life events totaling 150 or more points in one year was connected to a major illness (requiring physician's care) for 93 percent of the subjects. And the harmful effects of a high point total lasted as long as two years (Holmes and Masuda 50-56).

15

Even a collection of ordinary events in the lives of college students can place them in a danger category, as

14. *Establishing the link:* In this paragraph, Haley describes the major study that demonstrated the stress-illness connection. Here again, she refers us to an appendix for details.

15. *Focusing on college students:* Haley now interprets her general findings in specific relation to college students. This paragraph leads into a detailed discussion of studies done on college students.

6

shown in Table 1:

16

Table 1: A Life-Events Scale for College Students	
Event	Point Value
Beginning or ending of school	26
Change in living conditions	25
Revision of personal habits	24
Change in work hours or conditions	20
Change in residence	20
Change in church activities	19
Change in social activities	18
Loan of less than $10,000	17
Change in sleeping habits	16
Change in eating habits	15

Source: Adapted from Holmes and Rahe, Table 3: 216.

The life events in Table 1 alone total 200 points--
without considering any other points students collect
from experiences outside of school.

17

Studies of college students confirm the stress-
illness link. John Jemmott analyzed saliva of freshman
dental students for an antibody that fights tooth decay
and respiratory infections. Students who placed a higher
value on close friendship than on success consistently
secreted more of this antibody than students with a drive
for power and success did--especially during exams
(Stark 77). A popular interpretation of Jemmott's
findings is that highly motivated students are more
vulnerable to tooth decay and respiratory infections,
especially under stress (Taulbee 7).

Using a health questionnaire and a life-events scale
tailored for college students, other researchers have

16. *Using visuals:* To illustrate her numerical data, Haley decides to use a table. She is careful to number the table, to introduce it, to cite her source, and to interpret the data for her readers. If the table were longer than one text page, she would place it in an appendix (see pages 476–479). Besides tables, other visuals (charts, graphs, diagrams, maps, photos) can provide concrete and vivid illustrations.

17. *One topic sentence serving multiple paragraphs:* Haley discusses too many studies here to include in one paragraph. Instead, she breaks up her material into three paragraphs and lets her one topic sentence serve all three.

7

established a definite connection between "high levels
of life change and reported illness" (Kutash and
Schlesinger 194). More than half the medical students in
a study by Holmes and Masuda "experienced major health
changes" within two years after entering school. A
college life-events scale was given to 54 incoming
medical school freshmen; students with the highest
scores reported most illness before the end of sophomore
year (Holmes and Masuda 64). The stress of starting
school can strongly affect one's health.

In a related study, Holmes found a connection between
life changes and the number of injuries sustained by 100
college football players. High scores on the life-change
survey equaled more injuries on the field. Of the ten
players who had multiple injuries, seven were from the
group with highest scores in the life-events survey
(Holmes and Masuda 66).

Stress-induced illness among college students can be
self-perpetuating. A recent study suggests that
stressful events can initiate symptoms that then help
create further stressful events: "For example, divorce
of one's parents may lead to symptoms of depression
[anxiety, insomnia, loss of appetite, hopelessness,
etc.], which in turn may lead to disruption of
interpersonal relationships and poor performance in
school" (Compas 242). And so by merely treating the

18

18. *Citing supplementary sources:* Rather than giving a laundry list of all studies that confirm the stress-illness link, Haley merely states that such information is available, giving us a parenthetical citation so that we can locate the sources if we wish. Instead of listing every item she discovered in her research, Haley is *selective,* giving us only what we need.

8

symptoms--without confronting the causes--we ensure
that many students remain trapped in this endless cycle
of stress and illness.

Possible Solutions

Because stressful events in our lives are unlikely to
disappear, our only solution is to learn to cope with or
manage stress. In fact, the amount of stress caused by any
event depends precisely on how well we cope: "It is our
ability to cope with the demands made by the events in our
lives, not the quality or intensity of the events, that
counts. What matters is not so much what happens to us,
but the way we take it" (Selye, "Stress Concept" 83). And
"the way we take it" has a lot to do with heredity, with
the ways in which we've learned to manage stress in the
past, and with the helping resources available to us now.

To combat stress, we need both coping strategies and
help from others. Aaron Antonovsky uses the term
"resistance resources" to describe the things that come
between us and the effects of stress (246). Among the
coping strategies he lists are the ability to see all the
alternatives to a problem, the ability to see ourselves
in more than one role (so that failure in one role isn't
devastating), the capacity to recover our balance
quickly and to move on, and our ties to others (252). "On
the simplest level," says Antonovsky, "a person who has

19. *Transition:* Haley uses a transitional sentence to sum up the causes and to lead into her discussion of solutions, the final major section of her report.

20. *Arriving at solutions:* Notice Haley's line of reasoning throughout this section: from the importance of coping, to specific coping strategies, to students' coping needs, to programs designed to help students cope. The report is clear because Haley's line of thought is clear. She has taken the time to *shape* her material.

9

21 someone who cares for him [or her] is likely to more adequately resolve tension than one who does not" (252). The importance of ties to others is confirmed by Newton's findings that students have a great need for friendship and belonging (543).

22
23 Without coping mechanisms, we are likely to be overwhelmed. Richard Lazarus of the University of California at Berkeley suggests: "coping is the core problem [of stress]," and George Vaillant of Harvard speculates that "stress does not kill us so much as ingenious adaptation to stress . . . facilitates our survival" (Adler and Gosnell 108). Because of youth and relative inexperience in managing stress, typical college students face an immediate need to develop coping mechanisms.

24 Students' greatest coping need apparently is to develop more realistic expectations of college life. Newton's study at Kansas State produced a revealing picture of students' expectations: students are unrealistic about their chances of succeeding in college. They suffer from what Levine calls the Titanic Ethic: "They see doom in the world around them but still feel they [personally] will somehow survive" (qtd. in Newton 541). Students are so certain of survival, they make few plans for coping with anticipated problems;

21. *Punctuating quotations:* On page 1 of this report, we saw that Haley inserted no punctuation before the quotations she had integrated with her own sentences. When she inserts her own comments, however (as in "says Antonovsky"), within the quotation, she sets the comment off with commas.

　　　When using an independent clause to introduce a quotation, she precedes the quotation with a colon.

　　　Following a quotation, commas and periods belong inside the quotation marks. Any other punctuation following a quotation belongs outside the quotation marks—unless it belongs to the quoted material itself (*What did he mean when he said "I'm through"?* or *His response was "I'm through!"*).

22. *Using brackets in quotations:* To clarify some quotations, Haley inserts a word or phrase in brackets. The brackets are a signal that the writer has altered the original quotation; the bracketed comments are Haley's, not the author's.

23. *Using ellipses in quotations:* Haley uses ellipses (. . .), here and in the second paragraph of her report, to shorten otherwise long quotations. In fact, no quotation in the report is more than a few lines long. A research report does not merely catalog other people's ideas and words. Instead, writers filter this material, giving it their own concise shape—without, of course, distorting the original information.

　　　If Haley had used a quotation of more than four typewritten lines, she would have set it off by indenting it ten spaces and typing it double-spaced, without quotation marks.

24. *Quoting an indirect source:* In her research, Haley came across a key phrase—"the Titanic ethic"—to characterize college students. But she found this phrase quoted from the original in another source, and this second source gave no page number from the original. Unable to trace the original source, Haley includes the abbreviation "qtd."—for "quoted in"—in the parenthetical citation of her indirect source. As we will see, she includes in "Works Cited" all the bibliographic information available on the original source (that is, Lexine).

10

instead they rely on the hope that things will take care of themselves (Newton 540-542).

To help students avoid shattered expectations, college orientation should be more realistic. Newton suggests that, besides playing games, registering, testing, and waving good-bye until fall, orientation should include some stress-management counseling and a no-nonsense look at all sides of college life (541).

At least one school has begun offering, for credit, a course in stress management. University of Minnesota counselor John Romano offers "Psychology and the Management of Stress." The course's goal is to "teach students how to implement personal change strategies before emotional and physical crises develop." Focus is on three areas: diet, exercise, and life-style (Romano 533-534). In all three areas, students learn to accept responsibility for changing their lives.

College can be especially stressful, a time of massive and profound change. The stress from such change can cause serious illness. Although stress is unavoidable, it can be managed. Stress-management training should be offered to all students, to make them aware of the realities of college life and of their responsibility for their own well-being. Students who do learn to manage stress will be less likely to find that college makes them sick.

25. *Paraphrased and summarized material:* To save space and improve coherence, Haley paraphrases throughout her report. Here Haley derived her paraphrase and summary from this original passage:

Selective blindness may be a more difficult illness to prevent when the fantasy vision may seem more pleasant than reality. As a recommendation, to shock students into an awareness of reality now may be more beneficial than the rude awakening of tomorrow. So far, the best suggestion is to conduct "future shock" and "future cope" workshops that confront students with situations and problems that will need to be resolved. Perhaps, orientation programs should strive to show more of the realities of college life rather than the present-day programs of welcoming, testing, registering, and saying "I'll see you in the fall."

26. *Conclusion:* Haley's closing suggestions are keyed specifically to her thesis, thus summarizing and rounding out the discussion and reemphasizing the major points. Having followed Haley's line of thought throughout the report, we can readily accept her conclusions.

27

Appendix A: Warning Signals of Stress

Stress has definite warning signals, emotional and

physical. Here are the commonest:

Emotional Signs of Stress

- being emotionally very "up" or very "down"
- impulsive behavior and emotional instability
- uncontrollable urge to cry or run away
- inability to concentrate
- feelings of unreality
- loss of "joy of life"
- feeling "keyed up"
- being easily startled
- nightmares; insomnia
- a general sense of anxiety or dread

Physical Signs of Stress

- pounding heart (may indicate high blood pressure)
- constantly dry throat and mouth
- weakness; dizziness
- feelings of tiredness
- trembling; nervous tics
- high-pitched, nervous laughter
- grinding of teeth
- constant aimless motion
- excessive perspiring
- diarrhea; indigestion; queasy stomach
- headaches
- pain in neck or lower back (because of muscle tension)
- excessive or lost appetite
- proneness to accidents

Source: Adapted from Selye, The Stress of Life: 175.

27. *Appendixes* (including the one on the next two pages): To expand items in the report without cluttering the text, Haley includes two appendixes at the end of her text—but before her "Works-Cited" section.

An appendix is a catchall for material that is important but difficult to integrate into the body of a report. Typical material in an appendix includes:

- details of an experiment
- specific measurements
- maps
- quotations longer than one page of text
- photographs
- long lists or visuals using more than one full page
- texts of laws, regulations, literary passages, and so on

Haley is careful to use her appendixes correctly by including no needless information or by leaving no vital material out of the report itself. Readers should not have to turn to appendixes to understand the text of the report. Haley distills the essential facts from her appendixes and includes this distillation in the text of her report.

Each appendix is labeled clearly, and a separate one is used for each major item. At appropriate places in her report, Haley refers us to her appendixes for supplementary information: "(See Appendix A . . .)".

12

Appendix B: Stress Values of Common Life Events

In their 1967 study, Holmes and Rahe ranked life events in
descending order according to their stress value. This
table shows the rating scale.

Social Readjustment Rating Scale

Rank	Life Event	Mean Value
1	Death of spouse	100
2	Divorce	73
3	Marital separation from mate	65
4	Detention in jail or other institution	63
5	Death of a close family member	63
6	Major personal injury or illness	53
7	Marriage	50
8	Being fired at work	47
9	Marital reconciliation with mate	45
10	Retirement from work	45
11	Major change in the health or behavior of a family member	44
12	Pregnancy	40
13	Sexual difficulties	39
14	Getting a new family member (e.g., through birth, adoption, oldster moving in, etc.)	39
15	Major business readjustment (e.g., merger, reorganization, bankruptcy, etc.)	39
16	Major change in financial state (e.g., a lot worse off or a lot better off than usual	38
17	Death of a close friend	37
18	Changing to a different line of work	36
19	Major change in the number of arguments with spouse (e.g., either a lot more or a lot less than usual regarding child rearing, personal habits, etc.)	35
20	Taking out a mortgage or loan for a major purchase (e.g., for a home, business, etc.)	31
21	Foreclosure on a mortgage or loan	30
22	Major change in responsibilities at work (e.g., promotion, demotion, lateral transfer)	29
23	Son or daughter leaving home (e.g., marriage, attending college, etc.)	29

13

Appendix B (Continued)

Rank	Life Event	Mean Value
24	Trouble with in-laws	29
25	Outstanding personal achievement	28
26	Wife beginning or ceasing work outside the home	26
27	Beginning or ceasing formal schooling	26
28	Major change in living conditions (e.g., building a new home, remodeling, deterioration of home or neighborhood)	25
29	Revision of personal habits (dress, manners, associations, etc.)	24
30	Trouble with the boss	23
31	Major change in working hours or conditions	20
32	Change in residence	20
33	Changing to a new school	20
34	Major change in usual type and/or amount of recreation	19
35	Major change in church activities (e.g., a lot more or a lot less than usual)	19
36	Major change in social activities (e.g., clubs, dancing, movies, visiting, etc.)	18
37	Taking out a mortgage or loan for a lesser purchase (e.g., for a car, TV, freezer, etc.)	17
38	Major change in sleeping habits (a lot more or a lot less sleep, or change in part of day when asleep)	16
39	Major change in number of family get-togethers (e.g., a lot more or a lot less than usual)	15
40	Major change in eating habits (a lot more or a lot less food intake, or very different meal hours or surroundings)	15
41	Vacation	13
42	Christmas	12
43	Minor violations of the law (e.g., traffic tickets, jaywalking, disturbing the peace, etc.)	11

Source: "The Social Readjustment Scale": 216.

14

Works Cited

Adler, Jerry, and Mariana Gosnell. "Stress: How It Can
     Hurt." Newsweek 21 Apr. 1980: 106-108.

Antonovsky, Aaron. "Conceptual and Methodological
     Problems in the Study of Resistance Resources and
     Stressful Life Events." Dohrenwend and Dohrenwend.
     245-258.

Bower, Bruce. "Setting the Stage for Infection."
     Science News 26 August 1989: 141.

Brooks, Andre A. "Educating the Children of Fast-Track
     Parents." Phi Delta Kappan April 1990: 612-615.

Compas, Bruce E. et al. "A Prospective Study of Life
     Events, Social Support, and Psychological
     Symptomatology During the Transition from High
     School to College." American Journal of Community
     Psychology 14 (1986): 241-256.

Dohrenwend, Barbara Snell, and Bruce P. Dohrenwend. "A
     Brief Historical Introduction to Research on
     Stressful Life Events." Dohrenwend and Dohrenwend.
     1-5.

---, eds. Stressful Life Events. Their Nature and
     Effects. New York: Wiley, 1974.

Holmes, Thomas H., and Minoru Masuda. "Life Change and
     Illness Susceptibility." Dohrenwend and
     Dohrenwend. 45-72.

28. *Works Cited* (including the continuation on the next page): One inch from the top of the page is the centered heading "Works Cited." Two inches below the heading is the first entry. Each entry is double spaced, with the second line indented five spaces from the left margin. Entries are in alphabetical order, with double spacing between them. Each page of the "Works-Cited" section follows the numbering of the text pages.

29. An entry for a signed article in a weekly magazine.

30. To cite three works from the same collection, Haley uses the cross-reference "Dohrenwend and Dohrenwend" and the page numbers. Whenever two or more works from the same collection are cited, the only information you need is the editor's name and the page numbers—as long as the main entry itself (with complete information) is somewhere in the "Works-Cited" list.

31. The work compiled by the editors above, and the main entry for the cross-references just mentioned.

15

Holmes, Thomas H., and R. H. Rahe. "The Social

Readjustment Scale." Journal of Psychosomatic

Research 11 (1967): 213-218.

Kutash, Irwin L., and Louis B. Schlesinger, eds.

Handbook on Stress and Anxiety. San Francisco:

Jossey, 1980.

Levine, A. When Dreams and Heroes Died: A Portrait of

Today's College Student. San Francisco: Jossey,

1980.

Newton, Fred B., et al. "The Assessment of College

Student Needs: First Step in a Prevention Response."

Personnel and Guidance Journal 62 (1984): 537-543.

Romano, John L. "Stress Management and Wellness:

Reaching Beyond the Counselor's Office." Personnel

and Guidance Journal 62 (1984): 533-536.

Selye, Hans. "The Stress Concept: Past, Present, and

Future." Stress Research: Issues for the 80's. Ed.

Cary L. Cooper. Chichester, England: Wiley, 1983:

69-87.

---. The Stress of Life. Rev. ed. New York: McGraw,

1976.

Stark, Elizabeth. "Stressing Yourself Sick."

Psychology Today, Sept. 1983: 77.

"Study Pinpoints Stress-Illness Link." Science News 15

Dec. 1979: 40.

Taulbee, P. "Study Shows Stress Decreases Immunity."

Science News 2 July 1983: 7.

32. An entry for a scholarly journal.

33. An entry for a work compiled by editors.

34. An entry for a book with one author.

35. An entry for an article in a collection of works compiled by an editor.

36. An entry for a book that is a revised edition. If no edition number or name is given on the title page, assume the book is a first edition. Otherwise, identify the edition by number, name, or year, as given on the title page.

37. An entry for an unsigned article in a weekly newsletter.

Application 20–1

Prepare a research report by completing these steps. (Your instructor might establish a timetable for completing the phases outlined here.)

PHASE ONE: PRELIMINARY STEPS

1. Choose a topic of *immediate practical importance*, something that will provide information that *can be used*. (The list of research possibilities on pages 485–487 should give you some ideas.) Develop a tree chart that will enable you to ask the right questions.

2. Identify a specific audience and its intended use of your information.

3. Narrow your topic, and check with your instructor for approval and advice.

4. Identify the various viewpoints that will enable you to achieve your own balanced viewpoint.

5. Establish a working bibliography to ensure that your library holds sufficient resources. Don't delay this step!

6. List the information you already have about your subject.

7. Write a clear statement of purpose, and submit it to your instructor.

8. Create a working outline.

PHASE TWO: COLLECTING, EVALUATING, AND INTERPRETING DATA

1. In your research, move from the general to the specific; begin with broad discussions in general reference works in order to develop a good overview.

2. Skim the sources, looking for high points. In this way, you will cover the most ground in the least time.

3. Evaluate each finding for accuracy, reliability, fairness, and completeness.

4. Take notes selectively. Don't record everything! Use notecards.

5. Interpret your findings, and decide what they all mean.

6. Settle on your thesis.

PHASE THREE: ORGANIZING YOUR DATA AND WRITING YOUR REPORT

1. Revise and adjust your working outline, as needed.
2. Follow the introduction-body-conclusion format.
3. Concentrate on only *one* section of your report at a time.
4. Fully document all sources of information.
5. Write your final draft.
6. Proofread carefully.

DUE DATES

- List of possible subjects due:
- Final subject due:
- Working bibliography and working outline due:
- Notecards due:
- Revised outline due:
- First draft of report due:
- Final draft of report with full documentation due:

Here are some possible research projects for Phase One.

1. Identify a modern discovery in your field that dramatically advanced the state of the art (as the discovery of antibiotics revolutionized medical treatment). Establish how the discovery was made, and trace its beneficial effects along with any negative effects (antibiotics, for example, can cause severe allergic reactions and other complications, and they have caused resistant strains of organisms to develop).

2. Does jogging really promote good health?

3. Find out which geographic sections of the United States are experiencing greatest economic and population growth. What are the major reasons for this growth? Trace the recent history of this change.

4. Some observers claim that productivity in American industry is on the decline. Find out whether this claim is valid. If it is, identify the reasons.

5. Assume that you and a business partner have developed a desktop duplicating machine (or some other product) that can be manufactured at low cost. What are the intricacies involved in applying for and getting a patent for your product?

6. How safe are artificial sweeteners?

7. What is the present status of women and minorities in your specialty? Assess their hiring and promotional opportunities, relative salaries, and percentages in executive positions. Do comparative data over the past decade suggest a trend toward equal opportunity?

8. Is the present famine in Africa likely to worsen? What needs to be done?

9. Why have SAT scores declined? What needs to be done?

10. How will the computer revolution affect our lives by the year 2000?

11. The federal government is planning at least two national sites for disposal of spent nuclear fuel rods and other high-level radioactive waste. State governments plan many more sites for disposal of low-level nuclear waste and other toxic waste. Find out the proposed locations for these sites, and determine whether the site planned closest to your area poses any health or economic threat.

12. Home buyers (especially of older homes) face a frightening array of possible hazards, including chlordane sprayed for termites; wood preservatives; urea formaldehyde foam insulation; radon gas (radioactive) or chemical contamination in well water; lead paint; and asbestos. Research the effects of these hazards for someone you know who is buying a home.

13. Can peanut butter, black pepper, potatoes, and buttered toast cause cancer? Which of the commonest "pure" foods can be most carcinogenic? Find out, and write a report for your cafeteria dietitian.

14. Assume you are the health officer in a town less than 1 mile from a massive radar installation. Citizens are worried about the effects of microwave radiation. Do they need to worry? Find the facts, and write your report.

15. Assume you are the health officer in a town where a power company easement allows high-voltage lines to run immediately adjacent to the elementary school playground. Are the children

endangered by ionic disturbances? Parents and the school committee want to know. Find out, and write your report.

16. The "coffee generation" wants to know about the properties of caffeine and the chemicals used on coffee beans. What are the effects of these substances on the human body? Write your report, making specific recommendations about precautions coffee drinkers can take.

17. Are there any recent inventions that could help decrease our reliance on fossil fuels in ways that are economical and practical? Find out, and prepare a report for your U.S. senator.

18. What is the latest that scientists are saying about the implications of global warming caused by rain forest destruction and ozone depletion? Find out, and prepare a report to be published in your campus newspaper.

19. Are video display terminals (computer screens) a health hazard? Find out, and write a report for people who work in front of a computer.

20. Does acupuncture have measurable medical benefits? Your classmates want to know.

21. Assume that you and some classmates have been offered a great deal on the purchase of waterfront land in south Florida. Will the land be under water within a couple of decades? Find out and write a report for your classmates.

Application 20–2

Answer as many of these questions as your instructor requires. Write a complete citation for each source of information (author, title, place of publication, publisher, date, volume, page number).

1. What was the headline in *The New York Times* on the day you were born?

2. You have just heard that you have cyanoderma. Are you going to die?

3. List the titles and specific locations of three recent articles on rap music.

4. How and when was the word *communism* first used?

5. Who was the first woman elected to the U.S. Congress?

6. If someone called you a cockswain, would you feel insulted?

7. Which schools in the country have a horsemanship program?

8. What is the exact value of today's American dollar in French francs?

9. You're feeling run-down, and a friend offers you some of his Centrax prescription. Will the medication help?

10. What is the half-life of plutonium?

11. Who originated the statement "There's a sucker born every minute"?

12. What was the population of your hometown in 1980?

13. What is the world pole-vaulting record?

14. What is the difference between a digital and an analog computer?

15. What is the operating principle of a diesel engine?

16. Do you think you may have been a dolphin in a former life? Find an article discussing reincarnation.

17. Where would you find a brief description of your intended occupation?

Application 20–3

List five major reference works in your major or on your topic by consulting Sheehy, Walford, or a more specific guide to literature.

Application 20–4

Using the card catalog, locate and list the full bibliographic citation (author's name, title of work, place and publisher, date) for five books in your major or on your semester report topic, all published within the past two years.

Application 20–5

Using one of the latest book indexes, identify one book in your major or on your semester topic published within the past three years. Give the full bibliographic citation.

Application 20–6

Identify a major periodical index in your major or on your topic. Locate a recent article on a specific topic (say, the use of artificial intelligence in medical diagnosis). Photocopy the article, and submit it to your instructor along with the full bibliographic citation.

Application 20–7

Consult the appropriate librarian and identify two databases you would search for information on your semester topic.

Application 20–8

If your library offers students a free search of mainframe databases, ask your librarian for help in preparing an electronic search for your research report.

Application 20–9

Using the *Monthly Catalog* or *Government Reports Announcements and Index*, locate and photocopy a recent government publication in your major or on your topic.

Application 20–10

Determine whether your library offers OCLC and/or InfoTrac™ services. Through each service that is available, locate two current books or articles in your major or on your topic. Give full bibliographic citations.

21

Composing Business Letters and Memos

In business writing, you share information with readers who will use it for a practical purpose. Readers might use your information to perform a task, answer a question, solve a problem, or make a decision. Any business document is designed to give readers the exact information they need for taking specific action.

Uses of Business Writing Skills

In the work world, your value to any organization will depend on how well you communicate what you know. In any field, almost anyone in a responsible position writes daily. Managers write progress reports, personnel evaluations, requisitions, and instructions—among other documents. Computer specialists write documentation explaining to customers how to use software and hardware. Contractors write proposals, bids, and specifications for banks and customers. Engineers and architects plan, on paper, the structure of a project before contracts are awarded and construction begins. In this era of rapidly changing technology, good communication is more than ever crucial.

When you enter the work world, employers first judge your writing by your application letter and résumé. If you join a large organization, your retention and promotion may be decided by executives you've never met. Thus, your letters, memos, and reports will be seen as a measure of the overall quality of your work. As you advance, your ability to communicate will become even more important, and your technical background may become less important. The higher your goals, the more skill in writing you will need.

Specific Features of Business Writing

Besides having the general features of worthwhile content, sensible organization, and readable style, business writing has several specific features: (1) constant focus on the reader's need for information, (2) efficiency, (3) accuracy, (4) a "you" perspective, and (5) a professional format.

A FOCUS ON THE READERS' INFORMATION NEEDS

Business writing is for readers who will use your information for some purpose. You might write to *define* something—as to an insurance customer who wants to know what "variable annuity" means. You might write to *describe* something— as to an architectural client who wants to know what a new addition to her home will look like. You might write to *explain* something—as to a stereo technician who wants to know how to eliminate bass flutter in your company's new line of speakers. You might write to *persuade* someone—as to your vice president in charge of marketing who wants to know if it's a good idea to launch an expensive advertising campaign for a new oil additive. Whatever your specific purpose, as a business writer, you do not write for yourself, but to inform and persuade others.

Business writing does more than merely record information. Instead of telling readers everything you know, be selective; tailor your message to the specific needs of your readers.

When you write for a specific reader or a small group of readers, you can focus sharply on your audience by asking yourself these questions:

1. Who wants the letter or report? Who else will read it?

2. Why do they want it? How will they use it? What purpose do I want to achieve?

3. What is the technical background of the audience?

4. How much does the audience already know about the subject? What material will have informative value?

5. What exactly does the audience need to know, and in what format (letter, memo)? How much is enough?

6. When is the document due?

The more you can learn about your audience's exact expectations and needs, the more useful you can make your document. In your audience's view, which material will be most important? Be sure to answer this question before you decide what to say.

EFFICIENCY

Readers of business documents are busy and impatient. They never want to put more into reading a document than they can get from it. They hate waste and expect efficiency. Every sentence and word should carry its own weight, advancing the writer's meaning.

The efficiency of any system is the ratio of useful output to input. For the product that comes out, how much energy goes in?

In an efficient system, the output nearly equals the input.

A document's efficiency is measured by how hard readers have to work with the document to get the information they need. Is the product worth the reader's effort?

In other words, no reader should have to spend ten minutes deciphering a message worth only five minutes. Inefficient messages drain the reader's energy.

Make your message long enough to be understood but short

enough to be tolerated. If you are responding to a job applicant, don't write like this:

> We are in receipt of your recent correspondence indicating your interest in the position listed below. Your correspondence has been duly forwarded to the office with candidate selection responsibility for consideration. You may expect to hear from the aforementioned office relative to your application as the selection process progresses.

Notice how hard we work to extract information that could be expressed like this:

> We've received your application for the position listed below and have forwarded it to the office that will select candidates. At each stage in selection, we will inform you of the status of your application.

Never make readers work needlessly.

Here are some of the most frequent errors that cause a document to be inefficient:

- more information than readers need
- insufficient, irrelevant, or inaccurate information
- no clear organization
- more words than are needed
- fancier or less precise words than are needed
- poor appearance or confusing format

Inefficient documents are produced by writers who lack a clear sense of purpose, audience, meaning, organization, or style. In style matters, we *think* in plain English, but we sometimes forget to *write* that way. We might say to ourselves:

> I want a better job.

but instead we might write:

> I desire to upgrade my employment status.

Whatever their cause, inefficient documents make readers work too hard.

ACCURACY

Because readers use business writing to make decisions and take action, accuracy is vital. Names, dates, places, costs, and measurements have to be spelled out and exact.

A business letter can be considered a contract; therefore, if you write to a customer with an offer of a service or product at a specified cost, you are making a legal commitment. Be sure to tell customers exactly what they will and will not get for their money. Notice how, in Figure 21.1, the writer provides exact specifications and figures—and spells out exceptions to the repairs outlined in the estimate.

Business writing should convey only *one* meaning and should allow only *one* interpretation insofar as possible.

A "YOU" PERSPECTIVE

In speaking face to face with someone, you unconsciously modify your delivery as you read the listener's signals: a smile, a frown, a raised eyebrow, a nod. Even in a phone conversation, a listener provides cues that signal approval, anger, and so on. Writing, however, has one major disadvantage: because you face a blank page, you can too easily write only to please yourself, forgetting that a flesh-and-blood person will be reading and reacting to your document.

The "you" perspective comes from your tone; by careful word choice, you show respect for your readers— you create genuine contact. Put yourself in their place; ask yourself how readers will respond to what you've just written.

Business writing should create a relationship that encourages readers to be on your side. Always try to be sensitive to the reader's position. Show some intimacy by letting readers know you understand their way of seeing. Assume, for instance, that your tuition is due but your college loan is late. You write to ask the registrar for an extension. Which of these two closing paragraphs is more likely to get the reader on your side?

> (a) It is imperative that I receive this extension of my tuition due date. I appreciate your cooperation.

> (b) May I have this brief extension of my tuition due date, without causing too much inconvenience? Your patience in this difficult time would be a great help.

The second version has a "you" perspective; it focuses on the reader instead of the writer.

Even one carelessly chosen word can offend readers. In a letter

LEVERETT LAND & TIMBER COMPANY, INC.   creative land use
quality building materials
architectural construction

January 17, 1991

Mr. Thomas E. Muffin
Clearwater Drive
Amherst, Massachusetts   01002

Dear Mr. Muffin:

I have examined the damage to your home caused by the
ruptured water pipe and consider the following repairs to be
necessary and of immediate concern:

    Exterior:
      Remove plywood soffit panels beneath overhangs
      Replace damaged insulation and plumbing
      Remove all built-up ice within floor framing
      Replace plywood panels and finish as required

    Northeast Bedroom--Lower Level:
      Remove and replace all sheetrock, including closet
      Remove and replace all door casings and baseboards
      Remove and repair windowsill extensions and moldings
      Remove and reinstall electric heaters
      Respray ceilings and repaint all surfaces

This appraisal of damage repair does not include repairs and/
or replacements of carpets, tile work, or vinyl flooring.
Also, this appraisal assumes that the plywood subflooring on
the main level has not been severely damaged.

Leverett Land & Timber Company, Inc. proposes to furnish
the necessary materials and labor to perform the described
damage repairs for the amount of four thousand one hundred
and eighty dollars ($4,180).

                      Sincerely,

                      Gerald A. Jackson
                      President

GAJ/cb

Figure 21.1 A Letter-as-Contract

complaining about the monitor on your new personal computer, you have the choice of saying, "Although the amber screen causes very little eyestrain, the character resolution is not sharp enough for lengthy word-processing use" or "The monitor is lousy for word processing." Clearly, "lousy" would be a poor choice here because of the implied insult to the manufacturer or dealer and because it does not precisely describe the problem (i.e., poor resolution).

Put yourself in the reader's place as you consider these examples. Imagine you are an employer screening applicants for a position with your company. Which of these openings would you find appealing? Which applicants do you *like?*

(a) I recently read of your opening for a field geologist. One of my professors, Dr. R. D. Loner, worked for you and claims that your company was beneficial to his career. My taking the position would be a great opportunity to advance my career in geology. *(The tone here is self-serving; an employment letter should emphasize what the applicant can offer—not vice versa.)*

(b) I am applying for a position as a computer clerk. Most of my programming experience has been with PASCAL. I have experience programming in a variety of languages. I was referred to you by Chris Mather, who works as a computer clerk in your firm. His interest and enthusiasm encouraged me to write. *(The Dick-and-Jane sentence structure and diction, along with a nonexistent "you" perspective, add up to a dreary tone here.)*

(c) While attending Eastern University, I have closely followed your company's financial statements and have become highly interested in your sales growth. Therefore, when Roberta Lowny, Vice President of Sales for Bando Sportswear, told me of an opening in your fabric sales division, I decided to write immediately. *(This writer shows genuine interest in—and knowledge about—the company, focusing on the reader, not on himself.)*

(d) Does your company have a summer position for a student determined to become a technical writer? If so, I think you will find me qualified. *(Here again, the focus is on the company, with a confident but diplomatic tone that seems forceful but likable.)*

Here are some closings from employment letters. Which ones would make you want to meet the applicant?

(a) I would like to arrange an interview to discuss this position. Please phone me at your convenience. *(This sounds like a military order—a faceless writer telling a faceless reader what to do.)*

(b) I would like an interview as soon as possible. *(Being bossy with a prospective boss is no way to create a likable tone.)*

(c) I hope you agree that I am the type of engineer DGH is seeking. Please allow me to further discuss career opportunities with you. *(This closing is confident yet diplomatic, focusing on the company's needs and moving the reader to action.)*

(d) Hardworking, efficient, and eager to learn, I am anxious to apply my skills. Please consider me for a summer position. *(The "you" perspective is clearly implied by the writer's summation of what she can offer the reader.)*

Readers are much more likely to side with you if they *like* you. To have readers like you, make them feel they matter.

One way to destroy a "you" perspective and alienate readers is by inflating words (see pages 206–208) and using a category of trite expressions called *letterese:* overblown phrases some writers think they need to make their writing seem important. Here are a few of the clichés that invade letters, memos, and reports, creating artificial distance between writer and reader.

Letterese	Translation into plain English
As per your request	As you requested
It is imperative that you write.	Please write.
I am cognizant of the fact.	I know.
At the earliest possible date	As early as possible
I beg to differ.	I disagree.
This writer	I
At the present time	Now
I beg to acknowledge receipt of	I received
In the immediate future	Soon
Due to the fact that	Because
I wish to express my gratitude.	Thank you.
At this point in time	Now

Such artificial language denies contact. Write to a person as you would *speak* to that person.

A PROFESSIONAL FORMAT

Readers first react to the *appearance* of a document; they expect a professional format. Simply stated, format is the arrangement of words on the page: indention; margins; line spacing; typeface; and standard letter, memo, or report form. What your document looks like and how it is arranged may be just as important as what it says. A professional format helps you look good and invites the reader's attention.

To make any document pleasing to the eye, write it on high-quality (20-lb. bond, 8½ × 11-inch) white paper with a minimum fiber content of 25 percent. Type neatly, avoid erasures, and make sure you have clean typewriter keys and a fresh ribbon. If you write on a word processor, avoid using a dot-matrix printer for your final draft; instead, use a letter-quality printer or retype on a good typewriter.

In addition to these general requirements, letters and memorandums have their own specific format requirements, which are discussed later in this chapter.

Business Letters

The general purpose of any business letter is to create goodwill toward the writer and the company. Here is a sampling of the kinds of letters you can expect to write routinely:

- sales letters designed to create interest in a product or service

- letters of instruction outlining a procedure to be carried out by the reader

- letters of recommendation for friends, fellow workers, or past employees

- letters of transmittal to accompany mailed reports and other documents

- letters to inquire about a product, procedure, or person

- letters to complain about service or products and to request adjustment

- letters to apply for jobs

You may also write responses to letters received by your company.

A full discussion of letters would more than fill a textbook. In this chapter, therefore, we cover only three common types of letters: the inquiry letter, the complaint letter, and the letter of application, along with its accompanying résumé.

Regardless of type, all letters have definite format requirements. Be sure to use uniform margins, spacing, and indention: frame your letter with a 2½-inch top margin and side and bottom margins of 1 to 1¼ inches; single space within paragraphs, and double space between; avoid hyphenating at the end of a line.

If your letter extends to more than one page, begin the second page five lines from the top, with a notation identifying the addressee, the date, and the page number:

        Walter James, June 25, 1991, p. 2

Begin the text of your second page two spaces below this notation. Place at least two lines of your paragraph at the bottom of page 1 and at least two lines of your final text on page 2.

Your 9½-by-4⅛-inch envelope should be of the same quality as the stationery. Center your reader's address, and single space if it takes three lines or more. Use only accepted abbreviations. Place your own single-spaced address in the upper left corner.

Also, use an accepted letter form. Although several standard letter forms are used, and your company may have its own requirements, in this chapter we discuss one of the most familiar forms: semiblock, with no indentions, as shown in Figure 21.2. The line spacing from page top to the writer's address, and then to the reader's address, is variable. Depending on the length of your letter, adjust this upper spacing so that the letter appears centered on the page. All *other* spacing is fixed.

INQUIRY LETTERS

Letters of inquiry may be solicited or unsolicited. You often write the first type as a consumer requesting information about an advertised product. You can expect a solicited letter to be welcomed. After all, the reader stands to benefit from your interest, and so you can afford to be brief and to the point: "Please send me your brochure on . . .," for example.

Many of your inquiries will be unsolicited; that is, not in response to an ad, but requesting information for a research report or project you are working on. Here, you are asking a favor of your reader, who must take the time to read your letter, consider your request, collect the information, and write a response. Therefore, you need to apologize for any imposition, to express appreciation, and to state a reasonable request clearly and briefly (long, involved inquiries are unlikely to be answered). Begin your letter with something more cordial and less abrupt than "I need some information."

Before you can ask specific questions, do your homework. Don't expect the respondent to read your mind. A general question ("Please send me all your data on . . . ") is likely to be ignored. Only when you know your subject can you focus your questions.

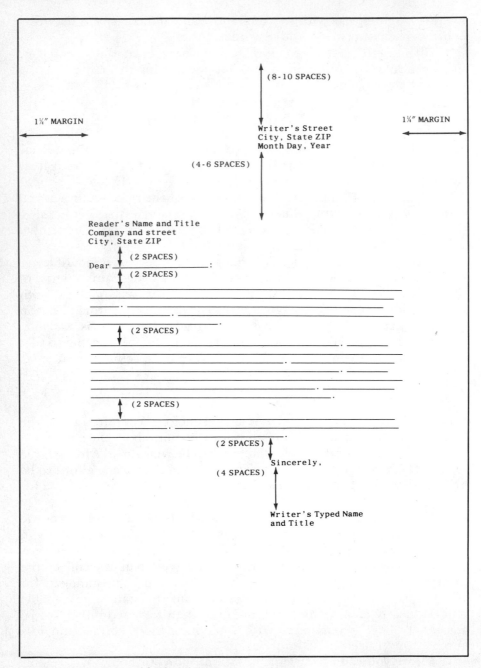

Figure 21.2   A Semiblock Letter Form

Don't wait until the last minute to write your letter. Write at least three weeks before your research report is due, politely indicating the due date in your letter.

Here is a typical inquiry situation. Imagine you are preparing a research report on the feasibility of harnessing solar energy for home heating in northern climates. You learn that a private, nonprofit research group has been experimenting with ecologically efficient energy systems. After deciding to write for details, you plan and compose your inquiry.

Like most good communication, a routine inquiry has a distinct introduction, body, and conclusion. Begin by introducing yourself and your purpose. The reader should be told who wants the information and why. Maintain the "you" perspective by opening with a statement that will spark the reader's interest and goodwill.

In the body, write specific and clearly worded questions that are easy to understand and answer. If you have several questions, list them. (Lists help readers organize their answers, increasing your chances of getting all the information you want.) Number each question, and separate it from the others, perhaps leaving space for responses right on the page. If you have more than five or six questions, you might place them in an attached questionnaire.

Conclude by explaining how you plan to use the information and, if possible, by saying how your reader might benefit. Offer to send a copy of your finished report. Close with a statement of appreciation; it will encourage your reader to respond. Include a stamped, self-addressed envelope.

When completed, your letter might look like this one:

234 Western Road
Arlington, VT 05620
March 10, 1990

Director of Energy Systems
The Earth Research Institute
Petersham, ME 04619

Dear Director:

While gathering data on home solar heating, I encountered references (in *Scientific American* and elsewhere) to your group's pioneering work. Would you please allow me to benefit from your experience?

I am a student at Evergreen College, preparing a report on the feasibility of solar energy as a major source of home heating in northern climates. Your answers to the questions below would help me complete my course project (April 15 deadline).

1. At this stage of development, have you found active or passive solar heating more practical?

2. Do you hope to surpass the 60 percent limit of heating needs supplied by the active system? If so, what efficiency do you expect to achieve, and how soon?

3. What is the estimated cost of building materials for your active system, per cubic foot of living space?

4. What metal do you use in collectors to get the highest thermal conductivity at the lowest maintenance costs?

Your answers, along with any recent findings you can share, will enrich a learning experience I will put into practice next summer by building my own solar home. I would be glad to send you a copy of my report, along with the house plans I have designed.

Sincerely yours,

Alan Greene

COMPLAINT LETTERS

Complaint (or claim) letters are a challenge—not because of what you need to say, but because you have to find a reasonable way of saying it. Although a complaint is an expression of your frustration and dissatisfaction, you would be mistaken to begin a complaint letter with the intention of telling someone off. Everyone likes to sound off now and then, but your real purpose is to achieve a desired result: a refund, a replacement, improved service, better business relations, or even an apology. Most businesses will grant all reasonable claims; they do so to retain customers' goodwill.

Imagine that you are in this situation: Recently you bought an expensive stereo, with top-of-the-line speakers, from a franchised dealer in New Jersey. Three weeks after your purchase you moved to Wisconsin, and five weeks later you noticed increasing distortion in heavy bass sounds in your speakers. The problem is that your guarantee requires that you return the equipment to the store where you bought it. You decide to write to the store, requesting they arrange for a local franchised dealer to repair or replace your speakers.

First, identify your reason for writing. Maintain the "you" perspective by stating your claim *objectively* (this exercise in patience will mean you have to choose your words carefully).

In the body section, explain the problem accurately and fully so that the reader understands the basis for your claim. (If you were writing to a jeweler, you would explain that your new wristwatch gains an hour a day, instead of merely saying it's defective.) Identify the faulty item clearly, giving serial and model numbers. Describe the deficiency, and explain how it has caused you inconvenience, expense, loss of time, and so on. Propose what you consider a fair adjustment, phrasing your statement so that the reader will feel inclined to honor your request. Be absolutely clear about whether you desire a replacement, a refund, or something else.

Conclude with a courteous but firm statement, indicating your goodwill and confidence in the reader's integrity. Thanking the reader in advance would be inappropriate. Once your claim has been resolved, you might write a thank-you note.

Here is how your letter to the stereo dealer might read:

534 Hartford Way
Madison, WI 20967
March 20, 1990

Stereo Components, Inc.
143 Main Street
Newark, NJ 10311

ATTENTION: Service Department

SUBJECT. Bass Distortion in Toneway Speakers

Because I've heard a great deal about your fine reputation, I'm sure you will do everything possible to help me with a perplexing service problem.

On December 10, 1989, I bought a component system (sales receipt #114621) from your outlet. Three weeks later, I moved to Wisconsin, and after eight weeks, I noticed distortion in heavy bass sounds in my speakers.

As a classical music fan, I bought your best speakers (Toneway 305's, #3624 and 3625) because of their extra-wide bass range. Their distortion of lower ranges of percussion and keyboard sounds, however, is increasing to the point of actual vibration, making my expensive system useless.

My speaker guarantee states that items for repair or replacement must be returned to the *original* retailer. But because we are now hundreds of miles apart, that arrangement would cost me considerable time and money—and further delay my use of the stereo. Under these circumstances, could you please arrange for a franchised dealer in the Madison area to honor my guarantee directly?

Yours truly,

Raymond Fields

Instead of the standard salutation ("Dear _____:"), the previous letter has an attention line and a subject line. Use an attention line when writing to an organization and when you want a specific person (whose name you don't know), title, or department to receive your letter. The subject line forecasts what your letter is about and is a good device for getting a busy reader's attention.

Sometimes we have to complain about *issues* rather than *things*. The following letter (with writer's and reader's addresses omitted) complains about a political decision.

Dear Governor King:

I protest your support of the sale of oil leases on the Georges Bank fishing grounds. As a registered voter of the Commonwealth and a resident of a coastal town, I am convinced that such oil leases would violate the interests of Massachusetts and New England citizens.

In 1988, New Bedford [*a nearby city*] was second in the nation in dollar value of seafood landed. Much of this catch was made up of such prized species as scallops, cod, haddock, flounder, and lobster. This revenue supported much of the local population in fishing and related jobs, such as fish processing and ship repair. Similar situations exist in many of our coastal communities, including Gloucester, Boston, and Provincetown. An industry with this much impact on the state cannot be ignored.

Offshore oil rigs certainly will affect the area's ecology. Sediment, garbage, and oil produced by normal operations on an oil platform will pollute the area surrounding the rigs—an area very close to the scallop and flounder grounds of Georges Bank.

Given the circular water current on the bank, a major blowout or oil spill would not be carried out to sea, but would concentrate on the fishing grounds, thus destroying one of the world's great seafood resources.

The possibility of such a disaster greatly outweighs the benefits from any oil found on the fishing grounds. I therefore ask, in the best interest of the Commonwealth, that you withdraw your support for offshore drilling and join the citizens who are fighting to prevent it.

Respectfully,

Carol C. Paine

Notice how this writer spells out her complaint, forcefully but diplomatically encouraging the reader to change his position.

RÉSUMÉS AND JOB APPLICATIONS

In the job market, many applicants compete for few openings. Whether you are applying for an attractive summer job, an internship, or your first professional job, or are changing careers in midlife, you have to wage an effective campaign to market yourself. Your résumé and application letter *must* stand out among those of other applicants.

The Résumé   The résumé is a summary of your experience and qualifications. Written before your application letter, it provides background information to support your letter. In turn, the letter will emphasize specific parts of your résumé and will discuss how your background is suited to that job. The résumé gets you the interview, not the job.

Most employers spend less than 60 seconds scanning a résumé. They look for an obvious and persuasive answer to this question: What can you do for us? Any employer expects a résumé

1. to look good (conservative and tasteful, on high-quality paper)

2. to read easily (headings, typeface, spacing, and punctuation that provide clear signals)

3. to provide information the employer needs for making an interviewing decision

Most employers discard immediately résumés that are mechanically flawed, cluttered, sketchy, or hard to follow. Don't leave readers guessing or annoyed; make your résumé perfect.

Organize your information within these categories:

- name, address, and phone number
- career objectives

- educational background
- work experience
- personal data
- interests, activities, awards, and skills
- references

Select and organize your material to best show what you have to offer. Don't just list *everything*; be selective. (We're talking about *communicating* instead of merely delivering information.) Don't abbreviate, because not all readers may know the referent. Use punctuation to clarify and emphasize, not to be "artsy" or "unique." Try to limit your résumé to one page.*

Begin preparing your résumé at least one month before your job search. You will need that much time to do a first-class job. Your final version can be duplicated for various targets (but each application letter has to be freshly typed or printed).

NAME, ADDRESS, AND PHONE NUMBER

At the top of the page, list your full name, mailing address, and phone number (many interview invitations and job offers are made by phone). If your school address and phone number differ from your summer address and number, include both, indicating dates on which you can be reached at each.

CAREER OBJECTIVES

Have a clear idea of the *specific* jobs for which you *realistically* qualify. Resist the impulse to be all things to all people. The key to a successful résumé is the image of *you* it projects—disciplined and purposeful, yet flexible. State your specific job and career goals:†

> Intensive care nursing in a teaching hospital, ultimately supervising and instructing.

Your statement of career objectives should show a clear sense of purpose.

---

*Of course, if you are changing jobs or careers, or if your résumé looks cramped, you might need a second page.

†To save space, you can omit your statement of career objectives from the résumé and include it in your letter instead.

EDUCATIONAL BACKGROUND

If your education is more impressive than your work experience, place it first. Begin with your most recent school and work backward, listing degrees, diplomas, and schools *beyond* high school (unless prestige, program, or your achievement warrants its inclusion). List the courses that have directly prepared you for the job. Include any schools attended or courses completed while you were in military service. If you finance part or all of your education by working, say so, indicating the percentage of your contribution.

WORK EXPERIENCE

If you have solid work experience, place it before your education. Beginning with your most recent job and working backward, list and clearly identify each job, giving dates and names of employers. Tell whether the job was full-time, part-time (hours weekly), or seasonal. Tell exactly what you did in each job, indicating promotions. If the job was major (and related to this one), describe it in detail; otherwise, describe it briefly. Include any military experience. If you have no real work experience, show you have potential by emphasizing your preparation and by writing an enthusiastic letter.

Do not use complete sentences in your job descriptions; they take up room best left for other items. But do use action verbs throughout (*supervised, developed, built, taught, opened, managed, trained, solved, planned, directed,* and so on). Such verbs emphasize your vitality and help you stand out.

PERSONAL DATA

An employer cannot legally discriminate on the basis of sex, age, race, color, religion, or national origin. Therefore, you aren't required to provide this information or a photograph. But, if you believe that any of this information could advance your prospects, include it.

INTERESTS, ACTIVITIES, AWARDS, AND SKILLS

List hobbies, sports, and other pastimes; memberships in teams and organizations; offices held; and any recognition for outstanding performance. Include dates and types of volunteer work. Employers know that persons who seek well-rounded lives are likely to take an active interest in their jobs. Be selective in this section. List only items that show the qualities employers seek.

REFERENCES

Your list of references should name four or five persons *who have agreed* to write strong, positive assessments. Often a reference letter is the key to getting an employer to want to meet you; choose your references carefully.

Select references who can speak with authority about your ability and character. Avoid members of your family and close friends not in your field. Choose instead among professors, previous employers, and community figures who know you well enough to write concretely on your behalf.

Ask each reference for only one letter, with no salutation, to be sent to the placement office for your placement dossier. Your dossier is a folder containing your credentials: college transcript, letters of recommendation, and any other items (such as a notice of a scholarship award or letter of commendation) that document your achievements. In your letter and résumé, you talk about yourself; in your dossier, others talk about you. An employer impressed by what you say about yourself will want to read what others think and will request a copy of your dossier. By collecting recommendations in one folder, you spare your references from writing the same letter over and over.

Visit your placement office to inquire about setting up a dossier (or placement folder).

Opinion generally is divided about whether the names and addresses of references should be included in a résumé. If saving space is important, simply state, "References available on request," keeping your résumé only one page long. But if your other résumé items take up more than one page, you probably should include names and addresses of references. (An employer might recognize a name, and thus notice *your* name among the crowd of applicants.) If you are changing careers, a full listing of references is especially important.

Composing the Résumé   With data collected and references lined up, you are ready to compose your actual résumé. Imagine you're a 23-year-old student at a community college, working on an A.A. degree in Hotel and Restaurant Management. Before college, you worked at related jobs for more than three years. You now seek a summer position with a resort. You have spent two weeks compiling and selecting information for your résumé and getting commitments from four references. Figure 21.3 shows your résumé. Notice that this résumé mentions nothing about salary. Wait until this matter comes up in your interview, or later.

When fully satisfied with your résumé, consider having your

James David Purdy

203 Elmwood Avenue
San Jose, California 90462
Tel.: (214) 316-2419

Professional Objective
To work in customer relations for a hospitality chain, to continue my education, and eventually to assume market management responsibilities.

Education
San Jose City College, San Jose, California
Associate of Arts degree in Hotel/Restaurant Management, expected June 1991. All college expenses financed by scholarship and part time job (20 hours weekly).

Employment

1988-1991
Peek-a-Boo Lodge, San Jose, California
Began as desk clerk and am now desk manager (part-time) of this 200-unit resort. Responsible for scheduling custodial and room service staff, convention planning, and customer relations.

1986-1988
Teo's Restaurant, Pensacola, Florida
Began as waiter, advanced to cashier, and finally to assistant manager. Responsible for weekly payroll, banquet arrangements, and supervising dining-room and lounge staff. Left to enroll in college.

1985-1986
Encyclopaedia Britannica, Inc., San Jose, California
Sales representative (part-time). Received top bonus twice.

1983-1985
White's Family Inn, San Luis Obispo, California
Worked as busboy, then waiter (part-time).

Personal
Awards
Captain of basketball team; Lions' Club Scholarship.

Special Skills
Speak French fluently; expert skier.

Activities
High school basketball and track teams (3 years); college student senate (2 years); Innkeepers' Club—prepared and served monthly dinners at the college (2 years).

Interests
Skiing, cooking, sailing, oil painting, and backpacking.

References
Available from: Placement Office, San Jose City College, San Jose, CA 94062

Figure 21.3 A Résumé for a Summer Job

model typeset or laser printed. At reasonable cost you can obtain a better-looking copy than a typewriter could produce. This one prototype, in turn, will yield as many copies as you need. For neat copies, use a photocopying machine, laser printing, or offset printing; *never* send out carbon, Thermofax, or mimeographed copies.

Now, with your résumé prepared, you are ready to plan and compose the application letter.

The Application Letter   Your application letter is one of the most important documents you will ever write. Although your letter expands your résumé, it should also emphasize your personal qualities and qualifications convincingly. In your résumé, you merely present raw facts; in your application letter, you relate these facts to the company to which you are applying. The tone and insight you bring to your discussion suggest a good deal about who you are. The letter is your chance to explain how you see yourself fitting into the organization. Your purpose is to interpret your résumé and show an employer how valuable you will be.

Unlike the résumé, the letter never should be photocopied. You can, however, base letters to different employers on the same model—with appropriate changes. But type or print each letter anew.

Sometimes you will apply for jobs advertised in print or by word of mouth (solicited applications). At other times you will write "prospecting" letters to organizations that have not advertised but might need someone like you (unsolicited applications). Either letter should be tailored to the situation.

THE SOLICITED LETTER

Imagine you are James Purdy (whose résumé appears on page 509). In *Innkeeper's Monthly*, you read this advertisement and decide to apply:

Resort Management Openings

Liberty International, Inc., is accepting applications for summer management positions at our new Lake Geneva Resort. Applicants must have three years' practical experience, along with formal training in hotel/restaurant management. Please apply by June 1, 1991, to:

> Elmer Borden
> Personnel Director
> Liberty International, Inc.
> Lansdowne, Pennsylvania 24135

Now plan and compose your letter.

Introduction. Create a confident tone by directly stating your reason for writing. Name the exact job, and remember you are talking to someone; use "you" often (especially important here, where you must talk about yourself without seeming conceited). If you can, establish a connection by mentioning the name of a mutual acquaintance. Say you learn that your professor of nutrition, Dr. H. V. Garlid, is a former colleague of Elmer Borden's; mention of Dr. Garlid's name—with permission—will call attention to your letter. Finally, after referring your reader to the enclosed résumé, discuss your qualifications.

Body. Concentrate on what you, specifically, can bring to *this* job. Don't come across as a jack-of-all-trades. Avoid flattery ("I am greatly impressed by your remarkable company"). Be specific. Replace "much experience," "many courses," or "increased sales" with "three years of experience," "five courses," or "a 35 percent increase in sales between June and October 1990." Always support your claims with *evidence,* and show how your qualifications will benefit this employer. Create a dynamic tone by using *active* voice and action verbs:

Weak	Increased responsibilities were steadily given me.
Stronger	I steadily assumed increasing responsibilities.

Trim the fat from your sentences:

Flabby	I have always been a person who enjoys a challenge.
Lean	I enjoy a challenge.

Express self-confidence:

Unsure	It is my opinion that I will be a successful manager because . . .
Certain	I will be a successful manager because . . .

Never be vague:

Vague	I am familiar with the 1022 interactive database management system and RUNOFF, the text-processing system.

Definite   As a lab grader for one semester, I kept grading
                          records on the 1022 database management system
                          and composed lab procedures on the RUNOFF
                          text-processing system.

Also, avoid "letterese." Write as you would speak, and remember that
an enthusiastic tone can go a long way. Your attitude can be as important as your background.

Conclusion. Restate your interest; emphasize your willingness to
retrain or relocate (if necessary); and review other important personal
qualities. If your reader is nearby, request an interview; otherwise,
request a phone call, stating times you can be reached. Leave your
reader with the impression you are worth knowing.

Revision. Never settle for a first draft—or even a second or third! And
because this letter is your model for letters serving a variety of circumstances, it must be your best effort. After several revisions, James Purdy
finally signed the letter shown in Figure 21.4.
      Purdy wisely emphasized practical experience because his back-
ground is varied and impressive. An applicant with less experience
would emphasize education instead, discussing courses and activities.

THE UNSOLICITED LETTER

Ambitious job seekers do not limit their search to advertised
openings. The unsolicited, or "prospecting," letter is a good way to
uncover other possibilities. Because your unsolicited letter is
unexpected, attract your reader's attention early, and make him or her
want to read on. Don't begin: "I am writing to inquire about the
possibility of obtaining a position with your company." By now, your
reader is asleep. If you can't establish a connection through a mutual
acquaintance, use a forceful opening:

> Does your resort have a place for a summer manager with college
> work in hospitality management, a proven commitment to high-
> quality service, and customer-relations experience that extends far
> beyond mere textbook learning? If so, please consider my
> application.

Many of your letters, solicited or unsolicited, can be versions of
one model, or prototype. Your prototype must, therefore, represent you
in the best possible light. Take plenty of time to compose your model
letter and résumé. Employers will regard the quality of your application
as an indication of the quality of work you will do. Businesses spend

203 Elmwood Avenue
San Jose, California   90462
April 22, 1991

Mr. Elmer Borden
Personnel Director
Liberty International, Inc.
Lansdowne, Pennsylvania   24135

Dear Mr. Borden:

Please consider my application for a summer management position at your Lake Geneva resort. I will graduate from San
Jose City College in June 1991 with an Associate of Arts
degree in Hotel/Restaurant Management. Dr. H. V. Garlid, my
nutrition professor, has told me of his experience as a consultant for Liberty International, and encouraged me to apply.

For two years I worked as a part-time desk clerk and I am now the
desk manager at a 200-unit resort. This experience, along with
customer relations work described in my resume, has given me a
clear and practical understanding of customers' needs and
expectations. As an amateur chef, I know of the effort, attention,
and patience required to prepare fine food. Also, my skiing and
sailing background might be useful in your recreation program.

I am determined to succeed in hospitality management. My
experience and education have prepared me to work well with
others and to respond creatively to changes, crises, and added
responsibilities.

I would make the most of my employment with Liberty International, and feel confident I would be considered an asset.
If my background meets your needs, please phone me at
(214)316-2419 any weekday after 4 p.m.

Yours truly,

James David Purdy

James David Purdy

Figure 21.4   An Application Letter

much money and time projecting favorable images. The image you project, in turn, must measure up to their standards.

Business Memorandum Reports

In the professional world, decision makers rely on reports. For every long report, countless short reports, usually in the form of memoranda, lead to *informed* decisions on matters as diverse as the most comfortable office chairs to buy or the best recruit to hire for management training.

On the job, personnel must communicate with speed and accuracy. Your success may depend on your skill in sharing useful information with colleagues and superiors. Here are some of the kinds of memorandum reports you might write on any workday:

- a request for assistance on a project

- a requisition for parts and equipment

- a proposal for a new project

- a set of instructions

- a cost estimate for materials and labor on a new project

- a report of your progress on a specific assignment

- an hourly or daily account of your work activities

- a report of your inspection of a site, item, or process

- a statement of reasons for equipment or project failure

- a record of a meeting's minutes

Memoranda (or memos) are the major form of written communication in an organization. Unlike conversations, memos leave a "paper trail" so that directives, inquiries, instructions, requests, recommendations, and so on can be used for future reference. Whereas letters go outside the organization, memos remain inside.

The standard memo (Figure 21.5) has a heading that names the organization and identifies the sender, recipient, subject (often in caps or underlined for emphasis), and date. (As with company letterheads, placement of these items differs slightly among firms.) A memo report might include topic headings for easier reading and better organization.

When your memo report is longer than one page, list on following pages the recipient's name, the date, and the page number (M. Roberts,

NAME OF ORGANIZATION

MEMORANDUM
Date: (also serves as a chronological record for future reference)
To: Name and title (the title also serves as a record for reference)
From: Your name and title (your initials for verification)
Subject: GUIDELINES FOR FORMATTING MEMOS

Subject Line
Announce the memo's purpose and contents on the subject line, to help readers
focus on the subject and assess its importance.

Introductory Paragraph
Unless you have reason for being indirect, state your main point immediately.

Topic Headings
When discussing multiple subtopics, include headings (as we do here).
Headings help you organize, and help readers locate information quickly.

Paragraph Spacing
Do not indent the first line of paragraphs. Single space within, and double
space between paragraphs.

Second-page Notation
When the memo exceeds one page, begin the second and subsequent pages with
(1) the recipient's name, (2) the date, (3) the page number. For example:
Ms. Baxter, June 12, 19XX, page 2. Place this information three lines from
the page top and begin your text three lines below.

Memo Verification
Do not sign your memos. Initial the "From" line, after your name.

Copy Notation
When sending copies to people not listed on the "To" line, include a copy
notation two spaces below the last line, and list, by rank, the names and
titles of those receiving copies. For example,

Copies: J. Spring, V.P., Production
           H. Baxter, General Manager, Production

Figure 21.5   Standard Memo Format

4/13/85, page 2). Place this information three lines from the top of the page. Begin your text three lines below.

Memos do not require a complimentary close and signature. If authentication is needed, initial the "FROM" line, after your name. When you are distributing the memo to a number of people, place a distribution notation at the end of the memo, listing recipients (Copies: C. Black, J. Capilona, G. Hopkins, P. Maxwell).

Memo reports cover any topic important to a company's operations. The two broad types are informational reports and recommendation reports.

INFORMATIONAL REPORTS

Informational reports supply knowledge about products, services, operations, or anything about which readers need to be informed.

In your own field, you may be asked to report, say, research findings comparing the cost or quality of similar products. These findings may lead to contracts with certain suppliers. The informational report in Figure 21.6 shows how data in memo form can serve as a basis for decision making. Notice that the writer *interprets* her information for the reader. Unless your reader requests otherwise, provide an interpretation of your findings.

RECOMMENDATION REPORTS

Beyond merely providing information (and interpretation, as needed), recommendation reports offer conclusions and recommend specific action. Sometimes a recommendation report is written in response to a reader's request; sometimes writers initiate the reports on their own. When the report is *solicited*, make your recommendation at the very beginning; then justify it.

Here is a typical situation in which a solicited report serves as a basis for action: Mark Noll, a biology major, works part-time as a lab technician for an environmental testing company. Customers have recently complained about waiting too long for results of tests they've ordered. During a staff meeting, Mark comments that one of the company's problems is that employees have too heavy a workload. The personnel director asks Mark for a report outlining the problem and recommending a solution. Mark's report appears in Figure 21.7.

When the report is *unsolicited*, begin by spelling out the problem in enough detail to alert the reader; justify your solution *before* giving it. When they have sufficient background, readers are more inclined to act favorably on a recommendation they haven't solicited. In Figure 21.8, the writer structures his unsolicited report so the reader will

CALVIN COLLEGE

MEMORANDUM

TO: Professor Smith   DATE: February 15, 1991
           Writing Instructor

FROM: Susan Grimes, Student

SUBJECT: CONSUMER SURVEY OF COMPARATIVE RETAIL PRICES FOR
           DILANTIN TABLETS

I surveyed comparative prices for a Dilantin prescription by
calling six local pharmacies.

SIX LOCAL PHARMACIES CLASSIFIED IN DESCENDING ORDER
OF THEIR RETAIL PRICE FOR DILANTIN

Pharmacy	Price/ 100 tablets
Hargrove Pharmacy, Harwich	$4.14
Cascade Village Pharmacy, Hyannis	4.14
Murphy's Rexall, Sandwich	4.10
Apothecary, Dennis Village	3.89
Consumer's Pharmacy, Harwich	2.79
Dunn's Pharmacy, Hyannis	2.19

These data are important to me because I must take Dilantin
every day. The 100 tablets last only about one month and the
expense of this medicine quickly adds up. From my data I
conclude that my best choice for future Dilantin purchases
is Dunn's Pharmacy in Hyannis.

Figure 21.6   An Informational Report in Memo Form

understand the basis for the recommendation. Whenever you expect your reader to react negatively or to need persuading, give the explanation *before* the main point.

For recommendation reports and other persuasive writing tasks covered in this chapter, review the advice in Chapters 18 and 19.

Application 21–1

These sentences need overhauling before being included in a letter. Identify the problems, and revise as needed.

1. Pursuant to your ad, I am writing to apply for the scholarship.
2. I need all the information you have about methane-powered engines.
3. You idiots have sent me a faulty disc drive!
4. It is imperative that you let me know of your decision by January 15.
5. You are bound to be impressed by my credentials.
6. I could do wonders for your company.
7. I humbly request your kind consideration of my application.
8. If you are looking for a winner, your search is over!
9. I have become cognizant of your experiments and wish to ask your advice about the following procedure.
10. You will find these instructions easy enough for an ape to follow.
11. I would love to work for your wonderful company.
12. As per your request, I am sending the county map.
13. I am in hopes that you will call soon.
14. We beg to differ with your interpretation of this leasing clause.
15. I am impressed by the high salaries paid for this kind of work.

Application 21–2

Bring to class a copy of a business letter addressed to you or a friend. Compare letters. Choose the most and the least effective. Working in small groups, revise the least effective letter, and then compare your revision with those from other groups.

Application 21–3

Write and mail an unsolicited letter of inquiry about the topic you have investigated, or will investigate, for a research assignment. In your letter you may request brochures, pamphlets, or other informational literature, or you may ask specific questions ("What chemicals are used to clean algae, barnacles, and other marine vegetation from the cooling system's filters?"; "Are these chemicals then discharged into the sea?"). Submit a copy of your letter and the response.

Application 21–4

Write and mail an inquiry letter about an item or service you've seen advertised. Ask no fewer than six questions, and provide any explanations you think necessary to help the reader answer your questions fully. Write as a prospective customer, not as a student. Turn in the advertisement with your letter. Your instructor might also ask for a copy of the reply.

Application 21–5

1. As a student attending a state college, you learn that your governor and legislature have cut next year's operating budget for all state colleges by 20 percent. This cut will cause the firing of many young and popular faculty members, drastic reduction in student admissions, reduction in financial aid, cancellation of new programs, and erosion of college morale and quality of instruction. Write a complaint letter to your governor or your legislative representative, expressing your strong disapproval and justifying a major change in the proposed budget.

2. Write a complaint letter to a politician about some issue affecting your school or community.

3. Write a complaint letter to an appropriate school official about a campus problem.

Application 21–6

Write a letter of complaint about some problem you have had with goods or services. Be sure to state your case clearly and objectively and to request a specific adjustment.

Application 21–7

Write a letter applying for a part-time or summer job. Choose an organization that can offer you experience related to your career goal. Identify the exact hours and calendar period during which you are free to work. Include a résumé.

Application 21–8

1. Identify the job you hope to have in a few years. Using the newspaper, library (see your reference librarian for assistance), placement office, and personal sources, write your own full description of the job: duties, responsibilities, work hours, salary range, requirements for promotion, highest promotion possible, unemployment rate in the field, employment outlook for the next decade, need for further education (advanced degrees, special training, and so on), and optimum age bracket (as in football, does one fade around age 35?).

2. Using the sources above and your good judgment, construct a profile of the ideal employee for this job. If you were the personnel director screening applicants, what specific qualifications would you require (education, experience, age, physical ability, appearance, special skills, personality traits, attitude, outside interests)? Try to locate an actual newspaper ad describing job responsibilities and qualifications. Better yet, assume you're a personnel officer, and compose an ad for the job.

3. Assess your own *anticipated* credentials against the ideal-employee profile. Review the plans you have made to prepare for this job: specific courses, special training, work experience, and so on. Assume you have completed your preparation. How do you measure up to the requirements in item 2, above? Are your goals realistic? If not, why not? What alternative plan should you formulate? (For this assignment, of course, you will want to make a complete list of the credentials you *plan* to have by the time you seek professional employment.)

4. Using your list from item 3, above, as raw material, construct your résumé. Revise until it is perfect.

5. Write a letter of application for the job described in item 1, above. Revise until you feel good about signing it.

Note: Use the sample letters in this chapter for guidance, but do not borrow specific expressions.

Application 21–9

Assume that this advertisement has appeared in your school newspaper:

Student Consultant Wanted

The office of Dean of Students invites applications for the position of student consultant to the Dean for the upcoming academic year. Duties will include (1) meeting with fellow students as individuals and groups to discuss issues, opinions, questions, complaints, and recommendations regarding all areas of college policy; (2) presenting oral and written reports to the Dean of Students on a regular basis; and (3) attending various college planning sessions in the role of student spokesperson. Time commitment: 15 hours weekly both semesters. Salary: $3500.

Candidates should be full-time students with at least one year of student experience at this college. The ideal applicant will be skilled in report writing and oral communication, will work well in groups, and will demonstrate a firm commitment to our college. Application deadline: May 15.

1. Compose a résumé and a letter of application for this position.

2. Split your class into screening, interview, and hiring committees.

3. Exchange your group's letters and résumés with another group.

4. As an individual committee member, read and evaluate each of the applications you have received. Rank each application, privately, on paper, according to the criteria in this chapter before discussing the applications with your group.

    Note: While screening applicants, you will be competing for selection by another committee who is reviewing your own application.

5. Compare your conclusions with those of your colleagues, and choose the winning candidate.

6. As a committee, compose a memo to your instructor, giving specific reasons for your final recommendations.

Application 21–10

Assume a friend has asked you for help with this application letter. Read it carefully, evaluate its effectiveness, and rewrite as needed.

Dear Mr. Brown:

Please consider my application for the position of assistant in the Engineering Department. I am a second-year student majoring in Electrical Engineering Technology. I am presently an apprentice with your company and would like to continue my employment in the Engineering Department.

I have six years' experience in electronics, including two years of engineering studies. I am confident my background will enable me to assist the engineers, and I would appreciate the chance to improve my skills through their knowledge and experience.

I would appreciate the opportunity to discuss the possibilities and benefits of a position in the engineering department at Concord Electric. Please phone me any weekday after 3:00 P.M. at (467) 568-9867. I hope to hear from you soon.

Sincerely,

Application 21–11

Research the writing skills you will need in your career. (Begin by looking at the *Dictionary of Occupational Titles* in your library's reference section. You might also interview a successful person in your profession.) Why and for whom will you write on the job? Explain in a memo to your instructor.

Application 21–12

Assume you are a training manager for XYZ Corporation. After completing this section of the text and the course, what advice about the writing process would you have for a beginning writer who will need to write frequent reports on the job? In a one-page (single-spaced) memo to new employees, explain the writing process briefly, and list general suggestions these beginning writers can follow.

Application 21-13

We all would like to see changes in our school's policies or procedures, whether they are changes in our major, school regulations, social activities, grading policies, registration procedures, or the like. Find some area of your school that needs obvious changes, and write a recommendation report to the appropriate decision maker. Explain why the change is necessary, and outline the benefits to be gained. Follow the format on page 519.

Application 21-14

You would like to see some changes in this course to better reflect your career plans. Perhaps you feel too much emphasis is placed on writing and too little on reading. Or maybe there's too much lecturing and not enough discussion. Write a recommendation report to your instructor, justifying the reasons for the changes you propose. Illustrate specific benefits resulting from your plan for you and your classmates. Do *not* try to justify spending less time doing course work.

Application 21-15

Think of an idea you would like to see implemented in your job. Write a recommendation report persuading your audience that your idea is worthwhile.

Application 21-16

Identify a dangerous or inconvenient area or situation on campus or in your community (endless cafeteria lines, a poorly lit intersection, slippery stairs, a poorly adjusted traffic light). Observe the problem for several hours during a peak-use period. Write a memo to a *specifically identified* decision maker describing the problem, listing your firsthand observations, making recommendations, and encouraging readers' support or action.

Application 21–17

Conduct a brief survey (e.g., of comparative interest rates from various banks for a car loan, comparative tax and property evaluation rates in three local towns, or comparative prices among local retailers for a certain item). Arrange your data and report your findings to your instructor in a memo that closes with specific conclusions and recommendations for making the most economical choice.

Application 21–18

Although the campus store (or cafeteria) is a convenient place to buy small items (or food), you believe students are overcharged for the convenience. To prove your point, you decide to do a comparative analysis of five items at the campus store (or cafeteria) and two local stores (or restaurants). Be sure to compare like sizes, weights, brands. Conduct your survey, analyze your findings, and submit the results in memo form to the student senate. Your instructor might want you to include recommendations.

Application 21–19

INFORMATIONAL REPORT TOPICS

Choose *one* for a memo or letter.

1. You are legal consultant to the leadership of a large auto workers' union. Before negotiating its next contract, the union needs to know what effects robotics technology will have on assembly line auto workers within ten years. Do the research, and write the report.

2. You are a consulting engineer to an island community of 200 families suffering a severe water shortage. Some islanders have raised the possibility of producing drinking water from salt water (desalination). Write a report for the town council, summarizing the process and describing cases where desalination has been successful or unsuccessful. Would desalination be economically feasible for a community this size?

3. How, specifically, has your school been affected by budget cuts in recent years? Write for the student senate.

4. Is a selected elementary or high school in your town free of dangers from urea formaldehyde insulation, asbestos, toxic art supplies, or dangerous fumes from cleaning fluids and solvents? Find out, and write a report for the PTA and school committee.

5. Find out if your school stores radioactive or other hazardous materials on campus. What precautions are taken? Are they adequate? Write a report for the student senate.

6. Dream up a scenario of your own; use specific information.

Application 21–20

RECOMMENDATION REPORT TOPICS

Choose *one* for a memo or letter.

1. You are an investment broker for a major firm. A longtime client calls to ask your opinion. She is thinking of investing in a company that is fast becoming a leader in fiber-optics communication links. "Should I invest in this technology?" your client wants to know. Find out, and give her your informed opinion in a short report.

2. The buildings in the condominium complex you manage have been invaded by carpenter ants. Can the ants be eliminated by an insecticide *proven* nontoxic to human beings and pets? (Many dwellers have small children and pets.) Find out, and write a report making recommendations to the maintenance supervisor.

3. Which area of your state has the cleanest air and groundwater, and which has the most polluted? Write for someone who wants the safest place to raise a family.

4. As a consulting dietitian to the school cafeterias in Blandville, you've been asked by the school board to report on the most dangerous chemical additives in foods. Worried parents want to be sure that foods containing these additives will be eliminated from school menus, insofar as possible. Write your report, making recommendations for modifying school menus.

5. Dream up a scenario of your own; answer your question with specific information and recommendations. (Perhaps the question could be one you've always wanted answered.)

Appendix: Review of Grammar, Punctuation, and Mechanics

Sentence Parts • Sentence Types • Common Sentence Errors
• Effective Punctuation • Effective Mechanics

No matter how vital and informative a message may be, its credibility can be damaged by basic errors. Any of these errors—an illogical, fragmented, or run-on sentence; faulty punctuation; or a poorly chosen word—stands out and mars otherwise good writing. Not only do such errors confuse and annoy the reader, but they also speak badly for the writer's attention to detail and precision. Your career will make the same demands for good writing that your English classes do. The difference is that evaluation (grades) in professional situations usually shows in promotions, reputation, and salary.

Table A-1 displays the standard correction symbols along with their interpretation and page references. When your instructor marks a symbol on your paper, turn to the appropriate section for explanations and examples that will help you make corrections quickly and easily.

Sentence Parts

Aside from a few exceptions we discuss later, a sentence is a statement that contains a subject and a verb and expresses a complete idea. More

Table A.1 Correction Symbols

Symbol	Meaning	Page*	Symbol	Meaning	Page
ab	abbreviaton	565	, /	comma	552
agr g	pronoun/referent agreement	543	-- /	dash	564
			... /	ellipses	562
agr sv	subject/verb agreement	541	! /	exclamation point	550
appr	inappropriate diction	204	- /	hyphen	566
bias	biased tone	211	*ital*	italics	563
ca	pronoun case	544	( ) /	parentheses	563
cap	capitalization	568	. /	period	549
chop.	choppiness	184	? /	question mark	549
cl	clutter word	181	" / "	quotation marks	561
coh.	paragraph coherence	132	; /	semicolon	550
cont.	contraction	560	*qual*	needless qualifier	181
coord.	coordination	166	*red*	redundancy	175
cs	comma splice	538	*rep*	needless repetition	175
dgl	dangling modifier	160	*ref*	faulty reference	161
¶ dev	paragraph development	114	*ro*	run-on sentence	540
			shift	sentence shift	546
euph	euphemism	195	*sp*	spelling	570
exact	inexact word	197	*str*	paragraph structure	124
frag.	sentence fragment	534	*sub*	subordination	167
gen	generalization	194	*trans*	transition	144
len.	paragraph length	135	*trite*	triteness	193
mod	misplaced modifier	159	*un*	paragraph unity	130
			v	voice	168
noun ad	noun addiction	178	*var*	sentence variety	187
over	overstatement	194	*w*	wordiness	174
par	parallelism	163	*ww*	wrong word	182
pct	punctuation	547	#	numbers	569
ap/	apostrophe	559	¶	begin new paragraph	125
[ ] /	brackets	564			
: /	colon	551	*no ¶*	no paragraph	124

*Numbers refer to the first page of major discussion in the text.

important than this textbook definition of *sentence*, however, is our innate understanding of how groups of words function as sentences. As an illustration, consider this nonsense statement:

> In the cronk, the crat midingly pleted the mook smurg.

Although the only words we recognize in the example are **in** and **the,** we can say that this is a sentence. Why? Because in some place, something did something to something else. Specifically, the statement has a subject, **crat,** which did the doing; it has a verb, **pleted,** which is in the past tense; it has an adverb, **midingly,** which modifies the verb, telling us how the crat pleted; it has an adjective, **mook,** which modifies **smurg;** it has three nouns, **cronk, crat,** and **smurg; cronk** is the object of the preposition **in,** and **smurg** is the object of the verb **pleted.** And so, without understanding the words, we can see we already know something about language—how words work to make up a sentence. We don't know what this particular idea is, but we do know that it is complete.

Let's look at these sentence parts, and others, in more detail.

SUBJECT

The subject is the actor of the sentence—the noun or pronoun that usually precedes the predicate (the verb and other words that explain it) and about which we say something or ask a question.

> The **cat** eats too much.
>
> Why does the **cat** eat too much?
>
> The **big, fat lazy cat sitting on the table** eats too much.

In this last sentence, the simple subject is **cat,** and the complete subject (with all the words that explain the simple subject) is **The big, fat, lazy cat sitting on the table.**

PREDICATE

The predicate is made up of the verb and any words that modify and explain it. The predicate usually is what is said about the subject's action or being.

> The cat **eats.**
>
> Who **is** a fat cat?
>
> The cat **eats until he can no longer stand up.**

In this last sentence, the simple verb is **eats,** and the complete predicate (with all the words that explain the simple predicate) is **eats until he can no longer stand up.**

OBJECT

An object is something that is acted on either directly or indirectly by a verb, or that is governed by a preposition.

Direct Object   A direct object is a noun or noun substitute that receives or is otherwise affected by the predicate's action.

> The cat drank the **bowl of milk.**
>
> Why did the cat eat **the mouse?**
>
> I don't know **where the cat is.**
>
> **What** did the cat eat?

Indirect Object   An indirect object is a noun or noun substitute that states to whom or for whom (or to what or for what) the predicate acts.

> I gave **the cat** a bowl of milk.
>
> He built **his friend** a house.

Usually the indirect object could be replaced by a prepositional phrase beginning with **to** or **for.**

> I gave a bowl of milk **to the cat.**
>
> He built a house **for his friend.**

Object of the Preposition   The object of the preposition is a noun or noun substitute that is joined to another part of the sentence by a preposition (**across, after, between, by, for, in, near, up, with,** and other "relationship" words). The words **cat** and **friend** in the two sentences above are objects of the preposition, as is **floor** in the next:

> The fat cat collapsed on the **floor.**

OBJECTIVE COMPLEMENT

An objective complement is a word or group of words that further explains the subject's action on the direct object.

The cats elected Jack **president.**

I consider him **a villain.**

SUBJECTIVE COMPLEMENT

A subjective complement is a word or group of words that further explains the subject. Subjective complements always follow linking verbs (**be, seem, feel, taste,** or any other verb that indicates a condition of being and that has no object).

Jack is **angry.**

All cats appear **alert and vigilant.**

PHRASE

A phrase is a group of related words that lacks either a subject or a predicate, or both. These are the kinds of phrases:

Infinitive phrase	Jack likes **to be fat.** [*functions as direct object*]
Prepositional phrase	Jack is content to sit **on the table.** [*functions as adverb*]
Verbal phrase	Jack **will be eating** until his dying day. [*functions as verb*]
Gerund phrase	**Eating constantly** can be damaging. [*functions as noun*]
Participial phrase	**Hoping for more food,** Jack meowed loudly. [*functions as adjective*]

CLAUSE

A clause is a group of related words that contains a subject and a predicate. It may be independent (main) or dependent (subordinate). An independent clause can stand alone as a sentence.

The cat eats too much.

A dependent clause cannot stand alone as a sentence; it can serve as a noun, an adjective, or an adverb. A dependent clause always needs an independent clause to complete its meaning.

Noun clause	Jack hopes **he can eat forever.** [*as direct object*] **Anyone Jack meets** is a potential meal ticket. [*as subject*]
Adjective clause	Jack, **who eats constantly,** is the fattest cat in town. [*modifies "Jack"*]
Adverb clause	Jack is fat **because he eats too much.** [*modifies the subjective complement "fat"*]

Now let's look at the types of sentences that can be made by combining these sentence parts.

Sentence Types

SIMPLE SENTENCES

A simple sentence contains one independent clause and expresses one complete thought.

Jack eats.

Jack eats too much.

On any given day, **Jack eats** too much.

On any given day, **Jack,** the fat, lazy cat, **eats** too much dry and canned food for any small animal.

Each of these sentences is a simple sentence. Although the subject and verb are gradually expanded, and objects, adjectives, adverbs, and prepositional phrases are added, the kernel sentence still is **Jack eats.**

COMPOUND SENTENCES

A compound sentence contains two or more independent clauses, each with a subject and a predicate. The clauses are usually joined by coordinating conjunctions (**and, but, or, nor, for**) or by a semicolon or colon.

Jack eats constantly **and** he gets fatter.

Jack eats constantly; he gets fatter.

Ideas in a compound sentence are roughly equal in importance; therefore, they are expressed in equal (parallel) grammatical form.

Jack **eats** all morning, and he **sleeps** all afternoon, and he **prowls** all night.

COMPLEX SENTENCES

A complex sentence has two or more clauses that are *not* equal in importance. Instead, it has a dependent clause and an independent clause; the former depends on the latter to complete its meaning.

Because Jack eats too much, **he is fat.** [*second clause is independent*]

Have you seen the cat who eats too much? [*first clause is independent*]

Because one clause depends on the other, they should not be separated by anything stronger than a comma. Words such as **which, although, after, when,** and **because** (subordinating conjunctions) placed at the beginning of an independent clause will make it dependent.

A complex sentence can have more than one dependent clause— as long as it has one independent clause.

After Jack eats all morning, sleeps all afternoon, and prowls all night, **he is ready to begin all over again,** even when he has the flu.

As discussed in the section on subordination (Chapter 8), complex sentences signal that some ideas merit more emphasis than others.

COMPOUND-COMPLEX SENTENCES

A compound-complex sentence has at least two independent clauses and one dependent clause.

Even though Jack's girlfriend has left town, **he remains optimistic, and he has an active social life.** [*second and third clauses are independent*]

Common Sentence Errors

Any piece of writing is only as good as each of its sentences. Here are common sentence errors, with suggestions for easy repairs.

SENTENCE FRAGMENT

A sentence expresses a logically complete idea. Any complete idea must contain a subject and a verb and must not depend on another complete idea to make sense. Your sentence might contain several complete ideas, but it must have at least one!

> [*incomplete idea*]   [*complete idea*]   [*complete idea*]
> Although he was hurt, he grabbed the line, and he saved the boat.

However long or short your statement, it should make sense to your reader. If the idea is not complete—if your reader is left wondering what you mean—you probably have left out an essential element (the subject, the verb, or another complete idea). Such a piece of a sentence is called a fragment.

> Grabbed the line. [*a fragment because it lacks a subject*]

> Although he was hurt. [*a fragment because—although it has a subject and a verb—it needs to be joined with a complete idea to make sense*]

The only exception to the sentence rule applies when we give a command ("Run!") in which the subject (you) is understood. Because "Run!" is a logically complete statement, it is properly called a sentence. So is this one:

> Sam is an electronics technician.

Readers cannot miss your meaning: somewhere is a person; the person's name is Sam; the person is an electronics technician.
Suppose instead we write:

> Sam an electronics technician.

This statement is not logically complete, therefore not a sentence. The reader is left asking, "What **about** Sam the electronics technician?" The verb—the word that makes things happen—is missing. By adding a verb, we can easily change this fragment to a complete sentence.

Simple verb	Sam **is** an electronics technician.
Verb plus adverb	Sam, an electronics technician, **works hard.**
Dependent clause, verb, and subjective complement	**Although he is well paid,** Sam, an electronics technician, **is not happy.**

Do not, however, mistake the following statement—which seems to contain a verb—for a complete sentence:

Sam being an electronics technician.

Such "-ing" forms do not function as verbs unless accompanied by such other verbs as **is, was,** and **will be.** Again, readers are left in a fog unless you complete your idea with an independent clause.

Sam, being an electronics technician, **was responsible for checking the circuitry.**

Likewise, remember that the "to + verb" form (infinitive) does not function as a verb.

To become an electronics technician.

The meaning is unclear unless you complete the thought.

To become an electronics technician, **Sam had to complete a two-year apprenticeship.**

Sometimes we inadvertently create fragments by adding certain words (**because, since, if, although, while, unless, until, when, where,** and others) to an already complete sentence, transforming our independent clause (complete sentence) to a dependent clause.

Although Sam is an electronics technician.

Such words subordinate the words that follow them so that an additional idea is needed to make the first statement complete. That is, they make the statement dependent on an additional idea, which must itself have a subject and a verb and be a complete sentence. (See "Complex Sentences" and "Subordination"—pages 534, 167.) Now we have to round off the statement with a complete idea (an independent clause).

Although Sam is an electronics technician, **he hopes to become an electrical engineer.**

Note: Be careful not to use a semicolon or a period instead of a comma to separate elements in the preceding sentence. Because the incomplete idea (dependent clause) depends on the complete idea (independent clause) for its meaning, you need only a *pause* (symbolized by a comma), not a *break* (symbolized by a semicolon), between these ideas. In fact, many fragments are created when the writer uses too strong a mark of punctuation (period or semicolon) between a dependent and an independent clause, thereby severing the needed connection. (See the discussion of punctuation.)

Here are some fragments from students' writing. Each is repaired in several ways. Can you think of any other ways of making these statements complete?

Fragment	She spent her first week on the job as a researcher. **Selecting and compiling technical information from digests and journals.**
Revised	She spent her first week on the job as a researcher, selecting and compiling technical information from digests and journals.
	She spent her first week on the job as a researcher. She selected and compiled technical information from digests and journals.
	In her first week on the job as a researcher, she selected and compiled technical information from digests and journals.
Fragment	**Because the operator was careless.** The new computer was damaged.
Revised	Because the operator was careless, the new computer was damaged.
	The operator's carelessness resulted in damage to the new computer.
	The operator was careless; as a result, the new computer was damaged.
Fragment	**When each spool is in place.** Advance your film.
Revised	When each spool is in place, advance your film.
	Be sure that each spool is in place before advancing your film.

ACCEPTABLE FRAGMENTS

For some purposes, a fragmented sentence is acceptable even though it lacks a subject or a verb; in commands or exclamations, the subject ("you") is understood.

Acceptable	Slow down.
	Give me a hand.
	Hurry.
	Look out!

Also, questions and answers are sometimes expressed as incomplete sentences.

Acceptable	How? By investing wisely.
	When? At three o'clock.
	Who? Bill.

These are the commonest situations that justify fragmented sentences. Some of the sample essays in Section Three show other examples. In general, however, avoid fragments unless you have good reason to use one for special tone or emphasis.

Application A–1

Correct these sentence fragments by rewriting each in two ways.

1. Fred is a terrible math student. But an excellent writer.
2. As they entered the haunted house. The floors began to groan.
3. Hoping for an **A** in biology. Sally studied every night.
4. Although many students flunk out of this college. Its graduates find excellent jobs.
5. Three teenagers out of every ten have some sort of addiction. Whether it is to alcohol or drugs.

COMMA SPLICE

In a comma splice, two complete ideas (independent clauses), which should be *separated* by a period or a semicolon, are incorrectly *joined* by a comma:

Sarah did a great job, she was promoted.

There are several possibilities for correcting this error:

1. Substitute a period followed by a capital letter:

    Sarah did a great job. She was promoted.

2. Substitute a semicolon to signal a relationship between the two items:

    Sarah did a great job; she was promoted.

3. Use a semicolon with a connecting adverb (a transitional word):

    Sarah did a great job; **consequently,** she was promoted.

4. Use a subordinating word to make the less important clause incomplete, thereby dependent on the other:

    Because Sarah did a great job, she was promoted.

5. Add a connecting word after the comma:

    Sarah did a great job, **and** she was promoted.

Your choice of construction will depend, of course, on the exact meaning or tone you wish to convey. These comma splices can be repaired in the ways described above.

Comma splice	This is a fairly new product, therefore, some people don't trust it.
Revised	This is a fairly new product. Some people don't trust it.
	This is a fairly new product; therefore, some people don't trust it.
	Because this is a fairly new product, some people don't trust it.
	This is a fairly new product, **and so** some people don't trust it.
Comma splice	Ms. Jones was a strict supervisor, she was well liked by her employees.
Revised	Ms. Jones was a strict supervisor. She was well liked by her employees.
	Ms. Jones was a strict supervisor; **however,** she was well liked by her employees.

Although Ms. Jones was a strict supervisor, she was well liked by her employees.

Ms. Jones was a strict supervisor, **but** she was well liked by her employees.

Ms. Jones was a strict supervisor; she was well liked by her employees.

Application A-2

Correct these comma splices by rewriting each in two ways.

1. Efforts are being made to halt water pollution, however, there is no simple solution to the problem.

2. Bill slept through his final, he had forgotten to set his alarm.

3. Sam must be a genius, he never studies yet always gets A's.

4. We arrived at the picnic late, there were no hamburgers left.

5. My part-time job is excellent, it pays well, provides good experience, and offers a real challenge.

RUN-ON SENTENCE

The run-on sentence, a cousin to the comma splice, crams in too many ideas without needed breaks or pauses.

Run-on
The hourglass is more accurate than the waterclock for the water in a waterclock must always be at the same temperature in order to flow with the same speed since water evaporates it must be replenished at regular intervals thus not being as effective in measuring time as the hourglass.

Like a runaway train, this statement is out of control. Here is a corrected version:

Revised
The hourglass is more accurate than the waterclock because water in a waterclock must always be at the same temperature to flow at the same speed. Also, water evaporates and must be replenished at regular intervals. These

temperature and volume problems make the
waterclock less effective than the hourglass in
measuring time.

Application A–3

Revise these run-on sentences.

1. The gale blew all day by evening the sloop was taking on water.

2. Felix felt hopeless about passing English however the writing center helped him complete the course.

3. The professor glared at John he had been dozing in the back row.

4. Our drama club produces three plays a year I love the opening nights.

5. Pets should not be allowed on our campus they are messy and sometimes dangerous.

FAULTY AGREEMENT—SUBJECT AND VERB

Failure to make the subject of a sentence agree in number with the verb is a common error. Happily, it's an error easily corrected and avoided. We are not likely to use faulty agreement in short sentences, where subject and verb are not far apart. Thus we are not likely to say "Jack eat too much" instead of "Jack eats too much." But in more complicated sentences—those in which the subject is separated from its verb by other words—we sometimes lose track of the subject–verb relationship.

Faulty   The lion's **share** of diesels **are** sold in Europe.

Although **diesels** is closest to the verb, the subject is **share,** a singular subject that must agree with a singular verb.

Revised   The lion's **share** of diesels **is** sold in Europe.

Errors in agreement are easy to correct when the subject and verb are identified.

Faulty   There **is** an estimated 29,000 **women** living in our city.

Revised   There **are** an estimated 29,000 **women** living in
                   our city.

Faulty   **A system** of lines **extend** horizontally to form a
                   grid.

Revised   **A system** of lines **extends** horizontally to form a
                   grid.

A second problem with subject–verb agreement occurs when we use
indefinite pronouns such as **each, everyone, anybody,** and **somebody.**
They function as subjects and usually take a singular verb.

Faulty   **Each** of the crew members **were** injured during the
                   storm.

Revised   **Each** of the crew members **was** injured during the
                   storm.

Faulty   **Everyone** in the group **have** practiced long hours.

Revised   **Everyone** in the group **has** practiced long hours.

Sometimes agreement problems can be caused by collective nouns such
as **herd, family, union, group, army, team, committee,** and **board.** They
can call for a singular or plural verb, depending on your intended meaning. When denoting the group as a whole, use a singular verb.

Correct   The **committee meets** weekly to discuss new
                   business.

                   The editorial **board** of this magazine **has** high
                   standards.

To denote individual members of the group, however, use a plural verb.

Correct   The **committee disagree** on whether to hire Jim.

                   The editorial **board are** all published authors.

Yet another problem occurs when two subjects are joined by **either . . .
or** or **neither . . . nor.** Here, the verb is singular if both subjects are singular and plural if both subjects are plural. If one subject is plural and
one is singular, the verb agrees with the one that is closer to the verb.

Correct   Neither **John** nor **Bill works** regularly.

                   Either **apples** or **oranges are** good vitamin sources.

Either Felix or his **friends are** crazy.

Neither the boys nor their **father likes** the home
team.

If, on the other hand, two subjects (singular, plural, or mixed) are joined
by **both . . . and,** the verb will be plural. Whereas **or** suggests "one or
the other," **and** announces a combination of the two subjects, thereby
requiring a plural verb.

Correct   **Both** Joe and Bill **are** resigning.

                     The **book and** the **briefcase appear** expensive.

FAULTY AGREEMENT—PRONOUN AND REFERENT

A pronoun can make sense only if it refers to a specific noun (its referent or antecedent), with which it must agree in gender and number.
It is easy enough to make most pronouns agree with their respective
referents.

Correct   **Joe** lost **his** book.

                     The **students** complained that **they** had been
                     treated unfairly.

Some instances, however, are not so obvious. When an indefinite pronoun such as **each, everyone, anybody, someone,** or **none** serves as the
pronoun referent, the pronoun itself is singular.

Correct   **Anyone** can get **his** degree from that college.

                     Anyone can get **his** or **her** degree from that
                     college.

                     Each candidate described **her** plans in detail.

Application A–4

Revise these sentences to make their subjects and verbs agree in
number or their pronouns and referents agree in gender and number.

1. Ten years ago the mineral rights to this land was sold to a
   mining company.

2. Each of the students in our dorm have a serious complaint about living conditions.

3. Neither the students nor the instructor like this classroom.

4. The team meet every Tuesday to discuss new plays.

5. Neither Fred nor Sam expect to pass this course.

6. Anyone wanting to enhance their career should take a computer course.

7. Everyone has their own opinion about nuclear power.

FAULTY PRONOUN CASE

A pronoun's case (nominative, objective, or possessive) is determined by its role in the sentence: as subject, object, or indicator of possession.

If the pronoun serves as the subject of a sentence (**I, we, you, she, he, it, they, who**), its case is *nominative*.

> **She** completed her graduate program in record time.
>
> **Who** broke the chair?

When a pronoun follows a version of the verb **to be** (a linking verb), it explains (complements) the subject, and so its case is nominative.

> It was **she.**
>
> The professor who perfected our new distillation process is **he.**

If the pronoun serves as the object of a verb or a preposition (**me, us, you, her, him, it, them, whom**), its case is *objective.*

Object of the verb	The employees gave **her** a parting gift.
Object of the preposition	To **whom** do you wish to complain?

If a pronoun indicates possession (**my, mine, our, ours, your, yours, his, her, hers, its, their, theirs, whose**), its case is *possessive.*

> The brown briefcase is **mine.**
>
> **Her** offer was accepted.
>
> **Whose** opinion do you value most?

Here are some frequent errors in pronoun case:

Faulty	**Whom** is responsible to **who?** [*The subject should be nominative and the object should be objective.*]
Revised	**Who** is responsible to **whom?**
Faulty	The debate was between Marsha and **I.** [*As object of the preposition, the pronoun should be objective.*]
Revised	The debate was between Marsha and **me.**
Faulty	**Us** students are accountable for our decisions. [*The pronoun accompanies the subject, "students," and thus should be nominative.*]
Revised	**We** students are accountable for our decisions.
Faulty	A group of **we** students will fly to California. [*The pronoun accompanies the object of the preposition, "students," and thus should be objective.*]
Revised	A group of **us** students will fly to California.

Hint: By deleting the accompanying noun from the two latter examples, we can easily identify the correct pronoun case ("We . . . are accountable . . ."; "A group of us . . . will fly . . .").

Application A–5

Select the appropriate pronoun case from each of these pairs (in parentheses).

1. Kevin was as fascinated by the Grand Canyon as (me, I).
2. By (who, whom) was the job offer made?
3. The argument was among Bill, Terry, and (I, me).
4. A committee of (we, us) concerned citizens is working to make our neighborhood safer.
5. (Us, we) students are being hurt by federal cuts in loan programs.
6. The liar is (he, him).

SENTENCE SHIFTS

Shifts in point of view damage coherence. If you begin a sentence or paragraph with one subject or person, don't shift to another.

Shift in person	When **you** finish such a great book, **one** will have a sense of achievement.
Revised	When **you** finish such a great book, **you** will have a sense of achievement.
Shift in number	**One** should sift the flour before **they** make the pie.
Revised	**One** should sift the flour before **one** makes the pie. (*Or better:* Sift the flour before making the pie.)

Don't begin a sentence in the active voice and then shift to the passive voice.

Shift in voice	He **delivered** the plans for the apartment complex, and the building site **was also inspected by him.**
Revised	He **delivered** the plans for the apartment complex and also **inspected** the building site.

Don't shift tenses without good reason.

Shift in tense	She **delivered** the blueprints, **inspected** the foundation, **wrote** her report, and **takes** the afternoon off.
Revised	She **delivered** the blueprints, **inspected** the foundation, **wrote** her report, and **took** the afternoon off.

Don't shift from one verb mood to another (as from imperative to indicative mood in a set of instructions).

Shift in mood	**Unscrew** the valve and then steel wool **should be used** to clean the fitting.
Revised	**Unscrew** the valve and then **use** steel wool to clean the fitting.

Don't shift from indirect to direct discourse within a sentence.

Shift in discourse	Jim wonders **if he will get the job** and **will he like it?**
Revised	Jim wonders **if he will get the job** and **if he will like it.** [*someone speaking for someone else*]
	Jim wonders, **"Will I get the job, and will I like it?"** [*speaker expressing himself directly*]

Application A–6

Revise these sentences to eliminate shifts in person, mood, voice, tense, number, or discourse.

1. People should keep themselves politically informed; otherwise, you will not be living up to your democratic responsibilities.

2. Sam made the Dean's List and the Junior Achievement award was also won by him.

3. Professor Jones said that our performance was excellent and that "I am proud to have worked with you all."

4. As soon as he walked into his dorm room, George sees the mess left by his roommate.

5. When one is being stalked by a bear, you should not snack on sardines.

6. First loosen the lug nuts; then you should jack up the car.

7 One should expect that you will face a competitive job market.

Effective Punctuation

Punctuation marks are like road signs and traffic signals. They govern reading speed and provide clues for navigation through a network of ideas; they mark intersections, detours, and road repairs; they draw attention to points of interest along the route; and they mark geographic boundaries. In short, punctuation marks provide us with a practical and simple way of making ourselves understood.

Before we discuss individual punctuation marks in detail, let's review the four used most often (period, semicolon, colon, and comma). These marks can be ranked in order of their relative strengths.

1. *Period.* The strongest mark. A period signals a complete stop at the end of an independent idea (independent clause). The first word in the idea following the period begins with a capital letter.

    Jack is a fat cat. His friends urge him to diet.

2. *Semicolon.* Weaker than a period but stronger than a comma. A semicolon signals a brief stop after an independent idea but does not end the sentence; instead, it announces that the forthcoming independent idea is **closely related** to the preceding idea.

    Jack is a fat cat; he eats too much.

3. *Colon.* Weaker than a period but stronger than a comma. A colon usually follows an independent idea and, like the semicolon, signals a brief stop but does not end the sentence. The colon and semicolon, however, are never interchangeable. A colon provides an important cue: it symbolizes "explanation to follow." Information after the colon (which need not be an independent idea) explains or clarifies the idea expressed before the colon.

    Jack is a fat cat: he weighs forty pounds. [*The information after the colon answers "How fat?"*]

    or

    Jack is a fat cat: forty pounds worth! [*The second clause is not independent.*]

    Note: As long as any two adjacent ideas are independent, they may correctly be separated by a period. Sometimes a colon or a semicolon may be more appropriate for illustrating the logical relationship between two given ideas. When in doubt, however, use a period.

4. *Comma.* The weakest of these four marks. A comma does not signal a stop at the end of an independent idea, but only a pause within or between ideas in the sentence. A comma often indicates that the word, phrase, or clause set off from the independent idea cannot stand alone but must rely on the independent idea for its meaning.

    Jack, **a fat cat,** is jolly. [*The phrase within commas depends on the independent idea for its meaning.*]

Although he diets often, Jack is a fat cat. [*Because the first clause depends on the second, any stronger mark would cause the first clause to become a fragment.*]

A comma is used between two independent clauses only if accompanied by a coordinating conjunction (**and, but, or, nor, yet**).

Comma splice	Jack is a playboy, he is loved everywhere.
Correct	Jack is a playboy, **but** he is loved everywhere.

And so we see that punctuation marks, like words, convey specific meanings to the reader. These meanings are further discussed in the sections that follow.

END PUNCTUATION

The three marks of end punctuation—period, question mark, and exclamation point—work like a red traffic light by signaling a complete stop.

Period   A period ends a sentence. Periods end some abbreviations.

Ms.	Assn.	N.Y.
M.D.	Inc.	B.A.

Periods serve as decimal points for figures.

$15.95

21.4%

Question Mark   A question mark follows a direct question.

Where is the balance sheet?

Do not use a question mark to end an indirect question.

Faulty	He asked if all students had failed the test?
Revised	He asked if all students had failed the test. [*someone speaking for someone else*]
	or
	He asked, "Did all students fail the test?" [*speaker expressing himself directly*]

Exclamation Point   Because exclamation points symbolize that you are excited or adamant, don't overuse them. Otherwise you might seem hysterical or insincere.

Use an exclamation point only when expression of strong feeling is appropriate.

Appropriate   Oh, no!

                         Pay up!

                         My books are missing!

SEMICOLON

A semicolon usually works like a blinking red traffic light at an intersection by signaling a brief but definite stop.

Semicolons Separating Independent Clauses   Semicolons separate independent clauses (logically complete ideas) whose contents are closely related and are not connected by a coordinating conjunction.

The project was finally completed; we had done a good week's work.

The semicolon can replace the conjunction-comma combination that joins two independent ideas.

The project was finally completed, and we were elated.

The project was finally completed; we were elated.

The second version emphasizes the sense of elation.

Semicolons Used with Adverbs as Conjunctions and Other Transitional Expressions   Semicolons must accompany conjunctive adverbs and other expressions that connect related independent ideas (**besides, otherwise, still, however, furthermore, moreover, consequently, therefore, on the other hand, in contrast, in fact**, and the like).

The job is filled; however, we will keep your résumé on file.

Your background is impressive; in fact, it is the best among our applicants.

Semicolons Separating Items in a Series   When items in a series contain internal commas, semicolons provide clear separation between items.

I am applying for summer jobs in Santa Fe, New Mexico; Albany, New York; Montgomery, Alabama; and Moscow, Idaho.

Members of the survey crew were John Jones, a geologist; Hector Lightweight, a draftsman; and Mary Shelley, a graduate student.

COLON

A colon works like a flare in the road. It signals you to stop and then proceed, paying attention to the situation ahead, the details of which will be revealed as you move along. Usually a colon follows an introductory statement that requires a follow-up explanation.

> We need this equipment immediately: a voltmeter, a portable generator, and three pairs of insulated gloves.

> She is an ideal colleague: honest, reliable, and competent.

> Two candidates are clearly superior: John and Marsha.

Except for **Dear Sir:** and other salutations in formal correspondence, colons follow independent (logically and grammatically complete) statements. Because colons, like end punctuation and semicolons, signal a full stop, they are never used to fragment a complete statement.

Faulty   My plans include: finishing college, traveling for two years, and settling down in Boston.

No punctuation should follow "include."
Colons can introduce quotations.

> The supervisor's message was clear enough: "You're fired."

A colon normally replaces a semicolon in separating two related, complete statements when the second statement directly explains or amplifies the first.

> His reason for accepting the lowest-paying job offer was simple: he had always wanted to live in the Northwest.

The statement following the colon explains the "reason" mentioned in the statement preceding the colon.

Application A-7

Insert semicolons or colons as needed in these expressions.

1. June had finally arrived it was time to graduate.

2. I have two friends who are like brothers Sam and Daniel.

3. Joe did not get the job however, he was high on the list of finalists.

4. The wine was superb an 1898 Château Lafitte.

5. Our student senators are Jim Blake, a geology major Helen Simms, a nursing major and Henry Drew, an English major.

COMMA

The comma is the most frequently used—and abused—punctuation mark. Unlike the period, semicolon, and colon, which signal a full stop, the comma signals a *brief pause*. Thus, the comma works like a blinking yellow traffic light, for which you slow down without stopping. Never use a comma to signal a *break* between independent ideas; it is not strong enough.

Comma as a Pause Between Complete Ideas   In a compound sentence in which a coordinating conjunction (**and, or, nor, for, but**) connects equal (independent) statements, a comma is usually placed immediately before the conjunction.

> This is an excellent course, but the work is difficult.

> This vacant shop is just large enough for our hot-dog stand, and the location is excellent for walk-in customer traffic.

Without the conjunction, each previous statement would suffer from a comma splice, unless the comma were replaced by a semicolon or period.

Comma as a Pause Between an Incomplete and a Complete Idea   A comma is usually placed between a complete and an incomplete statement in a complex sentence to show that the incomplete statement depends for its meaning on the complete statement (the incomplete statement cannot stand alone, separated by a break such as a semicolon, colon, or period).

> **Because he is a fat cat,** Jack diets often.

> **When he eats too much,** Jack gains weight.

Above, the first idea is made incomplete by a subordinating conjunction (**since, when, because, although, where, while, if, until**), which here connects a dependent with an independent statement. The first (incomplete) idea depends on the second (complete) for wholeness. When the order is reversed (complete idea followed by incomplete), the comma usually is omitted.

Jack diets often **because he is a fat cat.**

Jack gains weight **when he eats too much.**

Because commas take the place of speech signals, reading a sentence aloud should tell you whether or not to pause (and use a comma).

Commas Separating Items (Words, Phrases, or Clauses) in a Series   Use a comma to separate items in a series.

Sam, Joe, Marsha, and **John** are joining us on the term project.

The dorm room was **yellow, orange,** and **red.**

He works hard **at home, on the job,** and even **during his vacation.**

The new employee complained **that the hours were long, that the pay was low, that the work was boring,** and **that the foreman was paranoid.**

She came, saw, and **conquered.**

Use no commas when **or** or **and** appears between all items in a series.

She is willing to study in San Francisco or Seattle or even in Anchorage.

Add a comma when **or** or **and** is used only before the final item in the series.

Our luncheon special for Thursday will be coffee, rolls, steak, beans, and ice cream.

Without the comma, that sentence might cause the reader to conclude that "beans and ice cream" is an exotic new dessert.

Comma Setting Off Introductory Phrases   Infinitive, prepositional, or verbal phrases introducing a sentence usually are set off by commas.

Infinitive phrase   **To be or not to be,** that is the question.

Prepositional phrase   **In Rome,** do as the Romans do.

In fact, the essay was superb.

Verbal phrase **Being fat,** Jack was a slow runner.

Moving quickly, the army surrounded the enemy.

When an interjection introduces a sentence, it is set off by a comma.

Oh, is that the final verdict?

When a noun in direct address introduces a sentence, it is set off by a comma.

Mary, you've done a great job.

Commas Setting Off Nonrestrictive Elements A restrictive phrase or clause modifies or limits the subject in such a way that deleting the phrase would change the meaning of the sentence.

All students **who have work experience** will receive preference.

The clause **who have work experience** defines **students** and is essential to the meaning of the sentence. Without this clause, the meaning would be entirely different.

All students will receive preference.

This sentence also contains a restriction.

All students **with work experience** will receive preference.

The phrase **with work experience** defines **students** and thus specifies the meaning of the sentence. Because this phrase *restricts* the subject by limiting the category **students,** it is essential to the sentence's meaning and so is not separated from the sentence by commas.

In contrast, a nonrestrictive phrase or clause does not limit or define the subject; such a modifier is nonessential because it could be deleted without changing the essential meaning of the sentence.

Our new manager, **who has only six weeks' experience,** is highly competent.

This house, **riddled with carpenter ants,** is falling apart.

In each of those sentences, the modifying phrase or clause does not restrict the subject; each could be deleted.

Our new manager is highly competent.

This house is falling apart.

Unlike a restrictive modifier, the nonrestrictive modifier does not supply the essential meaning to the sentence; any nonessential clause or phrase is set off from the sentence by commas.

To appreciate how commas can affect meaning, consider this statement:

Restrictive   Office workers **who drink martinis with lunch** have slow afternoons.

Because the restrictive clause limits the subject, **office workers,** we interpret that statement as follows: some office workers drink martinis with lunch, and these have slow afternoons. In contrast, we could write:

Nonrestrictive   Office workers, **who drink martinis with lunch,** have slow afternoons.

Here the subject, **office workers,** is not limited or defined. Thus we interpret that *all* office workers drink martinis with lunch and therefore have slow afternoons.

Commas Setting Off Parenthetical Elements   Items that interrupt the flow of a sentence are called parenthetical and are enclosed by commas. Expressions such as **of course, as a result, as I recall,** and **however** are parenthetical and may denote emphasis, afterthought, clarification, or transition.

Emphasis   This deluxe model, **of course,** is more expensive.

Afterthought   Your report format, **by the way,** was impeccable.

Clarification   The loss of my job was, **in a way,** a blessing.

Transition   Our warranty, **however,** does not cover tire damage.

So, too, is direct address parenthetical.

Listen, **my children,** and you shall hear . . . .

A parenthetical expression at the beginning or the end of a sentence is set off by a comma.

Naturally, we will expect a full guarantee.

My friends, I think we have a problem.

You've done a good job, **Jim.**

Yes, you may use my name in your advertisement.

Commas Setting Off Quoted Material   Quoted items included within a sentence are often set off by commas.

The customer said, "I'll take it," as soon as he laid eyes on our new model.

Commas Setting Off Appositives   An appositive, a word or words explaining a noun and placed immediately after it, is set off by commas when the appositive is nonrestrictive. (See p. 554.)

Martha Jones, **our new president,** is overhauling all personnel policies.

The new Mercedes, **my dream car,** is priced far beyond my budget.

Alpha waves, **the most prominent of the brain waves,** typically are recorded in a waking subject whose eyes are closed.

Please make all checks payable to Sam Sawbuck, **school treasurer.**

Commas Used in Common Practice   Commas set off the day of the month from the year, in a date.

May 10, 1989

Commas set off numbers in three-digit intervals.

11,215

6,463,657

They also set off street, city, and state in an address.

Mail the bill to John Smith, 18 Sea Street, Albany, Iowa 01642.

When the address is written vertically, however, the commas that are omitted are those which would otherwise occur at the end of each address line.

John Smith
18 Sea Street
Albany, Iowa 01642

If we put "Albany" and "Iowa" on separate lines, we wouldn't have a comma after "Albany," either.

Use commas to set off an address or date in a sentence.

Room 3C, Margate Complex, is my summer address.

June 15, 1987, is my graduation date.

Use them to set off degrees and titles from proper nouns.

Roger P. Cayer, M.D.

Gordon Browne, Jr.

Sandra Mello, Ph.D.

Commas Used Erroneously   Avoid sprinkling commas where they are not needed or simply do not belong. In fact, you are probably safer using too few commas than using too many. Again, overuse of commas generally can be avoided if you read your sentences aloud.

Faulty	The instructor told me, that I was late. [*separates the indirect from the direct object*]
	The most universal symptom of the suicide impulse, is depression. [*separates the subject from its verb*]
	This has been a long, difficult, semester. [*second comma separates the final adjective from its noun*]
	John, Bill, and Sally, are joining us on the trip home. [*third comma separates the final subject from its verb*]
	An employee, who expects rapid promotion, must quickly prove his or her worth. [*separates a modifier that should be restrictive*]
	I spoke by phone with John, and Marsha. [*separates two nouns linked by a coordinating conjunction*]

The room was, 18 feet long. [*separates the linking verb from the subjective complement*]

We painted the room, red. [*separates the object from its complement*]

Application A-8

Insert commas where needed in these sentences.

1. In modern society highways seem as necessary as food water or air.

2. Everyone though frustrated by pollution can play a part in improving the environment.

3. The economic recession is deepening yet real estate continues to be a good investment.

4. Professor Jones who has written three books is considered an authority in his field.

5. Bill my best friend has just left town for the weekend.

6. Sam Ford Jr. of course is the best candidate for governor.

7. When Clem opened the barn door he saw the armadillo scurry behind a hay bale its tail wagging.

8. This car dying of body rot is ready for the junkyard.

9. Terrified by the noise Sally ran never looking back.

10. One book however will not solve all your writing problems.

Application A-9

Eliminate needless or inappropriate commas from these sentences.

1. Students, who smoke marijuana, tend to do poorly in school.

2. As I started the car, I saw him, dash into the woods.

3. This has been a semester of boring, dreadful, experiences.

4. Sarah mistakenly made dates on the same evening with Joe, and Bill, even though she had promised herself to be more careful.

5. In fact, a writer's reaction to criticism, is often defensiveness.

APOSTROPHE

Apostrophes serve three purposes: to indicate the possessive, a contraction, and the plural of numbers, letters, and figures.

Apostrophe Indicating the Possessive   At the end of a singular word, or of a plural word that does not end in **s**, add an apostrophe plus **s** to indicate the possessive.

> The people's candidate won.
>
> The chainsaw was Bill's.
>
> The men's locker room burned.
>
> The car's paint job was ruined by the hailstorm.
>
> I borrowed Doris's book.
>
> Have you heard Ray Charles's new song?

Convention sometimes requires no **s**, because the sound would be awkward.

> Moses' death
>
> for conscience' sake

Do not use an apostrophe to indicate the possessive form of either singular or plural pronouns.

> The book was hers.
>
> Ours is the best school in the country.
>
> The fault was theirs.

At the end of a plural word that ends in -**s**, add an apostrophe only.

> the cows' water supply
>
> the Jacksons' wine cellar

At the end of a compound noun, add an apostrophe plus **s**.

> my father-in-law's false teeth

At the end of the last word in nouns of joint possession, add an apostrophe plus **s** if both own one item.

Joe and Sam's lakefront cottage

Add an apostrophe plus **s** to both nouns if each owns specific items.

Joe's and Sam's passports

Apostrophe Indicating a Contraction   An apostrophe shows that you have omitted one or more letters in a phrase that is usually a combination of a pronoun and a verb.

I'm	they're
he's	you'd
you're	who's

Don't confuse **they're** with **their** or **there.**

Faulty	there books
	their now leaving
	living their
Correct	their books
	they're now leaving
	living there

Remember the distinction this way:

Their friend knows they're there.

Don't confuse **it's** and **its. It's** means "it is." **Its** is the possessive.

It's watching its reflection in the pond.

Don't confuse **who's** and **whose. Who's** means "who is," whereas **whose** indicates the possessive.

Who's interrupting whose work?

Other contractions are formed from the verb and the negative.

isn't	can't
don't	haven't
won't	wasn't

Apostrophe Indicating the Plural of Numbers, Letters, and Figures

The 6's on this new typewriter look like smudged G's, 9's are illegible, and the %'s are unclear.

QUOTATION MARKS

Quotation marks set off the exact words borrowed from another speaker or writer. At the end of a quotation, the period or comma is placed within the quotation marks.

"Hurry up," he whispered.

She told me, "I'm depressed."

The colon or semicolon always is placed outside the quotation marks.

Our student handbook clearly defines "core requirements"; however, it does not list all the courses that fulfill the requirement.

You know what to expect when Honest John offers you a "bargain": a piece of junk.

Sometimes a question mark is used within a quotation that is part of a larger sentence.

"Can we stop the flooding?" inquired the captain.

When a question mark or exclamation point is part of a quotation, it belongs within the quotation marks, replacing the comma or period.

"Help!" he screamed.

He asked John, "Can't we agree about anything?"

But if the question mark or exclamation point is meant to denote the attitude of the quoter instead of the person being quoted, it is placed outside the quotation mark.

Why did he wink and tell me, "It's a big secret"?

He actually accused me of being an "elitist"!

When quoting a passage of 50 words or longer, indent the entire passage ten spaces, and single space between its lines to set it off from the text. Do not enclose the indented passage in quotation marks.

Use quotation marks around titles of articles, paintings, book chapters, and poems.

> The enclosed article, "The Job Market for College Graduates," should provide some helpful insights.

The title of a published work (book, journal, or newspaper) should be underlined to represent italics.

Finally, use quotation marks (with restraint) to indicate your ironic use of a word.

> He is some "friend"!

Application A-10

Insert apostrophes and quotation marks as needed in these sentences.

1. Our countrys future, as well as the worlds, depends on everyone working for a cleaner environment.

2. Once you understand the problem, Professor Jones explained, you find its worse than you possibly could have expected.

3. Can we help? asked the captain.

4. Its a shame that my dog had its leg injured in the accident.

5. All the players hats were eaten by the cranky beaver.

ELLIPSES

Use three dots in a row (. . .) to indicate you have left some material out of a quotation. If the omitted words come at the end of the original sentence, a fourth dot indicates the period. Use several dots centered in a line to indicate that a paragraph or more has been left out. Ellipses help you save time and zero in on the important material within a quotation.

> " . . . Three dots . . . indicate you have left some material out. . . . A fourth dot indicates the period. . . . Several dots centered in a line . . . indicate . . . a paragraph or more. . . . Ellipses help you . . . zero in on the important material. . . . "

ITALICS

In typing or longhand writing, indicate italics by <u>underlining</u>. Use italics for titles of books, periodicals, films, newspapers, and plays; for the names of ships; for foreign words or scientific names; for emphasizing a word (used sparingly); for indicating the special use of a word.

The *Oxford English Dictionary* is a handy reference tool.

The *Lusitania* sank rapidly.

She reads *The Boston Globe* often.

My only advice is *caveat emptor*.

Bacillus anthracis is a highly virulent organism.

Do not inhale these fumes under any circumstances!

Our contract defines a *work-study student* as one who works a minimum of 20 hours weekly.

PARENTHESES

Use commas normally to set off parenthetical elements, dashes to give some emphasis to the material that is set off, and parentheses to enclose material that defines or explains the statement that precedes it.

An anaerobic (airless) environment must be maintained for the cultivation of this organism.

The cost of running our college has increased by 15 percent in one year (see Appendix A for full cost breakdown).

This new calculator (made by Ilco Corporation) is perfect for science students.

Notice that material between parentheses, like all other parenthetical material discussed earlier, can be deleted without harming the logical and grammatical structure of the sentence.

Also, use parentheses to enclose numbers or letters that segment items of information in a series.

This process entails three basic steps: (1) . . . , (2) . . . , and (3) . . . .

BRACKETS

Use brackets within a quotation to add material which was not in the original quotation but which is needed for clarification. Sometimes a bracketed word provides an antecedent (or referent) for a pronoun.

"She [Amy] was the outstanding candidate for the scholarship."

Brackets can enclose information taken from some other location within the context of the quotation.

"It was in early spring [April 2, to be exact] that the tornado hit."

Use brackets to correct a quotation.

"His essay was [full] of mistakes."

Use *sic* ("thus," or "so") when quoting a mistake in spelling, usage, or logic.

The assistant's comment was clear: "He don't [sic] want any."

DASHES

Dashes can be effective—as long as they are not overused. Make dashes on your typewriter by placing two hyphens side by side. Parentheses deemphasize the enclosed material; dashes strongly emphasize it.

Used selectively, dashes can provide dramatic emphasis for a statement, but they are not a substitute for all other punctuation. When in doubt, do not use a dash!

Dashes can denote an afterthought

Have a good vacation—but don't get sunstroke.

or to enclose an interruption in the middle of a sentence.

The designer of this college building—I think it was Wright—was, above all, an artist.

Our new players—Jones, Smith, and Brown—are already compiling outstanding statistics.

Although they often can be used interchangeably with commas, dashes dramatize a parenthetical statement more than commas do.

Mary, a true friend, spent hours helping me rehearse.

Mary—a true friend—spent hours helping me rehearse.

Notice the added emphasis in the second version.

Application A–11

Insert parentheses or dashes as appropriate in these sentences.

1. Writing is a deliberate process of deliberate decisions about a writer's purpose, audience, and message.

2. Have fun but be careful.

3. He worked hard summers at three jobs actually to earn money for agricultural school.

4. To achieve peace and contentment that is the meaning of success.

5. Fido a loyal pet saved my life during the fire.

Effective Mechanics

Correctness in abbreviation, capitalization, use of numbers, and spelling is an important sign of your attention to detail.

ABBREVIATIONS

In using abbreviations, consider your audience; never use an abbreviation that might confuse your reader. Often, abbreviations are not appropriate in formal writing. When in doubt, write the word out.

Abbreviate some words and titles when they precede or immediately follow a proper name.

Correct

Mr. Jones   Raymond Dumont, Jr.

Dr. Jekyll   Warren Weary, Ph.D.

St. Simeon

Do not, however, write abbreviations such as these:

Faulty

He is a Dr.

Pray, and you might become a St.

In general, do not abbreviate military, religious, and political titles.

Correct   Reverend Ormsby

                          Captain Hook

                          President Bush

Abbreviate time designations only when they are used with actual times.

Correct   400 B.C.

                          5:15 A.M.

Do not abbreviate these designations when they are used alone.

Faulty   Plato lived sometime in the B.C. period.

                          She arrived in the A.M.

In formal writing, do not abbreviate days of the week, individual months, words such as **street** and **road,** or names of disciplines such as **English.** Avoid abbreviating states, such as **Me.** for **Maine;** countries, such as **U.S.** for **United States;** and book parts, such as **Chap.** for **Chapter, p.** for **page,** and **fig.** for **figure.**
Use **no.** for **number** only when the actual number is given.

Correct   Check switch No. 3.

For abbreviations of other words, consult your dictionary. Most dictionaries have a list of abbreviations at the front or rear or alphabetically with the word entry.

HYPHEN

Use a hyphen to divide a word at your right-hand margin. Consult your dictionary for the correct syllable breakdown:

com-puter

comput-er

Actually, it is best to avoid altogether this practice of dividing words at the ends of lines in a typewritten text.

Use a hyphen to join compound modifiers (two or more words preceding the noun as a single adjective)

> the rough-hewn wood
>
> the well-written novel
>
> the all-too-human error

Do not hyphenate these same words if they *follow* the noun.

> The wood was rough hewn.
>
> The novel is well written.
>
> The error was all too human.

Hyphenate an adverb-participle compound preceding a noun.

> the high-flying glider

Do not hyphenate compound modifiers if the adverb ends in **-ly**.

> The finely tuned engine.

Hyphenate most words that begin with the prefix **self**. (Check your dictionary.)

> self-reliance
>
> self-discipline
>
> self-actualizing

Hyphenate to avoid ambiguity.

> re-creation [*a new creation*]
>
> recreation [*leisure activity*]

Hyphenate words that begin with **ex** only if **ex** means "past."

> ex-faculty member
>
> excommunicate

Hyphenate all fractions, along with ratios that are used as adjectives and that precede the noun.

a **two-thirds** majority

In a **four-to-one** vote, the student senate defeated the proposal.

Do not hyphenate ratios if they do not immediately precede the noun.

The proposal was voted down **four to one.**

Hyphenate compound numbers from twenty-one through ninety-nine.

Thirty-eight windows were broken.

Hyphenate a series of compound adjectives preceding a noun.

The subjects for the motivation experiment were **fourteen-, fifteen-,** and **sixteen**-year-old students.

CAPITALIZATION

Capitalize these proper nouns: titles of people, books, and chapters; languages; days of the week; the months; holidays; names of organizations or groups; races and nationalities; historical events; important documents; and names of structures or vehicles. In titles of books, films, and the like, capitalize the first word and all those following except articles or prepositions.

Joe Schmoe	Russian
A Tale of Two Cities	Labor Day
Protestant	Dupont Chemical Company
Wednesday	Senator John Pasteur
the *Queen Mary*	France
the Statue of Liberty	The War of 1812

Do not capitalize the seasons, names of college classes (**freshman, junior**), or general groups (**the younger generation, the leisure class**).
Capitalize adjectives that are derived from proper nouns.

Chaucerian English

Capitalize titles preceding a proper noun but not those following.

State Senator Marsha Smith

Marsha Smith, state senator

Capitalize words such as **street, road, corporation,** and **college** only when they accompany a proper noun.

> Bob Jones University
>
> High Street
>
> The Rand Corporation

Capitalize **north, south, east,** and **west** when they denote specific locations, not when they are simply directions.

> the South
>
> the Northwest
>
> Turn east at the next set of lights.

Begin all sentences with capitals.

USE OF NUMBERS

If numbers can be expressed in one or two words, you can write them out or you can use the numerals.
For larger numbers, use numerals.

> 4,364   2,800,357
>
> 543

Use numerals to express decimals, fractions, precise technical figures, or any other exact measurements. Numerals are more easily read and better remembered than numbers that are spelled out.

> 3¼   15 pounds of pressure
>
> 50 kilowatts   4000 rpm

Express these in numerals: dates, census figures, addresses, page numbers, exact units of measurement, percentages, ages, times with A.M. or P.M. designations, and monetary and mileage figures.

> page 14   1:15 P.M.
>
> 18.4 pounds   9 feet
>
> 115 miles   12 gallons
>
> the 9-year-old motorcycle $15

Do not begin a sentence with a numeral.

Six hundred students applied for the 102 available jobs.

If your figure consumes more than two words, revise your word order.

The 102 available jobs brought 780 applicants.

Do not use numerals to express approximate figures, time not designated as A.M. or P.M., or streets named by numbers less than 100.

about seven hundred fifty

four fifteen

108 East Forty-second Street

If one number immediately precedes another, spell out the first, and use a numeral for the second:

Please deliver twelve 16-inch anchovy pizzas.

In contracts and other documents in which precision is vital, a number can be stated both in numerals and in words:

The tenant agrees to pay a rental fee of three hundred seventy-five dollars ($375.00) monthly.

SPELLING

If you are bothered by spelling weaknesses, take the time to use your dictionary for all writing assignments. And when you read, notice the spelling of words that have given you trouble. Compile a list of troublesome words. Your college may have a learning laboratory where you can get assistance. Or your instructor may suggest books for spelling improvement.

Application A–12

In these sentences, make any needed mechanical corrections in abbreviations, hyphens, numbers, or capitalization.

1. Dr. Jones, our english prof., drives a Volkswagen Jetta.

2. Eighty five students in the survey rated self-discipline as essential for success in college.

3. Since nineteen seventy seven, my goal has been to live in the northwest.

4. Senator Tarbell has collected forty five hand made rugs from the middle east.

5. During my third year at Margate university, I wrote twenty three page papers on the Russian revolution.

Acknowledgments

Jay Allison. "About Men: Back at the Ranch" by Jay Allison from *The New York Times Magazine*, May 27, 1990, page 14. Copyright © 1990 by The New York Times Company. Reprinted by permission.

Roger Angell. Excerpt from *Five Seasons* by Roger Angell. Copyright © 1972, 1973, 1974, 1975, 1976, 1977 by Roger Angell. Reprinted by permission of Simon & Schuster, Inc.

Russell Baker. "Meaningful Relationships" by Russell Baker from *The New York Times Magazine*, March 19, 1978. Copyright © 1978 by The New York Times Company. Reprinted by permission.

David Blum. "The Evils of Gentrification" by David Blum from *Newsweek*, January 3, 1983. Copyright © 1983 by David Blum. Reprinted by permission of the author.

Ellen Goodman. "The Belated Father" from *Close to Home* by Ellen Goodman. Copyright © 1979 by The Washington Post Company. Reprinted by permission of Simon & Schuster, Inc.

Hendrick Hertzberg and David C. K. McClelland. Excerpt from "Paranoia." Copyright © 1974 by *Harper's Magazine*. All rights reserved. Reprinted from the June 1974 issue by special permission.

Thomas H. Holmes and R. H. Rahe. Table reprinted with permission from *Journal of Psychonomic Research*, Vol. 11, "The Social Readjustment Rating Scale." Copyright © 1967, Pergamon Press Inc.

Robert Jay Lifton and Eric Olson. Excerpts from *Living and Dying*. Copyright © 1974 by Robert Jay Lifton and Eric Olson. Reprinted by permission of Holt, Rinehart and Winston, Inc.

Anne Morrow Lindbergh. From *Gift from the Sea* by Anne Morrow Lindbergh. Copyright © 1955 by Anne Morrow Lindbergh. Reprinted by permission of Pantheon Books, a division of Random House, Inc.

Norman Mailer. Excerpt from *The Presidential Papers*. Copyright © 1960, 1961, 1962, 1963 by Norman Mailer. Reprinted by permission of the author and the author's agents, Scott Meredith Literary Agency, 845 Third Avenue, New York, New York 10022.

Donald Murray. *A Writer Teaches Writing*, Second Edition, by Donald Murray. Copyright © 1985 by Houghton Mifflin Company. Used with permission.

The New York Times. Excerpt from *The New York Times*, April 4, 1973. Copyright © 1973 by The New York Times Company. Reprinted by permission.

Index

A

Abbreviations, 565–566
Abstractions, 200–202
Abstract words, 42, 200, 201, 202, 228
Accuracy, in business writing, 494, 495
Action verbs
 for conciseness, 177
 for instructions, 165, 285
 in a job application letter, 511
 in a resume, 507
Active reading, 90, 96
Active voice, 168–171
 for conversational tone, 210
 for instructions, 285
 in a resume, 511
Adjective, 532
Adjective clause, 533
Adverb, 532
Adverb clause, 533
Agreement
 pronoun-antecedent (referent), 543
 subject-verb, 541–543
Ambiguity, 159, 162, 198, 209, 567
Analogy
 versus comparison, 319–322
 guidelines for, 322–323
Anecdote, as essay introduction, 65–66
Apostrophe, 559–561
Appeals
 to emotion, 369–375

to reason, 356–364, 371
to shared goals and values, 352–353
Appendix, to a research report, 458, 459, 476, 477, 478–479
Appositive, 556
Argument
 audience resistance to, 345–346
 debatable point in, 346–348
 deduction in, 356, 357, 360–364
 as a development strategy, 223–224
 emotional appeal in, 369–375
 ethics guidelines for, 389–390
 features of, 346
 goals of, 344, 352, 353, 390–391
 humor in, 373–374
 illogical reasoning, avoidance of, 364–369
 induction in, 356, 357, 358–360
 reader questions about, 345
 relation to other strategies, 223, 224, 344, 346
 standard shape for, 384–385
 support for, 346, 350–356
 thesis (main point) in, 346, 347, 348, 384
 tone in, 371–375, 388
Argument essay (samples), 348–350, 374–375, 386–388, 392–393, 397–398, 401–402, 404–405, 406–407
Argument guidelines, 385–388
Argument outline (shape), 384–385
Assertions, 105, 348. See also Thesis statement

Messiness in the writing process, the
   need for, 4, 5
Modifiers
   compound, hypenation of, 567
   dangling, 160–161
   misplaced, 159–160
   nonrestrictive, 554, 555
   restrictive, 554, 555
   sentence parts as, 530

N

Name calling, in argument, 367
Narration. See also Chronological
   order
   as development strategy, 223
   guidelines for, 249–250
   to make a point, 242–249
   to merely report, 241–242
   reader questions about, 240
Narrative essay (samples), 244–247,
   248, 251–252
Needless details, avoidance of, 115–
   116. See also Selecting, of
   writing material
Needlessly technical details,
   avoidance of, 113
Negative constructions, avoidance
   of, 179–181
Neutral expressions, to avoid sexist
   usage, 213
Nominalization. See Noun
   addiction
Nominative case, 544, 545
Nonrestrictive modifier (element),
   554, 555
Notation, in a formal outline, 441
Notecards, for recording research
   findings, 436, 437, 438, 441
Noun addiction, 178–179
Noun clause, 532, 533
Numbers, use of, 569–570

O

Objective case, 544, 545
Objective complement, 531–532

Objective versus subjective support
   for an argument, 351, 352,
   355, 356
Objectivity, 211, 229, 230, 231
Object of a preposition, 531, 544,
   545
Opening strategies, for essays, 65–69
Opinion. See also Fact
   and argument, 345, 347
   credibility and, 105–108
   fact and, 106, 107
   informed versus uninformed, 106,
   107, 413
   and research, 413, 414, 442
Order of ideas
   in an essay, 11, 71, 72
   in a paragraph, 133–141
Order of importance. See Emphatic
   order
Organization (shape)
   of an essay, 4, 10–11, 13, 17–18,
   43–46
   of a paragraph, 123–124
   of any useful writing, 10–11
Orienting statement, 67, 135, 139.
   See also Topic statement
Outline format, 441
Outlining. See also Essay; Essay
   body; Essay conclusion; Essay
   introduction
   an essay, 43–46
   a research report, 439, 440, 452,
   454–455
Overstatement, 14, 194, 363, 371
Overstuffed sentences, 163–187

P

Page numbering, in a research
   report, 457
Paragraph
   in relation to an essay, 18, 32,
   123, 124
   as single sentence, 125, 146
   as unit of meaning, 124
Paragraph body, 124. See also Body
   section, of a message